Hispanics in the U.S. Economy

Hispanics in the U.S. Economy

A 1982 Conference

SPONSORED BY

The National Commission for Employment Policy
The Institute for Research on Poverty of
The University of Wisconsin

This is a volume in the

INSTITUTE FOR RESEARCH ON POVERTY
MONOGRAPH SERIES

Hispanics in the U.S. Economy

Edited by

GEORGE J. BORJAS

Department of Economics
University of California
Santa Barbara, California

MARTA TIENDA

Department of Rural Sociology
and
Institute for Research on Poverty
University of Wisconsin–Madison
Madison, Wisconsin

ACADEMIC PRESS, INC.

(Harcourt Brace Jovanovich, Publishers)

Orlando   San Diego   New York   London
Toronto   Montreal   Sydney   Tokyo

This book is one of a series sponsored by the Institute for Research on Poverty of the University of Wisconsin.

ACADEMIC PRESS, INC.
Orlando, Florida 32887

United Kingdom Edition published by
ACADEMIC PRESS INC. (LONDON) LTD.
24/28 Oval Road, London NW1 7DX

Library of Congress Cataloging in Publication Data

Main entry under title:

Hispanics in the U.S. economy.

   Bibliography: p.
   Includes index.
   1. Hispanic Americans--Employment--Addresses, essays, lectures. 2. Wages--Hispanic Americans--Addresses, essays, lectures. 3. Hispanic Americans--Economic conditions--Addresses, essays, lectures. 4. Hispanic Americans --Social conditions--Addresses, essays, lectures.
I. Borjas, George J. II. Tienda, Marta.
HD8081.H7H58 1985   331.6'3'6873   84-14611
ISBN 0-12-118640-7 (alk. paper)

PRINTED IN THE UNITED STATES OF AMERICA

85 86 87 88   9 8 7 6 5 4 3 2 1

To Mother
G. J. B.

To Lucille Page
M. T.

P The Institute for Research on Poverty is a national center for research established at the University of Wisconsin in 1966. Its primary objective is to foster basic, multidisciplinary research into the nature and causes of poverty and means to combat it.

In addition to increasing the basic knowledge from which policies aimed at the elimination of poverty can be shaped, the Institute strives to carry analysis beyond the formulation and testing of fundamental generalizations to the development and assessment of relevant policy alternatives.

The Institute endeavors to bring together scholars of the highest caliber whose primary research efforts are focused on the problem of poverty, the distribution of income, and the analysis and evaluation of social policy, offering staff members wide opportunities for interchange of ideas, maximum freedom for research into basic questions about poverty and social policy, and dissemination of their findings.

Contents

1 Introduction
GEORGE J. BORJAS AND MARTA TIENDA

Part I EARNINGS AND LABOR SUPPLY

2 A Comparative Analysis of the Wages of Hispanics, Blacks, and Non-Hispanic Whites
CORDELIA W. REIMERS

3 Employment, Wages, and Earnings of Hispanics in the Federal and Nonfederal Sectors: Methodological Issues and Their Empirical Consequences
JOHN M. ABOWD AND MARK R. KILLINGSWORTH

4 Ethnic Differentials in Unemployment among Hispanic Americans
GREGORY DEFREITAS

Part II   YOUTH EMPLOYMENT AND SCHOOL ENROLLMENT

5 Educational Transitions of Whites and Mexican-Americans
NEIL FLIGSTEIN AND ROBERTO M. FERNANDEZ

6 Labor Market Turnover and Joblessness for Hispanic Youth
STANLEY P. STEPHENSON, JR.

11   Immigration and Industrial Change in the New York City Apparel Industry
ROGER WALDINGER

List of Tables and Figures

Tables

Figures

Contributors

Numbers in parentheses indicate the pages on which the authors' contributions begin.

JOHN M. ABOWD (77), Graduate School of Business, University of Chicago, Chicago, Illinois 60637

FRANK D. BEAN (221), Population Research Center and Department of Sociology, University of Texas at Austin, Austin, Texas 78712

GEORGE J. BORJAS (1), Department of Economics, University of California, Santa Barbara, California 93106

HARLEY L. BROWNING (277), Population Research Center and Department of Sociology, University of Texas at Austin, Austin, Texas 78712

GREGORY DEFREITAS (127), Department of Economics, Barnard College, Columbia University, New York, New York 10027

ROBERTO M. FERNANDEZ (161), Department of Sociology, University of Arizona, Tucson, Arizona 85721

NEIL FLIGSTEIN (161), Department of Sociology, University of Arizona, Tucson, Arizona 85721

PATRICIA GUHLEMAN (243), Department of Rural Sociology and Center for Demography and Ecology, University of Wisconsin–Madison, Madison, Wisconsin 53706

MARK R. KILLINGSWORTH (77), Department of Economics, Rutgers University, New Brunswick, New Jersey 08903

ALLAN G. KING (221), Department of Economics, University of Texas at Austin, Austin, Texas 78712

CORDELIA W. REIMERS (27), Department of Economics, Hunter College; and Graduate School of the City University of New York, New York, New York 10021

NESTOR RODRÍGUEZ (277), Department of Sociology, University of Houston–University Park, Houston, Texas 77004

SASKIA SASSEN-KOOB (299), Queen's College of the City University of New York, New York, New York 11367

STANLEY P. STEPHENSON, JR.,[1] (193), Department of Business Administration, The Pennsylvania State University, University Park, Pennsylvania 16802

C. GRAY SWICEGOOD (221), Department of Sociology, University of Illinois, Urbana, Illinois 61801

MARTA TIENDA (1, 243), Department of Rural Sociology and Institute for Research on Poverty, University of Wisconsin–Madison, Madison, Wisconsin 53706

ROGER WALDINGER (323), Department of Sociology, The City College of the City University of New York, New York, New York 10031

[1] Present address: The University of Hartford, West Hartford, Connecticut 06117.

Foreword

In 1980, 14.6 million Hispanics were counted in the U.S. census. Hispanics are the fastest-growing minority in the United States, and it has been estimated that because of continued immigration and a high birthrate, they will shortly become the largest minority. Their political impact has increased already, owing in part to their numbers and in part to their location: They make up a sizable proportion of the voting-age population of many Western states and Florida as well as large metropolitan areas in the Northeast and Midwest. Obviously, this growth is transforming the country at the same time that the immigrants are being transformed into mainstream Americans. What are the dynamics of the process by which Hispanics enter and participate in the labor market, and how does the market adjust to them? Now, for the first time, data and measurement techniques are available to study the process in detail.

Because Hispanic groups entering the United States share numerous characteristics and yet are widely diverse in other traits, they allow social scientists to isolate the causes of their labor market successes and failures, the factors that determine the rapidity of integration, the role discrimination plays in restricting their opportunities, the forces that determine where they settle, the differences between first- and second-generation Americans, and the impact immigration has on the job opportunities of non-Hispanic citizens.

Once differences become apparent, explanations become possible. We find, for example, that Puerto Ricans, all of whom are U.S. citizens from birth, are worse off economically than Mexican-Americans. Why should this be the case? And why are some other Hispanic groups, for example immigrants from Cuba and Central and South America, more likely to be employed than non-Hispanic whites? Why should education have a greater payoff in higher wages for some Hispanic groups than for others? The answers to such questions should tell us much about how the labor market functions and how Hispanics deal with it.

The chapters in this volume, reflecting the disciplines of the two editors, George Borjas and Marta Tienda, make use of both economic and sociological techniques to pose and answer just such questions. There are statistical comparisons among Hispanic groups and between Hispanic and non-Hispanic whites, and there are case studies. The latter explore in detail such seeming paradoxes as how undocumented immigrants, with limited English and no papers, find and hold onto jobs, and how New York City can continue to absorb immigrant labor in the apparel industries, where total employment is declining.

Special attention is given to the labor market experiences of Hispanic women, including a study of the extent to which the high fertility rates of some groups reduce female labor force participation. The employment problems of youth also receive special attention.

The studies in this volume were presented at a Hispanic Labor Conference in Santa Barbara in 1982, sponsored by the National Commission for Employment Policy and the Institute for Research on Poverty. These studies provide useful insights for public policy. They pinpoint many areas where appropriate policy could hasten and smooth transitions. For example, limited education, rather than discrimination in the labor market, is seen by several authors as the chief cause of the low wages of many Hispanics. This leads to further questions not addressed here: Why do Hispanic youth have so little schooling? and What policies can address the problem?

Increased knowledge of the socioeconomic standing of this significant and growing proportion of the populace and better understanding of the workings of the labor market of the sort supplied by this volume should lead to better opportunities for all minorities, which means greater progress for the entire economy.

SHELDON DANZIGER
Director, Institute for Research on Poverty

Acknowledgments

During the winter of 1980, the Human Resources Management and Development Program of the College of Business at the University of Texas at San Antonio (UTSA) sponsored a symposium on Hispanics and CETA (the Comprehensive Employment and Training Act) in collaboration with the U.S. Department of Labor. Among the noteworthy accomplishments of this event were, first, the bringing together of social scientists from various disciplines with interest or previous experience in conducting research about the labor market experiences of Hispanics, and, second, the reaffirmation of the need to promote high-quality research about the labor market experiences of Hispanic-origin groups. This conference volume is the culmination of our joint effort to pick up where the 1980 UTSA symposium left off. The general goal that guided the organization of the Hispanic Labor Conference held at the University of California–Santa Barbara, February 4–5, 1982, was to promote research about Hispanics in the labor market, research derived from theoretically elaborated relationships and evaluated with rigorous empirical analyses from both sociological and economic perspectives. We sought to advance the study of the Hispanic labor force beyond the descriptive aggregate comparisons among national-origin groups that dominated the labor market literature. As a secondary objective, we hoped to entice new and established scholars to undertake research about the labor market experiences of Hispanic-origin groups.

Our success in meeting these objectives, and especially in producing the first major collection of readings about the labor market experiences of Hispanics, must be shared with many colleagues and collaborators. Eugene Smolensky, as Director of the Institute for Research on Poverty, and Glen G. Cain, a faculty affiliate of the Institute, encouraged us to pursue the idea of the conference by providing institutional support and intellectual guidance. They reviewed the initial project proposal and made useful suggestions at the planning stage. Both served as formal discussants for the conference papers and provided excellent suggestions for revising the papers. With the encouragement of Carol Jusenius, staff economist at the National Council for Employment Policy, we obtained funding for the conference (NCEP Grant No. 99-1-463-50-42), and we are indebted to Carol for her continued assistance in planning the conference and for granting us relative autonomy in structuring its content and form.

Jeanette Schreier of the University of Wisconsin and Maritza Elias of the University of California handled the logistical aspects of the conference with efficiency, skill, and dedication.

Although the conference was the major building block for this volume, its production in large measure is attributable to invaluable editorial assistance from Elizabeth Evanson and Elizabeth Uhr, the editors at the Institute for Research on Poverty. Their incisive suggestions and dutiful sense of craft have greatly strengthened the final product.

The authors of chapters benefited greatly from the written and verbal commentary of several conference participants: Orley Ashenfelter, Princeton University; Robert Bach, State University of New York at Binghamton; Daniel Hamermesh, Michigan State University; Robert Mare, University of Wisconsin at Madison; Solomon Polachek, University of North Carolina at Chapel Hill; Alejandro Portes, The Johns Hopkins University; Ross Stolzenberg, Rand Corporation; and Finis Welch, University of California–Los Angeles. Several individuals were involved in the conference as session moderators: Carol Jusenius; Allan King, University of Texas at Austin; Ronald Oaxaca, University of Arizona; and Ralph Smith, National Commission for Employment Policy, currently at Vanderbilt University. Other conference participants who contributed to the research and policy debate were Burt Barnow, U.S. Department of Labor; Virgulino Duarto, National Commission for Employment Policy; Leo Estrada, University of California–Los Angeles; Randall King and Steven Myers, University of Akron; and Dan Saks, National Commission for Employment Policy.

Joyce Collins and Jack Sorenson skillfully administered the grant funds, allowing us to focus on the substance of the conference and volume. Wence and Luis Gabriel generously gave of their time when deadlines pressed into family time.

Any opinions, findings, conclusions, or recommendations are those of the authors and do not necessarily reflect the views of the National Commission for Employment Policy or other agencies supporting the work of the various authors.

CHAPTER 1

Introduction

George J. Borjas and Marta Tienda

Background

Few topics have intrigued social scientists more than inequality. Despite the vast number of studies on this subject, the existing literature is remarkable for its relative lack of interest in the social and economic status of groups other than blacks and women. This narrow emphasis is currently being broadened as social scientists begin to identify systematic differences *within* the black and white populations. These differences may exist along religious lines (Chiswick, 1983), by nationality (Sowell, 1978), by immigration status (Cafferty et al., 1983), and by language spoken in the household (McManus et al., 1983), as well as by socioeconomic origins (Featherman and Hauser, 1978). The growth of interest in the Hispanic population, especially recent immigrants, over the past two decades can be understood in this context.

A large share of the existing research about the economic well-being of Hispanics and immigrants analyzes labor market outcomes of men in the prime working ages (see review in Tienda, 1981) and, to a lesser extent, women and youth. These studies have helped us appreciate the variation in the social, economic, and demographic situations of the major Hispanic-origin groups. The ongoing immigration from Central and South America, however, continuously alters the composition of the Hispanic populations. These changes in composition, along with shifts in labor market conditions, modify the economic well-being and labor market opportunities for the different national-origin groups in different ways. Thus, to understand the meaning of "Hispanicity" as a dimension of ethnic inequality, it is necessary to document patterns of differentiation among the groups and to strive for an explanation of their sources. The chapters in this volume therefore attempt to distinguish between the national-origin groups—Mexicans, Cubans, Puerto Ricans,

TABLE 1.1
Summary Characteristics of Hispanic and Non-Hispanic White Women Age 18–64

Selected characteristics	Mexican	Puerto Rican	Cuban	Central and South American	Other Hispanic	All Hispanic	Non-Hispanic white
Mean age (years)	33.9	34.6	38.6	33.7	37.7	35.0	38.6
Native born	72.4%	17.7%	2.9%	8.7%	72.9%	57.1%	94.8%
English is language usually spoken	55.0	34.8	30.2	38.4	68.7	52.6	96.1
Speaks and/or understands English well[a]	77.5	68.6	60.5	57.7	88.2	76.2	99.0
12 or more years education	40.1	35.6	59.1	62.9	62.0	46.7	78.2
Marital status							
Married, spouse present[b]	67.2	51.4	64.3	57.9	65.8	64.1	68.3
Never married	16.7	16.8	18.1	20.6	15.8	16.9	17.3
Other	16.0	31.8	17.5	21.5	18.4	19.0	14.3
Female household heads[c]	16.7	37.6	14.6	18.1	20.2	20.0	16.6
Ages of children							
No children under age 18	26.2	31.8	37.8	41.3	43.0	32.0	50.2
No children under age 6, but at least one age 6–17	34.1	32.9	41.8	24.3	34.7	33.7	30.6
At least one child under age 6	39.7	35.3	20.5	34.4	22.3	34.2	19.2
Region							
Northeast	0.6	79.3	26.8	45.7	23.4	19.8	31.2
Northcentral	7.0	10.3	3.9	4.6	5.2	6.7	23.5
South	39.8	4.7	63.1	19.1	23.3	31.8	23.3
West	52.6	5.8	6.2	30.7	48.0	41.7	22.0
N	2,432	554	243	341	892	4,452	20,147

Source: 1976 Survey of Income and Education (U.S. Department of Commerce, 1978).

[a] Includes all women who speak only English. Information from two survey items regarding competency in speaking and understanding English is used to determine language proficiency for women who speak any other language.

[b] Spouses may be household heads or secondary family heads (i.e., related to the household head but having families of their own).

[c] Women who are household heads, including primary individuals (i.e., women who live alone or are unrelated to others in household).

TABLE 1.2
Summary Characteristics of Hispanic and Non-Hispanic White Men Age 18–64

Selected characteristics	Mexican	Puerto Rican	Cuban	Central and South American	Other Hispanic	All Hispanic	Non-Hispanic white
Mean age (years)	34.5	36.0	40.1	35.8	37.3	35.5	38.2
Native born	69.2%	26.7%	3.2%	5.7%	72.9%	42.0%	95.4%
English is language usually spoken	54.4	53.2	27.1	48.5	72.5	55.7	96.1
Speaks and/or understands English well[a]	70.2	65.3	47.0	52.9	80.5	78.4	99.1
12 or more years education	45.8	44.0	57.6	62.6	63.4	50.3	77.0
Marital status							
Married, spouse present	65.0	66.3	69.9	67.6	64.7	65.5	68.2
Never married	24.7	21.3	19.5	20.3	26.7	24.2	24.6
Other	10.3	12.4	10.6	12.1	8.6	10.4	7.2
Family head[b]	78.7	74.9	81.6	74.7	77.5	78.0	77.0
Children under age 18							
None	34.2	40.7	38.0	41.9	45.0	37.5	50.8
One or two	36.0	39.2	48.7	42.8	36.5	37.5	35.8
Three or more	29.8	20.1	13.3	15.3	18.5	25.0	13.4
Region							
Northeast	0.4	72.7	23.8	49.4	23.2	16.7	30.3
Northcentral	8.7	12.4	4.3	5.2	4.6	8.0	23.7
South	35.2	5.7	66.4	15.0	24.4	30.4	23.7
West	55.7	9.2	5.5	30.4	47.8	44.9	22.3
N	2,368	452	212	217	716	3,965	19,175

Source: 1976 Survey of Income and Education (U.S. Department of Commerce, 1978).

[a] Includes all men who speak only English. Information from two survey items regarding competency in speaking and understanding English is used to determine language proficiency for men who speak any other language.

[b] Men living with their spouses and/or children, including men in secondary families.

Central and South Americans, and others—as well as to compare Hispanic and non-Hispanic populations.

Available descriptive studies (Newman, 1978; Jaffe et al., 1980) hint at important scientific and policy implications of the research on Hispanics. Tables 1.1 and 1.2, which summarize differences in socioeconomic characteristics among Hispanic and non-Hispanic women and men, respectively, illustrate the nature of these implications. The source of these data is the 1976 Survey of Income and Education (SIE; U.S. Department of Commerce, 1978). Since the SIE is also the data base used in most of the empirical analyses reported in this volume, we have provided a detailed description of its construction and contents in an appendix following this chapter.

A Profile of Hispanic Groups

Tables 1.1 and 1.2 confirm the view that socioeconomic characteristics vary appreciably between the Hispanic and non-Hispanic populations. More interestingly, these statistics also show the remarkable socioeconomic differentiation within the Hispanic population, as evidenced by comparisons among the national-origin groups. Mexicans comprised more than half of all Hispanic-origin individuals between 18 and 64 years of age who were interviewed in 1976. Of these, approximately 70% were born in the United States. A similar share reported an ability to speak and understand English well, although only just over half reported that they usually spoke English. The average level of educational attainment among Mexican-origin men and women in 1976 was quite low, less than 50% having graduated from high school. About 60% of working-age Mexicans were under the age of 35, and their marital and family characteristics largely reflected this fact. This compares with less than 50% of working-age non-Hispanic white workers. Differences in educational attainment and the number of years in the labor force are directly related to the value that employers place on an individual's skills. Consequently, these attributes have major impacts on earnings differentials.

Marital and family conditions affect men's and women's labor force experiences in different ways, necessitating the use of variables specifically adapted to each sex group. Female household heads include women not currently living with a spouse or another adult relative who is the household head. They may have children or live alone. Male family heads may be living with their spouses and/or children. Obviously, these two forms of family headship imply different economic circumstances and needs, including eligibility for public assistance. The low percentage of households headed by women is a distinguishing feature of the type of household prevailing among Mexicans and Cubans, where intact marriages predominate. The marital status distribution is very similar among all the subgroups, except that a significantly lower proportion of working-age Puerto Rican women reported being married with spouse present.[1]

Mexicans and Puerto Ricans, the two largest groups, are similar in

---

[1] Although the marital status distributions are parallel for men and women of Mexican origin, note that the individuals in the samples of men and women are not necessarily

many ways, especially in their economic characteristics, but they also exhibit many important differences. In fact, persons of Puerto Rican origin, who represented about 11% of the Hispanic-origin population, differed from those of Mexican origin in two respects. First, they are concentrated in the Northeast, an area characterized by generally high wages as well as fewer low-skill jobs relative to other parts of the United States (Seidman, 1978; Cooney and Ortiz, 1983). This has clear implications for understanding the Puerto Rican's disadvantaged status in the U.S. labor market. Second, Puerto Ricans are much less likely than are Mexicans to be born in the United States. Less than 20% of all working-age Puerto Rican women and about one-fourth of working-age Puerto Rican men are "native born," which in their case refers to birth on the U.S. mainland rather than on the island of Puerto Rico. Although it is true that the island–mainland distinction is not strictly comparable to the native–foreign distinction applied to other immigrant populations, Puerto Rico's unique commonwealth status promotes a substantial two-way migration flow between the U.S. mainland and the island. One possible result of this geographic movement may be an undercount of mainland-born Puerto Ricans, as has been suggested by Wagenheim (1975), the U.S. Commission on Civil Rights (1976), Cooney and Colon (1979), and Bonilla and Campos (1981).

Puerto Rican–origin respondents are the least educated of the five Hispanic groups, although the lower educational attainment of this group relative to Mexicans is basically due to the limited schooling received by Puerto Rican women. Only approximately one-third of adult Puerto Rican women have a high school education. This corresponds closely to the proportion who claim that English is their primary language. In contrast, slightly over 53% of adult Puerto Rican men report English rather than Spanish as their usual language. Notice, however, that fully two-thirds of both sexes claim to speak and comprehend English well. This linguistic advantage is due to the strong U.S. influence in Puerto Rico from the time it became a U.S. territory following the Spanish–American War until the present.

Puerto Ricans are similar to Mexicans in their age composition, yet they differ in marital, headship, and residence characteristics. Although over 65% of the Puerto Rican–origin men in the 1976 SIE were married, only about half of all adult Puerto Rican–origin women were married,

---

married to one another. However, because the SIE data were collected using households as sampling units, many husband–wife couples are represented in the data shown in Tables 1.1 and 1.2. Exceptions are due to interethnic marriages as well as to the presence of secondary individuals.

and 38%—a notably high proportion—were single household heads. Puerto Rican–origin men were similar to other Hispanic-origin men in their marital-status distribution. Next to Mexicans, Puerto Rican men were also the most likely to have three or more children present in their households. This should serve to increase their labor force participation rates relative to those of non-Hispanic white men, of whom only 13% have three or more children residing in their households.

Persons of Cuban origin constituted about 5% of the sample of working-age Hispanics. The sociodemographic composition of this group has been heavily influenced by the political exodus from Cuba during the 1960s. Virtually all (97%) the adults who participated in the SIE were born in Cuba, and over 60% were 35 years or older at the time of the interview. Thus, Cubans represent the oldest of the Hispanic national-origin groups in the sample. The immigrant composition of Cuban adults is mirrored by their language characteristics. Approximately one-third of both men and women in the SIE reported English as their primary language, while almost two-thirds of the women and less than half of the men reported being proficient in English. Unlike Mexicans and Puerto Ricans, Cuban women were less likely to have very young children residing in their homes, and few Cuban men resided in households where there were three or more children present. This also reflects the age composition of this group.

Cuban women were less likely to head households than were any of the other Hispanic national-origin groups or non-Hispanic white women. A further indicator of Cuban family stability is the finding that 70%—the highest proportion observed among all groups—were in husband–wife couples. The majority of persons of Cuban origin were concentrated in the South (about 65%); an additional 25% lived in the Northeast. Of all the Hispanic groups, Cubans appear to be the most successful economically, partly a consequence of the selective character of the exodus from Cuba that took place during the 1960s.

Central and South Americans represented about 7% of the adult Hispanic-origin population. Like Cuban-origin men and women, this group is largely foreign born and well educated. Most of their training was acquired abroad, so it is not surprising that between 60% (women) and 50% (men) indicated that Spanish was their primary language. Despite similarity to Cubans in terms of nativity and educational characteristics, Central and South Americans were more similar to Mexicans and Puerto Ricans in age composition. With most of the working-age adults under 35 years old, a considerably higher share of Central and South American–origin women were in the prime childbearing ages compared to Cuban-origin women. The fact that only 15% of the men headed families with three or more children may partly reflect the incomplete fertility cycles of this group. Further support for the contention that Central and South Americans, as a group, may be in the early phases of the family-formation cycle can be found in the fact that approximately one-third of the women in the sample had at least one child under 6 years old in the home. This share is similar to that observed among Mexicans and Puerto Ricans.

The modal region of residence for Central and South Americans is the Northeast, where about 47% live. However, about 30% reside in the West and about 17% in the South, indicating a wider geographic distribution than is characteristic of Puerto Ricans, Mexicans, or Cubans. As a result, their labor market experiences are more varied, though still in general reflecting their favorable socioeconomic backgrounds.

The final Hispanic group, identified as Other Hispanics, is derived as a residual category. As such, it is quite heterogeneous in a number of important respects and is unusually large, making up almost 20% of the Hispanic population. Although common sense would suggest that this group mostly represents individuals from the Iberian peninsula, this inference is not supported by the data (also see Jaffe et al., 1980.) We suspect that the majority of the Other Hispanic category comprises Hispanos (i.e., descendants of the early Spanish settlers who were originally under the jurisdiction of the Mexican government and, after the signing of the Treaty of Guadalupe Hidalgo in 1848, came under the legal jurisdiction of the U.S. government).[2]

Other Hispanics are similar to those of Mexican origin in the high percentage of native born, but they differ in that they are somewhat older and have different linguistic attributes. The percentage who reported using English more than Spanish corresponds closely to the percentage of native born. Over 80% of both men and women claimed to speak and understand English well. The educational composition of this group is more similar to that of Cubans and Central and South Americans, and notably above levels characteristic of Mexicans and Puerto Ricans. Although about two-thirds of the Other Hispanic adults of working age were married, almost half had no children under the age of 18 at the time of the survey.

---

[2] The suspicion that many individuals classified as being of Other Spanish origin (Other Hispanic) are Hispanos is further reinforced by their disproportionate concentration in New Mexico, Colorado, and Arizona. However, those residing in the Northeast are likely to be true immigrants from peninsular Spain. The SIE data do not permit us to establish whether this classification consists predominantly of Hispanos, but the low proportion of foreign born and the socioeconomic characteristics of this group suggest that this is highly plausible.

TABLE 1.3
Labor Force Participation Rates of Hispanic and Non-Hispanic White Women
by Nativity, Language, and Education

Characteristics	Mexican	Puerto Rican	Cuban	Central and South American	Other Hispanic	All Hispanic	Non-Hispanic white
Nativity							
Native born	50.0%	54.2%	—[a]	75.4%	56.0	52.0%	57.2%
Foreign born	45.1	32.7	64.6%	59.3	53.3	47.9	52.1
Language usually spoken[b]							
English	55.1	46.6	74.0	76.8	59.8	57.5	57.0
Spanish	40.8	29.4	60.3	48.7	39.9	41.1	n.a.
English language proficiency							
Speaks and/or understands English well[c]	52.6	43.4	70.7	68.0	56.5	54.2	57.1
Does not speak and/or understand English well	34.3	21.3	54.2	50.3	46.2	37.6	40.3
Completed years of schooling							
Less than 12 years	41.3	30.2	57.3	52.9	36.4	40.2	42.1
12 years	55.7	44.8	67.5	64.5	63.9	58.1	57.8
More than 12 years	69.7	54.7	71.0	66.3	71.6	68.7	65.1

Source: 1976 Survey of Income and Education (U.S. Department of Commerce, 1978).
[a] There are too few native-born Cuban women for reliable estimates.
[b] Women whose primary language is neither English nor Spanish are omitted from this panel.
[c] Includes all women who speak only English. Information from two survey items regarding competency in speaking and understanding English is used to determine language proficiency for women who speak any other language.

The compositional differences between Hispanics and non-Hispanic whites as well as among the various Hispanic groups extends to the labor market. Tables 1.3 and 1.4 document the labor force behavior for women and men, respectively, permitting comparisons among Hispanic-origin groups as well as with non-Hispanics. They too indicate that such factors as nationality, nativity, and language influence individuals' labor supply. Again, the dispersion among the Hispanic-origin groups is dramatic. For instance, Cubans and Central and South Americans had labor force participation rates 3–8 percentage points higher than non-Hispanic whites, whereas Puerto Rican participation rates were about 10 percentage points lower than those of non-Hispanic whites.

Working women differ from nonworking women in many respects. As shown in Table 1.3, the labor force participation rates of Hispanic-origin women vary greatly according to birthplace, language proficiency, and education levels. Women who were born in the United States, who had a good command over the English language, or who were well-educated were more likely than their counterparts to be in the labor force in 1976. But these generalities mask very different profiles among the national-origin groups. For example, discrepancies in the probability of being in the labor force by nativity were most extreme among Puerto Rican–origin women. In contrast to the 54% of mainland Puerto Rican women who were in the labor force in 1976, less than one-third of those born on the island were economically active. Since more than 80% of working-age Puerto Rican women were born on the island, the patterns of labor force participation that characterized immigrants are dominant. The labor force participation rate of Cuban women, who were virtually all foreign born, exceeded that of native- and foreign-born non-Hispanic white women.

Women who frequently used English and those who were proficient in the language were more likely than others to be in the labor force. This pattern was uniform among all Hispanic-origin groups, although the magnitude of the differential varied by ethnicity. Use of the Spanish language does not appear to deter Cuban-origin women from being in the labor market to the same extent as it does other Hispanic females. Sixty percent of Cuban women who reported usually speaking Spanish and more than half of those who did not speak or understand English well were in the labor force in 1976. In contrast, less than 30% of Puerto Rican women and only a minority of Mexican-origin women with comparable language-use patterns were in the labor force.

The positive relationship between labor force participation and education emerged for women of all Hispanic national origins. Yet, for any given level of education, Puerto Rican women were much less likely to be in the labor market than either non-Hispanic white or other Hispanic-origin women. With the exception of Puerto Ricans, however, Hispanic women who had completed 12 or more years of formal schooling had higher labor force participation rates than similarly educated non-Hispanic women. The crucial distinction between Hispanic and non-Hispanic women resides in the overall percentage who obtained a high school diploma. This is especially important for understanding the impact of education on labor force participation for Mexican and Puerto Rican–origin women.

Differentials in labor force participation were much less pronounced among men than women. In 1976, 87% of non-Hispanic white men between the ages of 18 and 64 were in the labor force. Labor force

TABLE 1.4
Labor Force Participation Rates of Hispanic and Non-Hispanic White Men
by Nativity, Language, and Education

Characteristics	Mexican	Puerto Rican	Cuban	Central and South American	Other Hispanic	All Hispanic	Non-Hispanic white
Nativity							
Native born	85.6%	75.5%	—[a]	—[a]	85.8%	88.0%	87.3%
Foreign born	89.9	79.9	90.8%	95.1%	85.4	85.2	87.8
Language usually spoken[b]							
English	86.4	79.4	93.2	96.3	87.7	86.6	87.6
Spanish	87.8	76.9	90.2	95.0	80.5	86.3	n.a.
English language proficiency							
Speaks and/or understands English well[c]	86.5	81.3	93.1	92.2	88.0	86.8	87.4
Does not speak and/or understand English well	87.9	72.7	89.3	96.9	76.1	84.8	n.a.
Completed years of schooling							
Less than 12 years	86.0	75.8	90.5	96.3	86.9	85.5	80.8
12 years	89.2	85.0	89.4	89.5	83.9	87.5	89.7
More than 12 years	86.6	76.3	92.9	95.6	86.6	87.1	89.0

Source: 1976 Survey of Income and Education (U.S. Department of Commerce, 1978).
[a] Cell size is too small for reliable estimates.
[b] Men whose primary language is neither English nor Spanish are omitted from this panel.
[c] Includes all men who speak only English. Information from two survey items regarding competency in speaking and understanding English is used to determine language proficiency for men who speak any other language.

membership among Hispanic men was somewhat higher for Cuban and Central and South Americans: 91 and 94%, respectively. Mexican and Other Hispanic men participated in the labor force at about the same rate as non-Hispanic white men, while a smaller proportion of Puerto Rican men, 78%, were in the labor force in 1976.

In contrast to women, Table 1.4 shows that few sociodemographic characteristics differentiated Hispanic men who were in the labor force and those who were not, although some differences deserve mention. The labor force participation rates of immigrant Mexican and Puerto Rican–origin men were higher than those of their native-born counterparts. Also, for most groups, men who usually spoke English rather

TABLE 1.5
Median Earnings of Hispanic and Non-Hispanic White Men and Women by Full-Time–Full-Year Work Status, 1975

	Men workers				Women workers			
	All	N	Full time–full year	N	All	N	Full time–full year	N
Mexican	$7,066	2,111	$ 9,020	$ 1,290	$3,137	1,313	$5,615	493
Puerto Rican	7,798	367	9,125	226	4,782	205	6,913	84
Cuban	7,979	184	10,032	118	4,812	153	6,816	87
Central and South American	8,019	205	9,723	135	4,992	209	6,917	97
Other Hispanic	9,009	630	10,550	419	4,991	502	7,618	229
All Hispanic	7,819	3,497	9,613	2,188	3,987	2,382	6,381	991
Non-Hispanic white	11,156	17,519	13,649	11,752	4,855	12,399	7,965	5,368

Source: 1976 Survey of Income and Education (U.S. Department of Commerce, 1978).
Note: The population is limited to individuals with at least $100 earnings in 1975.

than Spanish, and men with proficiency in English, were more likely to be in the labor market.

The relationship between education and labor force participation was not the same for men of different Hispanic national origins. Mexican and Puerto Rican men were like non-Hispanic white men in that a greater share of those with high school diplomas were in the labor force than those with less education. Among Central and South American and Other Hispanic men, however, labor force participation was lower among high school graduates than among those with less than 12 years of education. Interestingly, labor force participation rates among Mexican and Puerto Rican men were roughly similar for men with less than 12 years education and men with more than 12 years schooling—lower than the rates of those with exactly 12 years of schooling (i.e., just a high school diploma). However, this effect was not observed for Cubans and Central and South Americans—the two Hispanic groups with the highest levels of schooling—nor was it obtained for Other Hispanic men. The reasons for these rather disparate patterns are not immediately obvious, but they may reflect the effects of different schooling distributions among the groups (see Neidert and Tienda, 1981).

Finally, Table 1.5 provides summary statistics on the annual earnings in 1975 among the various groups, by sex. These data reveal that Hispanic men and women, on the average, were worse off than non-Hispanic men and women, but the earnings gap was much smaller for women. This does not mean that Hispanic women are better off than Hispanic men, but rather that they are a low-paid minority within a minority. Note too that some Hispanic groups (Cubans and Central and South Americans) did substantially better than other Hispanic groups (Mexicans and Puerto Ricans).

Why Study the Labor Market Experience of Hispanics?

The descriptive profile of Hispanic national-origin groups as summarized in Tables 1.1–1.5 indicates that there exists extensive social and economic inequality between Hispanics and non-Hispanics, and among the Hispanic national-origin groups. Such a condition justifies both advocating and undertaking labor market research on Hispanics, but studies such as those presented in this volume have broader implications. The systematic study of the labor market experience of the Hispanic national-origin groups can furnish substantive findings regarding the operation of the U.S. labor market. For example, one-third of all Hispanics of labor force age are immigrants, and we are just beginning to understand the nature and dimensions of labor market adjustments required by large influxes of immigrants. Clearly any study of recent immigration to the United States must explicitly analyze the causes and consequences of the large Hispanic immigration in both the sending and receiving communities. Thus, the study of the immigration and social integration experiences of Hispanics should yield insights on such diverse and important topics as the value of language acquisition in the labor market, the accumulation of human capital investments by "new" labor market entrants (i.e., the immigrants), and the significance of the reason for immigration (i.e., "economic" immigrants vs. political refugees).

The study of Hispanics provides the opportunity to explore the extent to which intergenerational mobility determines labor market outcomes. For example, the 1970 census indicates that about 45% of all Mexican-origin individuals had foreign-born parents. This fact raises a multitude of possibilities for empirical research on the transmission of "culture" and human capital from the immigrant parents to their native-born children. Such analyses can provide an important addition to the developing literature on the intergenerational properties of the income distribution. (For a theoretical development of this issue, see the pathbreaking work of Becker, 1981.)

The study of Hispanics can also provide important insights into the

role of nationality and ethnicity in determining labor market success.
The fact that the labor market characteristics of the five major nationality
groups in the Hispanic population differ substantially suggests that nationality plays an important part in differentiating this population—one
that also bears upon labor market success. This is not surprising, as
national background has significantly influenced the economic integration of many non-Hispanic groups in the United States (Gordon, 1964;
Yancey et al., 1976). The analysis of the Hispanic population therefore
provides a unique opportunity to isolate the importance of nationality as
a determinant of success in the U.S. labor market, particularly since the
Hispanic national-origin groups share many cultural traits.

Finally, careful analysis of the Hispanic population should generate
insights concerning how the labor market adjusts to large shifts in the
supply (both in terms of numbers and skills) of workers. Because the
Hispanic immigrant population has grown so fast over the past decade,
it has been blamed for taking jobs away from other groups, such as
blacks and other poor minorities (see, for example, Briggs, 1973). An
important research task, therefore, is to estimate the impact of Hispanics
on local and regional labor markets. This type of analysis would shed
light on how Hispanics affect the earnings, employment, and occupational characteristics of other minority and nonminority groups. More
important, such studies would deal largely with a fundamental question
in economics and sociology: How do labor markets work?

Despite the intriguing research and policy problems posed by the
study of the labor market experiences of Hispanics, most of the available
studies do not address the broad theoretical issues we have identified.
Instead they offer us a multitude of descriptive empirical relationships
that need further exploration. We have learned that the occupational
status of the Hispanic population has improved steadily since 1930,
partly as a result of migration from rural to urban locations and the
accompanying occupational shifts from agricultural to service and from
low-skilled to semiskilled jobs. But we do not even know whether the
improvements have kept pace with the gains of the non-Hispanic population and to what extent they have differed for the various Hispanic
groups.[3]

---

[3] Because of the difficulties of adequately distinguishing among the Hispanic national-
origin groups until very recently, as well as the problems of comparability introduced by
changes in the Spanish identifiers used by the Census Bureau between 1950 and 1970, few
researchers undertook comparative analyses of the major Hispanic nationalities, even at a
highly descriptive level. This situation changed with the inclusion of Spanish identifiers in
the Census Bureau's annual Current Population Surveys during the early 1970s, and
especially with the release of the 1976 SIE (U.S. Department of Commerce, 1978) microdata file.

These descriptive studies are largely responsible for carving the re-search agenda for current researchers. The studies in this volume refine the empirical analysis found in the descriptive literature, and go further in that they develop a theoretical framework to aid in the interpretation of these findings and in the use of the analysis for policy purposes.

Organization of the Volume

STUDIES OF EARNINGS AND LABOR SUPPLY

The chapters by Cordelia W. Reimers and by John M. Abowd and Mark R. Killingsworth focus on the determination of wage rates for Hispanic individuals and on comparison of Hispanic and non-Hispanic wage rates. Their methodology draws heavily on the voluminous dis-crimination literature. Despite differences in the data sets, in the sub-populations analyzed, and in the statistical techniques used, the find-ings in both studies converge in several respects.

Reimers (Chapter 2) makes the standard argument that, in order to estimate the extent of wage "discrimination" among equally skilled groups, the statistical analysis must control for differences in the observ-able socioeconomic characteristics (e.g., education, labor market experi-ence, etc.). In addition, she argues that the *wage offer* distribution is likely to differ from the observed wage distribution. In essence, because a certain fraction of the population opts not to work, given their costs and opportunities, the observed wage distribution cannot be used to predict how much the average Hispanic, or black, or white individual would earn. Thus, it is necessary to correct for the decision about whether or not to work when comparing earnings differentials among various groups.

Using the Heckman (1979) correction for selectivity, Reimers finds that controlling for differences in socioeconomic characteristics reduces substantially the observed wage differences between Hispanic and non-Hispanic men. For example, among Mexicans, the largest Hispanic sub-group, the observed wage differential is about 30% for men. Yet, once Reimers controls for differences in socioeconomic characteristics, the wage differential drops to about 5%. In fact, Reimers finds a large num-ber of Hispanic groups for whom the wage—given similar socioeco-nomic characteristics—is roughly similar to that of white non-Hispanic men.

Extending her analysis of wage discrimination to Hispanic women,

Reimers finds that Hispanic women have lower returns to education than do non-Hispanic women, and that minority women have flatter age–wage profiles than do white non-Hispanics. As was true for men, low education and attainment rather than discrimination largely account for the lower wages of minority women. The 1982 report of the National Commission for Employment Policy identifies low levels of formal schooling as one of the major barriers to success in the labor market faced by Hispanic workers, but the question of why Hispanics have so little formal education requires further research. The possibility of pre-market discrimination has not been eliminated.

Overall, these studies indicate that the low wage levels of Hispanics in the U.S. wage labor market do not result primarily from the type of "wage discrimination" usually found in black–white or male–female comparisons. Rather, it is largely due to the fact that Hispanics, on the average, have relatively low levels of those human capital characteristics that are valued in the labor market, especially education. One fruitful avenue for future research suggested by these analyses is the study of differences in the costs and opportunities for human capital investments between Hispanics and non-Hispanics, as well as between natives and immigrants.

Abowd and Killingsworth (Chapter 3), despite a methodological approach different from that of Reimers, find that for Hispanics not of Puerto Rican origin the standardized wage differential is very close to zero. Overall, their findings are qualitatively similar to Reimers's. Both chapters report large observed wage differentials between Hispanics and non-Hispanics, and both identify unequal educational attainment as a major determinant of the observed wage differentials. The robustness of this result suggests that a solution to the problem of low Hispanic wage rates requires a policy to promote additional education for Hispanics. Higher education not only raises wage rates, it also lowers the probability and duration of unemployment spells, which ultimately translate to lower earnings.

Gregory DeFreitas (Chapter 4) provides a systematic empirical analysis of the unemployment experience of Hispanics, examining differences in both the incidence and duration of unemployment. He documents the effects of immigration, education, and other socioeconomic variables on the Hispanic unemployment propensities. DeFreitas found that, at the national and regional level, Hispanics were considerably more likely to be unemployed one or more times during 1975 than were non-Hispanics. Although Hispanics and non-Hispanics in his sample did not differ significantly either in the average duration of joblessness or in the effects of most personal and labor market characteristics on the total length of unemployment spells, the higher unemployment rates of Hispanics resulted from a greater probability of their experiencing one or more spells of joblessness. DeFreitas's analysis indicates that differences in worker characteristics explain most of the unemployment differentials among Hispanics, but the unexplained residual gap suggests that discrimination also plays an important role in generating the higher Hispanic unemployment rates.

YOUTH EMPLOYMENT AND SCHOOL ENROLLMENT

Available research reports (see National Commission for Employment Policy, 1982; U.S. Commission on Civil Rights, 1982) and the chapters described above identify low educational achievement, particularly among Mexicans and Puerto Ricans, as a major determinant of low Hispanic earnings and high unemployment rates. Unusually high school-dropout rates are characteristic of Hispanics. Using 1979 National Longitudinal Survey data (NLS, Borus et al., 1980), Neil Fligstein and Roberto M. Fernandez (Chapter 5) probe the question of the determinants of high dropout rates for Mexican-Americans. (Because of the small sample size, reliable analyses were not obtained for the remaining Hispanic groups.) The authors' model of the process of educational attainment for Mexican-Americans includes elements reflecting the general process of educational attainment in the United States, together with ethnic and cultural factors that are unique to Mexican-Americans. By comparing Mexican-Americans and non-Hispanic whites, they isolate factors that partly account for the observed differences and evaluate their relative importance.

Fligstein and Fernandez find that, for Mexican-Americans, failure to complete high school is the major barrier to further education. Those who graduate go on to college at higher rates than do non-Hispanic whites, despite their lower socioeconomic origins. Just as they influence the education of whites, general family background factors influence Chicano school attendance and delay (repeating a grade), but only one of the ethnic factors—migration history—consistently affects attendance in high school and college and delay in high school. Fligstein and Fernandez conclude that programs designed to improve the English proficiency of Chicanos should enhance their rates of completing school. This conclusion concurs with those of the National Commission for Employment Policy (1982) and the U.S. Commission on Civil Rights (1982). Two policy-relevant research questions remain for future analyst: Does the pattern observed for Chicanos also hold for other Hispanics? and, How do school curricula, including the availability of bilingual education programs, influence the school performance of Hispanic youth?

Using data from the NLS continuous work history files, Stanley P. Stephenson, Jr. (Chapter 6), addresses a different aspect of the Hispanic youth employment experience. He focuses on how individual and market characteristics influence the unemployment rates of Hispanic youth. Stephenson concludes that Hispanic youth joblessness rates are quite high, due largely to relatively long spells of nonwork after losing a job. Sex differences occur primarily because women experience a period of no work nearly 50% longer than their male counterparts. His results show that family income, marital status, postschool vocational experience, age, and local unemployment rates significantly influence unemployment propensities, especially among young women. What sort of influence extensive unemployment during the early stages of the work life has on adult work experiences remains to be examined.

As did the researchers discussed earlier, both DeFreitas and Stephenson identify the relatively low educational levels of Hispanics as an important factor determining the Hispanic–non-Hispanic unemployment differential among adults and youth.

LABOR SUPPLY AND OCCUPATIONAL ALLOCATION OF WOMEN

There has been a tendency for researchers interested in the labor market experiences of Hispanics to focus their attention on men, to the relative neglect of women. The two studies in this section attempt to fill this void by examining differences in occupational and labor supply patterns among women of Hispanic origin, and in comparison to non-Hispanic white women.

In their chapter, Frank D. Bean, C. Gray Swicegood, and Allan G. King (Chapter 7) address an important research problem that has not been studied by analysts of the female labor force: How does the high fertility of Hispanic women influence their labor market behavior? Bean and his associates test several specific hypotheses that derive from the "role-incompatibility hypothesis." This hypothesis proposes that the choices women make between child care and work outside the home are in conflict with one another. They base their analysis on a subsample of the SIE suited to evaluate this agreement: currently married women of Hispanic origin, aged 20–34. Although there are differences in the ex-

tent to which the role-incompatibility hypothesis describes the fertility
and labor force behavior of Mexican-, Puerto Rican-, and Cuban-origin
women, in general the pattern of results is consistent with its predictions; namely, high fertility depresses female labor supply when women
must choose between employment and mothering.

Marta Tienda and Patricia Guhleman (Chapter 8) analyze women's
occupational position using one measure representing the socioeconomic status of occupations and another representing broad occupational strata. Education, an achieved characteristic, emerges as the most
important determinant of women's occupational position. Ascribed
characteristics, namely national origin and nativity, also contribute to
the observed occupational differentiation among Hispanics. Overall
these results highlight key differences in the access to and effective use
of social resources among the Hispanic national-origin groups, and suggest that further research should focus on why some ethnic groups are
more successful in gaining access to resources, especially education, that
ensure greater degrees of labor market success. They conclude that if
one were to equalize the Hispanics and non-Hispanics in terms of their
educational and language characteristics, as well as their demographic
and residential characteristics, the occupational-status gap between Hispanic and non-Hispanic white women would be reduced by only 27 to
57%. This finding suggests that labor market discrimination may partly
explain the disadvantaged occupational position of Hispanic women vis-
à-vis non-Hispanic white women. Thus, the forms and functions of
premarket discrimination must be studied before effective employment
and training policies can be devised.

LABOR MARKET CASE STUDIES

Of all the issues that have turned policy and research attention toward
the Hispanic population, perhaps none has received as much popular
and academic attention as that of undocumented immigration. And yet
this is an area where researchers concede they have much to learn.
Based on an ethnographic study of two Southwestern cities, Harley L.
Browning and Nestor Rodríguez (Chapter 9) deal with the process by
which undocumented Mexican workers integrate themselves into U.S.
society and its labor market. Their chapter, along with those by Saskia
Sassen-Koob (Chapter 10) and Roger Waldinger (Chapter 11), differs
from the others in this volume in that the models elaborated are geared
for ethnographic rather than econometric analysis. The richly textured
evidence garnered from the fieldwork provides many insights into the

process by which undocumented laborers enter the labor force and reveals the multiple strategies they use to sustain themselves socially and economically.

An important finding from the Browning and Rodríguez chapter is that undocumented workers do not attain status through occupational or job mobility, as do Chicanos or other native-born minority groups, but rather by accumulation of financial and material resources. Their prospects for mobility in the U.S. occupational structure are largely intergenerational, for few undocumented workers escape the exploitation of low-skilled, low-paying jobs. The labor market prospects for these younger workers are contingent on the acquisition of educational credentials, which it is unlikely that they can obtain. Whether the presence of undocumented workers provides a net gain or loss in community revenues is not addressed by the study, but the Browning and Rodríguez focus on settlers (as opposed to sojourners) suggests the possibility of a net gain in the short run, which might possibly be offset in the longer run as the offspring of undocumented workers enter the educational system. The quantification of labor market impacts requires both quantitative and qualitative data of the kind provided by Sassen-Koob and Waldinger.

The chapters by Sassen-Koob and Waldinger contribute to our understanding of the processes by which Hispanic workers are absorbed in the labor market. Both are studies of Central and South American immigrants, a group about which we know relatively little in comparison to Mexican, Cuban, and Puerto Rican immigrants. Both attempt to explain why a rise in the absorption of immigrant labor in the apparel industries in New York City between 1970 and 1980 was coupled with a substantial absolute and relative loss of jobs in these industries. Their insights help to address the argument that immigrants take jobs away from native workers.

Sassen-Koob's chapter is a macrostructural analysis that examines data on the city's industrial and occupational structure and documents major changes in the supply of jobs. She notes that the interdecade process of industrial dispersion involved a constant dynamic between recomposition of industries—mainly the emergence of large, capital-intensive firms, coupled with relocation—and constant changes in production technology, chiefly mechanization and de-skilling. She concludes that the demand for immigrant labor does not result from the need for cheap labor in declining industries; instead, the absorption of immigrant labor results from conditions that alter the demand for immigrant labor and facilitate the supply and subsequent incorporation of immigrants into the labor market.

Waldinger carries this argument further, examining directly the interaction between immigration and the structure of the New York City apparel industry. He argues that the structure of competitive industries generates opportunities for ethnically organized small-business activities. Based on various field experiences, Waldinger illustrates how immigrants use ethnicity to exploit labor market opportunities and secure protected market niches. By combining social and economic roles through family ownership of apparel firms, network recruitment, and the employment of fellow nationals, immigrant firms may surmount organizational barriers that impede performance among ethnically diverse competitors. These case studies reveal how ethnic differentiation operates to stratify the Hispanic population and to produce the patterns of inequality reflected in quantitative measures of labor market outcomes—earnings, labor supply, and unemployment.

An Agenda for Future Research

The studies in this volume provide important insights into the broad issues of how Hispanic national-origin groups differ, and more specific questions about why these differences emerge, such as (1) What are the key determinants of the Hispanic–non-Hispanic wage differential? (2) Why do the incidence and duration of unemployment differ among Hispanics? (3) Is there labor market discrimination against Hispanics? (4) How do labor outcomes differ between Hispanic men and women? and (5) How do local labor markets work? Obviously these studies do not exhaust the theoretical and empirical questions posed above. Indeed they raise as many questions as they answer. Therefore we close by identifying several areas where further exploration should be especially fruitful.

The historical experience of Hispanics in the United States has been little studied, although the past has often served as a key for understanding the present, if not for predicting the future. With the exception of Mexicans and Puerto Ricans, most of what is known about Hispanics in the United States is based on analyses of cross-section data sets like the 1970 census and the 1976 SIE (U.S. Department of Commerce, 1978). While instructive, these "snapshot" glimpses of the Hispanic experience in the labor market cannot provide an understanding of the social processes by which Hispanics arrived in the United States, experienced acculturation, and transmitted the newly learned skills and values to their children. The microdata files from the 1940 and 1950 censuses present a unique opportunity to bolster the historical evidence with empirical analyses at the national and subnational level.

Although the issue of immigration is often raised in Hispanic studies, the companion issue of emigration is seldom discussed. The theory of human capital investments suggests that the expectation of emigration will have strong effects on the individual's (and employer's) incentive to invest in human capital. Thus, human capital differences among Hispanic and non-Hispanic individuals may be directly related to differences in the probability of emigration among the groups. Moreover, a study of emigration is vital to evaluate the net volume and impact of immigration to the United States from Latin America and the Caribbean.

Another issue that our volume barely discusses is illegal immigration. Although the number of illegal Hispanic immigrants in the United States is not precisely known (and reported numbers fluctuate wildly), there exist a large number of Hispanics (mainly Mexicans) residing and working illegally in the United States. Their illegal status creates incentives for the individuals and their employers to engage in different labor contracts than could otherwise be made. Fear of deportation may raise the costs to illegal aliens of complaining against unfair labor practices and wages below the minimum rate. If illegal aliens tend to engage in relatively harmful labor contracts, and if a substantial number of illegal aliens do reside in the United States on a regular basis, observed measures of aggregate Hispanic economic welfare may be seriously biased, depending on whether and how many illegal aliens are represented in the surveys analyzed.

Because this question clouds our understanding of the labor market experiences of the legally resident Hispanic population, it is worthwhile for researchers to differentiate labor market impacts of temporary versus semipermanent illegal residents, especially with respect to the amount of labor market displacement produced by each. It is conceivable that labor-certified legal immigrants contribute to labor market displacement of native workers, although this question has not been well researched. Only preliminary work about labor market competition and substitution between legal-immigrant and native workers has been conducted (Borjas, 1984). Further empirical research should be instructive in determining to what extent illegal immigrants displace native workers. Unfortunately, because representative data about illegal immigrants are difficult to obtain, no study has convincingly demonstrated the existence of displacement effects.

Perhaps the most important general finding in this volume is that a large fraction of Hispanic–non-Hispanic wage, occupation, and unemployment differentials can be directly attributed to the relatively low educational attainment of Hispanics. How Hispanics make educational decisions for themselves and their children is, therefore, of crucial importance. The analysis of the demand for education and other learning activities by Hispanics should help identify the financial (or social) obstacles preventing Hispanics from investing in human capital. This, more than any other topic, deserves immediate research attention. Decisions made today about education will affect Hispanic labor market entrants in 10 to 20 years, and continuously thereafter, as new birth cohorts enter the labor market. Socioeconomic parity among Hispanics and non-Hispanic workers in future generations depends on today's educational policies.

Appendix: The Survey of Income and Education (SIE), 1976

As part of its legislative mandate, the Department of Health and Human Services, formerly the Department of Health, Education, and Welfare (HEW), distributes funds authorized by Title I of the Elementary and Secondary Education Act of 1965. The formula used in the distribution of these funds is based upon an estimate of the number of children 5–17 years of age living in families with incomes below the official poverty level in each state. Previously, this was based upon estimates derived from the 1970 U.S. Census. However, given the enormous changes in the residential distribution of the population, the estimates became increasingly unreliable toward the middle of the decade. Though national estimates of the number of children in poverty can be obtained from the Current Population Survey (CPS) on a yearly basis, estimates generated from the CPS for geographical areas as small as states are not statistically reliable owing to small sample size.

In response to the problem of unreliable data, Congress enacted the Educational Amendments Act of 1974 (Public Law 93-380) to provide for the collection of current data sufficiently detailed to comply with the requirements of distributing educational funds. As a result of this legislation, the Survey of Income and Education (SIE) was conducted between April and July, 1976. The basic survey instrument consisted of questions from the March CPS dealing with current employment, work experience, and income sources and amounts. (For a description of the data set, see U.S. Department of Commerce, 1978.) In order to address various concerns of other HEW programs, additional questions covering school enrollment, disability, health insurance, food stamp recipiency, household assets, household composition, and language proficiency were included.

The SIE is based on a stratified multistage cluster design. Primary sampling units (PSUs) for the SIE consisted of counties and independent cities. These PSUs were grouped to form strata within each state according to the proportion of children 5–17 years of age living in families with incomes below poverty at the time of the 1970 census. Of approximately 158,500 households eligible for interview, 151,170 households were contacted and 150,975 families containing 440,815 individuals were interviewed.

Because of its large sample size, the oversampling of disadvantaged minorities, and the differentiating of ethnic groups according to specific national origins, the SIE is particularly well suited for the study of Hispanics. Ethnicity was determined on the basis of the respondent's answer to the question, "What is_____'s origin or descent?" Populations whose origins are Mexico, Puerto Rico, Cuba, or Central and South America are thus distinguished from one another on the basis of the respondent's self-identification. The SIE includes various terms, such as *Mexicano* and *Chicano*, in order to maximize unbiased coverage of the Hispanic population.

In spite of the numerous options available to respondents for identification with a particular Hispanic national-origin group, a relatively large share is categorized as Other Spanish (listed in the tables of this volume as Other Hispanic). Whereas this group should consist of Hispanic individuals who do not belong in any of the other designations, it is probable that a significant proportion of these individuals are descendants of the Spanish who settled the area (Grebler et al., 1970). The Mexican-American population differs greatly in the length of time families have been in the United States. Some Hispanics of Mexican heritage who reside in northern New Mexico no longer identify with more recent immigrants. These individuals consider themselves to be more Spanish than Mexican, and in response to survey probes about self-identified ethnicity may identify themselves as Hispanic but not as Mexican-American or Chicano. We cannot be sure to what extent this problem affects the studies in this volume. Nevertheless, in the interpretation of results we emphasize the fact that the category Other Hispanic is not a unique classification.

Relatively few Hispanics are interviewed in most national surveys, including the CPS, because they constitute a relatively small proportion of the total U.S. population and because they are regionally concentrated. The SIE contains interviews with 10,620 Hispanic men and women aged 14 to 64. Most of the analyses in this volume are limited to

Hispanics between 18 and 64 years of age. Among respondents between the ages of 18 and 64, interviews were obtained with the following number in each national-origin group: 4800 Mexicans, 1006 Puerto Ricans, 455 Cubans, 558 Central and South Americans, and 1608 individuals of Other Hispanic origin. In the same age range, 39,322 non-Hispanic white males and females were interviewed.

PART I

Earnings and Labor Supply

A Comparative Analysis of the Wages of Hispanics, Blacks, and Non-Hispanic Whites*

Cordelia W. Reimers

Introduction

Hispanics, like blacks, are often classified as a disadvantaged minority in the American labor market. This classification rests primarily on comparisons of labor market outcomes between minority men and white non-Hispanic men. For instance, the Hispanic–Anglo wage ratio for men in 1975 ranged from .72 for Mexicans to .89 for Cubans.[1] Similarly, minority men in the labor force work fewer hours on an annual basis than do white non-Hispanic men. These wage and hours differentials contribute to lower annual earnings and lower family incomes than those enjoyed by whites.

That Hispanic men are a disadvantaged group in the U.S. labor market is widely recognized; little is known, however, about the specific sources of this disadvantage. For example, how much do lower education levels, younger average age, recency of immigration, English language problems, or residence in low-wage areas of the country contrib-

* Portions of this paper were presented at the Hispanic Labor Conference, Santa Barbara, California, February 4–5, 1982; and at the Eastern Economic Association meeting, Washington, D.C., May 1982. This research was supported by the U.S. Department of Labor, Employment and Training Administration, Grant No. 21-34-78-60 for research on Hispanic-American labor market problems and issues. I am indebted to Gilles Grenier and Jesse Abraham for excellent research assistance. Barry Chiswick, Mark Killingsworth, Ralph Smith, Marta Tienda, and members of the Princeton University Labor Economics/Industrial Relations Seminar made useful suggestions.

[1] Author's tabulations from the 1976 Survey of Income and Education (U.S. Department of Commerce, 1978), as reported in Table 2.3.

ute to the Hispanics' lower wages? How important is labor market discrimination?

In the case of women our knowledge of the basic facts is even more limited. Are Hispanic and black women also disadvantaged in the labor market relative to white non-Hispanic women? Are their wage rates substantially lower than those of nonminority women? Do differential levels of labor supply contribute to observed differences in levels of family income?

This chapter analyzes the wage structure of Hispanic men and Hispanic women to provide a detailed picture of the factors contributing to observed differentials among national-origin groups and a comparison with black and white non-Hispanic men and women. I first look at the average values of various wage-related personal characteristics for each ethnic group. To find out how important these characteristics are in determining wages, I then estimate (within each gender group) a separate wage function for each ethnic group: Mexicans, Puerto Ricans, Cubans, Central and South Americans, Other Hispanics, black non-Hispanics, and white non-Hispanics. The data are from the 1976 Survey of Income and Education (SIE; U.S. Department of Commerce, 1978). The wage samples consist of civilian employees aged 14 and older who were not self-employed nor full-time students. These wage samples contain about 60% of the total number of men and 40% of the total number of women in the data set.

Because the observed wage structure is affected by the decisions individuals make about whether to participate in the wage and salary sector as well as by the wage offers they receive, I correct for possible sample-selection bias to obtain consistent estimates of the parameters of the wage-offer function facing each gender and ethnic group. A group's wage-offer function shows the effect of various personal characteristics on the average wage offered by employers to members of the group, whether or not the offers are accepted and the individuals appear in the wage sample. The group's observed-wage function, on the other hand, shows the effect of these characteristics on the average wage that is actually observed in the wage sample. The average observed wage will differ from the average wage offer if inclusion in the wage sample is not random with respect to the wage offer. For example, if those who receive unusually low wage offers are less likely to accept them, the average observed wage will be higher than the average wage offer.

Examination of the parameters of the wage function reveals, among other things, to what extent English-language deficiencies reduce wages, whether black Hispanics earn less than white Hispanics, and whether minorities earn more in the public than the private sector. They also tell how rapidly immigrants' earnings rise after they come to the United States, how the returns to foreign schooling and work experience compare with the returns to schooling and work experience acquired in the United States, and how these returns vary across gender and ethnic groups.

Finally, we want to know how much the differences in average personal characteristics—education, age, recency of immigration, and so on—and in parameters of the wage function contribute to the observed wage differentials between minority individuals and white non-Hispanics. To answer this question, I present a detailed breakdown of the observed wage differentials, showing the portions due to (1) differences in sample-selection bias; (2) geographical differences in price levels; (3) differences in average personal characteristics, broken down to show separately the importance of education, potential work experience, nativity and date of immigration, English fluency, and other characteristics; and (4) differences in parameters of the wage function due to labor market discrimination and other omitted factors.

The section following the discussion of the data and general model specification presents the empirical results for the male samples, and the next section presents the results for the female samples. In each of these sections I present the average wage-related characteristics of the various ethnic groups, discuss the estimated parameters of the wage functions, and describe the breakdowns of the minority–Anglo wage differentials for each ethnic group.

Data and Model Specification

This study made use of the 1976 SIE (described in the Appendix to Chapter 1). The most serious omissions in the SIE are measures of accumulated work experience, job training, and ability. Wage rates are not reported directly, but must be computed from reported annual earnings, total weeks worked, and usual hours worked per week in 1975. Despite these shortcomings, the SIE is an attractive data set for investigating Hispanic–Anglo earnings differentials because it contains immigration and language information and because the large sample enables one to examine relatively small ethnic groups, such as Cubans, separately.

The data in the SIE reflect the conditions of a recession year, 1975. Since all sorts of differentials in the labor market tend to widen in recessions, my findings may not represent "normal" conditions. I minimize this potential problem by focusing on wage rates, which fluctuate less over the cycle than employment or hours, and by taking account of sample-selection bias in estimating the wage functions. Therefore, inter-group variations in employment over the cycle should not affect the results.

From the SIE I took the records of all individuals aged 14 or older who identified themselves as being of Hispanic origin—i.e., Mexican-American, Chicano, Mexican, Mexicano, Puerto Rican, Cuban, Central or South American, and the residual category of Other Hispanic. The first four groups constitute my "Mexican" category. I also extracted random samples of households headed by white and black non-Hispanics. The seven samples of each gender are mutually exclusive: the Hispanics may be of any race; the whites and blacks include non-Hispanics only. Non-Hispanics who are neither white nor black (e.g., Asians) are excluded from this study.

For estimating the wage function, I restricted the samples to those for whom a reasonably accurate wage rate could be obtained by dividing annual earnings by annual weeks worked times usual hours worked per week in 1975. The wage samples were therefore composed of civilians who worked for pay in 1975; whose earnings were from wages and salaries only; who were either not enrolled in school on February 1, 1976, or had worked over 1250 hours in 1975 if they were enrolled; for whom I had complete information on the explanatory variables; and whose hourly earnings, adjusted for the cost of living, were between 10¢ and $50 for Hispanics and blacks and between 10¢ and $100 for white non-Hispanics.[2] Thus I excluded the self-employed, students working part time, armed forces personnel, unpaid family workers and others with no reported earnings, those lacking information on such explanatory variables as language fluency and health status, and a handful of outliers on hourly earnings. The reasons for the first three exclusions are as follows: for the self-employed, computed hourly earnings are likely to be a very poor measure of the wage rate; weeks and hours worked are not available for the armed forces; and students often choose part-time jobs for convenience, at wages that do not reflect their human capital.

The wage samples, thus restricted, contain only about 60% of the men and 40% of the women aged 14 or older in the data set. Moreover, inclusion in the wage sample is the consequence of several decisions by the respondents that might very well be nonrandom with respect to the

---

[2] Examination of the hourly earnings distributions for each group revealed a few cases with such extremely low or high values that it seemed they must result from errors in reporting earnings or weeks or hours; because such extreme values would exert a great deal of leverage in an ordinary least squares regression, it seemed desirable to exclude them from the samples rather than to treat them as ordinary errors-in-equation.

stochastic error in the wage equation, and which may therefore bias the results. They must have chosen to be civilian wage and salary employees rather than full-time students, self-employed persons, full-time homemakers or other nonmarket workers, retirees, or members of the armed forces. This decision was presumably the outcome of optimizing behavior with respect to the current use of their stock of human capital. Because omitted variables that affect individuals' productivity in the wage and salary sector probably affect their productivity differently in the education, armed forces, self-employment, and nonmarket sectors, I would expect some systematic censoring of the sample to occur, with attendant bias to the estimated coefficients of the wage equation.

To see this, let the wage-offer function for individual i in group j be

$$\ln W_{ij} = X_{ij}\beta_j + \varepsilon_{1ij}. \tag{1}$$

Let the rule governing participation in the wage and salary sector be as follows: individual i in group j participates if and only if

$$Z_{ij}\gamma_j + \varepsilon_{2ij} > 0. \tag{2}$$

In these expressions, $\ln W_{ij}$ is the natural logarithm of the wage rate, X_{ij} and Z_{ij} are vectors of known individual characteristics, β_j and γ_j are vectors of unknown coefficients that are common to the members of the group, and ε_{1ij} and ε_{2ij} are random errors that reflect unknown influences on the wage rate and the participation decision, respectively. I assume that ε_{1ij} and ε_{2ij} are jointly normally distributed, with

$$E(\varepsilon_{1ij}) = E(\varepsilon_{2ij}) = 0,$$

$$\text{Cov}(\varepsilon_{1ij}\varepsilon_{2i'j'}) = \begin{bmatrix} \sigma_{11j} & \sigma_{12j} \\ \sigma_{12j} & 1 \end{bmatrix} \quad \text{if} \quad i = i' \quad \text{and} \quad j = j',$$

$$= 0 \quad \text{if} \quad i \neq i' \quad \text{or} \quad j \neq j'.$$

Then, as Heckman (1979) has shown,

$$E(\ln W_{ij}|\text{in sample}) = X_{ij}\beta_j + E(\varepsilon_{1ij}|\text{in sample})$$

$$= X_{ij}\beta_j + \sigma_{12j}\hat{\lambda}_{ij} \tag{3}$$

where $\hat{\lambda}_{ij} = f(Z_{ij}\hat{\gamma}_j)/F(Z_{ij}\hat{\gamma}_j)$, in which $f(\cdot)$ is the standard normal density function, and $F(\cdot)$ is the standard normal distribution function. If participation in the wage and salary sector is not random, given one's observed characteristics, so that $\sigma_{12j} \neq 0$, then $E(\varepsilon_{1ij}|\text{in sample}) \neq 0$ and ordinary least squares estimates of β_j will be subject to a type of "omitted variable" bias.

Therefore, to get consistent estimates of β_j, I estimate a sample partici-pation probit to obtain $\hat{\gamma}_j$, compute $\hat{\lambda}_{ij}$, and include it as an additional regressor in the wage function, which is then estimated by ordinary least squares:

$$\ln W_{ij} = X_{ij}\beta_j + \sigma_{12j}\hat{\lambda}_{ij} + v_{ij}, \tag{4}$$

where $v_{ij} \sim N(0, \Sigma_j)$.[3]

The variables in the reduced-form probit equation are defined in Table 2.1, and their estimated coefficients are given in Table 2.2 (for men) and Table 2.11 (for women). In addition to the variables in the wage equa-tion, the probit includes marital status, certain determinants of the spouse's wage if married, number and ages of family members, exoge-nous family income, and the maximum AFDC (Aid to Families with Dependent Children) payment that would be available to the family if it had no other income.

For the wage equation itself, as indicated above, I computed the aver-age hourly wage rate as total wage and salary earnings in 1975, divided by the product of total weeks worked and usual hours worked in those weeks. To allow for differences in wages due to price-level variation across the country, I divided each person's hourly earnings by a cost-of-living index for his place of residence.[4] The dependent variable for the estimated wage equation was the natural logarithm of real hourly earn-ings, *real* in this case meaning adjusted in that manner for the cost of living. This is equivalent to entering the natural logarithm of the cost index as an explanatory variable, and constraining its coefficient to equal one. This adjustment eliminated 21% of the original wage differential between Mexican and white non-Hispanic females, but widened the differential for Puerto Picans, who tend to live in the high-cost North-east.

As explanatory variables I used the following aspects of human capi-tal: educational attainment, years of education obtained abroad, poten-tial work experience (i.e., age minus preschool and school years), mili-tary experience (for men), health status, and command of English.

---

[3] I thank James Heckman for supplying a computer program that estimates the probit and wage equation and correctly computes $Cov(\beta_j)$, taking account of $Cov(v_{ij}) = \Sigma_j$.

[4] I used the Bureau of Labor Statistics (BLS) index of comparative cost of living based on an intermediate budget for a four-person family in autumn 1975 (U.S. Department of Labor, 1977, p. 277). To the extent possible, I matched the person's SMSA (Standard Metropolitan Statistical Area) of residence with the same SMSA in the BLS survey. When a sample member lived in an SMSA not included in the BLS survey, I used the cost index for the closest comparable SMSA. When a sample member did not live within any SMSA, I used the "nonmetropolitan" cost index for the region of residence.

TABLE 2.1
Definitions of Variables Used in the Analyses

Variable	Definition
WAGE (W)	Hourly wage rate, calculated as annual earnings/weeks worked × usual hours worked per week) in 1975
LNWAGE (ln W)	Natural logarithm of WAGE
LNCOST (ln P)	Natural logarithm of BLS cost index for moderate family budget in SMSA or region of residence. If SMSA of residence was not in the BLS sample, another SMSA in the same state or region was used. If residence was not identified as being in an SMSA, the BLS index for nonmetropolitan areas in the region was used
LNRWAGE ln(W/P)	LNWAGE minus LNCOST
ED	Highest grade of school completed
FORED	Years attended school abroad (= 0 if born in U.S. mainland)
AGE	Age, in years
AGESQ	Square of AGE
EXP	Potential work experience; age minus highest grade attended minus 5
EXPSQ	Square of EXP
USEXP	Years of potential work experience in U.S.: if born in U.S. mainland, age minus highest grade attended minus 5; if born outside U.S. mainland, estimated time in U.S. (using midpoint of immigration period) or age minus highest grade attended minus 5, whichever is smaller
USEXPSQ	Square of USEXP
FOREXP	Years of potential work experience before immigrating to U.S.: age minus highest grade attended minus 5 minus USEXP
FOREXPSQ	Square of FOREXP
VET	= 1 if veteran; 0 otherwise (men only)
MAR	= 1 if married, spouse present; 0 otherwise
NUMKIDS	No. of children under 18
KIDSLT6	No. of children under age 6
KIDS611	No. of children aged 6–11
KIDS1217	No. of children aged 12–17
FAM1864	No. of family members aged 18–64
FAM65	No. of family members aged 65 or more
FBORN	= 1 if born outside U.S. mainland; 0 otherwise
US06	No. of years since immigrated to U.S., 1970 or after (= 0 if born in U.S. or immigrated before 1970)
US46	= 1 if immigrated to U.S. 1970–72; 0 otherwise
US711	= 1 if immigrated to U.S. 1965–69; 0 otherwise
US1216	= 1 if immigrated to U.S. 1960–64; 0 otherwise
US1726	= 1 if immigrated to U.S. 1950–59; 0 otherwise
US2799	= 1 if immigrated to U.S. before 1950; 0 otherwise
ENGNVG	= 1 if does not speak and understand English very well; 0 otherwise

(Continued)

TABLE 2.1 (*Continued*)

Variable	Definition
HEALTH	= 1 if health limits ability to work; 0 otherwise
GOVT	= 1 if government employee; 0 otherwise
FGOVT	= 1 if federal government employee; 0 otherwise
SGOVT	= 1 if state government employee; 0 otherwise
LGOVT	= 1 if local government employee; 0 otherwise
NONWHT	= 1 if race is nonwhite; 0 otherwise
PROPHIS	Percentage Hispanic of population in state of residence
$\hat{\lambda}$	Inverse of Mill's ratio, predicted from reduced-form probit equation for being in wage sample
INCOME	Exogenous family income: dividends, interest, rents, pensions, child support, and other non-earnings-conditioned transfers; other family members' unemployment insurance, workmen's compensation, and veterans' benefits; earnings of family members other than self and spouse (measured in $thousands per year)
WELF	Maximum AFDC payment available to family if no other income (depends on state of residence, whether a male head is present, and number of children under age 18) (measured in $thousands per month)
SPED	Spouse's highest grade of school completed (= 0 if MAR = 0)
SPAGE	Spouse's age, in years (= 0 if MAR = 0)
SPAGESQ	Square of SPAGE (= 0 if MAR = 0)
SPFBORN	= 1 if spouse born outside U.S. mainland; 0 otherwise (= 0 if MAR = 0)
INSAMPLE	= 1 if in sample for wage equation: employed in 1975, civilian, no self-employment income, not enrolled in school (or worked over 1250 hours if enrolled), $.10 < W/P < $50 for Hispanics, $.10 < W/P < $100 for white non-Hispanics; = 0 if not in wage sample

Source: Cordelia Reimers, "Labor Market Discrimination against Hispanic and Black Men," *Review of Economics and Statistics*, 65 (Nov. 1983), 576, Table 4. Reprinted by permission of the North-Holland Publishing Co., Amsterdam.

Because much of a person's human capital is country-specific, I also controlled for nativity and length of time in the United States. Since the data contain no measure of actual accumulated labor market experience, for women I included marital status and number of children as proxies for "home time," in conjunction with potential experience, to control for actual work experience.

In addition to the human capital variables, I included variables for government employment and for race. If, as Sharon Smith (1977) has found, government employees earn more than private-sector workers with the same human capital, and if one ethnic group has greater access to government jobs than another, this will affect the relative average wage. I would like to be able to distinguish this effect. Since we know blacks suffer from discrimination, and some Hispanics are black, I would like to know how much of the Hispanics' lower average wage is due to race, and how much discrimination affects Hispanics who are white. I did not control for urban versus rural location because this information was suppressed in a great many cases by census procedures to preserve confidentiality. Insofar as location is known, the effect of urban residence, as well as region, on the wage rate is captured by the cost-of-living adjustment.

Wage Determination of Hispanic Men

The estimated probit coefficients reported in Table 2.2, which predict the probability of men being in the sample, look reasonable. Age and health are the only consistently significant determinants of being a wage or salary earner. Education, welfare, exogenous income, marital status, and spouse's age and education also have the expected effect, either positive or negative, in all but 5 of the 49 instances (assuming that the effect of the spouse's wage on a person's labor supply is negative).

The mean values in Table 2.3 of the variables for the men in the sample of wage earners reveal a number of ways in which Hispanics are disadvantaged by possessing less human capital on average than white non-Hispanic men. Average education levels are around 12.5 years for white non-Hispanic male wage earners and 10.5 years for blacks, yet are less than 10 years for Mexicans and Puerto Ricans. The other three Hispanic groups average between 11 and 12 grades of school. The Mexicans and Puerto Ricans are younger than the other groups on average (see EXP), and the Cubans are even older than white non-Hispanics. Almost all of the Cubans and Central and South Americans are foreign-born, and members of the latter group arrived in the United States even more recently than the Cubans. Eighty percent of the Puerto Ricans were born on the island. Almost 75% of the Mexicans, on the other hand, were born in the United States. The Other Hispanics are overwhelmingly (90%) from the second or later generations in the United States. This group includes persons of mixed Hispanic ancestry as well as those who did not identify with any of the listed Hispanic groups.

Not surprisingly, the percentages of each group who are fluent in English (the complement of ENGNVG) and who have been in the armed forces reflect the percentages born in the United States. Government employment also tends to reflect birthplace, except that Mexican and

TABLE 2.2
Estimated Coefficients of Reduced-Form Probit Equations for the Probability of a Man's Being in the Wage-Earner Sample

Variable	White non-Hispanic	Mexican	Puerto Rican	Cuban	Central and South American	Other Hispanic	Black non-Hispanic
Intercept	−2.68* (.201)	−2.84* (.267)	−3.02* (.724)	−3.27* (1.20)	−3.10 (1.61)	−3.00* (.482)	−3.89* (.210)
ED	.023* (.0078)	−.020 (.011)	.020 (.030)	.066 (.043)	−.024 (.055)	.012 (.020)	.027* (.0085)
FBORN × FORED	.018 (.027)	.029 (.018)	.021 (.025)	−.042 (.036)	.0083 (.046)	−.015 (.036)	.010 (.053)
AGE	.146* (.010)	.188* (.014)	.157* (.038)	.143* (.050)	.257* (.072)	.179* (.025)	.204* (.010)
AGESQ	−.0017* (.0001)	−.0021* (.0002)	−.0016* (.0005)	−.0014* (.0005)	−.0029* (.0009)	−.0020* (.0003)	−.0022* (.0001)
FBORN	−1.85* (.797)	−.431 (.226)	−.562 (.453)	−.556 (.758)	−1.82* (.860)	.022 (1.02)	−1.14 (.839)
FBORN × US06	.497* (.216)	.150* (.054)	.187* (.093)	.122 (.124)	.215* (.091)	−.027 (.210)	.245 (.155)
FBORN × US711	2.07* (.886)	.692* (.257)	.712 (.437)	.699 (.624)	.690 (.460)	.013 (.973)	1.10 (.752)
FBORN × US1216	1.42 (.942)	.293 (.263)	.902* (.438)	.778 (.615)	.505 (.497)	−.678 (.977)	.815 (.884)
FBORN × US1726	1.86* (.782)	.354 (.239)	.930* (.409)	1.64* (.739)	1.28* (.627)	−.702 (1.03)	1.31 (1.03)
FBORN × US2799	1.77* (.776)	.361 (.249)	.655 (.459)	1.19 (.803)	2.39* (1.02)	−.128 (1.02)	−.140 (1.09)
ENGNVG	−.066 (.282)	.069 (.089)	.330 (.197)	.037 (.262)	−.083 (.280)	−.036 (.157)	−.028 (.544)
NONWHT	—	−.120 (.182)	−.590* (.220)	.637 (.520)	−.321 (.329)	.435 (.272)	—
HEALTH	−.505* (.057)	−.760* (.086)	−1.51* (.200)	−1.15* (.296)	−.962* (.455)	−.883* (.142)	−.916* (.063)
VET	.128* (.046)	.077 (.075)	.453* (.198)	.447 (.441)	.914 (.733)	.248* (.128)	.111 (.060)
PROPHIS	.0001 (.0036)	−.0061* (.0029)	−.020 (.017)	−.0070 (.028)	−.0009 (.020)	−.0038 (.0038)	.0047 (.0046)

TABLE 2.2 (*Continued*)

Variable	White non-Hispanic	Mexican	Puerto Rican	Cuban	Central and South American	Other Hispanic	Black non-Hispanic
MAR	2.22*	2.27*	1.81	1.46	.798	1.01	2.32*
	(.310)	(.391)	(1.03)	(1.43)	(2.16)	(.767)	(.377)
KIDSLT6	−.086*	.108*	.373*	−.118	.352	.197	−.060
	(.044)	(.046)	(.125)	(.200)	(.233)	(.110)	(.049)
KIDS611	−.067*	−.035	−.123	−.129	−.219	.013	.014
	(.033)	(.036)	(.090)	(.158)	(.222)	(.073)	(.034)
KIDS1217	−.156*	−.109*	−.111	−.071	−.077	−.153*	−.161*
	(.026)	(.028)	(.083)	(.114)	(.221)	(.050)	(.026)
FAM1864	.110*	.099*	.045	.149	.276	.100	.118*
	(.027)	(.031)	(.109)	(.137)	(.237)	(.058)	(.025)
FAM65	−.061	−.170	−.830*	−.267	−.807	.045	−.126*
	(.056)	(.102)	(.312)	(.242)	(.577)	(.143)	(.061)
INCOME ($thousands)	−.021*	−.023*	.0018	−.0080	−.067*	−.021*	−.023*
	(.0030)	(.0059)	(.017)	(.020)	(.032)	(.0092)	(.0045)
WELF ($thousands)	.384*	−.318	−.553	−.857	.706	−.752	−.017
	(.156)	(.202)	(.437)	(.890)	(.906)	(.428)	(.188)
SPED × MAR	−.040*	−.040*	−.013	−.026	−.0002	−.0048	−.037*
	(.011)	(.013)	(.031)	(.042)	(.054)	(.026)	(.013)
SPAGE × MAR	−.076*	−.075*	−.069	−.047	−.110	−.037	−.079*
	(.015)	(.021)	(.056)	(.071)	(.125)	(.038)	(.017)
SPAGESQ × MAR	.0007*	.0007*	.0008	.0004	.0018	.0003	.0008*
	(.0002)	(.0003)	(.0007)	(.0008)	(.0017)	(.0004)	(.0002)
SPFBORN × MAR	.260*	−.157	−.552*	.088	.262	.362	−.580*
	(.131)	(.102)	(.221)	(.381)	(.428)	(.246)	(.238)
No. of observations	5,168	2,859	525	266	228	923	4,050
Max log likelihood	−2765.33	−1324.19	−222.47	−130.77	−90.92	−424.21	−1863.22

Source: 1976 Survey of Income and Education (U.S. Department of Commerce, 1978).
Notes: Dependent variable is INSAMPLE for wage equation. Standard errors are in parentheses. Variables are defined in Table 2.1
* Statistically significant at the 5% level.

TABLE 2.3
Means of Variables for Men in the Sample of Wage Earners

Variable	White non-Hispanic	Mexican	Puerto Rican	Cuban	Central and South American	Other Hispanic	Black non-Hispanic
WAGE (W) (dollars/hr)	5.97	4.31	4.52	5.33	4.94	5.20	4.65
LNWAGE (ln W)	1.607	1.303	1.389	1.515	1.397	1.466	1.374
LNCOST (ln P)	-.025	-.068	.074	-.015	.051	-.043	-.028
LNRWAGE (ln W/P)	1.632	1.371	1.316	1.530	1.346	1.509	1.402
ED (grade)	12.41	9.44	9.75	11.32	11.79	11.04	10.54
EXP (years)	20.77	19.51	20.45	24.12	19.05	21.33	22.96
EXPSQ	669.08	597.75	602.54	788.37	487.16	693.76	788.59
VET	.486	.304	.255	.112	.085	.427	.374
FBORN	.028	.269	.793	.950	.921	.119	.015
FBORN × FORED (years)	.192	1.31	5.25	8.64	9.23	1.04	.149
FBORN × US46	.0024	.040	.073	.125	.262	.019	.0059
FBORN × US711	.0031	.048	.086	.250	.220	.040	.0041

FBORN × US1216	.0010	.029	.102	.331	.134	.023	.0018
FBORN × US1726	.010	.059	.350	.150	.116	.010	.0014
FBORN × US2799	.010	.045	.115	.056	.037	.015	.0005
ENGNVG	.0076	.321	.446	.538	.482	.186	.0018
HEALTH	.101	.092	.076	.056	.055	.090	.120
GOVT	.169	.177	.150	.081	.104	.226	.240
NONWHT	0	.022	.086	.056	.116	.052	1.0
λ	.536	.416	.395	.461	.309	.454	.472
Selection bias ($\hat{\sigma}_{12}\lambda$)	-.198	-.163	-.084	-.134	.015	-.113	-.202
ED × FBORN (grade)	.329	1.93	7.38	10.73	10.80	1.19	.174
USEXP (years)	20.56	16.74	15.50	12.19	9.72	20.07	22.79
FBORN × USEXP (years)	.574	3.64	12.02	11.04	8.20	1.51	.125
FBORN × FOREXP (years)	.208	2.77	4.94	11.92	9.33	1.25	.168
USEXPSQ	656.49	474.24	365.76	244.24	169.35	641.10	782.67
FBORN × USEXPSQ	17.79	90.80	264.10	196.42	126.95	32.50	1.63
FBORN × FOREXPSQ	4.18	60.71	91.38	293.52	191.01	27.95	3.56
PROPHIS (%)	3.40	14.89	5.22	6.12	6.68	17.11	3.41

Source: Cordelia Reimers, "Labor Market Discrimination against Hispanic and Black Men," *Review of Economics and Statistics, 65* (Nov. 1983), 571, Table 1. Reprinted by permission of the North-Holland Publishing Co., Amsterdam.

Notes: Variables are defined in Table 2.1. Unless otherwise indicated, means reflect fractions.

Puerto Rican men are about as likely as white non-Hispanics to hold government jobs, while blacks and Other Hispanics are much more likely to do so.

PARAMETERS OF THE MALE WAGE FUNCTIONS

The estimated wage equations, corrected for selectivity bias, are reported in Table 2.4. The coefficient of $\hat{\lambda}$, which represents the covariance between the errors in the sample participation probit and the wage equation, is negative for all groups except the Central and South Americans. It is significantly negative for the largest samples of men—whites, blacks, Mexicans, and Other Hispanics. Apparently men in these ethnic groups who have unusually high market wage offers, given their measured characteristics, have even higher productivity in other sectors and so are less likely to be in the wage sample.[5]

My significantly negative estimates of σ_{12} (the coefficient of $\hat{\lambda}$) are not simply a result of the broad age range (everyone over age 13) included in the samples I analyzed. When I estimated the same model for Mexican men aged 25 through 59, the coefficient of $\hat{\lambda}$ was also significantly negative, even though the sample participation rate was much higher (81% rather than 62%). This illustrates the point that there is no necessary connection between the sample participation rate and the correlation between the stochastic terms in the wage and the participation equations. A 50% sample may be randomly selected, while a 90% sample may systematically exclude the highest 10% of wage offers. Thus, choosing an age group with a high wage and salary-sector participation rate would not eliminate the possibility of selectivity bias (though it might reduce its quantitative impact on the estimated parameters).

An examination of the estimates of the coefficients of the wage-offer functions in Table 2.4 reveals that race (NONWHT) has no significant impact on the wages of Hispanic men; black Hispanics suffer from one handicap, not two. The sign on the NONWHT dummy variable is actually positive for Puerto Rican men. Poor health does not depress the wage rate a man is offered; the sign on the health disability dummy is

---

[5] To see what the sign of the coefficient of $\hat{\lambda}$ implies, assume a person participates if $W_m > W_r$, where W_m = market wage offer = $X\beta + \varepsilon_1$, and W_r = reservation wage = nonmarket productivity = $Y\alpha + \varepsilon_3$.

The participation rule can be expressed as follows: participates if $X\beta - Y\alpha + \varepsilon_1 - \varepsilon_3 > 0$, or participates if $Z\gamma + \varepsilon_2 > 0$, where $\varepsilon_2 = \varepsilon_1 - \varepsilon_3$. The coefficient of $\hat{\lambda}$ is $\sigma_{12} = \text{Cov}(\varepsilon_1, \varepsilon_2) = \text{Cov}(\varepsilon_1, \varepsilon_1 - \varepsilon_3) = \sigma_{11} - \sigma_{13}$, so $\sigma_{12} \gtrless 0$ as $\sigma_{11} \gtrless \sigma_{13}$. For σ_{12} to be negative, as in my results, the covariance between the errors in the market and reservation wages must be positive and larger than the variance of the error in the market wage offer.

usually positive, significantly so for black men. Black men get 7% more in the public (GOVT) than in the private sector, but public-sector wages are not significantly different from wages in the private sector for white or Hispanic men.

The wages of successive cohorts of immigrant men, compared with U.S.-born members of their ethnic group, can be plotted using the estimated coefficients of the wage equation. FBORN + FBORN × FORED tells how a newly arrived immigrant with a given level of schooling fares, compared with the U.S.-born members of his ethnic group who have the same education, age, and so forth. The dummy variables US46, US711, US1216, US1726, and US2799, when added to (FBORN + FBORN × FORED), tell how immigrants of these cohorts fare compared with the U.S. natives. An immigrant who has 8 years of foreign schooling, which is about average, can serve as an example.

White non-Hispanic immigrant men do not catch up with native whites until they have been here at least 27 years. Mexican immigrants with less than a sixth-grade education match U.S.-born Mexicans when they have been here 17–26 years, but the cohort that arrived before 1950 earns less than U.S. natives. Island-born Puerto Rican men apparently never catch up, unless they come with no education. Neither do Cubans. The unusual nature of the wave of Cuban political refugees who came in the early 1960s is reflected in their average wage rate, which is higher than that of the Cuban men who arrived before or after them.

Central and South American immigrant men with 10 years of schooling overtake the few who are U.S. natives in 4 to 6 years. Those who arrive with less schooling take longer to catch up. Black and Other Hispanic men show an erratic pattern: new arrivals and those who have been here 12 to 26 years earn more than U.S. natives, but this is not true of those who have been here 4–11 years or more than 26 years.

The estimated wage loss from a poor command of English varies across groups, from an insignificant 5% for Mexican men to 18 to 20% for Other Hispanics and Puerto Ricans. Blacks with poor English apparently earn more than other blacks, but there are so few of them (four) that this may be a coincidence.

All Hispanic groups have lower returns to education than Anglo men. Their returns range from 3.4% higher wages per grade for Other Hispanics to 5.4% for Mexicans, whereas Anglo men earn 6.1% more for each additional grade of school completed. The coefficient of FORED is always virtually zero, indicating that there is no appreciable difference between U.S. and foreign schooling in enhancing earnings capacity.

The initial returns to (potential) work experience are about the same for Puerto Rican, Cuban, Central and South American, and white non-

TABLE 2.4
Coefficients of Wage Equations for Men, Corrected for Sample-Selection Bias: Effect of Variables on Average Wage Offer

Variable	White non-Hispanic	Mexican	Puerto Rican	Cuban	Central and South American	Other Hispanic	Black non-Hispanic
Intercept	.618* (.077)	.764* (.091)	.837* (.227)	1.035* (.462)	.290 (.402)	.893* (.175)	.850* (.090)
ED	.061* (.0041)	.054* (.0053)	.036* (.013)	.035 (.019)	.050* (.022)	.034* (.010)	.049* (.0046)
EXP	.041* (.0033)	.024* (.0041)	.038* (.0082)	.040* (.015)	.039 (.020)	.029* (.0078)	.015* (.0038)
EXPSQ	-.0006* (.0001)	-.0003* (.0001)	-.0006* (.0002)	-.0007* (.0003)	-.0006 (.0004)	-.0004* (.0001)	-.0002* (.0001)
VET	-.0078 (.024)	.029 (.034)	-.0015 (.068)	.210 (.144)	.219 (.214)	.044 (.060)	.022 (.026)
FBORN	-.195 (.355)	-.258* (.082)	-.157 (.152)	-.167 (.300)	-.411 (.322)	.277 (.324)	.415 (.413)
FBORN × FORED	.0006 (.014)	-.0056 (.0077)	-.0048 (.0086)	-.0067 (.016)	.019 (.018)	-.0092 (.022)	-.036 (.028)
FBORN × US46	.036 (.394)	.229* (.087)	.025 (.141)	-.031 (.227)	.245 (.161)	-.307 (.289)	-.184 (.327)
FBORN × US711	.088 (.379)	.129 (.086)	.086 (.138)	-.0030 (.220)	.244 (.156)	-.364 (.260)	-.124 (.344)

FBORN × US1216	.104 (.468)	.191 (.098)	.044 (.135)	.147 (.226)	.275 (.190)	.125 (.281)	.231 (.395)
FBORN × US1726	.029 (.348)	.284* (.085)	.027 (.125)	.063 (.268)	.479* (.214)	-.191 (.343)	.039 (.427)
FBORN × US2799	.186 (.350)	.220* (.097)	.160 (.152)	.108 (.292)	.313 (.362)	-.394 (.337)	-.187 (.595)
ENGNVG	-.068 (.153)	-.048 (.039)	-.203* (.072)	-.159 (.098)	-.097 (.121)	-.184* (.080)	.487 (.282)
HEALTH	-.011 (.039)	-.017 (.051)	.214 (.133)	.124 (.216)	.152 (.238)	.011 (.105)	.114* (.045)
GOVT	-.014 (.027)	-.033 (.033)	-.023 (.074)	.011 (.143)	.121 (.164)	.064 (.060)	.070* (.025)
NONWHT	—	-.089 (.089)	.120 (.095)	-.153 (.183)	.011 (.151)	-.064 (.114)	—
$\hat{\lambda}$	-.369* (.058)	-.390* (.063)	-.212 (.120)	-.291 (.247)	.050 (.254)	-.250* (.118)	-.428* (.057)
N	2,911	1,778	314	160	164	522	2,209
R^2	.261	.227	.262	.320	.248	.210	.228
$(\hat{\sigma}_{11})^{1/2}$ (Corrected)	.591	.579	.448	.494	.582	.561	.575

Source: Cordelia Reimers, "Labor Market Discrimination against Hispanic and Black Men," *Review of Economics and Statistics*, 65 (Nov. 1983), 575, Table 3. Reprinted by permission of the North-Holland Publishing Co., Amsterdam.

Notes: Dependent variable is LNRWAGE. Corrected standard errors are in parentheses. Variables are defined in Table 2.1.
* Statistically significant at the 5% level.

Hispanic men. Mexicans, Other Hispanics, and blacks have flatter experience–wage profiles than the others. For each group one can find the value of EXP that corresponds to the maximum wage on the experience–wage profile. Let the coefficient of EXP be β_1 and the coefficient of EXPSQ be β_2. Then $\partial \ln W / \partial \text{EXP} = \beta_1 + 2\beta_2\text{EXP} = 0$ at the maximum point, and $\text{EXP} = -\beta_1/2\beta_2$ gives the value of EXP for which the wage is highest. For white non-Hispanic men, wages peak 36 years after leaving school; for Mexicans, after 46 years; for blacks and Other Hispanics, after 40 years; for Puerto Ricans, Cubans, and Central and South Americans, after 30 to 32 years. Veterans do not earn significantly more than nonveterans in any ethnic group, which suggests that time spent in the armed forces is no more and no less valuable than other types of work experience.

The coefficients of experience and education merit further investigation. My estimated coefficients of EXP and EXPSQ measure an average of the returns to U.S. work experience for the native-born and the returns to foreign and U.S. work experience for immigrants. The coefficient of ED averages the return to U.S. schooling across U.S.-born and foreign-born individuals. Chiswick (1978a) has found that immigrants have a lower estimated return to education than U.S. natives, and speculates that this is due to a weaker correlation among immigrants between schooling and the omitted variable, ability. One would therefore expect ethnic groups with larger percentages of the foreign-born to have smaller coefficients on EXP and ED.

To disentangle these effects, I estimate another set of wage equations for men. These equations include an interaction term, ED × FBORN, and separate variables measuring potential work experience in the United States (USEXP) and potential work experience abroad (FOREXP), along with quadratic and interaction terms: USEXPSQ, FOREXPSQ, USEXP × FBORN, and USEXPSQ × FBORN.[6] I also include as a variable the percentage Hispanic in the population in the state of residence, to see whether there is any evidence that the wages of Hispanics are depressed by "crowding" in labor markets with many Hispanics. The coefficients, corrected for selectivity bias, are reported in Table 2.5. (The variable definitions and their mean values are in Tables 2.1 and 2.3.)

From the signs of the coefficients, it appears that, except for Cubans and Other Hispanics, the foreign-born have lower returns to their U.S. schooling than the native-born men of their ethnic group. (The return to

[6] For immigrants who arrived before 1970, the SIE does not give the exact year of immigration. USEXP and FOREXP are constructed by using the midpoint of the period when the person arrived in the United States as the estimated immigration date. This introduces some measurement error into these variables.

U.S. schooling for the foreign-born is the sum of the coefficients of ED and ED × FBORN.) However, except for Mexican men, the differences are not precisely enough measured that one can be sure of the signs. U.S.-born Mexican men have as high a return to schooling as white non-Hispanics, about 6%, and Puerto Rican men born on the mainland get the same return as U.S.-born blacks, about 5%. Those born in Mexico have a 3.6% return per grade of U.S. schooling, and those born in Puerto Rico have a 3.0% return, while foreign-born white non-Hispanics have 5.2% and foreign-born blacks have 2.0%. For Central and South American men, the return to U.S. schooling is 5% for those born abroad and 12% for the very few born in the United States. The latter estimate is not at all precise, however.

Foreign-born Cuban men seem to have a higher rate of return to U.S. schooling (4.1%) than those born in the United States. The latter group's estimated coefficient on ED is negative, but there are only eight of them in the sample, so this may be a coincidence. Other Hispanics also have a higher rate of return to U.S. schooling if they were born abroad—4.7% as opposed to 3.2% for those who were born in the United States.

The returns to foreign work experience are much smaller than the returns to work experience in the United States. In fact, Mexican, Puerto Rican, Central and South American, and black immigrant men gain virtually nothing in wage rates from prior work experience. In this sense, an immigrant in one of these groups, no matter how old, resembles a new entrant to the U.S. labor force who has just finished school. On the other hand, Cuban, Other Hispanic, and white non-Hispanic immigrant men do start out in the United States with higher wages the older they are on arrival. Their foreign work experience is worth only 1 or 2% per year, however—much less than experience in the United States.

There is also a difference between immigrants and U.S. natives in returns to work experience acquired in the United States. Mexican, Other Hispanic, and black male immigrants have higher initial returns to U.S. work experience than their native-born counterparts. Their experience–wage profiles also peak much more quickly, as shown in Table 2.6. This indicates a relatively brief, intense period of investment in human capital after entering the U.S. labor force, as one might expect of adult immigrants adapting to a new country. However, Puerto Rican, Cuban, and Central and South American immigrant men have lower initial returns to U.S. work experience than those born in the mainland United States. The Puerto Rican migrants' investment period lasts as long as that of mainland natives, but the Cuban and Central and South American immigrants' investment period is shorter.

Earlier, I presented some estimates of how long it takes before male

TABLE 2.5
Coefficients of Wage Equations for Men, Including Interaction Terms, Corrected for Sample-Selection Bias: Effect of Variables on Average Wage Offer

Variable	White non-Hispanic	Mexican	Puerto Rican	Cuban	Central and South American	Other Hispanic	Black non-Hispanic
Intercept	.622* (.078)	.721* (.095)	.619 (.358)	1.320 (.944)	-1.321 (1.021)	.992* (.173)	.854* (.091)
ED	.061* (.0042)	.062* (.0060)	.049 (.026)	-.025 (.073)	.119 (.068)	.032* (.010)	.050* (.0046)
FBORN × ED	-.0094 (.022)	-.026* (.0093)	-.019 (.028)	.067 (.076)	-.069 (.070)	.015 (.034)	-.029 (.042)
FBORN × FORED	.0048 (.014)	-.0025 (.0078)	-.0028 (.0081)	-.0088 (.016)	.0083 (.016)	-.012 (.028)	-.017 (.041)
FBORN	.019 (.343)	.185 (.125)	.298 (.369)	-.548 (.907)	1.639 (1.061)	-.297 (.393)	.335 (.434)
ENGNVG	-.058 (.174)	-.040 (.039)	-.179* (.072)	-.137 (.096)	-.116 (.113)	-.135 (.081)	.443 (.277)
USEXP	.040* (.0033)	.024* (.0041)	.047* (.014)	.098* (.045)	.122* (.049)	.030* (.0076)	.015* (.0038)
FBORN × USEXP	-.0012 (.018)	.013* (.0064)	-.019 (.016)	-.050 (.046)	-.065 (.051)	.023 (.027)	.042 (.056)
FBORN × FOREXP	.016 (.017)	-.0021 (.0055)	-.0034 (.0097)	.014 (.011)	-.0002 (.017)	.027 (.019)	-.0014 (.025)

	(1)	(2)	(3)	(4)	(5)	(6)	(7)
USEXPSQ	-.0006*	-.0002*	-.0007*	-.0017*	-.0019	-.0004*	-.0002*
	(.0001)	(.0001)	(.0003)	(.0009)	(.0013)	(.0001)	(.0001)
FBORN × USEXPSQ	-.0000	-.0004*	.0003	.0007	.0007	-.0007	-.0013
	(.0004)	(.0001)	(.0004)	(.0009)	(.0013)	(.0006)	(.0022)
FBORN × FOREXPSQ	-.0004	.0001	.0001	-.0003	.0002	-.0005	.0002
	(.0005)	(.0001)	(.0003)	(.0003)	(.0005)	(.0004)	(.0007)
VET	-.0061	.015	.0003	.205	-.086	.033	.022
	(.025)	(.034)	(.067)	(.149)	(.240)	(.059)	(.026)
HEALTH	-.0079	-.020	.187	.101	.236	-.043	.117*
	(.039)	(.051)	(.134)	(.197)	(.237)	(.104)	(.045)
GOVT	-.014	-.032	-.019	-.0075	.087	.086	.070*
	(.027)	(.033)	(.074)	(.142)	(.157)	(.060)	(.025)
NONWHT	—	-.104	.109	-.126	.011	-.130	—
		(.091)	(.096)	(.175)	(.147)	(.113)	
PROPHIS	.0021	-.0039*	-.0079	.016	.0032	-.0060*	-.0011
	(.0020)	(.0013)	(.0068)	(.012)	(.0084)	(.0017)	(.0022)
$\hat{\lambda}$	-.378*	-.394*	-.195	-.253	-.064	-.194	-.432*
	(.058)	(.057)	(.117)	(.203)	(.215)	(.114)	(.058)
N	2,911	1,778	314	160	164	522	2,209
R^2	.261	.236	.256	.338	.293	.216	.228
$(\hat{\sigma}_{11})^{1/2}$ (Corrected)	.594	.577	.447	.480	.565	.549	.577

Source: 1976 Survey of Income and Education (U.S. Department of Commerce, 1978).

Notes: Dependent variable is LNRWAGE. Corrected standard errors are in parentheses. Variables are defined in Table 2.1.

* Statistically significant at the 5% level.

47

TABLE 2.6
Value (in Years) of USEXP at Peak of the U.S.
Experience–Wage Offer Profile: Native-Born
and Foreign-Born Men

Ethnic group	U.S. natives	Foreign-born
White non-Hispanic	35.7	32.7
Mexican	51.3	31.1
Puerto Rican	32.3	33.5
Cuban	28.6	24.9
Central and South American	31.4	23.1
Other Hispanic	38.2	25.3
Black non-Hispanic	40.4	19.0

Source: 1976 Survey of Income and Education (U.S. Department of Commerce, 1978).

Note: Value of USEXP derived from estimated wage equations in Table 2.5 by setting $\partial LNRWAGE/\partial USEXP = 0$ and solving for USEXP.

immigrants' wages match the wages of native-born members of their ethnic group of the same age, education, and other personal characteristics. These estimates were derived from the wage equations that included dummy variables for the year of immigration. I can obtain another set of estimates from the wage equations that include USEXP and FOREXP as continuous variables. The answer depends on the amount and location of the immigrant's education and his age when he arrived in the United States. For specified values of these variables, I use the coefficient estimates to derive the appropriate expressions for the wages of a U.S. native and an immigrant who are alike in other respects, set these expressions equal to one another, and solve for the value of the immigrant's USEXP that satisfies the equation. (Note that, for men of the same age and education, the U.S. native's USEXP is equal to the immigrant's USEXP plus his FOREXP.)

If we compare an immigrant who arrives at age 20 having an eighth-grade education (i.e., FORED = 8 and FOREXP = 7) with a U.S. native having an eighth-grade education, the "catch-up" period is 4 years for black men, 18 for Other Hispanics, 34 for whites, 42 for Puerto Ricans, and 51 for Cubans. Mexicans never catch up. Central and South American immigrants start out earning more than the native-born, but the gap narrows the longer they stay. These results are reasonably consistent with my earlier estimates.

Coefficients in Table 2.5 for PROPHIS show that, in states where Hispanics constitute larger fractions of the population, white and Cuban men earn at least as much as they earn elsewhere; but Mexican, Puerto Rican, and Other Hispanic men have lower wages than elsewhere. Moreover, the negative effect is significant for Mexicans and Other Hispanics. This may be evidence that discrimination affects Hispanics more when they are a large proportion of the labor force, as in the Southwest. It may also represent a "compensating differential," which could arise if Mexicans and Other Hispanics prefer to live and work where there are many other Hispanics, regardless of lower wages.

DECOMPOSITION OF MALE WAGE DIFFERENTIALS

One can use the estimated wage equations to sort out how much of the observed minority–Anglo wage differential is due to differences in average wage offers, and how much is due to differences in selection bias of the type discussed at the beginning of this chapter. Further, one can break down the wage-offer differential into the parts due to differences in average personal characteristics and in parameters. The part due to differences in parameters is often attributed to discrimination.

Define $\bar{X}_j = \sum_{i=1}^{n_j} X_{ij}/n_j$, $\bar{\lambda}_j = \sum_{i=1}^{n_j} \hat{\lambda}_{ij}/n_j$, and $\overline{\ln W_j} = \sum_{i=1}^{n_j} (\ln W_{ij})/n_j = \ln W_j$, where n_j is the number of persons with observed wages in group j and $\hat{W}_j$ is the geometric mean of the observed wage rate for group j. (X_{ij}, $\hat{\lambda}_{ij}$, and $\ln W_{ij}$ are defined above.)

Then $\overline{\ln W_j} = \bar{X}_j\beta_j + \sigma_{12j}\bar{\lambda}_j$, and

$$\overline{\ln W_H} - \overline{\ln W_L} = (\bar{X}_H\beta_H - \bar{X}_L\beta_L) + (\sigma_{12H}\bar{\lambda}_H - \sigma_{12L}\bar{\lambda}_L), \qquad (5)$$

where the subscript H refers to the high-wage group and the subscript L refers to the low-wage group. This shows that the observed wage differential, $\overline{\ln W_H} - \overline{\ln W_L}$, equals the difference of mean wage offers, $\bar{X}_H\beta_H - \bar{X}_L\beta_L$, plus the difference in average selectivity bias, $\sigma_{12H}\bar{\lambda}_H - \sigma_{12L}\bar{\lambda}_L$ or $E(\varepsilon_{1H} \mid$ in observed sample) $- E(\varepsilon_{1L} \mid$ in observed sample).

The offered-wage differential can be decomposed in the spirit of Oaxaca (1973), giving

$$\overline{\ln W_H} - \overline{\ln W_L} = (\bar{X}_H - \bar{X}_L)[D\beta_H + (I - D)\beta_L]$$
$$+ [\bar{X}_H(I - D) + \bar{X}_L D](\beta_H - \beta_L)$$
$$+ (\sigma_{12H}\bar{\lambda}_H - \sigma_{12L}\bar{\lambda}_L), \qquad (6)$$

where I is the identity matrix and D is a diagonal matrix of weights.

Since $\overline{\ln W_H} - \overline{\ln W_L} = \ln(\hat{W}_H/\hat{W}_L) \approx (\hat{W}_H - \hat{W}_L)/\hat{W}_H$, Equation (6) decomposes the percentage difference between the geometric means of the observed wage rates for the two groups into a part due to selectivity bias, a part attributable to differences between the groups' average values of each characteristic, and a part attributable to differences between the parameters of the wage-offer function. The first term on the right-hand side of Equation (6) can be interpreted as the wage difference that would exist in the absence of discrimination, if both groups had the same wage-offer function. The second term is then an estimate of the wage-offer difference due to discrimination.

One will in general get different estimates of discrimination depending upon the choice of the matrix D of weights. This choice amounts to an assumption about what the wage-offer function would be in a non-discriminatory world. For example, setting $D = I$ (a procedure followed by many analysts of earnings differentials) assumes that the majority group's wage-offer function would prevail; whereas $D = 0$ assumes that the minority group's wage-offer function would apply to everyone, in the absence of discrimination. Neither assumption seems warranted, since employers' preferences for the majority and their distaste for the minority probably distort both groups' wages. Having no way of knowing the true weights, I choose $D = (0.5)I$. This assumes that the no-discrimination wage-offer parameters would lie halfway between the ones currently estimated for the majority and minority groups. To show how sensitive the estimates of discrimination are to the choice of weights, in Table 2.7 I report these estimates for $D = I$ and $D = 0$, as well as for $D = (0.5)I$. In addition, I show in Table 2.7 the observed wage differential and the estimated wage-offer differential between white non-Hispanics and each minority group.

Table 2.7 shows that the difference in average wage offers between Hispanic and white non-Hispanic men is always larger than the observed wage differential. For blacks, the wage-offer differential is the same size as the observed wage differential. Selectivity bias is negative for all groups except Central and South Americans, but it is larger in absolute value for white men than for Hispanic men. Therefore it reduces the average observed wage more for white men, narrowing the observed wage differences between them and Hispanics.

The average wages offered to minority men are at least 15% below those offered to white non-Hispanics. How serious a problem is labor market discrimination in producing these differences? Table 2.7 shows the wage difference that cannot be explained by various differences in group characteristics (age, education, etc.) and which is therefore potentially due to discrimination. Column 3 in that table gives the estimates if the whites' wage function is assumed to be the no-discrimination one; Column 4 gives estimates when the minority group's wage function is used; and the last column shows the average of 3 and 4. In most cases, the three estimates are quite similar. Cuban men constitute the only case

TABLE 2.7
Wage Differences between White Non-Hispanic and Minority Men, and Estimated Effect of Discrimination

Ethnic group	Observed wage difference[a] (1)	Wage difference, corrected for selection bias[b] (2)	Wage difference due to difference in parameters[c]		
			$(D = I)^d$ (3)	$(D = 0)^e$ (4)	$(D = (0.5)I)^f$ (5)
Mexican	.304	.339	.051	.076	.064
Puerto Rican	.218	.332	.177	.177	.177
Cuban	.092	.156	.024	−.147	−.062
Central and South American	.210	.423	.350	.380	.365
Other Hispanic	.141	.225	.106	.133	.119
Black non-Hispanic	.233	.229	.132	.142	.137

Source: Cordelia Reimers, "Labor Market Discrimination against Hispanic and Black Men," *Review of Economics and Statistics*, 65 (Nov. 1983), 574, Table 2. Reprinted by permission of the North-Holland Publishing Co., Amsterdam.

[a] $\ln W_w - \ln W_h$ (approximately the percentage difference in the geometric mean observed wage between each group and white non-Hispanic men).

[b] $\ln W_w - \ln W_h - [(\hat{\sigma}_{12}\lambda)_w - (\hat{\sigma}_{12}\lambda)_h] = \ln P_w + \bar{X}_w\beta_w - \ln P_h - \bar{X}_h\beta_h$ (the "wage-offer" differential).

[c] $[\bar{X}_w(I - D) + \bar{X}_h D](\beta_w - \beta_h)$.

[d] Assuming whites' wage function reflects no discrimination; $\bar{X}_h (\beta_w - \beta_h)$.

[e] Assuming minority group's wage function reflects no discrimination; $\bar{X}_w(\beta_w - \beta_h)$.

[f] Assuming that the no-discrimination wage function is halfway between that of whites and minority.

in which the choice of weights makes a difference of more than three percentage points in the estimate of the wage difference due to discrimination.

If one takes the average estimates of discrimination, given in the last column, the largest (36%) describes the case of Central and South American men. This is 86% of the total wage-offer differential between them and white non-Hispanic men. For Puerto Rican men, discrimination may be responsible for as much as an 18% difference in wages, about half of the 33% wage-offer gap. Discrimination may cause a wage gap of up to 12% for Other Hispanic men, a little over half of the total gap. Black men are between the Puerto Ricans and Other Hispanics; the wage-offer difference due to racial discrimination may be as large as 14%, which is 60% of the total black–white male wage-offer differential.

For Mexican men, however, discrimination may result result in only a 6% wage difference at most. The rest of the 34% wage-offer gap is due to differences in characteristics such as education. And Cuban men apparently have higher wages compared with white non-Hispanic men than their human capital characteristics would warrant; the difference in parameters of the wage function goes in their favor.

It is possible that discrimination affecting many Hispanics is directed not against Hispanics per se, but against blacks, immigrants, and those not fluent in English. Since these groups constitute a larger fraction of the Hispanic ethnic groups than of white non-Hispanics, such discrimination would affect Hispanics' wages disproportionately. I include race as a characteristic in my wage equations in order to distinguish discrimination against Hispanics from discrimination against blacks. Language skills and duration of residence in the United States, as aspects of a worker's human capital stock, are also included in the wage equations. My decomposition method attributes wage differences due to these factors to differences in personal characteristics, not to discrimination. It is therefore of interest to examine how much of the Hispanic–white wage difference is due to the differences in race, nativity, and language skills. Beyond that, analysis of the portion of the Hispanic–white differential that is due to measured characteristics will tell us how much of the difference comes from differences in education levels, geographic location, government-sector employment, health, and age. In Table 2.8 I present a detailed decomposition of the geometric mean wage differential between each minority group and white non-Hispanics, assuming the no-discrimination parameters lie halfway between those of the whites and those of the minority group.

The figures in Table 2.8, being derived from the estimated coefficients of the wage function, are subject to sampling variability. The standard error of the estimated contribution of each characteristic to the intergroup wage difference is given in parentheses, as is the standard error of the sum of these contributions. This sum, plus the difference in area price levels, is the estimated wage-offer difference due to the differences in observed characteristics. The remainder of the wage-offer difference, which would exist even if the groups had the same characteristics, is often attributed to discrimination. The standard error of the total effect of observed background variables is thus also the standard error of this estimated effect of discrimination.

In Table 2.8, subtracting the area price-level difference from the wage-offer differential of 34% between Mexican and white non-Hispanic men would reduce the "real" wage-offer differential between these groups to 30%. Education is the source of half of the 34% wage-offer

TABLE 2.8

Decomposition of Wage Differences between White Non-Hispanic and Minority Men: Effect of Discrimination and Effect of Particular Variables

	Mexican	Puerto Rican	Cuban	Central and South American	Other Hispanic	Black non-Hispanic
Observed arithmetic wage difference: $(\overline{W}_w - \overline{W}_h)/\overline{W}_w$	.278	.243	.107	.173	.129	.221
Observed geometric mean wage difference (Table 2.7, col. 1): $\ln W_w - \ln W_h$	.304	.218	.092	.210	.141	.233
Difference in selection bias: $(\hat{\sigma}_{12}\bar{\lambda})_w - (\hat{\sigma}_{12}\bar{\lambda})_h$	−.035 (.041)	−.114 (.057)	−.064 (.118)	−.213 (.084)	−.084 (.062)	.004 (.041)
Wage difference, $\ln W_w - \ln W_h$, corrected for selection bias[a]	.339	.332	.156	.423	.225	.229
Effect of discrimination (Table 2.7, col. 5): $[(\overline{X}_w + \overline{X}_h)/2](\beta_w - \beta_h)$	.064	.177	−.062	.365	.119	.137
Difference of area price levels: $\overline{\ln P_w} - \overline{\ln P_h}$	.043	−.099	−.010	−.076	.018	.003
Total effect of background variables listed below: $(\overline{X}_w - \overline{X}_h)(\beta_w + \beta_h)/2$	.233 (.023)	.253 (.044)	.228 (.106)	.134 (.095)	.089 (.015)	.088 (.007)
ED	.171 (.010)	.129 (.018)	.053 (.010)	.034 (.007)	.065 (.008)	.103 (.006)
Total EXP	.011 (.001)	−.027 (.004)	−.062 (.011)	−.039 (.022)	−.008 (.001)	−.015 (.001)
VET	.002 (.004)	−.001 (.008)	.038 (.027)	.042 (.043)	.001 (.002)	.001 (.002)
Total FBORN	.029 (.015)	.101 (.046)	.127 (.113)	.052 (.112)	.005 (.008)	.001 (.003)
ENGNVG	.018 (.025)	.060 (.037)	.060 (.048)	.039 (.046)	.023 (.015)	.001 (.001)
HEALTH	−.0002 (.0003)	.002 (.002)	.003 (.005)	.003 (.006)	.000 (.001)	−.001 (.001)
Total GOVT	.0002 (.0002)	−.0004 (.001)	−.0001 (.006)	.004 (.005)	−.001 (.002)	−.002 (.001)
NONWHT (β_h)	.002 (.002)	−.010 (.008)	.009 (.010)	−.001 (.018)	.003 (.006)	— —

Source: Cordelia Reimers, "Labor Market Discrimination against Hispanic and Black Men," *Review of Economics and Statistics*, 65 (Nov. 1983), 577, Table 5. Reprinted by permission of the North-Holland Publishing Co., Amsterdam.

Note: Standard errors are in parentheses.

[a] $(\overline{X}_w\beta_w + \overline{\ln P_w}) - (\overline{X}_h\beta_h + \overline{\ln P_h})$ = difference in wage offers. See Table 2.7, Column 2.

differential; bringing the Mexicans up to the whites' average schooling level would bring the Mexican men to within 17% of the whites' average wage rate. This would entail an increase from 9.4 to 12.4 grades completed. The difference in average time in the United States accounts for a wage differential of 3%. Improving fluency in English to the level of white non-Hispanics would eliminate only two percentage points of the gap. Differences in potential work experience, armed forces experience, health, government employment, and race each accounts for a wage differential of 1% or less. Discrimination accounts for a difference of 6%. Race, time in the United States, and English together account for another 5% difference.

The wages offered Puerto Rican men are 33% less than those offered white non-Hispanics, on average (Table 2.8: Row 4). The observed wage differential (Row 2) is only two-thirds this size, due to selectivity bias. Adjusting for area prices widens the "real" wage-offer gap to 43%, since Puerto Ricans tend to live in the high-priced Northeastern cities. Differing characteristics account for 60% of this gap, leaving a wage-offer differential of 18% that may be due to discrimination. Just closing the education gap of 2.7 years would eliminate a differential of 13%, and improving Puerto Ricans' command of English would take care of 6%. The Puerto Rican–Anglo difference in length of residence on the U.S. mainland accounts for a 10% wage-offer gap. Race and the difference in potential work experience act to narrow the observed wage gap, not to widen it. Nothing else has much impact on the wage differential.

Cuban men fall short of the wages offered white non-Hispanic men by 16% after adjusting for selectivity bias (Row 4). If their background characteristics were the same, the differential would be 6% in the Cubans' favor (Row 5). The Cubans' recent arrival in the United States accounts for a differential of 13%. Improving the Cubans' command of English would eliminate a differential of 6%, and closing the education gap of 1.1 grades would eliminate a wage-offer differential of 5%. The Cubans' lack of experience in the U.S. armed forces (which is related to their recent immigration) accounts for a 4% differential. The lower wages of black Cubans account for a 1% difference in average wages offered Cuban and white non-Hispanic men. The fact that the Cubans are older on average tends to narrow the wage-offer differential; if they had the same potential experience as white non-Hispanics, the wage-offer differential would be 22% instead of 16%.

Central and South American men have average observed wages that are 21% below those of white non-Hispanic men, and their average wage offers are 42% lower than those of the Anglo men. The price-level adjustment widens the "real wage-offer" gap to 50%. A differential of only 13% can be explained by differing personal characteristics of the ethnic groups. In this case, a wage-offer differential as high as 36% may be due to discrimination. A 4% difference is due to lack of fluency in English, and a 4% difference results from lack of experience in the U.S. armed forces. Both of these differentials may be linked to the fact that the Central and South Americans are the most recent Hispanic arrivals in the United States, even more recent than the Cubans, on average. By itself, this accounts for a 5% wage-offer differential. As they already have nearly as much education as white non-Hispanic men (11.8 grades vs. 12.4 grades), increasing education to the level of the Anglos could only close a wage-offer gap of 3%.

The men of Other Hispanic origin have average wage offers that are 22% below those of white non-Hispanics, after correcting for selectivity bias. A differential of 12% could be attributed to discrimination. A gap of 7% is due to the difference in education of 1.4 grades, and a gap of 2% is due to poor command of English. Local price differences account for another 2%. Nothing else affects the differential in any important way.

By way of comparison, black and white men have a 23% wage-offer difference, of which less than half can be attributed to differing characteristics, so that as much as a 14% wage-offer differential may be due to discrimination. The education difference of nearly 2 years explains a wage-offer gap of 10%. No other observable differences contribute in a particularly important way to the wage gap.

SUMMARY OF MALE WAGE DETERMINATION ANALYSIS

My major findings, roughly in order of importance, are as follows: First, the five major Hispanic-American groups differ so much among themselves and from blacks that it makes little sense to lump them under a single "Hispanic" or "minority" rubric for either analysis or policy treatment.

Second, discrimination in the labor market may be responsible for a wage differential, compared to non-Hispanic white men, of 18% for Puerto Rican men, 14% for black men, and 12% for Other Hispanic men, but only 6% for Mexican men. Low levels of education are apparently a much more serious problem than discrimination for Mexicans. The Cuban–Anglo wage differential can be completely explained by differences in observable personal characteristics, especially recency of arrival in the United States and language handicaps. These factors, along with discrimination and little education, also seriously handicap Puerto Rican men.

Third, Mexican and Other Hispanic men, but not the other minority groups, have significantly lower wages in states where Hispanics are a larger fraction of the population. This may be evidence of "crowding" in a discriminatory environment, or of a preference for locating, despite lower earnings, where there are many other Hispanics.

Fourth, minority men (except for U.S.-born Mexicans) have lower wage returns to education than Anglos, and foreign work experience is worth much less than experience in the United States; indeed, it is virtually worthless for several groups. However, returns to education do not differ significantly between U.S. natives and immigrants within the same ethnic group (except for Mexicans), nor is the difference between foreign and U.S. schooling significant within a group. U.S.-born Mexican men have as high a return to education as U.S.-born Anglos, while the Mexican-born have a much lower return, as do the other minority groups. There is no clear evidence that Hispanic immigrants' wages ever overtake those of native-born members of their ethnic group who are of the same age, educational level, and so forth.

Fifth, English deficiencies do not depress the wages of Mexican men as much as the other four Hispanic groups.

Sixth, the wages of white and non-white Hispanics do not differ significantly, ceteris paribus. Public-sector wages are not significantly different from private-sector wages of Hispanic and Anglo men with the same human capital characteristics. Black men, however, do get higher wages in government employment.

Seventh, health disabilities do not depress wage offers; their often-found negative impact on observed wages is apparently due to sample-selection bias.

Finally, selectivity bias can be a problem even when estimating wage functions for men, using a sample restricted to wage and salary employees. I find a *negative* correlation between the error terms in the equations for the wage and for participation in the wage and salary sector. Moreover, sample-selection bias affects estimates of intergroup wage differences, making the difference in average *observed* wages smaller than the true difference in average wage *offers*.

Wage Determination of Hispanic Women

In this section I replicate the analysis presented for men on the sample of women from the Survey of Income and Education. The raw data show that Hispanic women differ from white women in ways that might well handicap them in the labor market and consequently lead to lower earnings. For example, the average educational level of wage-earning Mexican and Puerto Rican women in the data set is less than 10 grades, while that of Anglo women is 12.5 grades. These and other variable means are in Table 2.9. (The variables were defined in Table 2.1.) Mexican and Puerto Rican women wage earners are also 5 years younger, on average, than Anglo women. (Cuban women are a year older.) The black and Hispanic women (except for the Cubans) have more children, which means that they may have less actual work experience than Anglo women of the same age and education. The Hispanics are also more likely to be recent immigrants and to have some deficiencies in English. Finally, the groups are located in different areas of the country, with different price levels and different money wage levels. The Mexicans and Other Hispanics tend to be in lower-price areas than blacks and white non-Hispanics.

Reimers (1984) shows that Puerto Rican, Mexican, and Other Hispanic women who were wives or heads of families did have lower average annual earnings in 1975 than their white non-Hispanic counterparts. This was due to lower labor force participation, higher unemployment rates, and—in the case of Mexicans—much lower average hourly earnings. However, several groups of minority women (Cubans, Central and South Americans, and blacks) actually had higher average annual earnings than white non-Hispanics, despite higher unemployment and somewhat lower wage rates. This is because they had higher labor force participation and worked longer hours each week. Table 2.10 shows that, except for Mexicans and Other Hispanics, the women of all the minority groups had average hourly wages in 1975 within 90% of white non-Hispanic women. Mexican women, however, earned only 78% of the white non-Hispanic women's average hourly wage.

These wage comparisons raise a number of questions. How can the Cuban, Puerto Rican, and black women's wage rates be so close to those of the white non-Hispanic women when their human capital is lower? And why do Mexican women lag so far behind?

One possible answer to the first question lies in sample-selection bias. Human capital presumably affects the wage offered to a woman by employers, but we cannot observe everyone's wage offer. We observe wages only for those women who work in the wage and salary sector, not those who are self-employed or full-time students or full-time homemakers. As a result of selectivity bias, the observed wage differential may understate the difference in average wage offers between ethnic groups. Suppose, for example, that a woman will not participate in the wage and salary sector unless her wage offer is higher than some threshold or reservation wage, which is the same in both majority and minority groups for women with the same human capital characteristics. Now

TABLE 2.9
Means of Variables for Women in the Sample of Wage Earners

	White non-Hispanic	Mexican	Puerto Rican	Cuban	Central and South American	Other Hispanic	Black non-Hispanic
WAGE (W) ($)	3.67	2.88	3.36	3.47	3.31	3.04	3.46
LNWAGE (ln W)	1.111	.909	1.084	1.137	1.063	.966	1.068
LNCOST (ln P)	−0.025	−0.068	.077	−0.019	.043	−0.041	−0.029
LNRWAGE (ln W/P)	1.136	.977	1.007	1.156	1.020	1.007	1.097
ED (grade)	12.50	9.88	9.83	11.44	11.06	11.70	11.32
EXP (years)	19.83	16.87	17.05	22.26	17.52	18.47	20.68
EXPSQ	618.29	470.03	461.85	674.39	419.48	521.53	645.63
MAR	.663	.643	.607	.679	.601	.675	.474
NUMKIDS (number)	.903	1.77	1.33	.832	.978	1.30	1.39
FBORN	.034	.186	.816	.956	.893	.108	.016
FBORN × FORED (years)	.259	.928	5.03	8.46	8.49	.982	.155
FBORN × US46	.0020	.025	.070	.124	.197	.018	.0045
FBORN × US711	.0037	.037	.099	.241	.281	.025	.0061
FBORN × US1216	.0033	.034	.104	.314	.135	.028	.0020
FBORN × US1726	.010	.043	.343	.190	.146	.020	.0013
FBORN × US2799	.012	.026	.124	.044	.017	.0025	.0009
ENGNVG	.0073	.253	.468	.533	.545	.122	.0029
HEALTH	.084	.076	.095	.037	.045	.080	.118
GOVT	.225	.174	.164	.095	.101	.255	.313
FGOVT	.034	.032	.040	.022	.045	.043	.092
SGOVT	.060	.049	.035	.022	.034	.085	.075
LGOVT	.132	.094	.090	.051	.022	.128	.147
NONWHT	0	.019	.104	.037	.096	.033	1.0
$\hat{\lambda}$	.730	.801	.912	.519	.627	.768	.643
Selection bias $(\hat{\sigma}_{12}\hat{\lambda})$	−.035[a] / −.037[b]	−.039	−.065	−.096	.074	−.020	−.074

Source: 1976 Survey of Income and Education (U.S. Department of Commerce, 1978).
Notes: See Table 2.1 for definitions of variables. Data base is 1976 SIE. Unless otherwise indicated, means reflect fractions.
[a] Equation with GOVT.
[b] Equation with FGOVT, SGOVT, LGOVT.

TABLE 2.10
Average Hourly Earnings of Women Age 14+ in 1975, by Ethnic Group

Ethnic group	Female wage rate	Percentage of white non-Hispanic wage
White non-Hispanic	$3.67	100%
Cuban	3.47	95
Black non-Hispanic	3.46	94
Puerto Rican	3.36	92
Central and South American	3.31	90
Other Hispanic	3.04	83
Mexican	2.88	78

Source: 1976 Survey of Income and Education (U.S. Department of Commerce, 1978).

suppose that discrimination reduces the Cubans' or another minority group's wage offers below those of Anglos with the same human capital. Then more of the minority women will not accept the offer and will not appear in the wage-earning sector; therefore, the selectivity bias would be larger for the Cubans and would raise their average *observed* wage closer to that of Anglo women than their average wage *offer* really is. In other words, we only know what the offer is if it is accepted, which means that what we observe is a biased sample—it excludes the refused offers.

Another possible explanation for the Puerto Rican and Cuban women's wages being so close to Anglos is that their concentration in the high-price Northeast makes them appear better off in terms of nominal wages than they are in terms of real wages. Alternatively, perhaps the payoffs to various human capital characteristics differ across ethnic groups, or perhaps human capital differences exert little influence on women's wage rates.

To answer such questions, I estimate a wage function (correcting for sample-selection bias) for each ethnic group of women in the sample: Mexicans, Puerto Ricans, Cubans, Central and South Americans, Other Hispanics, black non-Hispanics, and white non-Hispanics. I can then find out whether selectivity bias is distorting the observed wage differentials. I can also see to what extent the parameters of the female wage-generating function differ across ethnic groups. I can ask to what extent wage differences (as between Mexicans and Anglos) can be attributed to differences in characteristics such as educational attainment, and to what extent labor market discrimination (as measured by the overall difference in parameters of the wage-offer function) may be a factor. I can also ask whether Puerto Rican, Cuban, black, and white non-His-

panic women with similar costs of living and other individual characteristics would get similar wage offers, or whether there is evidence of
ethnic wage discrimination among women lurking behind the observed
near-equality of average wage rates of these groups.

PARAMETERS OF THE FEMALE PROBIT
AND WAGE FUNCTIONS

The wage samples consist of women aged 14 and above who worked
for pay in 1975 but who were not self-employed or full-time students.
These samples contain from 30% to 50% of all the women aged 14 and
over in each ethnic group in the data set. Because the observed wage
structure is affected by the decisions women make about participating in
the wage and salary sector as well as by the wage offers they face, I
correct for possible sample-selection bias to get consistent estimates of
the parameters of the wage-offer function facing each ethnic group.

As was shown in the previous section, the correction for selection bias
first involves the estimation of a probit model to predict inclusion in the
observed wage sample. The probit parameter estimates are presented in
Table 2.11.

The coefficients in Table 2.11 show that age, health, and children are
always significant determinants of a woman's working in the wage and
salary sector, regardless of ethnic group. Education, exogenous income,
available AFDC, and husband's age and education have the expected
positive or negative effect in 31 out of 35 cases (assuming that a spouse's
higher wage reduces one's labor supply). The impact of being married
on women's participation in the wage and salary sector, evaluated at the
mean values of husbands' age, education, and nativity, is negative for
all groups except the Puerto Ricans. The point estimates of the coefficients on English proficiency and immigration date, though they are not
always significant, suggest that foreign-born women are more likely to
work in the wage and salary sector when they are more assimilated (i.e.,
when they have been in the United States longer and have better command of English).

The second stage of the analysis is the estimation of the wage function
itself. In the wage equation, W_{ij} is the woman's money wage rate, divided by a cost-of-living index for her place of residence to take account
of the differences in geographic concentration of these groups. The set
of explanatory variables, X_{ij} and λ_{ij}, were defined in Table 2.1: education
(in the United States and abroad), potential work experience, marital
status and number of children, nativity and date of immigration, fluency

in English, health disability, race, government employment,[7] and the inverse of Mill's ratio (predicted from the sample-inclusion probit; included to correct for sample-selection bias).

The estimated wage functions, corrected for selectivity bias, are reported in Table 2.12. The coefficients could be estimated precisely only for the larger samples (whites, blacks, and Mexicans); they are sometimes insignificant for the other groups even when the point estimates are fairly large. I will therefore occasionally take note of signs and magnitudes of the point estimates even for nonsignificant coefficients, but the uncertainty surrounding them should be borne in mind.

The coefficient of $\hat{\lambda}$, which represents the covariance between the errors in the sample participation probit and the wage function, is significantly different from zero only for black women, for whom it is negative. Apparently black women who have unusually high wage offers in the wage and salary sector, given their measured characteristics, have even higher productivity in the other sectors (e.g., school, household, self-employment) and so are less likely to be in the wage sample. For the other ethnic groups, I can detect no evidence of selectivity bias. The insignificant coefficient of $\hat{\lambda}$ for white and Hispanic women means that, for women with the same observed characteristics X_{ij}, participation in the wage and salary sector is random with respect to the wage offer.

Hispanic women in the sample have much lower returns to education than white and black non-Hispanic women. Only the Cubans, with wage gains of 4.1% per grade, have even half as high a return to schooling as Anglo women, with 7.6%. Puerto Rican and Central and South American women increase their wages by only about 1.8% by going to school an extra year, while Mexicans and Other Hispanics get 3.5%. Black women get about the same return as whites. For Mexican women, education obtained abroad yields a return of only 1.1% per year, significantly less than U.S. schooling. For the other groups, the difference between foreign and U.S. education is not significant.

The lower estimated returns to education for Hispanic women might be because more of them are foreign-born. The coefficient of ED averages the return to U.S. schooling across U.S.-born and foreign-born individuals. Chiswick (1978a) has found that immigrants have a lower estimated return to education than U.S. natives, but he does not distinguish between U.S. and foreign schooling.

---

[7] For the larger ethnic groups, I include three separate variables for federal, state, and local government employment. The Cubans and the Central and South Americans, however, have so few employees in any one level of government that for them I combine all levels of government into one category.

TABLE 2.11
Estimated Coefficients of Reduced-Form Probit Equations for the Probability of a Woman's Being in the Wage-Earner Sample

Variable	White non-Hispanic	Mexican	Puerto Rican	Cuban	Central and South American	Other Hispanic	Black non-Hispanic
Intercept	−3.44*	−2.75*	−3.03*	−4.99*	−2.20*	−3.64*	−4.03*
	(.141)	(.247)	(.643)	(1.28)	(.990)	(.468)	(.130)
ED	.067*	.052*	.046	.026	−.063	.110*	0.72*
	(.006)	(.010)	(.025)	(.042)	(.037)	(.020)	(.0058)
FBORN × FORED	.0003	−.033*	−.0023	.0075	.039	−.025	.016
	(.015)	(.016)	(.020)	(.033)	(.031)	(.035)	(.036)
AGE	.172*	.161*	.153*	.340*	.225*	.166*	.194*
	(.007)	(.013)	(.033)	(.062)	(.049)	(.024)	(.006)
AGESQ	−.0020*	−.0019*	−.0019*	−.0040*	−.0029*	−.0021*	−.0021*
	(.0001)	(.0002)	(.0004)	(.0007)	(.0006)	(.0003)	(.0001)
FBORN	−.967*	−.809*	−.491	−.674	−1.64*	−.467	−1.38*
	(.436)	(.256)	(.417)	(.831)	(.502)	(.649)	(.643)
FBORN × US06	.283*	.213*	.177*	.013	.140*	.104	.209
	(.113)	(.059)	(.088)	(.135)	(.062)	(.127)	(.116)
FBORN × US711	.922*	.984*	.545	.263	1.11*	.655	1.46*
	(.460)	(.261)	(.376)	(.689)	(.317)	(.626)	(.578)
FBORN × US1216	1.02*	.874*	.689	.983	1.22*	1.33*	1.66*
	(.450)	(.267)	(.385)	(.698)	(.367)	(.643)	(.687)
FBORN × US1726	1.13*	.764*	.857*	.487	1.27*	.287	1.02
	(.418)	(.261)	(.380)	(.719)	(.385)	(.636)	(.694)
FBORN × US2799	1.05*	.808*	.872*	.659	1.32*	−.841	1.98*
	(.417)	(.284)	(.425)	(.868)	(.675)	(.830)	(.876)
ENGNVG	−.015	.088	−.034	−.334	−.101	−.074	.123
	(.162)	(.079)	(.152)	(.276)	(.192)	(.154)	(.309)
NONWHT	—	.019	.016	−.265	−.180	.096	—
	—	(.189)	(.194)	(.466)	(.270)	(.268)	—
HEALTH	−.493*	−.508*	−.484*	−1.41*	−.942*	−.547*	−.869*
	(.042)	(.086)	(.177)	(.369)	(.326)	(.140)	(.039)
PROPHIS	−.0012	−.013*	−.047*	.0012	.020	−.0023	−.0023
	(.0025)	(.003)	(.018)	(.031)	(.014)	(.0034)	(.0029)

TABLE 2.11 (Continued)

Variable	White non-Hispanic	Mexican	Puerto Rican	Cuban	Central and South American	Other Hispanic	Black non-Hispanic
MAR	3.34*	1.98*	2.01*	3.87*	.663	2.37*	2.23*
	(.225)	(.383)	(.932)	(1.92)	(1.42)	(.713)	(.251)
KIDSLT6	−.431*	−.318*	−.366*	−.620*	−.457*	−.432*	−.196*
	(.029)	(.039)	(.096)	(.227)	(.141)	(.088)	(.026)
KIDS611	−.235*	−.064*	−.137	−.350*	−.304*	−.128*	−.043*
	(.023)	(.030)	(.072)	(.171)	(.133)	(.065)	(.018)
KIDS1217	−.115*	−.116*	−.164*	−.172	−.252*	−.047	−.109*
	(.018)	(.025)	(.069)	(.113)	(.122)	(.048)	(.015)
FAM1864	.085*	−.023	−.012	−.114	−.0043	−.0033	.0038
	(.019)	(.032)	(.094)	(.123)	(.118)	(.056)	(.016)
FAM65	−.038	.015	.204	−.135	.253	−.021	−.074
	(.042)	(.098)	(.204)	(.270)	(.313)	(.152)	(.040)
INCOME ($thousands)	−.023*	−.011	.028	−.0069	.0031	−.020*	−.0098*
	(.002)	(.006)	(.018)	(.017)	(.017)	(.008)	(.0030)
WELF ($thousands)	−.303*	−.345	−.760*	−3.77*	−.415	−.406	−.599*
	(.106)	(.181)	(.384)	(.982)	(.595)	(.358)	(.114)
SPED × MAR	−.030*	−.016	.0063	−.054	−.0019	−.015	−.013
	(.006)	(.010)	(.026)	(.034)	(.032)	(.019)	(.007)
SPAGE × MAR	−.135*	−.076*	−.067	−.150	−.023	−.100*	−.078*
	(.010)	(.018)	(.042)	(.085)	(.072)	(.033)	(.010)
SPAGESQ × MAR	.0012*	.0006*	.0005	.0014	.0000	.0010*	.0006*
	(.0001)	(.0002)	(.0005)	(.0009)	(.0009)	(.0004)	(.0001)
SPFBORN × MAR	.074	−.013	−.049	−.069	.065	.182	.016
	(.099)	(.088)	(.210)	(.334)	(.216)	(.218)	(.176)
No. of observations	11,034	2,931	649	296	350	1,041	10,027
Max log likelihood	−5867.14	−1658.60	−324.63	−126.41	−196.79	−542.05	−5088.98

Source: 1976 Survey of Income and Education (U.S. Department of Commerce, 1978).

Notes: Dependent variable is INSAMPLE for wage equation. Standard errors are in parentheses. Variables are defined in Table 2.1.

* Statistically significant at the 5% level.

TABLE 2.12
Coefficients of Wage Equations for Women, Corrected for Sample-Selection Bias: Effect of Variables on Average Wage Offer

	White non-Hispanic with GOVT	White non-Hispanic with FGOVT, SGOVT, LGOVT	Mexican	Puerto Rican	Cuban	Central and South American	Other Hispanic	Black non-Hispanic
Intercept	.0020 (.067)	-.014 (.068)	.492* (.129)	.804* (.307)	.605 (.317)	.696* (.352)	.481 (.278)	.170* (.080)
ED	.076* (.004)	.077* (.004)	.035* (.007)	.017 (.016)	.041* (.017)	.019 (.021)	.034* (.014)	.072* (.004)
EXP	.026* (.002)	.026* (.002)	.024* (.005)	.017 (.011)	.013 (.015)	.018 (.020)	.015 (.010)	.010* (.003)
EXPSQ	-.0005* (.0001)	-.0005* (.0001)	-.0004* (.0001)	-.0004 (.0002)	-.0001 (.0003)	-.0003 (.0005)	-.0003 (.0002)	-.0002* (.0001)
MAR	.0005 (.019)	.0011 (.019)	.0034 (.032)	-.044 (.069)	.074 (.082)	.048 (.091)	.029 (.062)	.039* (.016)
NUMKIDS	-.040* (.010)	-.040* (.010)	-.035* (.013)	-.017 (.034)	-.016 (.045)	-.034 (.059)	-.024 (.027)	-.0092 (.0064)
FBORN	-.324 (.214)	-.324 (.214)	.037 (.129)	-.234 (.176)	.302 (.274)	-.613* (.310)	-.429 (.339)	-.143 (.318)
FBORN × FORED	-.010 (.009)	-.010 (.009)	-.024* (.011)	.011 (.011)	-.014 (.012)	.0086 (.018)	.020 (.023)	-.013 (.020)
FBORN × US46	.654* (.256)	.656* (.256)	-.037 (.142)	-.224 (.165)	-.296 (.188)	.456* (.159)	.090 (.300)	.323 (.251)
FBORN × US711	.174 (.217)	.168 (.217)	.048 (.130)	.184 (.157)	-.175 (.180)	.439* (.188)	.457 (.289)	.517* (.249)
FBORN × US1216	.293 (.227)	.288 (.226)	.150 (.134)	.159 (.158)	-.024 (.184)	.576* (.213)	.109 (.302)	.398 (.282)

FBORN × US1726	.477* (.199)	.472* (.198)	.213 (.132)	.177 (.152)	-.172 (.195)	.654* (.218)	.147 (.293)	.408 (.314)
FBORN × US2799	.376 (.201)	.377 (.200)	062 (.153)	.261 (.185)	-.294 (.252)	.460 (.369)	.790 (.601)	-.120 (.360)
ENGNVG	.154 (.114)	.157 (.114)	-.020 (.047)	.030 (.083)	-.152 (.099)	-.075 (.096)	-.095 (.100)	.189 (.166)
HEALTH	-.065* (.033)	-.062 (.033)	-.160* (.064)	-.217 (.118)	-.233 (.208)	-.046 (.222)	-.294* (.116)	-.045 (.035)
GOVT	.129* (.021)	—	—	—	.088 (.121)	-.145 (.132)	—	—
FGOVT	—	.298* (.046)	.250* (.086)	.389* (.161)	—	—	.330* (.135)	.346* (.027)
SGOVT	—	.093* (.035)	.122 (.070)	.218 (.164)	—	—	.249* (.098)	.140* (.029)
LGOVT	—	.097* (.026)	.067 (.053)	.621* (.111)	—	—	.147 (.083)	.162* (.023)
NONWHT	—	—	.023 (.109)	-.165 (.103)	.049 (.190)	-.057 (.137)	-.078 (.161)	—
λ̂	-.048 (.041)	-.051 (.041)	-.048 (.084)	-.071 (.148)	-.185 (.140)	.117 (.249)	-.026 (.154)	-.115* (.048)
N	4,548	4,548	1,176	201	137	178	400	4,466
R^2	.168	.171	.124	.277	.303	.170	.153	.247
$(\hat{\sigma}_{11})^{1/2}$ (Corrected)	.555	.554	.505	.418	.390	.508	.528	.510

Source: 1976 Survey of Income and Education (U.S. Department of Commerce, 1978).

Notes: Dependent variable is LNRWAGE. Corrected standard errors are in parentheses. Variables are defined in Table 2.1.

* Statistically significant at the 5% level.

The coefficients of EXP and EXPSQ convey the return to potential work experience (i.e., time elapsed since leaving school), averaged across marital-status and number-of-children categories. These returns are low (starting at 2.6% per year and declining) for white non-Hispanic women, and lower still for minority women. In other words, older women's wages are not much higher than those of younger women, controlling for marital status, number of children, education, and so forth. If women do not stay in the labor market continuously after leaving school, we would expect elapsed time per se to have an attenuated effect on wages. Moreover, if many women, when they do work for pay, do so in jobs that provide little training and poor promotion possibilities, their wage-experience profile would be quite flat— that is, wages would not rise with experience.

The Hispanic women may have lower returns to potential work experience than white non-Hispanic women because more of them are foreign-born. The estimated coefficients of EXP and EXPSQ measure an average of the return to U.S. (potential) work experience for the native-born and the returns to foreign and U.S. (potential) experience for immigrants. One would expect foreign work experience to have a lower return in the U.S. labor market than experience acquired here. On the other hand, the minority women's potential experience–wage profile may be flatter because they work even less of the time for pay than Anglo women (controlling for number of children) and so acquire less actual experience per year, or because they work at jobs with less opportunity for on-the-job training and promotions. Further investigation of the labor supply behavior of Hispanic women is needed to determine what is in fact the case.

Marital status per se is not associated with wage offers for any group but black women, who have wages 4% higher if they are married. However, the presence of children does lower women's wages, probably because women with more children have spent more time out of the labor force in child-rearing and so have less accumulated work experience. This effect is significant for Mexican and Anglo women, whose wages are lowered by 4% for each child. The effect of children on wages is smallest for black women, perhaps because they are less likely to drop out of the labor market when they have children.

How female immigrants compare with U.S. natives of their own ethnic background depends upon how much education they bring with them and how long they have been in the United States. Eight years of schooling is about average, so such a woman can serve as an example. For every ethnic group, there is at least one immigrant cohort that has higher wages than U.S.-born women. I can discern a tendency for wages to rise with time since entry, but the pattern is erratic and the estimates are imprecise. For Puerto Ricans and Other Hispanics, the highest wages are apparently earned by women who came to the mainland before 1950; for Mexicans and Central and South Americans, by those who came in the 1950s; for blacks, by those who came in the late 1960s; for white non-Hispanics, by those who came in the early 1970s, followed by those who came in the 1950s; and for Cubans, by those who came in the mid-1970s or in the early 1960s.

Lack of fluency in English does not have a significant effect on wages for any female group. Cubans' wages are reduced an estimated 15% by poor English, but the estimate is imprecise, perhaps because the sample is so small. White and black women without fluent English actually seem to have higher wages than others of their education, age, and immigration cohort, but these effects are not significant either. With the possible exception of Puerto Ricans, race has no significant additional impact on Hispanic women's wages. The point estimate of the impact of being nonwhite for Puerto Rican women is −.16, but its standard error is relatively large.

Poor health significantly lowers women's wages. It hurts the earning power of Hispanic women much more than that of blacks or whites. White women with a health disability receive wages 6.5% below healthy white women. The estimates of the wage reduction due to poor health for Mexicans, Puerto Ricans, Cubans, and Other Hispanics range from 16 to 29%.

Women of several ethnic groups get higher wages in the public than the private sector, especially if they work for the federal government. White non-Hispanic women get 10% more in state and local government, and 30% more in the federal government, than from a private employer. Black women get about 15% more in state and local government and 35% more in federal employment than in the private sector; Other Hispanic women are similar to blacks in this respect, except that they get 25% more in state government jobs than in private firms. Mexican women earn 7% more in local government (not significantly greater than zero), 12% more in state government, and 25% more in federal jobs than in the private sector. Puerto Rican women seem to earn about 20% more in state government (though the standard error is large), 40% more in federal government, and an astounding 62% more in local public-sector jobs than they can get in the average private firm. This may reflect pay differences in New York City between city jobs and the private-sector jobs available to Puerto Rican women.

These higher wages for women in government reflect something other than a general pay premium received by government workers or a government practice of favoring minorities. Recall that I found no significant public-private sector wage differences for men in the same data set, except for black men, whose wages are 7% higher in government than in private employment. Sharon Smith (1977) found that in 1975 men with similar characteristics got higher wages in federal employment than in the private sector, but received lower wages from state and local governments than from private employers. (In my analysis of male wage offers, I had to aggregate all levels of government because of the small numbers of men in certain categories. This may explain why I found no public–private wage differential for men.) Smith also found that women's wages were higher at all levels of government than in private employment, with the public–private difference being greatest for federal, then state, and then local government employees. Apparently wage discrimination against women is considerably stronger in the private than the public sector. We can deduce that, relative to the federal government, private employers discriminate most against Puerto Rican women, then blacks, Other Hispanics, and white non-Hispanics, in that order, and least against Mexican women.

DECOMPOSITION OF FEMALE WAGE DIFFERENTIALS

Using the decomposition technique derived in the previous section, I show in Table 2.13 the contribution of each type of characteristic to the wage difference between minority and white non-Hispanic women. As

TABLE 2.13
Decomposition of Wage Differences between White Non-Hispanic and Minority Women: Effect of Discrimination and Effect of Particular Variables

	Mexican	Puerto Rican	Cuban	Central and South American	Other Hispanic	Black non-Hispanic
Observed arithmetic wage difference: $(\overline{W}_w - \overline{W}_h)/\overline{W}_w$	.215	.084	.054	.098	.172	.057
Observed geometric mean wage difference (Table 2.14, col. 1): $\overline{\ln W_w} - \overline{\ln W_h}$	.202	.027	−.026	.048	.145	.043
Difference in selection bias: $(\hat{\sigma}_{12}\overline{\lambda})_w - (\hat{\sigma}_{12}\overline{\lambda})_h$	.002 (.073)	.028 (.138)	.061 (.079)	−.109 (.159)	−.017 (.122)	.037 (.043)

TABLE 2.13 (*Continued*)

	Mexican	Puerto Rican	Cuban	Central and South American	Other Hispanic	Black non-Hispanic
Wage difference, $\overline{\ln W_w} - \overline{\ln W_h}$, corrected for selection bias[a]	.200	−.001	−.087	.157	.162	.006
Effect of discrimination (Table 2.14, col. 5): $[(\overline{X}_w + \overline{X}_h)/2] \times (\beta_w - \beta_h)$	−.024	−.041	−.129	.117	.095	−.073
Difference of area price levels: $\overline{\ln P_w} - \overline{\ln P_h}$	.043	−.102	−.007	−.068	.016	.004
Total effect of background variables listed below: $(\overline{X}_w - \overline{X}_h) \times$	.181	.143	.049	.108	.051	.075
$(\beta_w + \beta_h)/2$	(.017)	(.050)	(.089)	(.070)	(.011)	(.006)
ED	.146	.125	.062	.068	.044	.088
	(.010)	(.022)	(.009)	(.016)	(.006)	(.003)
Total EXP	.014	−.005	−.030	−.025	−.006	−.007
	(.003)	(.007)	(.011)	(.024)	(.005)	(.001)
MAR	.0001	−.001	−.001	.002	−.0002	.004
	(.0004)	(.002)	(.001)	(.003)	(.0004)	(.002)
NUMKIDS	.033	.012	−.002	.003	.013	.012
	(.007)	(.008)	(.002)	(.002)	(.006)	(.003)
Total FBORN	.002	.019	.015	.080	.009	−.002
	(.007)	(.043)	(.090)	(.071)	(.006)	(.002)
ENGNVG	−.017	−.043	−.0004	−.021	−.004	.001
	(.015)	(.032)	(.040)	(.040)	(.009)	(.0004)
HEALTH	−.001	.001	−.007	−.002	−.001	.002
	(.0003)	(.001)	(.005)	(.004)	(.0003)	(.001)
Total GOVT	.005	.017	.014	−.001	−.007	−.022
	(.001)	(.003)	(.008)	(.008)	(.002)	(.002)
NONWHT (β_h)	−.0004	.017	−.002	.005	.002	—
	(.002)	(.011)	(.007)	(.013)	(.005)	—

Source: 1976 Survey of Income and Education (U.S. Department of Commerce, 1978).
Note: Standard errors are in parentheses.
[a] $(\overline{X}_w \beta_w + \overline{\ln P_w}) - (\overline{X}_h \beta_h + \overline{\ln P_h})$ = difference in wage offers. See Table 2.14, col. 2.

before, the standard errors of the estimated contributions of the characteristics to the intergroup wage difference are given in parentheses.

The first column of Table 2.13 shows that Mexican women's average
wage offers would be about 2% higher than those of white non-Hispanic
women, if their characteristics were the same. As it is, the Mexican
women average 20% lower, before correcting for local cost-of-living differences, and 16% lower after the adjustment is made. The difference in
education is responsible for 93% of this "real wage-offer" differential
(i.e., the wage differential, adjusted for selectivity bias and cost-of-living
differences). Larger family size (1.8 vs. 0.9 child per woman) is responsible for another 21%. If the average education of Mexican women were
raised from its present level of 9.9 grades to the level of white women,
which is 12.5 grades, the Mexicans' "real" wages would be within 1% of
the "real" wages of white women. None of the other differences between Mexican and white women are large enough and significant
enough in determining wages to have much effect on the differential.

The wage offers of Puerto Rican women average the same as those for
white non-Hispanic women, but after adjusting for the cost of living,
they get 10% less in "real" terms. Their wages would be 4% higher than
those of white women if their characteristics were the same. Closing the
2.7-grade difference in education would more than eliminate the entire
"real wage-offer" differential. Each difference between Puerto Rican and
white women—in family size (Puerto Ricans have 1.5 times more children), time on the U.S. mainland, race, and government employment—
accounts for a wage differential of only 1 to 2%. The government employment effect occurs because Puerto Rican women with similar
human capital characteristics get 62% higher wages from local government than from private employers, and white non-Hispanic women get
10% more. Thirteen percent of the Anglo women are employed by local
governments, as compared with only 9% of the Puerto Rican women.
Since English-language problems, ceteris paribus, are estimated to have
a positive effect on wages for both white and Puerto Rican women, the
larger percentage of Puerto Rican women with language problems tends
to raise their average wage relative to that of white women. Eliminating
the Puerto Ricans' language deficiency would therefore tend to widen
the wage differential, according to these estimates.

Although the arithmetic mean observed wage of Cuban women is 5%
less than that of white non-Hispanic women, their geometric mean observed wage is 3% higher, and their mean wage offer is 9% higher. This
Cuban advantage exists despite the differences in education, time in the
United States, and government employment, which tend to create a
differential in favor of white non-Hispanic women. The higher average

age of Cuban women does work in their favor, but the overall effect of the observed differences between them and white non-Hispanic women would be to create a wage differential of 5% in favor of the whites.

Central and South American women have average observed wages 5% below those of white non-Hispanic women, and average wage offers 16% below them. The price adjustment puts them 23% behind. A gap of 7% is due to the education difference of 1.4 grades, and another 8% is due to the short time they have been in the United States.

Other Hispanic women have average wage offers 16% below their white non-Hispanic counterparts; however, only two-fifths of this gap can be accounted for by differences in personal characteristics. Raising the Hispanics' educational level from its present average of 11.7 grades to the 12.5 grade level of whites would close 4.4 percentage points of the wage gap. The Hispanics' larger family size accounts for a gap of 1.3%, and local price levels account for 1.6%. Nothing else accounts for even a 1% wage differential.

Black women, on the other hand, have wages nearly as high as white women; there is only a 4% difference in observed wages and less than a 1% difference in wage offers. Moreover, if the blacks had the same characteristics as the whites, there would be a 7% difference in favor of the black women. The existing wage differential is largely due to the difference in education (1.2 grades) and the difference in average number of children (1.4 vs. 0.9). On the other hand, the greater potential work experience of blacks narrows the wage difference, as does their greater rate of employment in the higher-paying government sector, especially in the federal government.

In summary, the most important single reason for the lower wages of minority women is their lower levels of education. For Puerto Ricans and Mexicans, this accounts for a 13 to 15% difference in wages from white non-Hispanics. For blacks, the differential due to education is 9%. For the other Hispanic groups, who have more than 11 years of schooling, on average, education still accounts for a 4 to 7% shortfall in wages relative to white non-Hispanics.

Other factors also account for some of the Hispanic–Anglo wage differential. Differences in local price levels, for instance, account for a wage difference of 4% between white non-Hispanics and Mexicans, many of whom live in the low-price Southwest. For Puerto Ricans and Central and South Americans, who live in the high-price Northeast and West Coast, respectively, the variation in local prices narrows the wage gap—by ten percentage points for Puerto Ricans and seven points for Central and South Americans. Average price levels are similar in the areas where whites, blacks, Cubans, and Other Hispanics live.

Immigration is also a factor in explaining wage differences. The larger numbers of Hispanics who are immigrants result in wage differentials ranging from 0.2% for Mexican women to 8% for Central and South American women. Poor English is associated, ceteris paribus, with 15% higher wages for white women. When we assume the no-discrimination coefficients would be halfway between the current coefficients of whites and Hispanics, it appears that the English-language problems of Hispanics actually narrow the wage differential. If we assume that the Hispanics' coefficients would apply to everyone in the absence of discrimination, poor English causes a wage-offer differential ranging from −1.4% for Puerto Rican women to 8% for Cuban women.

Lack of access to public-sector jobs, which pay more than those in the private sector for the same measured human capital, has a small effect in the cases of Puerto Rican and Cuban women, resulting in a wage differential of about 1.5% between them and white non-Hispanics. Black women, on the other hand, gain a 2.2% advantage over whites from their higher rate of employment in the public sector.

Larger families account for a gap of 3% between Mexican women and their Anglo counterparts, and of 1.2% for Puerto Rican, Other Hispanic, and black women. Differences in health and marital status, however, are never large enough to be important.

One might suspect that the fact that some Hispanics are black would contribute to their earnings disadvantages. Race is not, however, an important factor in the lower average wage of Hispanics. Puerto Ricans and Central and South Americans are the only groups that are more than 5% nonwhite, and they are only about 10% nonwhite. Moreover, within these groups the impact of race on wages is not very large, except for Puerto Rican women. At most, race explains a 1.7% wage difference, between Puerto Rican and white non-Hispanic females.

Table 2.14 compares the observed wage differential, the wage-offer differential, and the wage differential attributable to differences in parameters under the three assumptions about the no-discrimination wage function discussed in the section about men. The first two columns demonstrate that for Mexican, Central and South American, and Other Hispanic women, the average wage offered to the minority group is at least 15% below that offered to white non-Hispanic women. Black and Puerto Rican women, on the other hand, have virtually the same geometric mean hourly earnings as white non-Hispanic women, especially if one corrects the observed average wage for selectivity bias. Cuban women actually have a higher geometric mean observed wage than white non-Hispanic women, and the difference in wage offers is even more in the Cubans' favor. (In these three cases, as well as for Mexican

TABLE 2.14
Wage Differences between White Non-Hispanic and Minority Women, and Estimated Effect of Discrimination

Ethnic group	Observed wage difference[a] (1)	Wage difference, corrected for selection bias[b] (2)	Wage difference due to difference in parameters[c]		
			$(D = I)^d$ (3)	$(D = 0)^e$ (4)	$(D = (0.5)I)^f$ (5)
Mexican	.202	.200	−.061	.013	−.024
Puerto Rican	.027	−.001	−.085	.003	−.041
Cuban	−.026	−.087	−.123	−.136	−.129
Central and South American	.048	.157	.125	.108	.117
Other Hispanic	.145	.162	.089	.101	.095
Black non-Hispanic	.043	.006	−.081	−.065	−.073

Source: 1976 Survey of Income and Education (U.S. Department of Commerce, 1978).
[a] $\ln W_w - \ln W_h$ (approximately the percentage difference in the geometric mean observed wage between each group and white non-Hispanic women).
[b] $\ln W_w - \ln W_h - [(\hat{\sigma}_{12}\lambda)_w - (\hat{\sigma}_{12}\lambda)_h] = \ln P_w + \bar{X}_w\beta_w - \ln P_h - \bar{X}_h\beta_h$ (the "wage-offer" differential).
[c] $[\bar{X}_w(I - D) + \bar{X}_h D](\beta_w - \beta_h)$.
[d] Assuming whites' wage function reflects no discrimination; $\bar{X}_h(\beta_w - \beta_h)$.
[e] Assuming minority group's wage function reflects no discrimination; $\bar{X}_w(\beta_w - \beta_h)$.
[f] Assuming that the no-discrimination wage function is halfway between that of whites and minorities.

women, the selectivity bias, while negative, is larger in absolute value than for white non-Hispanic women. Therefore the observed average wage is reduced more for the minority group, and the observed wage difference exaggerates the size of the wage-offer gap.)

The last three columns of Table 2.14 address the question, What would the wage differences be if the minority and majority groups had the same average characteristics? These wage differences would be entirely due to differences in the parameters of the wage function. Insofar as the parameter differences are due to discrimination in the labor market, then, these wage differences measure the impact of racial and ethnic discrimination on women's wages. The last three columns measure this effect, using as weights $D = I$, $D = 0$, and $D = (0.5)I$. In most cases, the three estimates are quite similar. Only for Mexican and Puerto Rican women does the choice of weights make a difference of more than two percentage points.

These wage differences due to differences in parameters are, of course, subject to sampling variability. It can be measured by the standard error of the total effect of background variables given in Table 2.13, because the wage difference due to differences in parameters is the residual wage-offer difference after subtracting the difference that can be explained by observed characteristics. This standard error is large relative to the observed wage differential for Puerto Ricans, Cubans, and Central and South Americans, whose average wages are very close to those of white non-Hispanic women in the first place.

When we look at the point estimates for Mexican, Puerto Rican, Cuban, and black women, the differences in characteristics appear to favor the white women, but the differences in parameters appear to favor the minority women. There is no evidence of wage discrimination based on ethnicity against Mexican, Puerto Rican, or Cuban women, nor of racial wage discrimination against black women. The women of these minority groups, given their human capital characteristics, fare at least as well (or as badly) as white women in their rates of pay.

Central and South American women may suffer from discrimination to the extent of a 12% gap in wage offers between them and white non-Hispanic women. Differences in observed characteristics explain only one quarter of the total difference in average wage offers. For Other Hispanic women, the unexplained wage gap is 10%, three-fifths of the total gap.

SUMMARY OF FEMALE WAGE DETERMINATION ANALYSIS

To sum up, the findings indicate that Hispanic women get very small returns to a year of schooling—less than half as large as white non-Hispanic women. Women of all groups get very low returns to potential work experience. This may be because they lack access to jobs with training and promotion possibilities, or because they do not participate in the labor force continuously. The fact that the presence of children significantly lowers the wages of Mexican and Anglo women suggests that lack of participation is at least part of the story. In any case, the wage differences among otherwise similar women of different ages are small, and are even smaller for minority women than for white non-Hispanics.

The analysis does not reveal a clear-cut pattern of wage growth accompanying time in the United States for women, such as Chiswick (1978a) and I (see Table 2.4) have found for men. Surprisingly, English deficiencies do not significantly affect women's wages, within groups having the same education and time in the United States. Nor does race have a significant impact on wages within Hispanic groups. This is consistent with my finding that black and white women have similar wage offers.

The main factors that do affect women's wage offers—besides education, age, number of children, and immigration date—are health and public-sector employment. Having a health problem lowers women's wages. Women get much higher wages (given their human capital characteristics) in local, state, and federal government jobs than in the private sector. Except for Puerto Ricans, women's pay is highest in the federal government. Puerto Rican women, however, get much higher wages in the local government sector than anywhere else. This may reflect a pay difference in New York City between municipal and private-sector jobs of similar skill levels, especially for the types of jobs (e.g., in the garment industry) that Puerto Rican women tend to hold. Since white and Hispanic men get no wage premium in the public sector as a whole, the public–private wage difference for women suggests that gender discrimination is worse in the private than in the public sector.

When comparing the wage offers of women of different ethnic groups and asking about the possible impact of racial or ethnic discrimination among women, one should first note that Puerto Rican, Cuban, and black women have geometric mean wage offers on a par with (or greater than) white non-Hispanic women, even without taking human capital differences into account. How can this be explained, given their apparent disadvantages in terms of human capital? For one thing, the Puerto Ricans live in the high-price, high-wage Northeast. Also, differences between minority and white non-Hispanic women in occupational and industrial distribution may be part of the story: white non-Hispanic women tend to be in white-collar jobs, while minority women with comparable education, experience, and so forth are in blue-collar jobs, and the minority women's wages in such jobs may include a compensating differential for their less desirable job status and working conditions.

Clearly, differences in education, and not labor market discrimination against the ethnic group, are the overwhelming reason for the shortfall in wages for Mexican-American women. Mexican women's average level of schooling is so low that closing the education gap would eliminate almost all of the "real" wage difference between them and white non-Hispanic women, despite their low returns to education. Ethnic discrimination is possibly an important factor for Central and South American and Other Hispanic women, but not for the other groups. Female Mexicans, Puerto Ricans, Cubans, and blacks fare no worse in wage offers than otherwise-comparable white non-Hispanic women.

CHAPTER 3

Employment, Wages, and Earnings of Hispanics in the Federal and Nonfederal Sectors: Methodological Issues and Their Empirical Consequences*

John M. Abowd and Mark R. Killingsworth

Introduction

A major reason for studying employment and earnings differences by race and ethnicity is to determine what such differences imply about both potential employer discrimination and other sources of economic disadvantage resulting from race or ethnic origin. Much domestic policy is concerned with such questions, and information about the extent to which low economic status is related to employer discrimination or to other factors may have important implications for the allocation of re-

* This chapter is based on a report prepared for the Employment and Training Administration, U.S. Department of Labor, under Research and Development Grant No. 21-36-78-61. Since grantees conducting research and development projects under government sponsorship are encouraged to express their own judgment freely, this chapter does not necessarily represent the official opinion or policy of the Department of Labor. The authors are solely responsible for the contents of this chapter and the associated report. We wish to acknowledge the assistance of Anthony Abowd, who performed most of the calculations for this chapter and for the detailed report in conjunction with his Ph.D. thesis, completed at the University of Chicago. Research assistance was provided by Paul McCudden and Leslie Brown of the University of Chicago.

sources to different domestic social programs such as antidiscrimination efforts, manpower training, and education programs.[1]

A major stylized (i.e., abstracted for purpose of analysis) fact about wage and earnings differentials is that the black–white differential, even after adjustment for differences in schooling and many other factors, remains statistically and economically important regardless of the economic model or the statistical technique used to analyze the data. Specifically, black–white "labor market discrimination" has not been fully explained by either structural economic theories or statistical adjustments designed to eliminate a plethora of potential biases. In this chapter, we devote special attention to employer wage discrimination and to the extent to which employers in the federal and nonfederal sectors discriminate by race or ethnicity in making wage offers.[2] We show that the stylized fact just noted does not apply to Hispanic–Anglo wage and earnings differentials. Rather, on the whole, Hispanic–Anglo wage and earnings differences can generally be explained by human capital differences, self-selection biases, and statistical biases arising from imperfect measurement of human capital differences. In particular, most of the difference between Hispanics and white non-Hispanics arises from human capital differences. A smaller but still important part of the difference arises from statistical biases due to measurement problems. Cor-

---

[1] Studies that attempt to decompose earnings differentials into portions attributable to employer discrimination and portions attributable to differences in productivity characteristics such as education include, among others, Blinder (1973), Oaxaca (1973), and Smith (1977). Litigation under Title VII of the Civil Rights Act and other antidiscrimination laws and regulations is implicitly or explicitly concerned with the extent to which observed employment and earnings differences between sexes or between racial or ethnic groups are attributable to employer discrimination per se rather than to other factors such as differences in productivity-related characteristics. Discussions of analyses of earnings differences in the context of legal proceedings include Baldus and Cole (1980), Ehrenberg (1979), Finkelstein (1980), and Bloom and Killingsworth (1982).

[2] One important reason for studying employment and earnings differences by sector is that such differences may reveal the extent to which a particular sector is unusual compared to the rest of the economy. (For example, see Smith, 1977.) A second reason is that nonpecuniary rewards to employment may vary by sector: for example, federal government employment may entail greater job security or better working conditions than employment elsewhere in the economy (Smith, 1977). We define *wage discrimination* as a differential in the total reward to employment, including both pecuniary and nonpecuniary rewards. This reinforces the usefulness of an intrasectoral analysis of wage discrimination, since important differences in nonpecuniary compensation across sectors are, in effect, held constant. On the other hand, the fact that such an analysis may have conceptual advantages over an intersectoral study does not necessarily mean that statistical procedures suitable for the latter kind of study are also suitable for the former kind of study.

recting for self-selection bias gives essentially the same results as ordinary regression analysis.

Before proceeding, we define a number of concepts that figure prominently in what follows.

By *federal* and *nonfederal* employment we mean, respectively, employment in the federal government and employment elsewhere in the economy.

By *ethnicity* we mean Hispanic or non-Hispanic ethnic origin, based on the self-declared origin of individuals as either Hispanic or not Hispanic. We subdivide Hispanics into two groups: those of Puerto Rican origin, and other Hispanics.[3] *Black* refers to blacks who are not Hispanic. Persons who are neither black nor Hispanic are called *white non-Hispanics* or simply *whites*. Note, however, that the group we call whites includes a relatively small number of Orientals, American Indians, and others who are not necessarily Caucasian.

By *labor force status* we mean the conventional trichotomy used in most government surveys, modified so as to distinguish between employment in the federal sector and employment in the nonfederal sector. Thus, in our analyses, any individual's labor force status is always one of the following mutually exclusive and exhaustive conditions: employed in the federal sector, employed in the nonfederal sector, unemployed (that is, not employed but seeking employment), or not in the labor force.

Finally, by *ethnic wage discrimination* we mean any difference in total compensation—including both pecuniary and nonpecuniary compensation—that is associated with differences in ethnicity but is not associated with differences in productivity. This definition seems to be standard (for example, see Arrow, 1973, p. 4). Our definition emphasizes something that, while implicit in most definitions of wage discrimination, is worth noting explicitly: Wage discrimination means differences in total compensation, rather than just in pecuniary compensation per se. For example, under our definition, pay differentials that are purely compensating or equalizing in nature are not discriminatory even if they are associated with ethnicity but not productivity. By the same token, the

[3] We do this in order both to analyze Puerto Ricans as such—because this is a sizable and, in geographic terms, relatively homogeneous Hispanic group that has not been the subject of extensive empirical investigation by economists—and to permit comparisons between Puerto Ricans and other Hispanics, taken as a group. Of course, non–Puerto Rican Hispanics are a heterogeneous group, consisting of Cubans, Mexicans, Europeans, Central and South Americans, and others. Thus, conclusions about this Hispanic group refer to the aggregate of such persons and do not necessarily apply to each group within this overall aggregate.

absence of a difference in pecuniary compensation may also entail wage discrimination. For example, an employer who offers Hispanic workers the same pecuniary pay but less desirable working conditions than equally productive non-Hispanic workers is behaving in a discriminatory manner, in our sense of that term.

This chapter is organized as follows. We first present the economic theory underlying our statistical models, and then discuss the statistical models. We next present a summary of the data used, discuss our results regarding ethnic differences in labor force status, and describe the direct regression results from the Survey of Income and Education (SIE; U.S. Department of Commerce, 1978) data. The reverse regression results from the SIE data follow. We then discuss the structural regression results from the same data. The next section discusses statistical results on federal compensation derived using an alternative data set, followed by comparison of all the statistical results. The final section presents our conclusions.

The Theoretical Model

Like most branches of economics, labor economics is concerned with the analysis of supply and demand. As actual or potential employees, individuals are chiefly concerned with the labor supply decision and are constrained utility-maximizers in the neoclassical sense: They select the combination of work hours, leisure hours, and job characteristics (including both pecuniary and nonpecuniary compensation) that brings the highest possible level of happiness consistent with the constraints. Note that it makes sense to say that individuals' choices are voluntary only if one adds that they are made subject to whatever constraints exist.

Whereas individuals, considered as agents in the labor market, are concerned with the labor supply decision, the major concern of the firm, as an actual or potential employer, is the labor demand decision. The firm must decide how high a wage it is willing to offer and what types of jobs it requires. Faced with a competitive market for hiring employees, firms do not offer more than is necessary to attract proper employees nor less than is necessary to fill all positions.

Firms may be viewed as continually making job offers, consisting of pecuniary compensation and a package of job characteristics which, in effect, constitute nonpecuniary compensation. Individuals may be viewed as continually seeking job offers and accepting or rejecting them. What is observed in a collection of data—for example, a sample survey—is the outcome of this job offer and job acceptance (or job rejection) process. The observed wage and employment outcome is the result of the process, not the process itself. For example, the fact that a given person selects a job in the federal sector over a job elsewhere is correctly called endogenous both to the individual's labor supply decision and to the labor demand decisions of employers.

Since firms seek to maximize profits and understand that workers seek to maximize utility, firms will, on average, offer job packages consisting of pecuniary pay and working conditions that will fill the available positions at minimum cost. A firm whose offers are unnecessarily attractive will be flooded with applicants. It, and any competing enterprise, then knows that it can reduce the generosity of its offers, broadly defined, and still attract adequate numbers of applicants. Subject to some important qualifications to be noted below, the utility associated with a given job offer will then fall to the minimum level required to attract the number of workers the firm wants. In this way, then, firms rely on the nature of utility-maximizing behavior of individuals and on the nature of a competitive market to bring labor supply and labor demand into balance. In all cases, individuals decide which of the options available to them is best, subject to the constraints they face.

Of course, employers may sometimes decide, as a matter of conscious policy, to operate out of equilibrium, at least in the sense of an imbalance between the number of persons willing to work for the employer at the current level of generosity of the employer's job package (supply) and the number of positions the employer wants to fill (demand). For example, the federal sector may continually and deliberately make job offers with compensation in excess of the minimum necessary to fill the number of positions it wants to fill. This will result in a waiting list, or queue, for federal jobs. When such a queue exists, the various jobs available need to be allocated or rationed out among the applicants according to some method, formal or informal. For federal government employment, one such method of allocation is political—some of the available jobs may be allocated through a process of explicit or implicit payoffs. In this situation, different groups in the population have an incentive to compete for the political clout necessary for influence over the allocation process. The resources spent competing for such clout eventually bring the system back into equilibrium. If a federal job offers a premium over the minimum amount that the individual would require in order to be willing to accept it, then the individual will be willing to spend resources up to the amount of that premium to get enough clout to be offered that job.

Political allocation may help explain why the federal government can make better job offers and have higher minority employment relative to total employment than other employers. This higher relative minority employment may be in regions where minority political clout is higher. For example, minorities may have political clout in regions where minority population proportions are higher than they are in the country as a whole. This is one reason why measures of local population proportions for minorities may be relevant to analyses of federal employment.

Of course, nonfederal employers, including employers in the private sector, may also—like the federal sector—make wage offers in excess of the minimum necessary to fill the number of positions they want to fill. Marginal private-sector employers cannot do so because their profits would be driven below the minimum required for survival. Intramarginal private-sector employers may do so if they choose. For example, a private-sector employer with access to superior production technology will be more profitable than average; while this greater potential profitability may accrue to shareholders, it may instead take the form of wage offers to some groups that exceed the minimum required to fill the jobs the firm wants to fill. Similarly, a private-sector employer may make unnecessarily high or excessive offers as a result of a collective-bargaining agreement. In cases such as these, as in our previous discussion of job allocation through political clout, there will be a disequilibrium in the sense that, at the prevailing wage offer, defined broadly so as to include nonpecuniary as well as pecuniary rewards, supply will exceed demand. This will induce adjustments that will eventually bring the market back into equilibrium; as before, such adjustments involve expenditures of resources up to the amount of the premium implicit in the employer's offer. In some cases, such expenditures are implicit and occur through queueing. In other cases, such expenditures are explicit. In still other cases, supply and demand are equated through a rationing mechanism that has little to do with productivity considerations, such as when the employer makes offers based on factors like race rather than on the basis of productivity.

The labor market, then, settles into an equilibrium in which the observed distribution of wages and the observed sectoral composition of employment are the result of demand and supply decisions. In what follows, we are concerned in general terms with intrasectorial differentials in employment and wage rates by ethnicity, with special reference to Puerto Ricans. To clarify the nature of some of the issues in which we are particularly interested, consider the following two questions:

Question 1. On average, if a randomly selected set of persons were placed in a particular sector, would the employer(s) in that sector pay those persons differently, depending on whether they were Hispanic or non-Hispanic, other things being equal?

Question 2. On average, are the Hispanic persons who are actually in a particular sector (i.e., the self-selected group) paid differently by the employer(s) in that sector from the non-Hispanic persons actually in the same sector who are comparable in terms of observed characteristics?

The answers to these two questions need not be identical. Both questions are of interest for most discussions of employer discrimination in the labor market. However, as we emphasize below, a particular statistical technique may provide a satisfactory answer to one of these questions without yielding any direct or useful evidence on the other.

Statistical Models

DIRECT WAGE REGRESSION

The vast majority of studies of wage differentials by race, ethnicity, or sex rely on the methodology of direct wage regression. Under this procedure, one fits an earnings function—with a measure of pay such as earnings or wages as the dependent variable, and with measures of productivity-related characteristics and hypothetically irrelevant characteristics (sex, race) as independent variables—by applying least squares to data on individuals actually employed in some sector of interest. In some cases, as in Mincer's (1974) seminal work, *sector* means all employed persons. In other cases, *sector* refers to a single employer, as in the studies by Malkiel and Malkiel (1973), Oaxaca (1976), Smith (1977), Ehrenberg (1979), Osterman (1979), and many others. Regardless of how sector is defined, however, all such studies are investigating wages given that the individuals in the analysis are all in the sector being studied and have both received and accepted an offer from that sector.

It is important to understand what kind of evidence about the source and magnitude of wage and earnings differentials is contained in direct wage regression results. While direct wage regression may provide useful information on some questions, it may provide little or no direct evidence on others. Direct wage regressions analyze wage offers that have been received and accepted. Thus, while it appears that results derived from direct wage regressions may be quite useful for answering what we have called Question 2, they may be much less useful for answering what we have called Question 1.

At the statistical level, it is important to note that, considered only in terms of questions on which it can reasonably be expected to provide useful information, direct wage regression may provide evidence that is misleading—in particular, estimates that may be biased or inconsistent in a statistical sense. Such bias or inconsistency can arise owing either to exclusion of relevant variables or to inclusion of inappropriate (more generally, endogenous) variables. (The problem of omitted-variable bias has sometimes been misinterpreted or misunderstood, however. A regression coefficient on a particular independent variable of interest will be biased due to omission of a relevant variable only if the omitted variable is correlated with both the dependent variable and the independent variable of interest at the margin, i.e., when all included independent variables other than the one of interest are held constant.)

A different but related bias is induced by errors of measurement in the included variables. It would be surprising if such variables were always perfect surrogate or proxy measures of productivity, and it is possible that such variables measure actual or expected productivity with error. In this case the coefficients in a direct wage regression may be subject to what Roberts (1979, 1981) has called underadjustment bias. A statistical procedure used to address this problem is called reverse regression.

REVERSE WAGE REGRESSION

The general phenomenon of measurement error bias in regression models has received attention for many years, and is a standard topic in many econometrics texts (e.g., Kmenta, 1971, pp. 307–322; Maddala, 1977, pp. 292–305). The problem of measurement error bias in direct wage regression, however, has received relatively little attention; most work on this subject is quite recent (e.g., Welch, 1973; Hashimoto and Kochin, 1979; Roberts, 1979, 1980, 1981; Kamalich and Polachek, 1982; A. Abowd, 1983; Conway and Roberts, 1983).

In the Appendix, we present a formal discussion of our reverse wage regression procedure and compare it with the conventional direct wage regression approach. We show the following:

1. Direct wage regression will tend to indicate the existence of pay discrimination *against* one group of persons, Group A, relative to persons in another Group B when no such discrimination exists—or, more generally, will tend to overstate the magnitude of such discrimination— provided that (a) productivity is measured with error, and (b) persons in Group A have less productivity, on average, than persons in Group B.

2. Reverse wage regression will tend to indicate the existence of pay discrimination *favoring* one group of persons, Group A, relative to persons in another Group B when no such discrimination exists—or, more generally, will tend to understate the magnitude of discrimination

against persons in Group A—provided that (a) pay is measured with error and (b) persons in Group A receive lower pay, on average, than persons in Group B.

In an important sense, the direct and reverse regression procedures are not really different: If they could be implemented using correct measures of pay and productivity, then either procedure would yield the same (unbiased) estimate of the actual extent, if any, of discrimination. However, in general, true pay cannot be measured exactly, since the appropriate measure would include current compensation, fringe benefits, the monetary value of future promotion possibilities, future benefits, and on-the-job amenities. Similarly, true productivity cannot be measured exactly, since the true index depends on schooling, types and quantities of previous experience, and various other factors that may be difficult to quantify. The importance of the analysis of direct and reverse regression methods is that, under typical conditions, the two statistical methods will result in estimates that bound the actual magnitude of discrimination.

We have derived a version of the reverse wage regression method for use in analyses comparable to the direct regression models. The procedure involves two steps. In the first or "direct" stage, we compute an underlying direct regression using a randomly selected half of the white non-Hispanic observations available to us. We use only half of the available observations to fit the direct regression because these estimated coefficients will be used to form a productivity index for the remaining half of the white non-Hispanics and all the black and Hispanic observations. (Splitting the sample avoids inducing spurious correlation between the computed productivity index and the wage rates in the reverse regressions.) The direct regressions used in the first stage involve all the productivity indicators used in the direct regression except, of course, the ethnicity indicators and interactions involving these indicators.

In the second or "reverse" stage, we use the conventional wage or earnings function coefficient estimates from the direct stage to compute predicted wages or earnings $\bar{y}$ for the remaining observations. We treat this constructed variable $\bar{y}$ as a proxy measure of productivity. Accordingly, $\bar{y}$ becomes the dependent variable in our second-stage reverse wage regression. We compute

$$\bar{y} = a + b_0' d + b_1 y + \eta,$$

where d is a vector of race and ethnicity indicators, y is a measure of pay (e.g., the logarithm of the hourly wage), and η is the regression error term. Thus $\bar{y}$ is a linear function of y (and d).

STRUCTURAL WAGE REGRESSION

Both direct and reverse wage regression are concerned with conditional wage relationships. Such techniques are therefore directly concerned with what we have called Question 2—identifying the within-sector differences in wages and earnings for different race–ethnic groups. However, they do not, in general, estimate the parameters governing the structure of the underlying process of supply and demand that generates wage offers; rather, they constitute analyses of the outcome of that process. Neither direct nor reverse wage regression addresses what we have called Question 1—identifying the across-sector differences in wages and earnings opportunities for different race–ethnic groups.

In order to obtain answers to Question 1, it is necessary to address directly the question of the determinants of wage offers. Unfortunately, most data sets, particularly survey data sets, contain information on only a subset of all wage offers—namely, the ones that have been both received and accepted. In particular, in terms of our federal–nonfederal sector dichotomy, most cross-sectional survey data on any given individual contain information on only one offer (from either the federal or the nonfederal sector) for employed persons, and do not contain information on any offer, from either sector, for persons who are unemployed or not in the labor force.

To ignore this completely, as in an intrasectoral direct or reverse wage regression analysis, may subject a study to sample-selection bias, at least insofar as answers to Question 1 are concerned (see Heckman, 1979; Heckman et al., 1981; Bloom and Killingsworth, 1982). Sample-selection bias may arise in such a study because the data to be used contain only observations on persons who have received and accepted an offer from the sector in question. For example, the observations contained in data for a given sector are in part self-selected, in the sense that, having received an offer from employers in that sector, the persons observed in the data for that sector have all selected themselves into the sample to be analyzed. Application of direct or reverse wage regression to a self-selected sample of this kind may not yield consistent estimates of the parameters of the employer's wage offer function. More generally, a sample of this kind has a sampling distribution determined by both the survey design and the respondent in the sense that it consists of persons who have accepted offers. This makes it not only a self-selected sample, in the sense used above, but also a "selected sample" in the sense that such persons must first have received offers from, and thus must have been selected by, employers.

This suggests that one way to avoid the self-selection biases that may

arise in the context of direct or reverse regression analysis of an intrasectoral sample is to derive a model that not only (1) specifies the determinants of wage offers—the relation of primary interest—but also (2) describes the process of selection by which the individuals in such a
sample got into the sample. For details, see the Appendix at the end of
this chapter.

Data Used in Empirical Studies

Most of the data used in the empirical studies described in this report
are derived from the 1976 Survey of Income and Education (SIE), described in the Appendix to Chapter 1 and in U.S. Department of Commerce (1978).

We base our analyses on a sample of the SIE that excludes persons
under 21 years old. Among persons 21 years or older in the SIE data
base, 8168 are Hispanics, 19,501 are black non-Hispanics, and the remainder (246,837) are whites (that is, persons neither Hispanic nor
black). Ethnicity is self-reported. Race, however, is determined by inter-
viewer observation. The data excluded persons residing in Hawaii and
Alaska, and, of course, persons living in Puerto Rico.

The SIE therefore refers to a sample of persons in the country as a
whole, and geography undoubtedly has major effects on pay through its
association with such factors as (1) regional cost-of-living differentials,
(2) regional differences in amenities and also, to the extent that labor is
immobile, (3) regional differences in factor proportions (for example, see
Kiefer and Smith, 1977). Moreover, there are important regional differences in the location of minority populations and the location of various
industries, including the federal government. In all of our analyses,
geography, specifically locational choices, is taken as exogenous. Nevertheless, we have taken several measures to ensure that minority groups
are compared with nonminority groups from the same geographic region. The sampling design of the SIE oversampled less populated states,
meaning that the geographic distribution of employment opportunities
is not sampled randomly.

In order to control for the differences in labor demand across geographic regions, we have used two sets of geographically matched samples in our analysis. The logit models of the labor force status were
estimated using samples of blacks and of white non-Hispanics that were
geographically matched to our sample of Hispanics. Regression analyses
were performed on federal and nonfederal samples that were geographically matched to the federal sample.

We did this geographic matching by state and by what the SIE calls central city code, which categorizes persons according to residence in the following way: (1) located in the central city of a Standard Metropolitan Statistical Area (SMSA); (2) located in an SMSA but not in a central city; (3) located outside an SMSA; and (4) location not disclosed (in order to avoid breaching Bureau of the Census regulations governing confidentiality). Relatively small numbers of persons, mainly persons residing in outlying areas, fall into the last of these four categories. Thus, for example, after determining the total number of Hispanics living in the central city area of the Los Angeles–Long Beach SMSA in California, we randomly selected equal numbers of black non-Hispanics and of whites from the total populations of such persons in the same area; and similarly for all other areas. The result of this process of matching was three samples (of Hispanics, black non-Hispanics, and whites, respectively) with the same sampling probabilities for each state and central city code. In addition, we produced two samples (of federal and nonfederal employees, respectively) with the same sampling probabilities for each state and central city code. Therefore, five analysis samples were produced: three that were geographically matched to the Hispanic data and two that were geographically matched to the federal data.

For the samples geographically matched to the Hispanic sample from the SIE, the sampling probabilities for Hispanics and whites are identical for each state and central city code. However, because there were not enough black non-Hispanics in the original SIE sample for the West and Southwest regions, this group is undersampled for these regions in our sample. All federal employees in the SIE are included in the federal sample. In the nonfederal sample, whites are exactly matched geographically but Hispanics and black non-Hispanics are oversampled. Since ethnicity and location are always conditioning variables in the analyses using the federal and nonfederal samples, the oversampling of blacks and Hispanics can be expected to reduce sampling error on ethnicity effects without inducing a location bias.

Because we are not able to observe the actual work experience of the individuals in our data, we must use a measure of potential work experience (Mincer, 1974) defined as current age less years of schooling less 5. The problems associated with this proxy are well known, particularly as regards male–female differences in potential versus actual work experience. Accordingly, we think it appropriate in analyzing differentials in employment status, wages, and earnings to consider men and women separately.

Annual earnings, as defined in our studies, is the total amount of income from work received during the year 1975. The *hourly wage,* as used in our studies, is computed as the ratio of annual earnings to annual hours of work, where the latter is computed as the products of weeks worked during the year 1975 and usual hours worked per week during the year 1975. *Labor force status* is defined according to standard Current Population Survey concepts (U.S. Department of Commerce, 1978) as of the week preceding the actual survey date.

The period 1975–1976 was part of an unusually severe recession. This may have implications for the interpretation of our results. In particular, differentials of any kind (skill, racial, etc.) may tend to widen during business-cycle slumps and narrow during booms. To the extent that this is true, the various effects we discuss in this report may overstate somewhat the effects that would be observed during more normal (less recessionary) times.

In addition to the SIE we also used the federal government's Central Personnel Data File (CPDF). The CPDF is a payroll data set based on federal personnel files. CPDF data are derived from various federal payroll documents and are used by the federal Office of Personnel Management and other federal agencies in studying characteristics of the federal civilian work force, in personnel planning, and in other related activities. The CPDF is longitudinal in nature, having begun in 1972 and having been updated on an annual basis since that time; thus, it permits analyses of several different years. Finally, since the CPDF covers essentially all federal employees, it contains large numbers of Hispanics as well as large numbers of persons in other racial and ethnic groups. (For further details on the CPDF, see Schneider, 1974.)

In computing results using the CPDF, we started with samples of 5000 Hispanics and 5000 non-Hispanics, selected randomly from the total CPDF populations present in each of the years 1975, 1976, and 1977. As in our work on the SIE data, we then excluded persons who either (1) were not living in the continential United States or (2) were under 21 years old. This reduced a given year's sample by about 12% to about 8800 people. About 15% of the persons remaining in any given year's sample after application of this exclusion could not be included in the regression for that year owing to missing data (mainly for educational attainment or, to a lesser extent, race or sex). Also, we computed regressions for each year separately for each sex. Thus, the total size of the sample used for regressions for a given sex for a particular year is between about 2000 (in the regressions for women) and about 5600 (in the regressions for men).

In order to provide a basis for comparisons between the various statistical procedures described earlier, we estimated a set of different wage and earnings models using the same data and definitions. We briefly discuss the design of these models. All regression models for wages and earnings based on the SIE use the same sets of explanatory variables. The regression models for wages and earnings based on the CPDF use different but similar explanatory variables. The logit models for employment sector based on the SIE use an abbreviated set of explanatory variables. We describe each explanatory variable list in turn.

The dependent variable for the wage and earnings analyses based on the SIE is either the log of the hourly wage rate or the log of annual earnings. Independent variables capture effects on wages associated with human capital, ethnicity, race, age, geography, and other factors. Table 3.1 contains a list of all variables used in the wage and earnings regressions based on the SIE data.

The Group A and Group B variables in Table 3.1 are indicators for minority status. Group A identifies Hispanics and blacks who are not

TABLE 3.1
Variables Used in Regression Analyses of SIE Data

Dependent variables
    Either the natural logarithm of the hourly wage rate or the natural logarithm of annual earnings
Independent variables
    Group A variables (ethnicity and race indicators—variant 1)
        1 if Hispanic, 0 otherwise
        1 if black and not Hispanic, 0 otherwise
    Group B variables (ethnicity and race indicators—variant 2)
        1 if Puerto Rican, 0 otherwise
        1 if Hispanic but not Puerto Rican, 0 otherwise
        1 if black and not Hispanic, 0 otherwise
    Group C variables (human capital, geography, and other factors)
      Number of years of formal education
        1 if graduated from high school, 0 otherwise
        1 if graduated from college, 0 otherwise
        1 if any postgraduate education, 0 otherwise
        1 if currently a full-time student, 0 otherwise
        1 if currently a full-time public school student, 0 otherwise
      Number of years of education received outside the U.S.
        1 if had any education outside the U.S., 0 otherwise
        1 if taught in English, 0 if taught in any other language
        1 if U.S.-born, spoke English as a child, and speaks English now; 0 otherwise
        1 if not U.S.-born, 0 otherwise
      Number of years lived in U.S. (equal to zero, for persons born in U.S.)
        1 if English not the primary language spoken as a child, 0 otherwise
        1 if English not the primary language spoken now, 0 otherwise
        1 if English not spoken or understood very well, 0 otherwise
        1 if has any physical condition limiting ability to work, 0 otherwise
        1 if age is over 30 and under 41, 0 otherwise
        1 if age is over 40 and under 51, 0 otherwise

TABLE 3.1 (*Continued*)

1 if age is over 50 and under 65, 0 otherwise
1 if age is over 64, 0 otherwise
Potential experience (age minus years of schooling minus 5)
Square of potential experience
    1 if employed part-time, 0 otherwise
    1 if a veteran, 0 otherwise
    1 if lives in New England area (Maine, New Hampshire, Vermont, Massachusetts, Rhode Island, Connecticut), 0 otherwise
    1 if lives in Middle Atlantic area (New York, New Jersey, Pennsylvania), 0 otherwise
    1 if lives in East North Central area (Ohio, Indiana, Illinois, Michigan, Wisconsin), 0 otherwise
    1 if lives in West North Central area (Minnesota, Iowa, Missouri, North Dakota, South Dakota, Nebraska, Kansas), 0 otherwise
    1 if lives in South Atlantic area (Delaware, Maryland, District of Columbia, Virginia, West Virginia, North Carolina, South Carolina, Georgia, Florida), 0 otherwise
    1 if lives in East South Central area (Kentucky, Tennessee, Alabama, Mississippi, Arkansas, Louisiana, Oklahoma, Texas), 0 otherwise
    1 if lives in Pacific area (Washington, Oregon or California), 0 otherwise
Group D variables (population proportions and interactions)
    Proportion of population in area (classified by state, SMSA, and central city) that is black non-Hispanic
    Proportion of population in area that is Hispanic
    Proportion black non-Hispanic in area times years of school
    Proportion Hispanic in area times years of school
    Proportion black non-Hispanic in area times potential experience
    Proportion Hispanic in area times potential experience
Group E variables (interactions with race, ethnicity indicators)
    Hispanic indicator times years of school
    Black non-Hispanic indicator times years of school
    Hispanic indicator times high school graduation indicator
    Black non-Hispanic indicator times high school graduation indicator
    Hispanic indicator times college graduation indicator
    Black non-Hispanic indicator times college graduation indicator
    Hispanic indicator times postgraduate education indicator
    Black non-Hispanic indicator times postgraduate education indicator
    Hispanic indicator times potential experience
    Black non-Hispanic indicator times potential experience
    Hispanic indicator times square of potential experience
    Black non-Hispanic indicator times square of potential experience
Group F variables (interactions between race, ethnicity indicators, and population proportions)
    Black non-Hispanic indicator times percentage black non-Hispanic in area
    Black non-Hispanic indicator times percentage black non-Hispanic in area times years in school
    Black non-Hispanic indicator times percentage black non-Hispanic in area times potential experience
    Hispanic indicator times percentage Hispanic in area
    Hispanic indicator times percentage Hispanic in area times year in school
    Hispanic indicator times percentage Hispanic in area times potential experience

Hispanics. Group B uses the same black non-Hispanic indicator but distinguishes between Hispanic subgroups; that is, those of Puerto Rican origin and other Hispanics.

Group C variables are forms of the basic human capital variables normally found in direct wage regressions. The exact form of these variables is, of course, limited by the nature of the data available in the SIE. These variables—for education, age, potential work experience, and the like—are proxies intended to capture the employer's attempt to estimate the productivity of potential employees.

Some variables in Group C go beyond the basic proxies used in most previous research. Variables for years of education outside the United States and for not speaking English as one's primary language are intended to capture effects of immigration and language skills that may affect earnings (see Chiswick, 1978a, 1980). Indicators of geographic location reflect the possible impact of region (that is, regional price differentials, capital-labor ratios, etc.) on job offers.

Group D variables reflect local Hispanic and black non-Hispanic population proportions. These population proportions are also multiplied by years of school or potential experience in order to capture possible interactions. Group E variables are interactions between human capital variables (schooling and potential experience) and minority status. Group F variables are triple-interaction effects; that is, minority indicators multiplied both by minority population proportions and by either years of school or years of potential experience.

Since the CPDF is similar to the personnel data files of a single employer, the variable list for the regression analyses based on these data includes more detailed information on the individual's work history. The variable list does not include the detailed educational, language, and immigrant background data found in the SIE. The variables used in the regressions based on the CPDF are listed in Table 3.2.

The Group A and Group B variables in Table 3.2 differ only in that, in the latter group, we distinguish between Orientals and American Indians, on the one hand, and all other persons who are neither black nor Hispanic, on the other. More or less by definition, this group of all other persons might be called majority white.

Note that our Group C variables in Table 3.2 (reflecting human capital, geographic location, and the like) are quite similar to the ones used in our SIE regression models in some respects, but are rather different in other respects. In particular, the CPDF data permit us to derive educational attainment indicators that are more detailed than the ones that can be obtained from the SIE data: for example, the latter do not contain any measures of the number of years elapsed since highest degree, or of the

TABLE 3.2
Variables Used in Regression Analyses of CPDF Data

Dependent variable
  Natural logarithm of annualized salary
Independent variables
  Group A (race and ethnicity indicators)
    1 if Hispanic, 0 otherwise
    1 if black, 0 otherwise
  Group B (expanded race and ethnicity indicators)
    1 if Hispanic, 0 otherwise
    1 if black, 0 otherwise
    1 if Oriental, 0 otherwise
    1 if American Indian, 0 otherwise
  Group C (human capital, geographic location, etc.)
    Educational attainment indicators (1 if possesses the indicated characteristics, 0 other-
      wise) for each of the following mutually exclusive categories:
      Completed elementary school, did not complete high school
      Has some high school education, but did not complete high school
      Has high school diploma or equivalent
      Attended terminal occupational training program, but did not complete it
      Completed terminal occupational training program
      Attended less than 1 year of college
      Attended 1 year of college
      Attended 2 years of college
      Has associate-in-arts or equivalent degree
      Attended 3 years of college
      Attended 4 years of college, but did not receive B.A. or equivalent degree
      Has B.A. or equivalent degree
      Has B.A. or equivalent and some post-B.A. training
      Has first professional degree (e.g., J.D., M.D.)
      Has first professional degree and some post-first-professional degree training
      Has M.A. or equivalent degree
      Has M.A. or equivalent and some post-M.A. training
      Has a sixth-year degree (e.g., Advanced Certificate in Education)
      Has a sixth-year degree and some post-sixth-year degree training
      Has Ph.D. or equivalent degree
      Has Ph.D. or equivalent degree and some post-Ph.D. training
    Years since highest degree, for persons with at least a B.A. or equivalent (for persons
      with less than a B.A., this variable is set at zero)
    Square of years since highest degree
    Indicators for field of highest degree, for persons with at least a B.A. or equivalent (1 if
      field of highest degree is the one indicated and 0 otherwise; set at 0 for all persons
      with less than a B.A.), as follows:
      Medical doctors (M.D., D.D.S., D.V.M., etc.)
      Allied health professions (nursing, therapy, etc.)
      Mathematics, architecture, engineering, data processing
      Physical or biological sciences
      Arts or humanities

(Continued)

TABLE 3.2 (*Continued*)

Social sciences
Law
Age
Square of age
Years employed in federal government
Square of years employed in federal government
Product of age and years employed in federal government
1 if has physical or mental disability, 0 otherwise
Indicators for veterans' preference (1 if possesses the indicated type of veterans'
    preference, 0 otherwise), as follows:
  5-point veterans' employment preference
  10-point disability veterans' employment preference
  10-point compensable veterans' employment preference
  10-point other veterans' employment preference (e.g., spouse, survivor)
Indicators for state of residence (1 if lives in a particular state, 0 otherwise) for all 48
    states in the continental United States and the District of Columbia

field of the highest degree, while the CPDF data do; and while the SIE measures the number of years of school completed, the CPDF data provide somewhat more information about the amount and kind of educational attainment than the simple amount of time spent in school. The CPDF data also contain a measure of years of employment in the federal government, while the SIE data do not contain any measure of actual work experience, even with one's present employer. Of course, on the other hand, the CPDF data do not contain measures of some variables of interest that are available in the SIE. For example, the CPDF data do not contain any information on language skills and also do not differentiate between race and ethnicity. That is, the SIE data classify persons according to both race and ethnicity (which, for example, permits one to differentiate between black and white Hispanics), while in the CPDF classification scheme race and ethnicity are defined in such a way as to make black and Hispanic mutually exclusive.

We use the variables listed above to form two different regression models. The first model uses the simple Group A race–ethnicity indicators and the Group C variables, while the second model uses the expanded Group B race–ethnicity indicators and the Group C variables. Note that the first model, comprising Group A and Group C variables, is most comparable to the basic model used in our SIE regressions.

Because of the problems associated with estimating many parameters in logit models, we use a smaller set of the available variables in our analysis of labor force status (which, as noted in the Appendix, is the

TABLE 3.3
Variables Used in Logit Analyses

Dependent variable
  Labor force status, categorized as follows:
    Employed in the federal sector
    Employed in the nonfederal sector
    Unemployed
    Not in the labor force
Independent variables
  Number of years of formal education
  Potential experience (= age minus years of schooling minus 5)
  1 if age is over 30 and under 41, 0 otherwise
  1 if age is over 40 and under 51, 0 otherwise
  1 if age is over 50, 0 otherwise
  Number of years lived in United States (equal to age, for persons born in United States)
  1 if born in U.S., spoke English as a child, and speaks English now, 0 otherwise
  1 if married with spouse present, 0 otherwise
  Number of persons in household
  Percentage of population in area (classified by state, SMSA, and central city) that is
    Hispanic
  Percentage of population in area that is black non-Hispanic
  Percentage Hispanic in area times years of school
  Percentage black non-Hispanic in area times years of school
  Percentage Hispanic in area times potential experience
  Percentage black non-Hispanic in area times potential experience
  1 if of Puerto Rican origin, 0 otherwise

first stage in our structural wage regression analysis). Table 3.3 contains
the variable list for the logit analyses based on the SIE data.

We estimate various logit models, containing alternative combinations
of these variables, separately for each sex, using separate samples of
Hispanics, black non-Hispanics, and white (that is, other) non-Hispanics. Note that an indicator for Puerto Rican ethnicity cannot be included
in logits for samples of black or white non-Hispanics because, by definition, this indicator has a value of zero for all such persons. On the other
hand, we do include such an indicator in logits for samples of Hispanics
in order to distinguish between Puerto Ricans and other Hispanics.

Labor Force Status Results

One of our principal interests in this research is to compare the federal
and nonfederal sectors. The implications of our logit models with respect to employment in these two sectors are summarized in Table 3.4,

TABLE 3.4
Comparison of Minorities' Predicted Employment Proportions

	Federal employees			Private employees		
	Actual %	Predicted %	% Diff.	Actual %	Predicted %	% Diff.
Men						
Hispanic	4.53	3.57	26.9	75.82	75.08	1.0
Puerto Rican	4.58	2.49	83.9	68.64	77.22	−11.1
Hispanic non–Puerto Rican	4.53	3.71	22.1	76.89	77.22	2.8
Black	5.07	2.98	70.1	67.62	73.17	−7.6
White	3.91	—	—	78.41	—	—
Women						
Hispanic	1.65	1.62	1.9	46.61	47.45	−1.8
Puerto Rican	1.35	1.00	35.0	34.28	51.64	−33.6
Hispanic non–Puerto Rican	1.69	1.71	−1.2	48.43	47.06	2.9
Black	3.53	1.29	173.6	50.96	52.08	−2.2
White	1.60	—	—	43.95	—	—

Source: 1976 Survey of Income and Education (U.S. Department of Commerce, 1978).
Notes: Predictions use logit coefficients from the sample of whites. See text for description of analysis.

which compares the actual and predicted employment sector for each race–ethnic group. The comparison is based on the characteristics of each individual in the sample (regardless of actual sector). A predicted probability was generated using the estimated logit coefficients for labor force status from the white sample. All comparisons in this table concerning under- or overrepresentation are made relative to white non-Hispanics (men, in the case of the other male ethnic groups; or women, in the case of the other female ethnic groups). A positive entry for a given sector in the "% Diff." column indicates that the group in question is overrepresented in that sector relative to white non-Hispanics of the same sex with the same educational attainment, age, and so forth; a negative entry indicates underrepresentation.

The main implications of Table 3.4 may be summarized as follows: First, virtually all minority ethnic groups (that is, groups other than white non-Hispanics) are substantially overrepresented in federal employment relative to white non-Hispanics. (The only exceptions to this generalization are Hispanic non–Puerto Rican women, who are slightly underrepresented in federal employment, and Hispanic women generally, who are only slightly overrepresented in federal employment, on average.) However, note that such overrepresentation in federal employment is only a small proportion of any given group's population. (For example, Table 3.4 indicates that men of Puerto Rican origin are overrepresented in federal employment in the sense that the actual proportion of such men in federal employment is 4.58%, as opposed to the 2.49% that would be expected if this group acted and were treated in regard to labor force status as white men with identical schooling, age, etc.) In this sense, an end to such overrepresentation would not involve the reallocation of a large number of persons. Second, Puerto Ricans of either sex are also substantially underrepresented in nonfederal employment relative to comparable white non-Hispanics. Third, black non-Hispanic males are also underrepresented in nonfederal employment. Recall that these differences in labor force status cannot be attributed exclusively to either supply or demand factors (e.g., to individual tastes or to employer discrimination) since the estimated version of the logit model does not identify either of these two behavioral relationships separately.

To complement Table 3.4, we present in Table 3.5 a summary of the

TABLE 3.5

Comparison of Minorities' Predicted Unemployment and Proportions Not in Labor Force

	Unemployed			Not in labor force		
	Actual %	Predicted %	% Diff.	Actual %	Predicted %	% Diff.
Men						
Hispanic	5.83	5.43	7.4	18.03	20.23	−10.9
Puerto Rican	8.92	7.24	23.2	21.51	17.09	25.9
Hispanic non–Puerto Rican	5.43	5.20	.2	17.58	20.63	−14.8
Black	7.16	5.20	37.7	27.38	21.64	26.5
White	3.45	—	—	22.54	—	—
Women						
Hispanic	4.90	4.96	7.5	52.80	53.52	−1.3
Puerto Rican	6.37	4.87	30.8	62.74	49.73	26.2
Hispanic non–Puerto Rican	4.70	4.52	4.0	51.44	54.04	−4.8
Black	7.21	4.78	50.8	41.20	46.69	−11.8
White	3.32	—	—	51.13	—	—

Source: 1976 Survey of Income and Education (U.S. Department of Commerce, 1978).
Notes: Predictions use logit coefficients from the sample of whites. See text for description of analysis.

implications of our logit results concerning the relation between ethnicity and nonemployment (i.e., either unemployment or absence from the
labor force). This shows that both men and women in each of the minority ethnic groups considered in our analyses are overrepresented among
the unemployed, relative to whites with comparable schooling, age,
family composition, and so forth. Non–Puerto Rican Hispanics of either
sex, and black women, tend to be underrepresented among persons not
in the labor force; Puerto Ricans of either sex, and black men, tend to be
overrepresented.

All things considered, our logit results suggest that ethnicity as such
does not have a particularly pronounced association with labor force
status once one holds constant the effects of other supply and demand
factors such as age, schooling, family composition, and the like. One
simple way to illustrate this is shown in Table 3.6. In this table, we show
how changing the ethnicity of *all* ethnic groups to white non-Hispanic
(without changing their age, schooling, etc.) would alter the distribution
of our total sample by labor force status. As shown there, changing the
ethnicity of all persons in our sample to white would produce rather
small shifts in the distribution of our total sample by labor force status.
For example, the proportion unemployed among men would fall about

TABLE 3.6
Comparison of Predicted and Actual Labor Force Distribution for Entire Sample

	Men		Women	
	Actual %	If white, predicted %	Actual %	If white, predicted %
Labor force status				
Employed	72.86	73.94	45.78	44.89
In federal sector	4.40	3.57	2.09	1.53
In nonfederal sector	68.46	70.37	43.69	43.36
Unemployed	5.22	4.62	4.86	4.14
Not in labor force	21.92	21.44	49.36	50.97
Ethnicity				
Hispanic	38.51		37.91	
Puerto Rican	4.36		4.56	
Other	34.15		33.35	
Black	22.99		24.16	
White	38.49		37.93	
N		10,025		11,361

Source: 1976 Survey of Income and Education (U.S. Department of Commerce, 1978).
Notes: Predictions use logit coefficients from the sample of whites. See text for description of analysis.

0.6 of a percentage point, while the proportion unemployed among women would fall by about 0.7 of a percentage point. (Recall, also, that our total sample for each sex consists of roughly equal numbers of Hispanics and white non-Hispanics, with somewhat smaller numbers of black non-Hispanics. Thus, minorities are substantially overrepresented in our sample relative to their representation in the population—meaning that any changes of the kind shown in Table 3.6 would be much smaller in the actual population than they are in our sample.)

Direct Regression Results from the SIE Data

In this section we discuss our direct (conventional least squares) regression results on ethnic pay differences, taking each sex in turn. (See J. Abowd and Killingsworth, 1981, for detailed tables; A. Abowd, 1983, for alternative specifications; and Tables 3.7 and 3.8 for a summary.)

RESULTS FOR MEN

Magnitudes

The pay differential for a given ethnic group relative to comparable white non-Hispanics varies considerably by ethnic group (and, as noted below, to a lesser extent by sector). All differentials are negative, implying that minority ethnic groups tend to be paid less than whites who are otherwise comparable (in terms of the other variables in the regression model from which the differential is derived). They are largest in absolute value (between about $-.14$ to $-.25$) for black non-Hispanics, smallest in absolute value (between about $-.01$ to $-.05$) for non-Puerto Rican Hispanics, and of intermediate size (between about $-.07$ to $-.13$) for Puerto Ricans.

Statistical Significance

As measured by t statistics, the statistical significance of these pay differentials is generally quite substantial for blacks (t ratios for most black–white differentials are between about 5.9 and 9.9); t ratios for most Puerto Rican–white differentials are considerably lower (between about 0.8 and 2.2). Most differentials between non–Puerto Rican Hispanics and comparable whites would not be judged statistically different from zero at conventional levels (t ratios for most of these differentials are between about 0.3 and 1.5).

TABLE 3.7
Summary of Direct, Reverse, and Structural Wage Regression Estimates of Ethnic Differentials in Pay for Men Evaluated at Mean Values of Whites

	Federal sector			Nonfederal sector		
	Hispanics of Puerto Rican origin	Hispanic non–Puerto Ricans	Blacks	Hispanics of Puerto Rican origin	Hispanic non–Puerto Ricans	Blacks
Without Population Proportion Variables						
Log wages						
Direct	−.1241	−.0466	−.1789	−.0799	−.0265	−.1426
	(.0820)	(.0321)	(.0183)	(.0481)	(.0232)	(.0192)
Reverse	.0201	.1097	−.0471	.0619	.0509	.0215
	(.0497)	(.0186)	(.0111)	(.0201)	(.0085)	(.0897)
Structural	−.1413	−.0513	−.1987	−.0783	−.0257	−.1409
	(.0856)	(.0342)	(.0191)	(.0482)	(.0232)	(.0191)
Log earnings						
Direct	−.0857	−.0186	−.1650	−.1340	−.0441	−.2476
	(.1072)	(.0419)	(.0238)	(.0628)	(.0303)	(.2503)
Reverse	.0042	.1362	−.0517	.0479	.0403	.0133
	(.0682)	(.0255)	(.0151)	(.0323)	(.0137)	(.0145)
Structural	−.1083	−.0404	−.1887	−.1344	−.0437	−.2472
	(.1118)	(.0447)	(.0250)	(.0629)	(.0303)	(.0250)
With Population Proportion Variables						
Log wages						
Direct	−.1279	−.0476	−.1612	−.0697	−.0080	−.1420
	(.0821)	(.0337)	(.0204)	(.0482)	(.0241)	(.0202)
Reverse	.0056	.0945	.0390	.0818	.0682	.0093
	(.0521)	(.0195)	(.0116)	(.0211)	(.0090)	(.0095)
Structural	−.1444	−.0503	−.1750	−.0676	−.0070	−.1386
	(.0856)	(.0356)	(.0214)	(.0482)	(.0241)	(.0202)
Log earnings						
Direct	−.0965	−.0108	−.1564	−.1304	−.0443	−.2497
	(.1073)	(.0440)	(.0267)	(.0630)	(.0315)	(.0264)
Reverse	−.0140	.1083	.0584	.0587	.0235	.0030
	(.0705)	(.0264)	(.0156)	(.0325)	(.0137)	(.0146)
Structural	−.1134	−.0278	−.1726	−.1299	−.0438	−.2475
	(.1118)	(.0465)	(.0280)	(.0631)	(.0315)	(.0264)

Source: 1976 Survey of Income and Education (U.S. Department of Commerce, 1978).
Note: Standard errors are in parentheses.

TABLE 3.8

Summary of Direct, Reverse, and Structural Wage Regression Estimates of Ethnic Differentials in Pay for Women Evaluated at Mean Values of Whites

	Federal sector			Nonfederal sector		
	Hispanics of Puerto Rican origin	Hispanic non–Puerto Ricans	Blacks	Hispanics of Puerto Rican origin	Hispanic non–Puerto Ricans	Blacks
Without Population Proportion Variables						
Log wages						
Direct	.1209	−.1268	−.0501	−.0590	−.0267	−.0119
	(.1576)	(.0567)	(.0236)	(.0619)	(.0262)	(.0189)
Reverse	.0320	.0127	−.0512	.1398	.0659	.0329
	(.0765)	(.0264)	(.0110)	(.0276)	(.0183)	(.0095)
Structural	.2943	−.3615	−.0025	.0472	−.0290	−.0147
	(.3268)	(.1784)	(.0387)	(.0621)	(.0263)	(.0189)
Log earnings						
Direct	−.3962	−.0327	−.0378	−.0075	−.0350	.0537
	(.2522)	(.0907)	(.0377)	(.1074)	(.0454)	(.0327)
Reverse	−.1133	.0574	−.1665	−.0394	.0176	.0444
	(.1340)	(.0462)	(.0194)	(.0258)	(.0196)	(.0182)
Structural	−.5281	.1889	−.0945	−.0185	.0332	.0563
	(.5908)	(.3224)	(.0699)	(.1007)	(.0456)	(.0329)
With Population Proportion Variables						
Log wages						
Direct	.1363	−.1328	−.0485	.0622	−.0199	−.0149
	(.1575)	(.0586)	(.0263)	(.0621)	(.0273)	(.0195)
Reverse	.0548	−.0050	−.0205	.1349	.0802	.0174
	(.0820)	(.0283)	(.0118)	(.0281)	(.0105)	(.0097)
Structural	.2474	−.3516	−.0045	.0508	−.0242	−.0173
	(.3264)	(.1759)	(.0381)	(.0622)	(.0273)	(.0195)
Log earnings						
Direct	−.3997	−.0911	−.0507	−.0144	.0350	.0402
	(.2523)	(.0938)	(.0421)	(.1077)	(.0473)	(.0338)
Reverse	−.0754	.0208	−.1228	−.0513	.0581	.0216
	(.1392)	(.0480)	(.0202)	(.0548)	(.0203)	(.0189)
Structural	−.3938	−.1211	−.0112	−.0256	.0321	.0415
	(.5611)	(.3025)	(.0655)	(.1080)	(.0474)	(.0339)

Source: 1976 Survey of Income and Education (U.S. Department of Commerce, 1978).
Note: Standard errors are in parentheses.

Sectoral Patterns

For all three minority ethnic groups, minority–white differentials in wages are larger in absolute value (that is, more negative) in the federal sector than in the nonfederal sector, while minority–white differentials in earnings are larger in the nonfederal sector than in the federal sector. For example, the black–white wage differential in the federal versus nonfederal sector is about −.16 to −.18 (−.14), while the comparable figure for the earnings differential in the federal versus nonfederal sector is about −.16 to −.17 (−.25).

Alternative Dependent Variables

For all three minority groups, the wage differential is larger than the earnings differential in the federal sector, but smaller than the earnings differential in the nonfederal sector. For example, for Puerto Ricans, the wage (earnings) differential is about −.12 to −.13 (−.08 to −.10) in the federal sector, while in the nonfederal sector the wage (earnings) differential is about −.07 to −.08 (−.13).

Alternative Models

For all three minority groups, estimates of a given differential are relatively robust with respect to alternative models (that is, use of alternative sets of independent variables). For example, regression estimates of the Puerto Rican–white differential are about −.08 to −.12 when population proportion variables are not included, and are about −.10 to −.13 when such variables are included among these regressors. (Changes in differentials for most other race–ethnic groups attendant upon inclusion of these variables are smaller still.)

RESULTS FOR WOMEN

Magnitudes

With a few exceptions, minority–white pay differentials among women are smaller than among men, and many are either positive (implying that certain groups of minority women are paid more than comparable white women) or else essentially zero, in a statistical sense. The black–white pay differential among women is about .05 to −.05; the Puerto Rican–white female pay differential is about .12 to about −.40; and the non–Puerto Rican Hispanic–white pay differential is about .04 to −.13.

Statistical Significance

On the whole, the statistical significance of minority–white pay differentials, as measured by their t ratios, is lower among women than among men. Black–white differentials among women have t ratios in the range 0.6 to 2.1; Puerto Rican–white differentials have t ratios between .07 and 1.6; and non–Puerto Rican Hispanic–white differentials have t ratios between .7 and 2.3.

Sectoral Patterns

With a few exceptions, minority–white pay differentials among women are more negative (that is, lower in absolute value) in the federal than in the nonfederal sector. For example, the black–white pay differential is about −.04 to −.05 in the federal sector, while differentials in the nonfederal sector are between about .05 and −.05.

Alternative Dependent Variables

Black–white and non–Puerto Rican Hispanic–white differentials in wages are typically more negative (that is, larger in absolute value if negative, or smaller in absolute value if positive) than are earnings differentials; while in the case of Puerto Rican–white differentials just the reverse holds. For example, the Puerto Rican–white wage differential is about .06 to .12, while the earnings differential is about −.01 to −.40; black–white and non–Puerto Rican Hispanic–white differentials in wages (earnings) are about −.02 to −.13 (.04 to −.09).

Alternative Models

For all three minority groups, estimates of pay differentials are relatively robust with respect to alternative models (that is, use of alternative sets of independent variables). For example, regression estimates of the Puerto Rican–white wage (earnings) differential are about .06 to .12 (−.01 to −.40) when population proportion variables are not included, and about .06 to .14 (−.01 to −.39) when such variables are included among the regressors in a given model.

Reverse Regression Results from the SIE Data

In this section we present the results of our reverse regression analysis for each sex. (See J. Abowd and Killingsworth, 1981, for detailed tables;

A. Abowd, 1983, for a discussion of alternative specifications; and Tables 3.7 and 3.8 for a summary).

RESULTS FOR MEN

Magnitudes

The pay differential for a given ethnic group relative to comparable white non-Hispanics varies considerably by ethnic group (and, as noted below, to a lesser extent by sector). Unlike the direct regression differentials, most of which are negative (implying that minorities tend to receive lower pay than comparable whites), most of the reverse regression differentials are positive (implying that minorities tend to receive higher pay than comparable whites). The black–white differential is between about .06 and −.05; the non–Puerto Rican Hispanic–white differential is between about .14 and .02; and the Puerto Rican–white differential is between about .06 and −.01.

Statistical Significance

As measured by their t statistics, the statistical significance of these pay differentials is generally quite substantial for non–Puerto Rican Hispanics (t statistics for this group are between about 3.7 and 5.9). Black–white differentials in the federal sector, and Puerto Rican–white differentials in the nonfederal sector, also have relatively high t ratios (between about 3.4 and 4.2, and between about 1.5 and 3.1, respectively). However, black–white differentials in the nonfederal sector and Puerto Rican–white differentials in the federal sector would not generally be judged different from zero, in a statistical sense, at conventional levels of significance.

Sectoral Patterns

The magnitudes and even the signs of these differentials vary considerably by sector. Puerto Rican–white differentials are always smaller in algebraic value (either negative, or else positive but small) in the federal sector than in the nonfederal sector (the range of federal sector differentials is about .02 to −.01, while the nonfederal sector differential is about .06). On the other hand, differentials between non–Puerto Rican Hispanics and comparable whites in the nonfederal sector (which are in the range .07 to .02) are smaller than the differentials in the federal sector (which are in the range .14 to .09). Finally, introducing population proportion variables changes completely the sectoral pattern of the black–white differentials. In models in which these variables are not included, the black–white differential in the federal versus nonfederal sector is −.04 to −.05 (.02 to .01), but when such variables are included the differential in the federal versus nonfederal sector is between about .04 and .06 (.01 and .00).

Alternative Dependent Variables

For all three minority groups, the wage differential is about the same as the earnings differential both in the federal and in the nonfederal sector. For example, for Puerto Ricans, the wage (earnings) differential is about .02 to .01 (.00 to −.01) in the federal sector, while in the non-federal sector the wage and earnings differentials are both about .06 and .05.

Alternative Models

For Puerto Ricans and other Hispanics, estimates of differentials are relatively robust with respect to alternative models (that is, use of alternative sets of independent variables). On the other hand, the federal black–white differential seems to be fairly sensitive to inclusion of population proportion variables. When such variables are excluded, the federal (nonfederal) black–white pay differential is between about −.04 and −.05 (.02 and .01), and when such variables are included the differential is between about .06 and .04 (.01 and .00).

RESULTS FOR WOMEN

Magnitudes

Minority–white pay differentials among women exhibit few obvious patterns; very roughly speaking, there appear to be about as many positive differentials (implying that minority women are paid more than comparable white women) as negative differentials (implying that minority women are paid less than comparable white women), and a large number do not appear to be different from zero (in a statistical sense) at conventional levels of significance. The black–white pay differential is between about .04 and −.17; the Puerto Rican–white pay differential is between about .14 and −.11; the non–Puerto Rican Hispanic–white pay differential is between about .08 and −.01.

Statistical Significance

On the whole, the statistical significance of minority–white pay differentials, as measured by their t ratios, is lower among women than among men. Black–white differentials among women have t ratios in the range 1.1 to 8.6; Puerto Rican–white differentials have t ratios between .4 and 5.1; and non–Puerto Rican Hispanic–white differentials have t ratios between .2 and 7.6.

Sectoral Patterns

With a few exceptions, minority–white pay differentials among women are lower in algebraic value (that is, larger in absolute value if negative, and smaller if positive) in the federal than in the nonfederal sector. For example, the black–white pay differential is about −.02 to −.17 in the federal sector, while differentials in the nonfederal sector are between about .04 and .02.

Alternative Dependent Variables

Black–white and Puerto Rican–white differentials in earnings are typically more negative (that is, larger in absolute value if negative, or smaller in absolute value if positive) than are wage differentials. For example, the Puerto Rican–white wage differential is about .14 to .03, while the earnings differential is about −.04 to −.11. On the other hand, non–Puerto Rican Hispanic–white differentials in wages are greater in algebraic value in the federal sector, and are smaller in the nonfederal sector, than are non–Puerto Rican Hispanic–white differentials in earnings.

Alternative Models

For all three minority groups, estimates of pay differentials seem fairly robust with respect to alternative models (that is, use of alternative sets of independent variables). For example regression estimates of the Puerto Rican–white wage (earnings) differential are about .14 to .03 (−.04 to −.11) when population proportion variables are not included, and about .13 to .05 (−.05 to −.08) when such variables are included among the regressors in a given model.

Structural Regression Results from the SIE Data

We now discuss our structural (instrumental variable) regression results for each sex. (See J. Abowd and Killingsworth, 1981, for detailed tables; A. Abowd, 1983, for a discussion of alternative specifications; and Tables 3.7 and 3.8 for a summary.)

RESULTS FOR MEN

Magnitudes

The pay differential for a given ethnic group relative to comparable white non-Hispanics varies considerably by ethnic group (and, as noted below, to a lesser extent by sector). In most cases, these differentials are negative (implying that minority groups are paid less than comparable whites), and many of them are quite close to the corresponding direct wage regression differential. (We say more about this below.) Differentials are largest in absolute value (between about $-.14$ to $-.25$) for black non-Hispanics, smallest in absolute value (between about $-.01$ to $-.05$) for non–Puerto Rican Hispanics, and of intermediate size (between about $-.07$ to $-.14$) for Puerto Ricans.

Statistical Significance

As measured by their t statistics, the statistical significance of these pay differentials is generally quite substantial for blacks (t ratios for most black–white differentials are between about 6.2 and 10.4); t ratios for most Puerto Rican–white differentials are considerably lower (between about 1.0 and 2.1). Most differentials between non–Puerto Rican Hispanics and comparable whites would not be judged statistically different from zero at conventional levels (t ratios for most of these differentials are between about 0.3 and 1.5).

Sectoral Patterns

For all three minority ethnic groups, minority–white differentials in wages are larger in absolute value (that is, more negative) in the federal sector than in the nonfederal sector, while minority–white differentials in earnings are larger in the nonfederal sector than in the federal sector. For example, the black–white wage differential in the federal versus nonfederal sector is about $-.18$ to $-.20$ ($-.14$), while the comparable figure for the earnings differential in the federal versus nonfederal sector is about $-.17$ to $-.19$ ($-.25$).

Alternative Dependent Variables

For all three minority groups, the wage differential is larger than the earnings differential in the federal sector, but smaller than the earnings differential in the nonfederal sector. For example, for Puerto Ricans, the wage (earnings) differential is about $-.14$ ($-.11$) in the federal sector, while in the nonfederal sector the wage (earnings) differential is about $-.07$ to -.08 ($-.13$).

Alternative Models

For all three minority groups, estimates of a given differential are relatively robust with respect to alternative models (that is, use of alternative sets of independent variables). For example, regression estimates of the Puerto Rican–white differential are about −.08 to −.14 when population proportion variables are not included and are about −.07 to −.14 when such variables are included among the regressors.

RESULTS FOR WOMEN

Magnitudes

With a few exceptions, minority–white pay differentials among women are smaller than among men; most are fairly similar to the corresponding direct wage regression estimate; many are essentially zero, in a statistical sense. The black–white pay differential among women is about .06 to −.09; the Puerto Rican–white female pay differential is about .29 to −.53; and the non–Puerto Rican Hispanic–white pay differential is about .03 to −.36.

Statistical Significance

On the whole, the statistical significance of minority–white pay differentials, as measured by their t ratios, is lower among women than among men. Black–white differentials among women have t ratios in the range 0.1 to 1.7; Puerto Rican–white differentials have t ratios between 0.2 and 0.9; and non–Puerto Rican Hispanic–white differentials have t ratios between 0.4 and 2.0.

Sectoral Patterns

Black–white and non–Puerto Rican Hispanic–white pay differentials among women are usually somewhat more negative (that is, lower in absolute value) in the federal than in the nonfederal sector. For example, the black–white differential is about .00 to −.09 in the federal sector, while differentials in the nonfederal sector are between .06 and −.02. Finally, the Puerto Rican–white differential is always larger in absolute value in the federal sector than it is in the nonfederal sector—but the estimated wage differentials imply that Puerto Ricans are paid more than comparable whites, particularly in the federal sector, while the estimated earnings differentials imply that Puerto Ricans are paid less than comparable whites, especially in the federal sector (see below).

Alternative Dependent Variables

Black–white and non–Puerto Rican Hispanic–white differentials in wages are typically more negative (that is, larger in absolute value if negative, or smaller in absolute value if positive) than are earnings differentials; while in the case of Puerto Rican–white wage differentials just the reverse holds. For example, the Puerto Rican–white wage differential is about .25 to .29 in the federal sector (vs. about .05 in the nonfederal sector), while the differential in earnings in the federal sector is about −.39 to −.53 (vs. −.02 to −.03 in the nonfederal sector).

Alternative Models

For all three minority groups, estimates of pay differentials are fairly robust with respect to alternative models (that is, use of alternative sets of independent variables). For example, regression estimates of the black–white wage (earnings) differential are about .05 to .29 (−.02 to −.53) when population proportion variables are not included and about .05 to .25 (−.03 to .39) when such variables are included among the regressors in a given model.

Direct and Reverse Wage Regression Results from the CPDF Data

In this section we discuss direct and reverse regression results derived from the federal government CPDF (see Schneider, 1974) data. (See Table 3.9 for a summary.)

RESULTS BY RACE–ETHNICITY AND SEX

In general, the CPDF results seem fairly similar to the SIE results as regards racial and ethnic pay differentials by sex within the federal sector. As in the SIE results, the CPDF results imply that both Hispanics and blacks are paid less within the federal sector than are whites (that is, either nonblack non-Hispanics, including American Indians and Orientals as well as majority whites; or majority whites as such). In general, black–white pay differentials in the CPDF results are larger in absolute value than Hispanic–white pay differentials; and, for either racial–ethnic group, the minority–white differential among men is larger than the minority–white differential among women. Most of the CPDF differen-

TABLE 3.9
Comparison of Ethnic Pay Differentials for Men and Women for 1975 Derived from SIE and CPDF Data

	Men		Women	
	SIE	CPDF	SIE	CPDF
Hispanics				
Direct	−.0558	−.0543	−.1020	−.0134
	(.0304)	(.0080)	(.0542)	(.0114)
Reverse	.0993	.0283	.0146	−.0017
	(.0176)	(.0062)	(.0251)	(.0107)
Blacks				
Direct	−.1787	−.1381	−.0503	−.0603
	(.0182)	(.0130)	(.0236)	(.0151)
Reverse	−.0471	−.0421	−.0512	−.0441
	(.0111)	(.0110)	(.0110)	(.0147)

Sources: 1976 Survey of Income and Education (U.S. Department of Commerce, 1978); Central Personnel Data File (see Schneider, 1974).

Notes: Standard errors are in parentheses. SIE columns present regression differentials derived from the Survey of Income and Education for men and women in the federal sector; dependent variable = natural logarithm of hourly wages. CPDF columns present regression differentials derived from the federal Central Personnel Data File; dependent variable = natural logarithm of annualized salary.

tials are statistically different from zero at reasonable levels of significance.

RESULTS BY TYPE OF STATISTICAL MODEL

In our CPDF results, as in our SIE results, reverse wage regression generally produces estimates of differentials that are less negative than those derived using direct wage regression; indeed, in several instances (notably for Hispanics), the direct wage regression estimate of the minority–white differential has a negative sign (implying that minority persons are paid less than comparable whites), but the reverse wage regression estimate is positive (implying that minority persons are paid more than comparable whites). Black women are an exception to this generalization, however; in some cases, the reverse wage regression estimate of the black–white differential for women is slightly more negative than the corresponding direct wage regression estimate. Finally, the shrinkage in the estimated differential (that is, the extent to which use of reverse wage regression makes a given differential less negative) seems, in general, to be smaller in the CPDF data than in the SIE data.

COMPARISON WITH RESULTS DERIVED FROM THE SIE

On the whole, both the direct and reverse wage regression estimates of the black–white differential derived from the CPDF are similar to the direct and reverse wage regression estimates of this differential derived from the SIE. (However, the CPDF direct wage regression black–white differentials among men seem somewhat smaller, in absolute value, than the corresponding SIE estimates.) On the other hand, the CPDF estimates of the Hispanic–white differential seem, in general, to be somewhat closer to zero (either smaller if positive, or less negative, if negative) than the corresponding SIE estimates. However, the differences between the SIE and CPDF estimates do not, in general, seem particularly large.

Comparison of Alternative Estimators and Results

We now consider the alternative estimation techniques that we have used in evaluating the determinants of pay. We do this using our preferred results from the SIE for men and for women, which we set out in Tables 3.7 and 3.8, respectively. These results are all evaluated at the mean values of all variables for white non-Hispanics and are derived from either our basic regression model (in which case they are labeled "without population proportion variables") or from our detailed regression model with population proportions but without three-way interactions (in which case they are labeled "with population proportion variables").

In drawing conclusions about our three different estimation techniques from Tables 3.7 and 3.8, it is worth recalling that these techniques are concerned with different statistical and conceptual issues. First, structural regression is concerned with estimating the answer to the first methodological question; that is, with estimating differences in employer wage offers. It does not, however, make a correction for possible measurement error bias. Second, both direct and reverse wage regressions are concerned with estimating the answer to the second methodological question; that is, with estimating differences in compensation conditional on employment. Direct regression does not make a correction for possible measurement error bias, whereas reverse regression does make a correction of this kind. Thus, it would be reasonable to expect that these three different techniques would produce different results. The key issue is, of course, the extent to which results derived from these techniques do in fact differ.

As before, it seems advisable to consider each sex separately. As regards men, it is evident from Table 3.7 that the reverse regression differentials contrast sharply with both the direct and the structural regression differentials: Differentials estimated using either of the latter two techniques are usually negative (and often significantly different from zero, in a statistical sense), while differentials estimated using the former technique are frequently positive. As regards the federal sector, both structural and direct regression differentials are negative, but the latter are usually somewhat smaller in absolute value than the former. On the other hand, structural and direct regression differential for the nonfederal sector, while usually negative, are also generally quite close to each other; indeed, in many instances, a structural wage regression differential for the nonfederal sector is usually slightly smaller than its direct wage regression counterpart, although the difference is generally very small. Finally, in most instances (particularly as regards the federal sector), t ratios for structural wage regression differentials are somewhat larger than t ratios for their direct wage regression counterparts: Standard errors of estimated structural wage regression differentials are slightly larger than standard errors of estimated direct wage regression differentials, but the estimates themselves are larger still, particularly for the federal sector.

While Table 3.7 thus suggests a variety of generalizations concerning the impact of using alternative estimation techniques as far as estimates for men are concerned, Table 3.8, for women, suggests little in the way of patterns or stylized facts. The three estimation techniques, applied to the federal sector, seem to produce three rather different sets of estimated ethnic differentials among women. Estimates for the nonfederal sector derived using the three techniques seem, on the whole and roughly speaking, to be somewhat closer together. However, in many cases—and to a much greater extent than is true of our results for men—the differentials for women reported in Table 3.8 would not be judged different from zero, at conventional levels of significance, regardless of the technique used in estimating them. In this sense, then, the results of these different estimation techniques are closer together than cursory inspection of Table 3.8 might suggest.

Table 3.9 compares the results obtained from both the SIE and the CPDF for the year 1975. For the two estimation techniques considered, direct and reverse, the results from these data sources are quite similar. Essentially the same inferences are supported in either data set.

Summary and Conclusions

There is not much consistent or compelling evidence in our results to suggest that minority women generally suffer substantial wage discrimination (in either the Question 1 or Question 2 sense) relative to comparable white women. One possible exception to this statement concerns black women in the federal sector, where our results usually show negative pay differentials. (However, a considerable number of these differentials do not differ from zero, in a statistical sense, at reasonable levels of significance.) An important caveat in this respect is that our data do not contain measures of actual work experience (Garvey and Reimers, 1980). We are, therefore, forced to use a proxy, potential experience.

Second, as regards ethnic differentials in pay among men, our results suggest (1) that minority men may suffer discrimination both in terms of conditional differentials and in terms of offers, and (2) that estimates of the magnitudes of both kinds of discrimination may be subject to serious measurement error bias. Part (1) of this conclusion follows in a straightforward way from consideration of our direct and structural wage regression results; note that our results provide much stronger support (in the sense of statistical significance) for this proposition with respect to blacks than with respect to Puerto Rican or other Hispanics. Part (2) of this conclusion is prompted by our reverse wage regression results.

Third, our results also suggest that *wage* discrimination against minority males (particularly blacks) is *greater* in the federal than in the nonfederal sector, while *earnings* discrimination against minority males (particularly blacks) is *smaller* in the federal than in the nonfederal sector. At first sight, this may seem paradoxical: If the nonfederal sector is better than the federal sector as regards wage discrimination, why is it not also better as regards earnings discrimination? One possible explanation of this apparent paradox has to do with employment instability, which is greater in the nonfederal sector than in the federal sector: If minorities suffer substantially and disproportionately (relative to comparable whites) from the relatively greater employment instability (layoffs, etc.) in the nonfederal sector, then the nonfederal sector could well be worse than the federal sector as regards earnings differentials even if it is better as regards wages. Our logit results on labor force status appear to suggest that minority groups generally are overrepresented among the unemployed. While this finding does not prove the validity of our conjecture about sectoral patterns in wage versus earnings differentials, it is certainly consistent with it.

Of course, the notion that discrimination within the federal sector may be substantial is not new. Our results not only support this view but also suggest something else: Discrimination against minority males, particularly in terms of wages and with respect to blacks, is of greater magnitude in the federal than in the nonfederal sector. This is particularly noteworthy because previous studies have tended to suggest just the opposite. We suspect that one reason for this is that, in contrast with previous work, we have attempted to control in a fairly detailed fashion for purely geographic effects on pay (via differences in the cost of living and the like). Since minorities are generally overrepresented in federal employment, and since much federal employment is concentrated in urban areas in particular states, sorting out purely geographic effects on pay (in effect, purely compensating or equalizing premia) from other kinds of effects, including ethnicity, obviously need not be a trivial matter. Indeed, the difference between our results and those found in previous work suggests that such effects may be important.

Appendix: The Reverse Wage Regression Procedure

In this Appendix we present formal discussions of direct, reverse, and structural regression estimators of discrimination in pay.

DIRECT AND REVERSE WAGE REGRESSION

We begin by discussing direct and reverse wage regression and the problem of measurement error bias. Our discussion of measurement error bias in direct wage regression and the conditions under which reverse wage regression may avoid such bias will focus on the bivariate case: the relationship between pay and a single productivity-related characteristic. Either variable may be measured with error. (The analysis of the theory of reverse wage regression in the multivariate case involving the relationship between pay and a vector of productivity-related characteristics is much less tractable.)

Assume that the first two moments of the random variables y^*, p^*, e_1^*, and e_2^* are given by

$$
E\begin{bmatrix} y^* \\ p^* \\ e_1^* \\ e_2^* \end{bmatrix} = \begin{bmatrix} \mu_y \\ \mu_p \\ 0 \\ 0 \end{bmatrix} = \mu, \quad \mathrm{Var}[\cdot] = \begin{bmatrix} \omega_{11} & \omega_{12} & 0 & 0 \\ \omega_{12} & \omega_{22} & 0 & 0 \\ 0 & 0 & \omega_{33} & 0 \\ 0 & 0 & 0 & \omega_{44} \end{bmatrix} = \Omega,
$$

(1)

where y^* is the appropriate pay variable, measured perfectly; p^* is the productivity index, measured perfectly; e_1^* is the measurement error in the pay variable; and e_2^* is the measurement error in the productivity variable. The observable pay, y, and observable productivity, p, are defined as

$$y = y^* + e_1^* \tag{2a}$$

$$p = p^* + e_2^* \tag{2b}$$

Accordingly, the first two moments of $[y, p]$ are given by

$$
E\begin{bmatrix} y \\ p \end{bmatrix} = \begin{bmatrix} \mu_y \\ \mu_p \end{bmatrix} \quad \mathrm{Var}[\cdot] = \begin{bmatrix} \omega_{11} + \omega_{33} & \omega_{12} \\ \omega_{12} & \omega_{22} + \omega_{44} \end{bmatrix}.
$$

(3)

The system described by Equations (2)–(3) is a standard bivariate measurement error model. True pay, y^*, and true productivity, p^*, are subject to measurement errors e_1^* and e_2^*, respectively, which are assumed uncorrelated with each other and uncorrelated with the other variables in the true system. Since the measurement errors have zero expectation, the true variables, y^* and p^*, have the same expected values as the measured proxies, y and p, respectively. Since the measurement errors are uncorrelated with any other variables in the system, the measured proxies have the same covariance as the true variables. However, the variance of each measured variable exceeds the variance of its true counterpart by the variance of the measurement error.

We consider next the regression relationships connecting the true variables and the proxy variables. By definition, the regression of y^* on p^* can be decomposed into the conditional expectation of y^* given p^* and an expectation error that is uncorrelated with the conditional expectation. We will assume that the conditional expectations are linear in the conditioning variables. In addition, assume that the mean vector μ and the system covariance matrix Ω are different for each race–ethnic group i, where i is Hispanic, white non-Hispanic, and black non-Hispanic. For each race–ethnic group i, then, the regression relationships connecting the true variables are given by

$$y^* = E[y^* \mid p^*]_i + \eta_1^* = a_i^* + b_i^* p^* + \eta_1^* \tag{4a}$$

$$p^* = E[p^* \mid y^*]_i + \eta_2^* = \alpha_i^* + \beta_i^* y^* + \eta_2^*, \tag{4b}$$

where η_1^* and η_2^* are the errors of the conditional expectations and a_i, b_i, α_i, and β_i are the parameters of the linear functional form for the conditional expectations. When the true system is multivariate normal or the system is estimated by least squares using the true variables, the conditional expectation parameters are the following functions of the underlying system parameters:

$$b_i^* = \frac{\omega_{12i}}{\omega_{22i}}, \qquad a_i^* = \mu_{yi} - b_i^* \mu_{pi}, \tag{5a}$$

$$\beta_i^* = \frac{\omega_{12i}}{\omega_{11i}}, \qquad \alpha_i^* = \mu_{pi} - \beta_i^* \mu_{yi}. \tag{5b}$$

When the true model is multivariate normal, these relationships hold exactly. When the true model is only specified up to its first two moments, as in Equation (1), the relationships in (5) hold as the probability limits of the least squares estimators of the theoretical parameters when the true variables are used in the analysis.

Of course, only y and p are directly observable. Consequently, we must know the regression relationship connecting these variables in order to state the implications of the measurement error problem for the discrimination analysis of interest. The regression of y on p is defined as the conditional expectation of y given p. Once again, by the assumption of linear conditional expectations, the regression relationships connecting the observable variables for each race–ethnic group i are given by

$$y = E[y^* \mid p^* + e_2^*]_i + \eta_1 = a_i + b_i p + \eta_1 \tag{6a}$$

$$p = E[p^* \mid y^* + e_1^*]_i + \eta_2 = \alpha_i + \beta_i y + \eta_1. \tag{6b}$$

When the true system (1) is multivariate normal or when the conditional expectations are estimated by least squares using the observed variables, the conditional expectation parameters in (6) have the following relationship to the theoretical parameters of the underlying system:

$$b_i = \frac{\omega_{12i}}{\omega_{22i} + \omega_{44i}}, \qquad a_i = \mu_{yi} - b_i \mu_{pi}, \tag{7a}$$

$$\beta_i = \frac{\omega_{12i}}{\omega_{11i} + \omega_{33i}}, \qquad \alpha_i = \mu_{pi} - \beta_i \mu_{yi}. \tag{7b}$$

When the true model is multivariate normal, these relationships hold exactly. When the true model is only specified up to its first two mo-

ments, as in Equation (1), the relationships in (7) hold as the probability
limits of the least squares estimators of the theoretical parameters when
the observed variables are used instead of the true variables. Notice that
the presence of measurement errors e_1^* and e_2^* causes the theoretical
regression parameters in Equation (5)—the starred values—to deviate
from the theoretical regression parameters in Equation (7)—the un-
starred values. Technically, the symmetric measurement error model
has the property that the least squares estimators for the regression
parameters a_i, b_i, α_i, and β_i are inconsistent estimators of the regression
parameters a_i^*, b_i^*, α_i^*, and β_i^* connecting the true variables. However, it
is straightforward to verify that the conditional expectation of the proxy
pay variable given the true value of the productivity variable is identical
to the conditional expectation in (4a). Similarly, the conditional expectation of the proxy productivity variable given the true pay variable is
identical to the conditional expectation in (4b).

The inconsistency in the estimators based on the observed variables is
at the heart of the criticisms leveled by Hashimoto and Kochin (1979)
and Roberts (1979, 1981) against the direct regression methodology in
statistical discrimination analyses. Direct regression is identical to least
squares estimation of a_i and b_i. These estimators are inconsistent for the
theoretical quantities a_i^* and b_i^* (or μ_i and Ω_i). The effect of the inconsistency on the potential reference of statistical discrimination based on the
direct regression estimates can be seen by considering the case in which
each race–ethnic group has the same theoretical values of a_i^* and b_i^*.
Then, the theoretical average difference in observed pay between a
member of race–ethnic group i and a member of group j, conditional on
the same true value of productivity, p^*, is given by

$$E[y_i \mid p^*] - E[y_j \mid p^*] = a_i^* + b_i^* p^* - (a_j^* + b_j^* p^*) = 0, \tag{8}$$

since, by hypothesis, $a_i^* = a_j^*$ and $b_i^* = b_j^*$. However, if the least squares
estimates of a_i and b_i are used, the estimated difference in pay between a
member of race–ethnic group i and a member of group j, conditional on
the same value of observed productivity, p, is given by

$$E[y_i \mid p] - E[y_j \mid p] = a_i + b_i p - (a_j + b_j p)$$

$$= a_i^* - a_j^* + (b_i^* - b_j^*)p + b_i^* \frac{\omega_{44i}}{\omega_{22i} + \omega_{44i}} \mu_{pi} - b_j^* \frac{\omega_{44j}}{\omega_{22j} + \omega_{44j}} \mu_{pj}$$

$$= b^* \frac{\omega_{44}}{\omega_{22} + \omega_{44}} (\mu_{pi} - \mu_{pj}), \tag{9}$$

since $a_i^* = a_j^*$ and $b_i^* = b_j^*$, by hypothesis. Notice that the expression in (9)
is not necessarily zero unless $\mu_{pi} = \mu_{pj}$—that is, unless the average

observed productivity index is the same for both groups. Normally, a test of the hypothesis of equal theoretical coefficients in the direct regression is considered a basis for an inference of statistical discrimination. Apparently, this test may support an inference of discrimination even though the theoretical coefficients of interest are equal when productivity is measured with error and the groups have different average values of the productivity proxy.

The analysis is symmetric in its implications for the reverse regression methodology. The least squares estimators of α_i and β_i are inconsistent for the theoretical parameters α_i^* and β_i^*. Reverse regression is identical to least squares estimation of α_i and β_i. The effect of the inconsistency on the potential inference of discrimination based on the reverse regression estimates can be seen by considering the case in which each race–ethnic group has the same theoretical values of α_i^* and β_i^*. Then, the theoretical average difference in observed productivity between a member of race–ethnic group i and a member of group j, conditional on the same true value of pay y^*, is given by

$$E[p_i \mid y^*] - E[p_j \mid y^*] = \alpha_i^* + \beta_i^* y^* - (\alpha_j^* + \beta_j^* y^*) = 0, \qquad (10)$$

since, by hypothesis, $\alpha_i^* = \alpha_j^*$ and $\beta_i^* = \beta_j^*$. However, if the least squares estimates of α_i and β_i are used, the estimated difference in pay between a member of the race–ethnic group i and a member of group j, conditional on the same value of observed productivity, p, is given by

$$E[p_i \mid y] - E[p_j \mid y] = \alpha_i + \beta_i y^* - (\alpha_j + \beta_j y^*)$$

$$= \alpha_i^* - \alpha_j^* + (\beta_i^* - \beta_j^*)y + \beta_i^* \frac{\omega_{33i}}{\omega_{11i} + \omega_{33i}} \mu_{yi} - \beta_j^* \frac{\omega_{33j}}{\omega_{11j} + \omega_{33j}} \mu_{yj}$$

$$= \beta^* \frac{\omega_{33}}{\omega_{11} + \omega_{33}} (\mu_{yi} - \mu_{yj}), \qquad (11)$$

since $\alpha_i^* = \alpha_j^*$ and $\beta_i^* = \beta_j^*$, by hypothesis. As we noted for expression (9), the mean difference in Equation (11) is not necessarily zero unless $\mu_{yi} = \mu_{yj}$; that is, unless the average observed pay is the same for both groups. Apparently, the reverse regression also may support an inference of statistical discrimination even though the theoretical coefficients of interest are equal.

Although Equations (9) and (11) are symmetric in their implications for the type of inconsistency induced by least squares analysis of the system (1) when only the system (2) is observed, the two inconsistencies lead to quite different errors in a statistical discrimination analysis. In general, the covariance between pay and productivity is positive ($\omega_{12} >$ 0). Therefore, the estimated regression slope parameter is expected to be positive whether one estimates b^*, β^*, b, or β. Consequently, the sign of the inconsistency depends on the sign of the difference in the mean values of productivity or pay for each race–ethnic group. If ethnic group i has a higher value of the observed productivity index than ethnic group j, then Equation (9) implies that direct regression analysis of the observable variables y and p will be biased in the direction of finding discrimination favoring group i even when all coefficients of interest are equal. However, if race–ethnic group i has a higher mean value of observed pay than race–ethnic group j, then Equation (11) implies that reverse regression analysis of the observable variables will be biased in the direction of finding discrimination favoring group j even when all coefficients of interest are equal.

As Equation (9) shows, direct regression estimation of the conditional expectation of observed y given observed p may give spurious evidence of statistical discrimination in the case where one group simply has a higher average value of the productivity proxy p than the other. On the other hand, as Equation (11) shows, reverse regression estimation of the conditional expectation of observed p given observed y may also give spurious evidence of statistical discrimination in the case where one group simply has higher average measured pay y than the other group. In principle, however, the errors involved in using direct or reverse regression are in the opposite direction. That is, if the observed average pay of group i is greater than the observed average pay of group j, then the observed average productivity of group i is very likely to be higher than the observed average productivity of group j. Under these conditions, direct regression analysis of the proxy variables y and p may lead to an inference of discrimination against group j while reverse regression analysis of the same proxy data may lead to an inference of discrimination against group i.

Thus, as we say in the text, the importance of direct and reverse wage regression is that, when both pay and productivity are measured with error, the two procedures will result in estimates that bound the actual magnitude of discrimination. (However, as noted below, a potential problem with either direct or reverse regression methodology is the implicit assumption that, if the structure in Equation (1) differs across race–ethnic groups in such a way that either Equation (8) or (10) is not zero, then such structural differences can erroneously be interpreted as differences in the behavioral equations governing the employment practices of the employer or sector being analyzed.)

STRUCTURAL WAGE REGRESSION

To obtain a statistical procedure that addresses the self-selection (or, more generally, selection bias) problems noted in the text, we first derive a model of the way in which individuals are selected into different sectors—that is, of the determinants of the labor force status of individuals, categorized, as before, as being (1) employed in the federal sector, (2) employed in the nonfederal sector, (3) unemployed, or (4) not in the labor force. This model provides a means of computing labor force status probabilities (i.e., the probability that labor force status will be any one of these four distinct categories), using logit analysis, for every individual. We then show how these probabilities may be used to form instrumental variables for structural wage regression.

The basic notion underlying our model of labor force status determination is the idea of an index function model (see Heckman et al., 1981), or, more or less equivalently, a discrete choice model (see McFadden, 1974, 1975). An index function model represents the decision-making process of an agent who is faced with the problem of having to choose the best of several alternatives. Associated with each alternative is a particular payoff or reward that is represented by the value of an index. The alternative actually chosen is the one with the highest index—that is, the one with the biggest payoff.

Specifically, recall that we have established four alternative possibilities for labor force status, and let the utility or payoff U associated with each possibility, or sector, s, be given by

$$U_s = V(w_s, q_s, x) + v(w_s, q_s, x), \tag{12}$$

where V, the systematic component of U, is a function of the wage offered to the individual by employers in that sector; q_s is an index of the characteristics associated with that sector (e.g., one's home or school environment, for the "not in the labor force" sector; the work environment, for the federal employment sector); x is a vector of observed characteristics of the individual; and v is an error term (the stochastic component of U). Note that no wage is relevant to being in the unemployed sector or the "not in the labor force" sector. The individual will choose to be in a particular sector s if the utility associated with that choice exceeds the utility associated with any other choice. For example, the individual will choose the federal sector if and only if

$$U_f > \text{Max}(U_n, U_u, U_o), \tag{13}$$

where the f subscript refers to the federal sector, n refers to the nonfederal sector, u refers to the unemployment sector, and o refers to the "not in the labor force" sector. Expressions similar to (13) define the circumstances under which the individual will choose nonfederal employment, unemployment, or absence from the labor force. Note that all such choices are subject to the values of the wage offers received from the federal and nonfederal sectors, w_f and w_n. Thus, as before, choice is subject to constraints, and statements that choice is voluntary make sense only if one understands both that such choices are constrained and, thus, that the fact that such choices are voluntary has no particular normative implications. Note also that nonreceipt of an offer from the federal or nonfederal sector may be treated as, and is treated in this analysis as, the equivalent of receipt of a very low offer from that sector.

To specify the decisions process (12)–(13) in a manner suitable for empirical estimation, let the systematic component V of the utility function for sector s ($s = f, n, u,$ or o) be given by

$$V(w_s, q_s, x) = a_1(q_s)w_s + x'a_2(q_s), \tag{14}$$

where $a_1(\cdot)$ and $a_2(\cdot)$ are, respectively, a scalar and a vector function of q_s, which vary across sectors because of their dependence on the characteristics q_s of that sector. Next, assume that the logarithm of the (best) wage offer available to the individual from employers in sector s ($s = f$ or n) is given by

$$w_s = z'b_s + e_s, \tag{15}$$

where z is a vector of observed variables that affect the wage offer w_s and e_s is an error term whose population mean is zero. Substitute (15) into (14) and rearrange terms, to obtain

$$U_s = z'\gamma_{1s} + x'\gamma_{2s} + v_2^* = V_s^* + v_s^*, \tag{16}$$

where

$$\gamma_{1s} = b_s a_1(q_s)$$
$$\gamma_{2s} = a_2(q_s)$$
$$v_s^* = e_s a_1(q_s) + v(w_s, q_s, x),$$

which is linear in all observed variables z and x. (Note that some elements in z may also appear in x, and vice versa.)

Finally, let the distribution of the random term v_s^* in (16) be approximately independent Weibull. This means that intersectoral differences between these errors, $v_f^* - v_n^*, v_f^* - v_u^*, v_f^* - v_o^*$, and so forth, are all approximately independent logistic.

Together with (13), the independent logistic assumption implies that

$$\text{Pr\{in sector } s\} = \frac{\exp(V_s^*)}{\exp(V_f^*) + \exp(V_n^*) + \exp(V_u^*) + \exp(V_o^*)} \quad (17)$$

for $s = f, n, u,$ or o. Thus, (17) gives the probability that an individual will be in any given sector s as a logistic function of x and z. Note that (17) is therefore a reduced-form expression, since it contains both supply and demand variables.

We now consider how to use estimates of parameters governing labor force status, that is, estimates of (17), to obtain estimates of the parameters of the wage-offer equation. We refer to this as structural wage regressions.

As noted earlier, we consider two kinds of employment in our analyses: federal and nonfederal employment. Let N_s be the number of persons in sector s; $s = f$ or n. Let w_s be the logarithm of the (best) wage offer for work in sector s available to an individual with characteristics x, z, and assume that w_s is given by (15) above.

Now, (15) is an expression for the wage w_s that the individual will receive if he works in sector s and, by assumption, the mean value of w_s in the population as a whole, given z, is

$$E[w_s \mid z] = z'b_s. \quad (18)$$

On the other hand, the mean value of w_s, given z, among persons actually working in sector t is

$$E[w_s \mid z, s = t] = z'b_t + E[e_s \mid z, s = t]. \quad (19)$$

Note that (18) and (19) are equivalent only if the conditional mean of e_s is independent of the condition $s = t$; that is, only if the population mean of the error term e_s and the mean of e_s among persons actually employed in sector t are the same. If not, then, in terms of the discussion in the previous section, persons in sector s are a selected sample. The sampling distribution of the e_s in the data is not the same as the distribution of the e_s in nature. This is the case in which conventional least-squares analysis of the regression based on a sample restricted to persons actually in sector s will yield biased estimates of the parameters of the wage offer function b_s. Such a regression in effect ignores the second term on the right-hand side of (19), and so will suffer from omitted variable bias, where the omitted variable in question is the conditional mean of e_s. (For further discussion of this point, see Heckman, 1979.)

To derive an alternative to conventional regression that may be used to obtain consistent estimates of the parameters of the wage offer function, note that

$$E[w_s \mid z, s = f] = \frac{\int_{-\infty}^{\infty} \int_{-\infty}^{\infty} w_f \pi_f(w_f, w_n, x) \, p(w_f, w_n \mid z) \, dw_f \, dw_n}{\int_{-\infty}^{\infty} \int_{-\infty}^{\infty} \pi_f(w_f, w_n, x) \, p(w_f, w_n \mid z) \, dw_f \, dw_n}, \tag{20}$$

where $\pi_s(w_f, w_n, x) = \Pr\{$in sector $s \mid w_f, w_n, x\}$ and $p(w_f, w_n \mid z) =$ the joint density function of w_f, w_n conditional on z. Approximate the numerator of (20) with a first-order Taylor series around the means of w_f and w_n. Approximate the denominator of (20) with the unconditional probability of choosing sector s to obtain an overall approximation:

$$E[w_s \mid z, s = t] = z'b_t \frac{\pi_t(z'b_f, z'b_n, x)}{\overline{\pi}_t}, \tag{21}$$

where $\pi_s(w_f, w_n, x)$ has been evaluated at mean values of w_f and w_n, and $\overline{\pi}_s$ is the average value of π_s in the population. Note that π_s is the probability that an individual will be in sector s and may be computed using estimates of the parameters of (17), while $\overline{\pi}_s$ is the proportion of all persons in sector s.

Equation (21) suggests an instrumental variable estimator of the coefficients b_s in the structural wage equation (15). The basis for this claim is the form of the approximation to the conditional expectation of the wage given the sector of employment in Equation (21). This is the approximate regression function for w_s given employment in sector s and the exogenous variables z. Therefore, by construction, the variables on the right-hand side of (21) are orthogonal to the error term in the sector-specific wage regression. These right-hand-side variables depend on an unknown ratio $\lambda = \pi(z'b_f, z'b_n, x)/\overline{\pi}_s$, which is the ratio of the probability of being employed in sector s evaluated at the mean value of the wage in each sector, given z, to the average probability of being employed in sector s. This ratio fluctuates around unity. It is higher for individuals with higher than average probabilities of being in sector s and lower for individuals with lower than average probabilities of being in sector s. This ratio may be estimated by using as the numerator probability the fitted value of the estimated logit probability developed above and using as the denominator probability the sample proportion in sector s.

Having developed an estimator for this ratio, we are faced with a choice of strategies for estimating b_s. First, we could regress the sector-specific wages on the product of z and the ratio λ. Since the ratio λ is estimated, this strategy will lead to problems in determining the appropriate measure of precision for this estimator. Alternatively, one may use λ to develop a set of instruments that are correlated with z but uncorrelated with the error in the conditional wage expectation given z and the sector of employment. These instruments are exactly the right-hand-side of Equation (21). The λ must still be estimated; however, this approach does not lead to problems in estimating standard errors because the convergence of the moment matrix of the instruments is guaranteed by the consistency of the logit parameter estimates and by the fact that no nonlinear instruments are used as right-hand-side variables in the equation being estimated. The estimated residuals may be heteroskedastic; however, in estimation we allow for this possibility.

Each row of the instrument matrix Q is defined as

$$q_{1i} = z_i \lambda_{si}, \tag{22}$$

where $\lambda_{si} = \pi(z_i' b_f, z_i' b_n, x_i)/\overline{\pi}_s$, $i = 1, \ldots, N_s$, and N_s is the total sample in sector s. To allow for potential misspecification of the probability-generating process we add a set of instruments, q_{2i}, defined as

$$q_{2i} = z_i \lambda_{si}^2. \tag{23}$$

The complete instrument matrix Q, then, consists of N_s rows of $[q_{1i}', q_{2i}']$. The b_s are estimated using instrumental variables:

$$\hat{b}_s = [Z_s' Q_s (Q_s' Q_s)^{-1} Q_s' Z_s]^{-1} Z_s' Q_s (Q_s' Q_s)^{-1} Q_s' w_s, \tag{24}$$

where Z is the N_s by k matrix of wage equation variables, Q is the N_s by $2k$ matrix of instruments, and w_s is the N_s by 1 vector of wages observed in sector s. The estimator of the asymptotic variance–covariance matrix is

$$\text{Var}[\hat{b}_s] = \hat{\sigma}_s^2 [Z_s' Q_s (Q_s' Q_s)^{-1} Q_s' Z_s]^{-1}, \tag{25}$$

where $\hat{\sigma}_s^2$ is the sum of squared structural residuals divided by the sample size N_s

$$\hat{\sigma}_s^2 = (w - Z'\hat{b}_s)'(w - Z'\hat{b}_s)/N_s. \tag{26}$$

Conceptually, the structural estimator of the parameters relating w_s to z is quite different from both the direct and reverse regression estimators of those parameters. If z includes a vector of race–ethnic indicators, say d, then the structural model developed in this paper estimates the coefficients on d for the population conditional expectation of w_s given z and not for the subpopulation conditional expectation of w_s given z and $s = t$ for some sector t. This difference is important, since the structural model attributes behavioral significance to the population conditional expectation and not to the self-selected subpopulation conditional expectation. In a direct or reverse regression analysis of race–ethnic pay differences, the conditional expectation of pay, given the productivity index $z'b_s$ and given the sector of employment s, may differ across groups because of systematic differences in the employers' pay practices (the usual assumption in statistical discrimination analyses) or because of systematic differences in the workers' preferences, as modeled by the sectoral choice model above. In general the conditional expectation of pay, given $z'b_s$ and sector s, may differ across race–ethnic groups because of variation in labor demand (employer policies) or labor supply (employee policies). The structural model developed in this chapter makes assumptions sufficient to identify the parameters underlying labor demand (but not labor supply), permitting estimation of the conditional expectation of pay offers given only z.

CHAPTER 4

Ethnic Differentials in Unemployment among Hispanic Americans*

Gregory DeFreitas

Introduction

Throughout the recent past, the unemployment rate of the Hispanic labor force has persistently exceeded the national average. In 1980, when 6.1% of white men were out of work, the annual rate for Hispanic men was 9.7% (see Table 4.1).[1] Among Hispanics, there are marked differences across ethnic groups, ranging in 1980 from a low of 8.9% of Cubans jobless to a high of 13.1% for Puerto Rican men. Unemployment among black men was, at 13.2%, well above either white or Hispanic levels, and the high black jobless rate has been the subject of some, though still too little, analysis by economists (see, e.g., Gilroy, 1974; Flanagan, 1978). Far less research has been done on the disproportionate share of unemployment experienced by Spanish-origin workers, despite their fast-growing importance in particular urban and regional labor

---

* I am indebted to Jacob Mincer, Orley Ashenfelter, Robert Mare, Finis Welch, and Barry Chiswick for their comments and suggestions on earlier drafts. I am also grateful to Machiko Osawa for research assistance. This research was supported by the National Institute of Child Health and Human Development, Grant No. 1-R01-HD-15435-01.

[1] Note that the relative unemployment differential appears to move countercyclically: from a high of 1.69 in the slack labor market situation of 1976, it fell from 1977 to 1979, then rose again in the 1980 recession. This is, of course, far too brief a period to permit drawing firm conclusions about broad cyclical patterns in Hispanic unemployment.

TABLE 4.1
Unemployment Rates of Men 16 Years and Over by Race
and Hispanic Ethnic Group, 1976–1980

	1976	1977	1978	1979	1980
All white	6.4%	5.5%	4.5%	4.4%	6.1%
All Hispanic	10.8	9.0	7.6	6.9	9.7
Mexican	9.9	8.5	7.0	6.5	9.6
Puerto Rican	15.7	13.7	12.4	11.4	13.1
Cubans	12.5	7.6	6.7	6.1	8.9

Source: U.S. Department of Labor, unpublished tabulations.

markets[2] and despite the increased availability of relevant national data sets since the mid-1970s.[3]

The purpose of this study is to examine differences in both the incidence and duration of unemployment among Hispanic men. Comparisons are also made between Hispanics and non-Hispanics. Among the most important questions to be addressed are the following:

1. Can the higher unemployment rates of Hispanic ethnic groups be largely attributed to more frequent spells of unemployment or to the longer duration of those spells?
2. Do ethnic groups differ in the relative importance of human capital variables—such as education, fluency in English, and work experience—as determinants of the probability and duration of joblessness?
3. Are there substantial differences among the ethnic groups in the impacts of such structural factors as local labor market conditions, industry of employment, and occupation?
4. Are Hispanic immigrants particularly prone to frequent and/or lengthy spells of unemployment, at least during their first few years of adjustment to U.S. labor markets? If so, to what extent can the sizable numbers of recent immigrants among certain ethnic groups account for the unemployment levels of those groups?

[2] According to 1980 census figures, persons of Spanish extraction accounted for 55.9% of the population in Miami, 27.5% in Los Angeles, 19.9% in New York City, and 19.6% in the Southwest as a whole (U.S. Department of Commerce, 1981a).

[3] Since April 1974, separate tabulations of labor force information on the Spanish-origin population have been published quarterly by the Bureau of Labor Statistics (BLS). Until that time, the only sources of government data on Hispanics were the decennial census and once-a-year supplements to the Current Population Survey in 1969, 1971, and 1972. For a description of the available BLS data and comparability problems with earlier series, see McKay (1974).

The data base, the principal variables of interest and the economic rationale behind their selection, and the empirical methodology are discussed in the following section. In the subsequent section I first present summary statistics on various dimensions of unemployment, including spells and duration, as well as quit and layoff rates, for the sample stratified by ethnic group, nativity, age, and geographic region. Maximum likelihood logit analysis of the determinants of the probability of unemployment in 1975 is then performed for individual Hispanic ethnic groups as well as for white non-Hispanics. Conducting separate regional analyses permits controlling for the possible confounding effects of divergent patterns of settlement across the country. After exploring differences in the probability of multiple spells of unemployment, ordinary least-squares estimates of the determinants of the duration of unemployment are presented for both the national sample and a regional subsample. Finally, differences in the likelihood of unemployment between Hispanics and non-Hispanics are decomposed into portions attributable to differences in schooling, job characteristics, and labor market treatment. The last section draws together the separate strands of the analysis.

Data, Variables, and Methodology

The empirical analysis employs data from the 1976 Survey of Income and Education (SIE; U.S. Department of Commerce, 1978). (See Chapter 1 and its Appendix for a description of the data set.) To investigate differences in the incidence of unemployment, the following unemployment probability function is estimated separately by ethnic group:

$$P(\text{UNEMP75} = 1) = f(\text{EDFOR, EDUS, EX, EXSQ, MSP, CHILD5,}$$
$$\text{CHILD517, HEALTH, IMM7475, IMM7073,}$$
$$\text{IMM6569, IMM6064, IMMPRE60,}$$
$$\text{NONWHITE, FLUENT, OTHINC,}$$
$$\text{PARTTIME, UNRATE, OCC, IND,}$$
$$\text{HISPROP),} \tag{1}$$

where UNEMP75 = 1 if unemployed 1 week or more in 1975, 0 otherwise. All other variables are defined in Table 4.2. The effects of the independent variables given above on two other dependent variables—the probability of more than one spell of unemployment during the year (SPELLGT1) and the total number of weeks of unemployment in 1975 (WKSUN75)—will also be explored. Both UNEMP75 and WKSUN75 are constructed from responses to the survey question item: "You said

TABLE 4.2
Definitions of Variables

Variable	Definition
UNEMP75	1 if out of work and looking for a job or on layoff 1 week or more in 1975; 0 otherwise.
SPELLGT1	1 if more than 1 stretch of time spent looking for work in 1975; 0 otherwise.
WKSUN75	Number of weeks looking for work or on layoff in 1975.
EDFOR	Years of schooling completed abroad.
EDUS	Years of schooling completed after moving to United States (total years of schooling minus EDFOR).
EX	Potential labor market experience (age minus total years of schooling minus six).
EXSQ	Potential labor market experience, squared.
MSP	1 if married, spouse present; 0 otherwise.
CHILD5	Number of children in family under 5 years old.
CHILD517	Number of children in family ages 5 to 17.
HEALTH	1 if amount or kind of work limited by health; 0 otherwise.
IMM7475	1 if foreign-born and moved to U.S. 1974 or after; 0 otherwise.
IMM7073	1 if foreign-born and moved to U.S. 1970–1973; 0 otherwise.
IMM6569	1 if foreign-born and moved to U.S. 1965–1969; 0 otherwise.
IMM6064	1 if foreign-born and moved to U.S. 1960–1964; 0 otherwise.
IMMPRE60	1 if foreign-born and moved to U.S. before 1960; 0 otherwise.
NONWHITE	1 if nonwhite; 0 otherwise.
FLUENT	1 if speaks and understands English very well; 0 otherwise.
OTHINC	Other family income, excluding labor earnings and unemployment benefits (respondent and spouse), and earnings-related transfers.
PARTTIME	1 if worked fewer than 35 hours/week when employed in 1975; 0 otherwise.
UNRATE	Annual unemployment rate for SMSA of residence or nearest SMSA.
OCC	1 if employed as craftsman, operative, laborer or service worker on longest job in 1975; 0 otherwise.
IND	1 if employed in durable manufacturing or construction industries on longest job in 1975; 0 otherwise.
HISPROP	Percentage of state population Hispanic.
UI	1 if received any unemployment insurance in 1975; 0 otherwise.

(household member) worked about __ weeks in 1975. How many of the remaining weeks was (household member) looking for work or on layoff from job?" Interviewers were instructed to ask the question only of those individuals who worked fewer than 50 weeks that year. (For a detailed description of the survey methodology and questionnaire, see U.S. Department of Commerce, 1977).

Predicting the signs of all the explanatory variables is particularly difficult in Equation (1) because the dependent variable includes both the probability of quitting and the probability of being laid off. However, with unemployment in 1975 at a postwar high and layoffs accounting for an unusually large share of all joblessness, the unemployment variable is doubtless weighted toward the layoff rather than the quit dimension. In light of this, previous theoretical and empirical work enables us to speculate on the probable effects of a number of the independent variables. Most of the relatively few recent studies on Hispanic unemployment have stressed the importance of ethnic differences in age, schooling, immigration patterns, and occupation or industry of employment (e.g., Gray, 1975a, 1975b; Newman, 1978; Piore, 1979). Insofar as older workers represent a larger investment in firm-specific capital by the employer, such workers would be less vulnerable to layoffs than younger individuals. Likewise, the greater the volume of worker-financed specific capital, the lower the probability of quitting. (For a full description of the specific capital framework, see Parsons, 1972). Education and proxies for on-the-job training, such as experience and tenure with the firm, are usually viewed as increasing specific capital. We would thus expect years of schooling completed to be negatively related to the probability of being unemployed one or more times. To distinguish between the effects of foreign and U.S. schooling, educational attainment was divided into premigration (EDFOR) and postmigration (EDUS) components. The effects of these same variables on the duration of joblessness are ambiguous. On the one hand, better-educated, more highly skilled individuals may have higher expected returns from job search, thus lengthening unemployment spells. However, search costs are also higher for those with more firm-specific capital, and these individuals may also be more efficient in their use of search techniques. The latter considerations would seem more compelling in slack labor markets, suggesting a negative relationship between education, experience, and duration.[4]

The implications of migratory differences across groups are even less obvious. Recent immigrants may be at some disadvantage in the labor market relative to earlier immigrants and the native-born due to a

[4] See Lippman and McCall (1976a) for a review of the job-search literature. Note that, unlike many studies in this literature, *duration* as used here refers not to duration per completed spell of unemployment (information not asked in the SIE survey), but rather to the full "unemployment experience" in the course of the year; that is, to the total number of weeks jobless and looking for work in 1975.

When this chapter was already at an advanced stage, I learned of two recent studies whose findings are relevant to this issue. Tienda et al. (1981, Chapter 9) look at job-search techniques and the duration of unemployment among Hispanics, also using SIE data. Their findings appear to be generally consistent with my own on duration. Chiswick (1982) used both 1970 census and SIE data to look at weeks worked by immigrants, and finds generally fewer weeks among recent cohorts. These findings are discussed in more detail in DeFreitas (1982).

smaller stock of U.S. labor market information, language problems, the imperfect international mobility of skills, and a variety of legal restrictions on the employment of aliens in certain fields. Chiswick (1978b, 1982) suggests that their quit rates may be high, at least in the initial adjustment period, as they hunt for jobs in various occupations and locales. Writing from a labor market segmentation perspective, Piore (1979) argues that recent immigrants are among those most likely to be confined to the typically unstable, low-skill jobs common in secondary-sector industries. Relatively high rates of job turnover and unemployment, generated by both supply and demand forces, may thus be expected for recent cohorts.

On the other hand, much of the sociological literature on immigrants has stressed their high motivation to locate jobs quickly in order to end dependence on friends and relatives, to begin accumulating savings for self-support and to remit to their families at origin, and to acquire U.S.-specific and firm-specific training. Kinship networks already established at destination may play an important role in advising on the optimal timing of the immigration, arranging initial housing accommodations, social contacts, and assistance in job search (see, e.g., Levy and Wadycki, 1973; Rogg and Cooney, 1980; Tienda, 1980). Prior migrants thus reduce the economic and psychic costs of immigration for newcomers as well as accelerate the newcomers' successful entry into the job market.

The relatively rapid earnings progress of most foreign-born groups relative to their native-born counterparts (Chiswick, 1978a, 1978b) likewise suggests that the initial employment disadvantages are typically overcome after an adjustment period of variable length. Among Hispanic immigrants, the unemployment experience of two ethnic groups are especially difficult to predict. Research on Cubans by Chiswick (1978a), Reimers (1980), and Borjas (1982) has pointed to the different earnings patterns of political refugees and economic migrants. The suddenness of most Cuban emigration prevented much premigration job search, and the steep downward occupational mobility many appear to undergo upon arrival may cause job dissatisfaction and a preference for general human capital investments to improve future occupational prospects over firm-specific investments, at least in the initial period after arrival. (On the occupational mobility of Cuban immigrants, see Moncarz, 1973, and Chiswick, 1978b. Borjas, 1982, provides evidence on the high rate of investment in U.S. education by Cuban immigrants relative to otherwise-comparable Hispanics.) The result may be high quit and/or layoff rates. Puerto Rican–born men are not formally classifiable as immigrants because they are U.S. citizens and are not impeded by legal restrictions on entry or exit from the United States. Whether they nonetheless have unemployment experiences similar to other Hispanics born outside the United States is a matter for empirical analysis.

To control for industrial characteristics, a dichotomous variable (IND) is set equal to 1 if the respondent's longest recent job was in the durable manufacturing or construction industries. In the course of 1975, durable goods manufacturers, led by auto and related industries, experienced the largest absolute employment reduction of any industrial group, accounting for two-thirds of the overall drop in manufacturing employment. The highest unemployment rate of any single industry (18.1% on an annual basis) was in contract construction, where the work force was cut sharply as housing starts plummeted with the tightening of the money market (St. Marie and Bednarzik, 1976). Although joblessness in white-collar occupations reached postwar highs, semiskilled and unskilled workers were, as in previous recessions, the most vulnerable to cyclical fluctuations (Cohen and Gruber, 1970; St. Marie and Bednarzik, 1976). The dummy variable OCC equals 1 if employed in craft, operative, service, laborer, or farm occupations, 0 otherwise. A dummy variable was also included for part-time employment (PARTTIME), which is likely to be especially unstable, characterized as it is by few seniority or union protections against layoffs and by employers' perceptions of part-time workers as especially quit-prone.

Three approaches were adopted to take into account the markedly different regional distributions of various ethnic groups. First, the annual unemployment rate of the SMSA (Standard Metropolitan Statistical Area) of residence or the nearest SMSA (UNRATE) was included in all regressions. (See U.S. Department of Labor, 1979a, for the annual unemployment rates of selected SMSAs.) The reduced number of vacancies and increased costs of search in slack labor markets are likely to be associated with increased layoffs, falling quit rates, and, among the unemployed, longer-duration joblessness. Second, in an effort to test the common view that the "crowding" of Hispanic workers in particular areas restricts local employment opportunities, the variable HISPROP was defined as the proportion of Hispanics in each state's population. Finally, where sample size permitted, separate regressions were estimated for particular regions of the country with high concentrations of Hispanic residents.

Although recent research indicates that black workers tend to have lower quit rates than whites with similar personal and job characteristics (Blau and Kahn, 1981), insofar as employers perceive them as high-turnover workers the employers will be less willing to finance firm-specific capital. Together with discriminatory factors, this would tend to increase the vulnerability of nonwhites to layoffs.

Finally, controls were included for two types of income: nonlabor income (OTHINC) and unemployment insurance (UI). The probable effects of nonlabor income on the incidence of unemployment are not apparent, a priori. But to the extent that such income can be used to finance extended job search, it may be positively related to the duration of unemployment. Likewise, a number of studies have found a positive correlation between the receipt of unemployment benefits and duration. (See, for example, Ehrenberg and Oaxaca, 1976. For a review of relevant studies, see Hamermesh, 1977.) A dichotomous variable (UI), set equal to 1 if the individual received unemployment insurance in 1975, has thus been included in the duration equations.

Empirical Results

The summary statistics presented in Table 4.3 reveal striking differences between Hispanics and non-Hispanic whites, as well as among Hispanic ethnic groups, in a number of characteristics. With an average of less than 10 years of schooling, Mexican and Puerto Rican men are 3 years below the non-Hispanic level and 1–2 years below the other Hispanic groups. Cubans are, on average, older (mean age: 41 years[5]), with more work experience than any other group, but much of that work experience was in the Cuban labor market—about 95% of the Cubans were foreign-born, and nearly 42% had been in the United States 10 years or less by 1975. Central and South Americans are even more recent immigrants: 39.2% arrived in the 1970s and another 24.7% in the period

TABLE 4.3
Means of Explanatory Variables among Men in Various Ethnic Groups

Variable	White non-Hispanic	Mexican	Puerto Rican	Cuban	Central and South American	Other Hispanic
EDFOR	1.137 (3.458)	1.237 (2.847)	5.019 (4.677)	8.764 (4.909)	9.572 (6.010)	1.146 (3.474)
EDUS	11.350 (4.476)	8.360 (5.130)	4.729 (5.555)	2.717 (4.321)	2.497 (4.459)	10.049 (4.497)
EX	20.960 (15.753)	18.770 (14.883)	20.222 (13.705)	23.696 (14.370)	18.868 (11.423)	21.401 (15.943)

[5] Findings cited in the text but not included in the tables are in an appendix available on request.

TABLE 4.3 (Continued)

Variable	White non-Hispanic	Mexican	Puerto Rican	Cuban	Central and South American	Other Hispanic
EXSQ	687.065	575.990	607.220	774.699	483.414	703.576
	(824.641)	(793.396)	(701.534)	(741.162)	(535.978)	(848.661)
MSP	.745	.700	.771	.739	.687	.728
	(.436)	(.458)	(.421)	(.441)	(.465)	(.445)
CHILD5	.221	.457	.356	.180	.380	.254
	(.519)	(.740)	(.619)	(.446)	(.618)	(.548)
CHILD517	.889	1.385	1.111	.919	.795	1.103
	(1.248)	(1.633)	(1.384)	(1.178)	(1.168)	(1.434)
HEALTH	.079	.079	.070	.062	.042	.075
	(.271)	(.269)	(.255)	(.242)	(.202)	(.263)
IMM7475	.007	.029	.041	.037	.102	.004
	(.083)	(.169)	(.199)	(.190)	(.304)	(.060)
IMM7073	.012	.054	.092	.124	.289	.025
	(.109)	(.227)	(.290)	(.331)	(.455)	(.156)
IMM6569	.021	.048	.086	.255	.247	.037
	(.143)	(.213)	(.280)	(.437)	(.433)	(.190)
IMM6064	.015	.028	.102	.342	.139	.025
	(.129)	(.165)	(.303)	(.476)	(.347)	(.156)
IMMPRE60	.103	.097	.448	.186	.151	.043
	(.304)	(.295)	(.498)	(.391)	(.359)	(.202)
NONWHITE	—	.022	.086	.037	.133	.050
	—	(.146)	(.280)	(.190)	(.340)	(.218)
FLUENT	.911	.671	.540	.422	.506	.792
	(.285)	(.470)	(.499)	(.496)	(.502)	(.406)
OTHINC	45.887	30.607	22.100	34.399	24.341	34.473
(hundreds)	(83.385)	(55.441)	(44.730)	(53.160)	(59.848)	(67.849)
PARTTIME	.094	.088	.060	.042	.053	.072
	(.292)	(.284)	(.237)	(.202)	(.225)	(.259)
UNRATE	8.322	8.144	9.486	10.947	9.635	8.780
	(2.254)	(2.561)	(1.658)	(2.023)	(1.919)	(2.040)
OCC	.576	.808	.806	.702	.729	.741
	(.494)	(.394)	(.396)	(.459)	(.446)	(.439)
IND	.276	.268	.329	.258	.306	.258
	(.442)	(.432)	(.463)	(.439)	(.462)	(.436)
HISPROP	3.080	12.741	4.299	5.533	5.628	15.284
	(4.923)	(9.400)	(3.425)	(2.859)	(5.190)	(14.089)
UI	.179	.185	.194	.162	.127	.172
	(.147)	(.388)	(.396)	(.369)	(.333)	(.378)
N	8,480	1,937	328	163	170	566

Source: 1976 Survey of Income and Education (U.S. Department of Commerce, 1978).
Note: Standard deviations are in parentheses.

1965–1969. Less than one-fourth of all Puerto Rican men were born on the U.S. mainland. In contrast, 74.5% of those of Mexican origin and 87% of the Other Hispanics were native-born (i.e., U.S.-born).[6]

In light of the high proportions of Puerto Ricans, Cubans, and Central and South Americans born abroad, it is not surprising to find that the majority of their schooling took place in their countries of origin and that many lack fluency in English. In fact, only 42% of Cubans and somewhat more than half of the Puerto Ricans and Central and South Americans in the sample could speak and understand English very well. Cuban and Central and South American immigrants are, however, far more likely than Puerto Ricans to have been drawn from the urban middle classes and skilled occupations of their homelands.[7]

These three groups—Puerto Ricans, Cubans, and Central and South Americans—tend to reside in labor markets with average unemployment rates well above those for the other groups. Whereas the majority of Mexicans and Other Hispanics live in the Southwest and over two-fifths are outside metropolitan areas, over 80% of each of the other Hispanic groups reside in SMSAs, principally in the Northeast and, in the case of Cubans, in Florida. Puerto Ricans and Central and South Americans tend to be more concentrated in cyclical industries, and Puerto Ricans as well as Mexicans are far more likely than either non-Hispanics or the other Hispanic ethnic groups to be in low-wage occupations.

Table 4.4 provides information on various dimensions of unemployment for the sample, stratified by ethnicity, nativity, age, and region. Nationally, as well as within specific regions, Hispanics were substantially more likely to have been unemployed at some point in 1975 than non-Hispanic whites. Of the full Hispanic sample, 21.5% experienced joblessness compared with 14.9% of non-Hispanics. Within each of the two subpopulations, the foreign-born rate was somewhat above the native-born level, but the difference was statistically significant only for non-Hispanic whites. Among Hispanics, rates vary from 21 to 23% for Mexicans, Puerto Ricans, and Cubans to less than 18% for Central and South Americans and Other Hispanics. Controlling for age, the ranking remains the same among prime-aged males, ages 35–54. When particular regions are examined separately, Other Hispanics continue to have relatively low rates, but nearly 23% of Central and South American in New York or New Jersey SMSAs were unemployed, the highest level of

[6] The Other Hispanic grouping is a residual category including individuals identifying themselves as Hispanics of mixed ethnic background (e.g., Portuguese–Cuban).

[7] For evidence on the above-average socioeconomic backgrounds of Dominican and Colombian immigrants, the two largest Central–South American groups in New York City, see Sassen-Koob (1979).

any Hispanic group. Central and South Americans in this region are, on average, younger (mean age of 35.6 years), more likely to be recent immigrants, and more concentrated in unskilled and semiskilled occupations than other ethnic groups or than Central and South American men elsewhere in the country. The largest disparity in unemployment is in Florida, where Cubans were over 1.5 times more likely to be jobless than were non-Hispanic whites.

Turning to the key components of unemployment, the duration of time out of work averaged about 18 weeks for Hispanics and non-Hispanics alike. The importance of long-term joblessness is revealed by the finding that, among the unemployed, about 30% were without work for 6 months or more, regardless of ethnic groups. The higher Hispanic unemployment rate thus reflects more frequent spells: 13.5% of Hispanics had one spell and 7.3% had two or more, while the corresponding frequencies for non-Hispanics were 10.3 and 4.7%.[8] Whether one looks

---

[8] While the principal difference between Hispanics and non-Hispanic whites is in the incidence of unemployment, the single most important component of unemployment for all ethnic groups in 1975 was the duration of time unemployed. This can be most clearly seen by defining the personal unemployment rate for the ith individual during the year as the ratio of the number of weeks unemployed (W_{ui}) to the total number of weeks in the labor force (W_{li}):

$$u_i = \frac{W_{ui}}{W_{li}}.$$

It can be easily shown (see Leighton and Mincer, 1979) that a weighted average of these rates for a given group can be computed as

$$\frac{\sum W_{ui}}{\sum W_{li}} = \frac{U}{L} \cdot \frac{W_u}{52} \cdot \frac{1}{(1 - W_{olf}/52)},$$

where U is the number of individuals unemployed during the year, L, the number of individuals in the labor force during the year, and W_{olf}, the number of weeks spent out of the labor force by labor force participants during the year.

The following calculations, based on the data in Columns 1, 2, and 4 of Table 4.4, reveal the primary importance of the duration component ($W_u/52$) relative to the incidence of unemployment (U/L) and the nonparticipation component ($1/(1 - W_{olf}/52)$:

	U/L	$W_u/52$	$1/(1 - W_{olf}/52)$
Non-Hispanic white	.148	.340	1.086
Mexican	.214	.346	1.103
Puerto Rican	.228	.362	1.063
Cuban	.228	.381	1.037
Central and South			
American	.171	.311	1.063
Other Hispanic	.179	.321	1.091

TABLE 4.4

Selected Characteristics of Unemployment by Ethnicity, Nativity, Age, and Region of Residence

	% Unemployed (1)	Weeks unemployed (2)	% With multiple spells (3)	Weeks out of labor force (4)	% Quits (5)	% Layoffs (6)	% Entrants (7)
Nativity							
White non-Hispanic	14.9	17.7	4.7	4.1	0.7	2.9	1.5
Native	14.5	17.6	4.7	4.1	0.7	2.8	1.5
Foreign	16.7	18.8	5.0	3.9	0.5	3.5	1.2
Hispanic	21.5	18.0	7.3	4.3	0.7	4.7	2.2
Native	20.5	17.6	7.9	4.9	0.7	4.2	2.4
Foreign	21.4	18.8	6.1	3.3	0.9	5.6	1.8
Mexican	21.4	18.1	7.9	4.9	0.8	4.5	2.1
Puerto Rican	22.8	18.8	5.6	3.1	1.4	5.3	2.5
Cuban	22.8	19.8	7.2	1.8	1.2	9.6	2.4
Latin American[b]	17.1	16.2	3.5	3.1	0.0	4.1	0.6
Other Hispanic	17.9	16.7	7.2	4.3	0.2	3.5	2.5
Age (35–54 Years Old)							
White non-Hispanic	11.1	17.7	3.4	1.1	0.4	2.5	0.5
Mexican	17.6	17.5	6.2	2.6	0.4	3.7	0.6

138

Puerto Rican	20.7	18.6	4.3	1.7	0.7	3.6	1.4
Cuban	19.5	24.4	5.8	0.1	0.0	10.3	1.2
Latin American[b]	12.7	16.3	0.0	1.2	0.0	3.8	0.0
Other Hispanic	9.3	15.9	3.6	1.7	0.0	1.8	1.3

Region of Residence

New York-New Jersey							
White non-Hispanic	14.3	22.7	4.1	2.7	0.2	5.8	1.9
Puerto Rican	19.7	18.2	3.8	2.7	0.0	3.0	2.3
Cuban	21.7	21.6	4.4	2.1	0.0	6.5	4.4
Latin American[b]	23.0	17.7	3.3	3.3	0.0	8.2	0.0
Other Hispanic	17.2	13.0	3.5	3.0	0.0	3.5	3.5
Southwest							
White non-Hispanic	12.7	17.1	5.0	3.8	1.0	1.0	1.4
Mexican	20.0	18.1	7.4	5.0	0.7	5.0	2.4
Other Hispanic	15.5	17.1	7.8	4.3	0.4	4.2	2.8
Florida							
White non-Hispanic	16.1	17.7	11.8	9.8	1.1	2.2	3.2
Cuban	27.9	21.8	13.1	0.8	0.0	16.4	1.6

Source: 1976 Survey of Income and Education (U.S. Department of Commerce, 1978).

Notes: Mean values of variables. All variables refer to 1975, except for quits, layoffs, and entrants, which are for 1976.

[a] Sample restricted to men unemployed 1 week or more in 1975.

[b] Refers to Central and South America.

at figures adjusted or unadjusted for age differences, Cubans, Puerto Ricans, and Mexicans had the longest mean duration of unemployment, while South Americans and Other Hispanics are below even the white non-Hispanic level.

Parenthetically, it is of interest to note that calculations of a measure of average duration per spell, obtained by dividing total weeks unemployed by the number of spells for each respondent with some unemployment in 1975, result in a similar ranking for all groups except Mexicans, who suffer more spells of shorter average length than white non-Hispanics or most Hispanic groups:

Weeks	White non-Hispanic	Mexican	Puerto Rican	Cuban	Central and South American	Other Hispanic
Average	14.25	13.53	15.77	15.85	13.84	12.09
Duration per spell	11.52	10.94	11.02	12.40	12.22	11.44

In contrast to the pattern for Mexicans and Cubans, the unemployment of Puerto Ricans appears to be concentrated in single rather than multiple spells. This may in part reflect labor market conditions in New York City and the higher unemployment benefits available there. This is borne out by the finding that, in New York and New Jersey SMSAs, all groups experienced above-average durations of joblessness but no more than 4% had multiple spells. The difference in spell length between Mexican and other Hispanic men observed in the national subsamples does not persist when we focus solely on the Southwest. In contrast, the duration differential between non-Hispanics and Cubans doubles when we shift from the national to the Florida subsample. The unemployment of Cubans is characterized by both longer and more frequent spells.

Despite a much higher incidence of unemployment, Hispanics appear no more likely than non-Hispanics to drop out of the labor force. Although the proportion of "discouraged workers" doubtless increased in all groups as the recession deepened, Puerto Ricans and Central and South American men averaged 1 week less spent out of the labor force than non-Hispanics, and Cubans had briefer spells of nonparticipation than any other group, both in the national and in the regional subsamples.

To explore further the determinants of unemployment associated with interjob and inter-labor-force mobility, it would be most desirable to have comparable data on the relative frequencies of quits, layoffs, entrants, and reentrants for each ethnic group in 1975. Unfortunately, the only information in the SIE on specific reason for unemployment is for the survey week of 1976 and is restricted to those currently unemployed. However, since unemployment remained at historically high levels well into 1976 (unemployment in New York and in Florida still averaged above 10% that year), comparisons across ethnic groups by reason for unemployment in 1976 may give at least some indication of the previous year's pattern.

As one would expect in depressed labor markets, quit rates were low for all groups, with insignificant differences between native- and foreign-born men and among ethnic groups. The last two columns of Table 4.4, however, reveal a tendency for most Hispanic groups to have higher probabilities of unemployment due to layoff and to labor market entry or reentry than non-Hispanic whites. By far the highest layoff rate observed was that of Cubans in Florida, who were almost 8 times more likely to be unemployed as a result of layoff than white non-Hispanics in that state.[9] This appears to be at least partly attributable to the high proportion of recent immigrants among the Cuban sample. Although the difference in layoff rates between native- and foreign-born Hispanics is relatively small and only significant at the 10% level, separate tabulations by immigration cohort (unadjusted for human capital or labor market variables) revealed that Mexicans, Puerto Ricans, and Cubans moving to the United States since 1965 average higher rates than earlier waves from their homeland or than non-Hispanics. In contrast, native-born Hispanics have higher unemployment due to labor market entry or reentry than the foreign-born; in fact, native-born Puerto Ricans have three times the rate of those born on the island.

[9] Unpublished BLS tabulations of Current Population Survey data on annual male unemployment rates by reason for unemployment in 1976 (the first year for which annual rates by reason among Cubans were available) likewise indicate an above-average unemployment rate due to job loss among Cubans, though the rate for Puerto Ricans is well above that found in the SIE. Unemployment rates in 1976, and reasons for unemployment, for men aged 16 and over are shown in the following table:

	Job losers	Quits	Entrants
All whites	3.90	0.70	1.80
All Hispanics	7.82	1.03	3.24
Mexican	6.77	0.97	3.20
Puerto Rican	13.78	1.06	3.54
Cuban	10.60	1.68	2.24

REGRESSION ANALYSIS OF INCIDENCE

Table 4.5 presents maximum likelihood logit estimates of the unemployment probability equations for white non-Hispanics, all Hispanics, and individual Hispanic ethnic groups.[10] As expected, more highly educated individuals are less vulnerable to unemployment among all groups, although the coefficients are not statistically significant for Puerto Ricans and Cubans (whose extremely small sample size helps

TABLE 4.5
Logit Estimates of Probability of Unemployment Equations, White Non-Hispanic and Hispanic Men, by Ethnic Group

Variable	White non-Hispanic	All Hispanic	Mexican	Puerto Rican	Cuban	Other Hispanic
EDFOR	−.120***	−.078***	−.125**	−.092	−.042	.093
	(.020)	(.022)	(.037)	(.060)	(.074)	(.071)
EDUS	−.098***	−.120***	−.156***	−.069	−.053	−.106*
	(.015)	(.020)	(.025)	(.066)	(.101)	(.054)
EX	−.041***	−.060***	−.052***	−.144***	−.035	−.069**
	(.008)	(.012)	(.015)	(.045)	(.067)	(.029)
EXSQ	.0002	.0004**	.0000	.002***	.0004	.0007
	(.0002)	(.0002)	(.0003)	(.0008)	(.001)	(.0005)
MSP	−.335***	−.166	−.061	.079	−.074	−.425
	(.091)	(.127)	(.165)	(.417)	(.562)	(.330)
CHILD5	.003	−.019	−.048	−.054	−.760	.146
	(.066)	(.074)	(.087)	(.257)	(.684)	(.239)
CHILD517	−.080***	−.009	−.049	.105	.027	.081
	(.028)	(.032)	(.039)	(.111)	(.181)	(.086)
HEALTH	.341***	.251	.126	.522	1.042	.330
	(.112)	(.172)	(.220)	(.516)	(.813)	(.430)
IMM7475	.364	−.201	−.776*	2.024**	−.364	−.245
	(.416)	(.295)	(.401)	(.877)	(1.421)	(1.591)
IMM7073	.332	−.689***	−.793**	.228	−1.765	−2.530**
	(.317)	(.255)	(.359)	(.700)	(1.212)	(1.133)
IMM6569	.499**	−.883***	−1.034***	1.208*	−1.674	−2.395**
	(.241)	(.253)	(.373)	(.676)	(1.122)	(1.080)

[10] Tests of the equality of the coefficients of Hispanics and non-Hispanics and among the Hispanic groups yielded chi-square statistics (37.21 and 48.5, respectively) above the critical value (37.2), indicating significant differences in the unemployment parameters. Significant differences were also found between the coefficients of each Hispanic group and white non-Hispanics, except in the case of Puerto Ricans.

TABLE 4.5 (*Continued*)

Variable	White non-Hispanic	All Hispanic	Mexican	Puerto Rican	Cuban	Other Hispanic
IMM6064	−.092	−.509**	−.220	.669	−1.005	−2.117*
	(.295)	(.259)	(.386)	(.671)	(1.082)	(1.100)
IMMPRE60	.414***	−.252	−.141	.569	−.930	−.588
	(.140)	(.187)	(.254)	(.469)	(1.075)	(.775)
NONWHITE	—	.284	.482	.441	−.094	−.091
	—	(.222)	(.356)	(.504)	(1.227)	(.553)
FLUENT	.132	−.179	−.127	−.750***	−.861	−.061
	(.118)	(.112)	(.144)	(.350)	(.565)	(.299)
OTHINC	−.002***	−.001	−.0002	−.0006	−.003	−.061
	(.0004)	(.001)	(.001)	(.004)	(.005)	(.299)
PARTTIME	.142	.389**	.433**	.535	1.489	.412
	(.111)	(.165)	(.200)	(.556)	(1.071)	(.473)
UNRATE	.085***	.057***	.072***	−.095	.002	−.023
	(.014)	(.020)	(.023)	(.087)	(.122)	(.070)
OCC	.681***	.528***	.519***	.094	1.448**	.448
	(.084)	(.145)	(.192)	(.461)	(.650)	(.355)
IND	.683***	.605***	.580***	.395	.408	.941***
	(.068)	(.098)	(.128)	(.304)	(.470)	(.248)
HISPROP	−.011	−.019***	−.019***	.012	.019	−.012
	(.007)	(.005)	(.007)	(.047)	(.079)	(.011)
Mexican	—	.002	—	—	—	—
		(.169)				
Cuban	—	.372	—	—	—	—
		(.251)				
Central and South American	—	−.186	—	—	—	—
		(.264)				
Other Hispanic	—	.015	—	—	—	—
		(.200)				
Constant	−1.042***	.141	.395	1.247	−.071	.450
	(.290)	(.401)	(.457)	(1.405)	(2.511)	(.973)
−2 × log likelihood	6597.03	3039.18	1872.27	324.31	151.72	479.30
N	8,480	3,164	1,937	328	163	566

Source: 1976 Survey of Income and Education (U.S. Department of Commerce, 1978).
Notes: Dependent variable is UNEMP75. Standard errors are in parentheses.
* Statistically significant at the 10% level.
** Statistically significant at the 5% level.
*** Statistically significant at the 1% level.

account for their relatively few significant coefficients). To the extent that schooling in the United States provides language training and country-specific labor market information, one might predict that EDUS would have a larger impact (in absolute value) than EDFOR, and this is the case for the pooled Hispanic, Mexican, and Other Hispanic subsamples. Among non-Hispanic whites and Puerto Ricans, however, schooling prior to arrival appears to have a relatively stronger influence,[11] although the point estimates for the latter are not significant.

The anticipated inverse relationship between years of work experience and the probability of unemployment is confirmed for all groups except Cubans. Likewise, marriage and additional dependents appear generally to contribute to employment stability, though the coefficients are significant only for non-Hispanics. Among otherwise similar Hispanic men, health limitations and race do not appear to exert a significant impact on unemployment probabilities. Puerto Ricans able to speak and understand English very well have a significant advantage over other Puerto Rican men, but the effect of fluency in English seems to be weak for the other Hispanic groups.

Despite the adjustment difficulties confronting recent immigrants in a new labor market, results for individual cohorts indicate that, whether due to high motivation, assistance by kin in the United States, or other factors, most have unemployment probabilities either insignificantly different from or significantly lower than their native-born counterparts. Thus, among all Hispanics, men who have been in this country only since 1974 (IMM7475) are about 5% less likely to be out of work than otherwise similar indigenous Hispanics. The differential is larger (12–15%) for those who arrived between 1965 and 1973 and is highly significant. After about 25 years in the United States, however, foreign-born Hispanics are about as susceptible to unemployment as the native-born.

Among white non-Hispanics, the results are less consistent and more difficult to interpret. Immigrants arriving since 1970 have a probability of unemployment insignificantly different from the native-born.[12] But the coefficients change sign and are significantly positive for two earlier cohorts (1965–1969 and pre-1960), for reasons which are unclear. One

[11] Recent studies of the earnings of foreign-born men have found that the partial effect on earnings of an extra year of schooling following arrival in the United States is either slightly lower than or insignificantly different from the effect of an additional year of schooling abroad for a pooled sample of foreign-born whites (Chiswick, 1978a), but that postimmigration schooling has a higher effect than preimmigration schooling for men from Mexico and Central and South America (DeFreitas, 1979).

[12] These results are consistent with findings for native- and foreign-born white males based on 1970 census data in DeFreitas (1979, Chapter 4).

must bear in mind that non-Hispanic immigrants are a heterogeneous group of widely varying ethnic and national origins about whom it is hard to generalize.

The pattern observed for the pooled Hispanic sample is no doubt much influenced by the tendency among Mexican men, the largest single component of the subsample, for immigrants to have unemployment probabilities 13.5–18% lower than U.S.-born Mexican Hispanics during the first 10 years in the United States. The Other Hispanic group, also concentrated in the southwestern states, exhibits a similar pattern, and the differentials are even larger than among Mexicans.

Similarly, the coefficients of the Cuban subsample are consistently negative, and nearly attain significance at the 10% level for the 1965–1969 and 1970–1973 cohorts. However, the regression results for Cuban immigrants must be interpreted with extreme caution because the native-born reference group consists of only 9 individuals, 4 of whom reported being unemployed at some time in 1975.

Puerto Ricans are the only ethnic group in which the most recent cohort of newcomers to the mainland United States has a significantly greater likelihood of unemployment than the native-born. Although the coefficients rapidly fall in magnitude and significance for successive cohorts, they remain consistently positive. Part of the explanation for this pattern may be the unique status among Hispanic immigrants of persons born in Puerto Rico. As mentioned above, men born in Puerto Rico are, as U.S. citizens, able to move more freely back and forth between the two countries than are most immigrant groups. High rates of temporary, as well as permanent, return migration are facilitated by fast, low-cost air transportation and the transferability of social security and unemployment insurance. Indeed, Gray (1975b) found that, in the period 1959–1972, unemployment insurance claims filed in Puerto Rico on the basis of mainland work experience rose dramatically. Insofar as those born on the island are more prone to periodic return visits, they are more likely than the native-born to have an impermanent attachment to the mainland labor market, discontinuous work histories, and a higher probability of unemployment. The increasingly rural, unskilled backgrounds of recent migrants, only weakly controlled for in our regressions, also put them at a disadvantage in urban northeastern job markets. The limited data available on premigration residence indicates that, by the late 1950s, three-fourths of all migrants to the mainland originated in areas outside San Juan and other major cities, urban areas that had been the source of most earlier migrants. Of those arriving on the mainland between 1957 and 1961, the largest single group of previously employed migrants came from the agricultural sector, the source of one-third of all those with some work experience. Farm laborers are thus disproportionately represented among recent cohorts (Gray, 1975b).[13]

Some might object that rural, unskilled backgrounds are also characteristic of Mexican immigrants, yet they exhibit exactly the opposite pattern of significantly lower probabilities of unemployment than native-born members of their ethnic group. Although the limited evidence on apprehended illegal entrants from Mexico does suggest that the majority are from rural areas and are concentrated in seasonal farm labor in the United States (Fogel and Corwin, 1978), this no longer appears to hold true for those able to acquire proper documents. For example, a survey of legal entrants arriving in Texas in 1973–1974 found that nearly two-thirds were from urban areas of 10,000 or more and over one-third were from cities with 100,000 or more inhabitants (Tienda, 1980). Their ability to locate employment quickly was facilitated by the fact that over 60% had lived in the United States previously (many apparently in an undocumented status) and 9 out of 10 had relatives waiting at their U.S. destination. Following a trend begun after the Second World War, the majority of Mexicans now live and work in urban areas and increasing numbers reside in regions outside the Southwest, though they continue to be disproportionately employed in agriculture. Their more diversified geographic, occupational, and industrial patterns, in combination with more urbanized backgrounds, may count as important advantages over Puerto Rican migrants still clustered in marginal and declining sectors of the New York City economy. However, since persons illegally in the country are doubtless underreported in any government survey, our estimates of Mexican immigrant unemployment may be biased downward if illegal entrants experience above-average rates of joblessness.

Higher unemployment in the local labor market, part-time employment, and employment in unskilled and semiskilled occupations have the expected positive impact on unemployment for Hispanics and non-Hispanics alike. The latter two variables are more consistently positive and have especially large, significant coefficients for Cubans, raising unemployment probabilities by 35 and 25%, respectively. Likewise, workers in the durable manufacturing and construction industries (IND) are, as expected, more prone to joblessness in the course of the year than are men in other industries: The unemployment probability is increased by about 9% for non-Hispanics and by 11% for the full Hispanic subset. Of individual ethnic groups, probabilities increase by over 11% for both Mexicans and Other Hispanics and by roughly 6% for Puerto

---

[13] From 1951 to 1961, over one-half of migrants interviewed prior to departure from Puerto Rico had no previous work experience.

Ricans, the group most concentrated in industries with high unemployment. (See Gray, 1975a, for an analysis of the occupational and industrial distributions of Puerto Ricans in New York City.)

Although some economists have cited the crowding of Hispanic workers in particular labor markets as contributing to higher unemployment rates, residence in states with a high proportion of Hispanics produced an insignificant effect on the probability of non-Hispanics being unemployed, and a significantly lower probability of unemployment among Hispanics. This may reflect certain regional labor market differences, as well as the advantages of job search in areas with already settled populations of one's own ethnic group.

UNEMPLOYMENT BY REGION

In the national and separate regional regressions (Table 4.6), dummy variables were included for each ethnic group, with Puerto Ricans serving as the reference group. Among all Hispanics nationally, Cubans alone appeared to have a somewhat higher (by about 6%) probability of being unemployed in 1975, though the coefficient is on the borderline of significance at the 10% level. In the New York–New Jersey subsample, however, the coefficient is well below standard significance levels, suggesting that the national result may be due to the experiences of Cubans elsewhere, particularly in Florida, where the most recent immigrants are concentrated.[14] This group is quite different from most other Hispanic immigrants in that, as refugees, they entered the U.S. labor market without much opportunity for premigration preparation or job search and, on average, at a much older age than other immigrants. The relatively large number with professional and managerial backgrounds appear to experience considerable difficulty finding jobs in their prior occupations and suffer sharp downward mobility for some time. These factors may contribute to a greater vulnerability to unemployment during the first few years in the United States than is observed for most other groups. It could also be argued that the exclusion of self-employed individuals and labor force participants unable to find work all year biases our results, since Cubans are about twice as likely to be self-employed as all Hispanics. Regressions run on an expanded sample including all labor force participants in 1975 revealed that the self-employed were less likely to be unemployed, but the coefficient did not

---

[14] Separate regressions could not be estimated for a Florida subsample due to inadequate sample size.

TABLE 4.6
Logit Estimates of Probability of Unemploymnt Equations, White Non-Hispanic and Hispanic Men, by Region

	New York and New Jersey		Southwest	
Variable	White non-Hispanic (1)	All Hispanic (2)	White non-Hispanic (3)	Mexican (4)
EDFOR	−.195***	−.038	−.110	−.084*
	(.066)	(.063)	(.075)	(.047)
EDUS	−.153**	−.157*	−.023	−.154***
	(.062)	(.093)	(.051)	(.032)
EX	−.017	−.165***	−.042	−.060**
	(.033)	(.054)	(.030)	(.019)
EXSQ	−.0003	.003***	.0003	.0002
	(.0006)	(.001)	(.0006)	(.0003)
MSP	−.343	−.570	−.806***	−.120
	(.391)	(.468)	(.308)	(.207)
CHILD5	−.216	.128	−.112	−.088
	(.303)	(.316)	(.292)	(.113)
CHILD517	−.040	.033	.066	−.024
	(.135)	(.163)	(.094)	(.049)
HEALTH	.479	1.414**	.578	−.278
	(.458)	(.683)	(.386)	(.309)
IMM74	1.012	.717	.447	−.493
	(1.385)	(1.208)	(1.352)	(.520)
IMM7073	.840	−.651	1.233	−1.259***
	(.865)	(1.106)	(1.358)	(.482)
IMM6569	.028	−1.563	.735	−1.324***
	(.812)	(1.108)	(1.397)	(.453)
IMM6064	.370	−.723	.171	−.163
	(.785)	(1.044)	(.932)	(.447)
IMMPRE60	1.052**	−.942	.273	−.294
	(.498)	(.934)	(.543)	(.322)
NONWHITE	—	.093	—	—
		(.643)		
FLUENT	.181	−.635	−.240	−.135
	(.371)	(.477)	(.508)	(.187)
OTHINC	.002	−.005	−.001	−.001
	(.002)	(.005)	(.002)	(.002)
PARTTIME	.334	−.120	.042	.627**
	(.463)	(.875)	(.355)	(.238)

TABLE 4.6 (*Continued*)

Variable	New York and New Jersey		Southwest	
	White non-Hispanic (1)	All Hispanic (2)	White non-Hispanic (3)	Mexican (4)
UNRATE	.113	−.039	.021	.093***
	(.104)	(.183)	(.045)	(.028)
OCC	.587*	.348	.777***	.392*
	(.349)	(.545)	(.271)	(.228)
IND	.766***	.697*	.483**	.679***
	(.296)	(.392)	(.243)	(.160)
HISPROP	.102	.073	−.013	−.021**
	(.138)	(.228)	(.016)	(.010)
Cuban	—	.334	—	—
		(.648)		
Central and South American	—	.092	—	—
		(.523)		
Other Hispanic	—	.333	—	—
		(.588)		
Constant	−1.970	1.685	−.859	.404
	(1.999)	(3.493)	(1.113)	(.600)
−2 × log likelihood	375.13	225.41	573.64	1217.44
N	525	266	806	1,321

Source: 1976 Survey of Income and Education (U.S. Department of Commerce, 1978).
Notes: Dependent variable is UNEMP75. Standard errors are in parentheses.
* Statistically significant at the 10% level.
** Statistically significant at the 5% level.
*** Statistically significant at the 1% level.

approach significance. The coefficient of the Cuban variable (.446), however, was positive and statistically significant at the 10% level, suggesting that Cubans were indeed especially affected by the 1975 recession, relative to other Hispanics.[15]

The coefficients of most variables in the regional subsamples are similar to national estimates in Table 4.5, suggesting that the national results

[15] When the UNEMP75 regression was run on an expanded sample of all Hispanic labor force participants in 1975 (OCC and IND were excluded, since no information on occupation or industry was available for nonworkers that year), the estimated ethnic group and

were not solely reflecting regional variations. Some interesting differences are, however, discernible in the estimates for work experience, health limitations, and industry in the New York–New Jersey Hispanic subset. All are statistically significant and considerably larger (in absolute value) than those of non-Hispanics in the region or those of Hispanics nationwide. In the subsample of Mexicans in the five southwestern states, it is noteworthy that, despite the limited variability possible in the variable for the proportion of Hispanics in the respondent's state of residence, HISPROP continues to be associated with a significantly lower probability of unemployment.

An analysis of the determinants of multiple spells of joblessness showed that education, work experience, and marital status all appear to be stabilizing influences, significantly reducing the likelihood of multiple spells for both non-Hispanic whites and Hispanics. Hispanic immigrants are generally less susceptible to multiple jobless spells than the native-born, but the coefficients were only significant at the 5% level for one cohort. Both Hispanic and non-Hispanic employees in unskilled and semiskilled occupations and in cyclical industries were found to have significantly higher probabilities, as were Hispanics in part-time jobs. Only Cubans have a significantly (10% level) higher probability of multiple spells than the Puerto Rican reference group.[16]

DURATION OF JOBLESSNESS

Having focused thus far on the incidence of unemployment in my regression analysis, I now consider the role of various factors in deter-

---

self-employment coefficients were as follows (standard errors in parentheses):

Self-Employed, all Hispanics	−.114	(.214)
Mexican	.083	(.156)
Cuban	.446*	(.228)
Central & South American	.041	(.246)
Other Hispanic	.036	(.185)
N = 3,432		

* Statistically significant at the 10% level.

Coefficient estimates of the other variables bore similar signs and magnitudes to those in Table 4.6, Column 2.

[16] Estimation of the multiple-spells equation for the expanded sample of all male labor force participants resulted in an insignificantly positive differential between the self-employed and other workers and a highly significant (5% level) positive coefficient (.896) for the Cuban dummy variable.

mining the duration of time spent looking for work by men with some unemployment in 1975. The dependent variable is WKSUN75, and the independent variables differ only in the addition of a dummy variable (UI) equal to 1 if the individual received any unemployment insurance during the year. In restricting the sample here to men with some unemployment, the sample size for individual ethnic groups other than Mexicans becomes so small as to make it impractical to run separate regressions for each group. The OLS estimates for non-Hispanics and all Hispanics in all states, as well as for non-Hispanics and Mexicans residing in the Southwest, are presented in Table 4.7.

Although better-educated individuals tend to have higher expected returns from job search, it appears that their higher search costs and perhaps also more efficient use of search techniques lead to slightly

TABLE 4.7
Ordinary Least-Squares Estimates of Total Duration of Unemployment, 1975, for White Non-Hispanic and Hispanic Men

	All states		Southwest	
Variable	White non-Hispanic	Hispanic	White non-Hispanic	Hispanic
EDFOR	−.376*	−.205	−1.729	−.178
	(.219)	(.229)	(1.405)	(.510)
EDUS	−.180	−.647***	−.405	−1.028**
	(.160)	(.220)	(.716)	(.408)
EX	.078	−.106	.398	−.068
	(.090)	(.136)	(.451)	(.234)
EXSQ	−.002	.003	−.003	.000
	(.002)	(.003)	(.010)	(.005)
MSP	−2.276**	−3.761***	−12.463***	−4.293*
	(.965)	(1.308)	(3.695)	(2.365)
CHILD5	.519	.539	5.153	1.400
	(.771)	(.759)	(4.698)	(1.296)
CHILD517	−.051	−.703**	1.126	−.712
	(.299)	(.316)	(1.171)	(.510)
HEALTH	.925	1.328	1.704	3.661
	(1.175)	(1.772)	(4.406)	(3.591)
IMM7475	4.584	−1.079	26.378	−4.714
	(4.668)	(3.051)	(19.508)	(5.800)
IMM7073	4.415	−2.652	29.469	−5.131
	(3.393)	(2.735)	(20.252)	(5.528)
IMM6569	−1.833	−.743	11.463	−5.389
	(2.424)	(2.786)	(20.062)	(5.736)

(Continued)

TABLE 4.7 (*Continued*)
Ordinary Least-Squares Estimates of Total Duration of Unemployment, 1975, for White Non-Hispanic and Hispanic Men

Variable	All states		Southwest	
	White non-Hispanic	Hispanic	White non-Hispanic	Hispanic
IMM6064	4.056	−2.406	—	—
	(3.208)	(2.680)		
IMMPRE60	−.047	−2.819	4.083	1.152
	(1.512)	(1.976)	(6.527)	(3.489)
NONWHITE	—	1.224	—	—
	—	(2.223)		
FLUENT	−.604	1.154	−.657	.842
	(1.303)	(1.186)	(6.874)	(2.083)
OTHINC	.005	.007	−.006	.008
	(.005)	(.010)	(.016)	(.017)
PARTTIME	2.190**	1.872	4.822	.974
	(1.106)	(1.543)	(3.799)	(2.470)
UNRATE	.586***	.595***	.754	.529
	(.164)	(.213)	(.562)	(.324)
OCC	−.125	−1.279	−2.507	−3.854
	(.968)	(1.652)	(3.390)	(2.825)
IND	.249	1.286	1.571	1.422
	(.761)	(1.033)	(3.142)	(1.849)
HISPROP	.039	.002	.057	.041
	(.078)	(.055)	(.197)	(.110)
UI	3.529***	4.027***	6.702**	4.276**
	(.771)	(1.055)	(2.921)	(1.856)
Mexican	—	.126	—	—
		(1.726)		
Cuban	—	−.978	—	—
		(2.581)		
Central and South American	—	−4.524	—	—
		(2.840)		
Other Hispanic	—	−1.514	—	—
		(2.068)		
Constant	12.731***	19.854***	13.293	26.268***
	(3.202)	(4.183)	(15.369)	(7.143)
R^2	.053	.092	.245	.114
N	1,305	678	109	269

Source: 1976 Survey of Income and Education (U.S. Department of Commerce, 1978).
Notes: Dependent variable is WKSUN75. Standard errors are in parentheses.
* Statistically significant at the 10% level.
** Statistically significant at the 5% level.
*** Statistically significant at the 1% level.

shorter periods of time out of work. For all Hispanics, an additional year of U.S. schooling is associated with some two-thirds of a week less in job search, and for Mexicans in the Southwest the reduction is even larger. The coefficients are highly significant at the 5% level for Hispanics, but are lower and insignificant for white non-Hispanics. Additional work experience has a very weak effect for all groups. In contrast, married Hispanic men have jobless durations nearly 4 weeks below single Hispanics, and the coefficient is highly significant.

Just as most Hispanic immigrant cohorts have probabilities of unemployment lower than or insignificantly different from their native-born counterparts, so also do they appear to have briefer spells out of work, although the differentials are uniformly insignificant. The same is true of the positive cohort differentials of non-Hispanics. Although, as expected, a higher local unemployment rate contributes significantly to lengthier job search (by over one-half week for both Hispanics and non-Hispanics nationwide), differences by occupational and industrial sectors appear to be insignificant. Receipt of unemployment insurance is, as previous studies have shown, associated with longer jobless periods. Among otherwise similar unemployed Hispanics, there do not appear to be significant differences by ethnic group.

Analysis of Predicted Unemployment Differentials

To what extent are the sizable differences in the unemployment probabilities of white non-Hispanics and Hispanic ethnic groups attributable to their different characteristics, and to what extent do they reflect differential treatment in the labor market? To answer this question, each group's estimated coefficient vector in Table 4.5 and the mean values of characteristics were first used to predict probabilities of unemployment. The differences in predicted probabilities between white non-Hispanics and the various Hispanic groups are presented in the first row of Table 4.8.

The predicted difference between all Hispanics and non-Hispanics is identical to the actual average difference of .066 in Table 4.8. The model was especially successful in predicting the Mexican and Puerto Rican probabilities, but underestimated the actual Cuban–non-Hispanic differential and the Other Hispanic–non-Hispanic differential by about one-third.

The average characteristics of each Hispanic group were next substituted into the white non-Hispanic logit function to evaluate the role of

TABLE 4.8
Decomposition of Differences in Unemployment Probabilities
between White Non-Hispanics and Hispanics

Assumption	Hispanic–non-Hispanic differential	Mexican–non-Hispanic differential	Puerto Rican–non-Hispanic differential	Cuban–non-Hispanic differential	Other Hispanic–non-Hispanic differential
Group's own characteristics and coefficients	.066	.068	.085	.057	.020
Group's own characteristics, non-Hispanic coefficients	.042	.047	.084	.025	.011
Group's own coefficients, non-Hispanic schooling characteristics	.019	.005	.070	.037	.003
Group's own coefficients, non-Hispanic job and labor market[a] characteristics	.073	.083	.095	.051	.035
Group's own coefficients, all non-Hispanic characteristics	.024	.013	−.015	.108	.017

Source: 1976 Survey of Income and Education (U.S. Deparment of Commerce, 1978).
[a] Average non-Hispanic values for PARTTIME, UNRATE, OCC, IND, and HISPROP were assigned to each Hispanic group.

differential treatment. If Hispanic characteristics were treated in the same manner as those of non-Hispanics, the findings in Row 2 reveal that the difference in their unemployment probabilities would fall from an unadjusted .066 to .042, a reduction of over 36%. The reductions by ethnic group range from 30.9% for Mexicans to 56.1% for Cubans. Only Puerto Ricans would be largely unaffected by such a change, due mostly to the greater impact of occupation and industry in the non-Hispanic equation. Overall, it appears that relatively unfavorable treatment of Hispanic characteristics in the labor market accounts for a substantial fraction of the unemployment differential.

To examine the relative importance of various characteristics, it was assumed that each Hispanic group kept its own coefficient vector and its own values of all characteristics except educational attainment (EDFOR and EDUS). The large "schooling gap" (over 3 years in the sample) between Hispanics and white non-Hispanics has often been cited as one of the most serious disadvantages hindering Hispanic earnings and employment progress. Its singular importance for unemployment is confirmed by the results reported in Row 3 of Table 4.8: over 70% of the difference in unemployment probabilities between Hispanics and non-Hispanics would be eliminated solely by equalizing educational attainment levels. For Puerto Ricans, the differential falls by only 18%, and for Cubans by one-third, both resulting from lower EDUS coefficients. But the differentials of Mexicans and of other Hispanics fell by 85 to 90%.

When non-Hispanic job and labor market characteristics alone are substituted into the Hispanic equations, the difference in unemployment propensities between all Hispanics and non-Hispanics is diminished by only one-half of 1%. For most groups, the differential increases, reflecting the fact that, for example, Mexicans are less likely than non-Hispanics to be part-time workers, to live in SMSAs with high rates of joblessness, or to be in the durable manufacturing or construction industries. Only the Cuban–non-Hispanics' differential is reduced, due primarily to non-Hispanics' lower local unemployment rates and smaller proportion of workers employed in unskilled and semiskilled occupations, as well as to the unusually large impact of such employment estimated in the Cuban unemployment equation.

Finally, the full set of non-Hispanic personal and labor market characteristics was substituted into the Hispanic equations. The results in the last row of Table 4.8 show that, with the same average characteristics as non-Hispanic whites, Mexicans would have nearly the same probability of unemployment and Puerto Ricans a slightly lower probability of unemployment than non-Hispanics. But the Other Hispanic–non-Hispanic differential falls by only 19%, as the impact of increased schooling levels is largely canceled out by the deleterious effects of being assigned non-Hispanic job and labor market characteristics. The Cuban–non-Hispanic differential is the only one to rise, nearly doubling as a result of non-Hispanics' smaller proportion of schooling abroad and smaller immigration cohorts, both of which are given considerable weight in the Cuban function.

Overall, the difference in the probability of unemployment between all Hispanics and white non-Hispanics is reduced by 63.4%. It thus appears that the unemployment differential is largely attributable to differences in personal and other characteristics. The remaining one-third of the differential may reflect differences in unmeasured characteristics and discrimination. The impact of the latter may, of course, be even greater if, as a number of studies have suggested, differences in certain characteristics such as schooling are at least in part due to previous and anticipated discrimination against Hispanics (see Fligstein and Fernandez, Chapter 5 in this volume).

Summary and Conclusions

This chapter has investigated differences in the incidence and duration of unemployment among Hispanic men and between Hispanics and non-Hispanic whites. It was found that, both nationally and within particular regions, Hispanics were far more likely to be unemployed one or more times in the course of 1975 than were non-Hispanics. The severity of the 1974–1975 recession was reflected in the finding that nearly one-third of the unemployed were out of work for 6 months or more. But there does not appear to have been a significant difference between Hispanics and non-Hispanics either in the average duration of joblessness or in the effects of most personal and labor market characteristics on total spell length. Rather, the principal difference is in the higher probability of Hispanics experiencing one or more spells without work.

Differential treatment appears to play a significant role in generating the higher unemployment of Hispanics, but differences in characteristics seem to be the most important explanatory factors. Our findings point to substantial differences among Hispanic ethnic groups in the nature of the unemployment experience and in the key characteristics influencing it. Mexican, Puerto Rican, and Cuban men had both a higher incidence and longer average duration of unemployment than Central and South Americans and the Other Hispanic group. For Mexicans, lower schooling levels are the single most important factor accounting for their above-average probability of unemployment. If Mexicans had the same amount of schooling as white non-Hispanics, their unemployment rates would be nearly equalized. Whereas, among Mexicans, immigrants tend to have significantly lower probabilities of unemployment, the opposite appears to be the case for Puerto Rican men. The large inflow of recent, increasingly rural and unskilled migrants from the island may contribute to their higher incidence of unemployment. Low educational levels play an influential but secondary role.

Despite relatively low unemployment rates during most years for which data are available, Cuban men appear to have been especially vulnerable to unemployment in the course of the 1975 recession. They experience higher probabilities of being unemployed and having multiple jobless spells than the Other Hispanic groups, even after controlling for a wide variety of personal and labor market variables. The results of a decomposition analysis of the Cuban–non-Hispanic unemployment differential suggest that the concentration of largely foreign-born Cuban workers in certain low-wage occupations in high-unemployment SMSAs may be among the principal causes of this pattern. However, because of the extremely small size of the Cuban subsample in both the SIE and the periodic Current Population Surveys, larger data sets will be required in the future to explore more fully what appear to be significant differences in the unemployment experience among Hispanic ethnic groups.

PART II

Youth Employment and School Enrollment

Educational Transitions of Whites and Mexican-Americans*

Neil Fligstein and Roberto M. Fernandez

Introduction

It is well known that Mexican-Americans attain lower levels of education than whites in American society (U.S. Commission on Civil Rights, 1978; U.S. Department of Commerce, 1979; National Center for Education Statistics, 1980). The reasons for this are the subject of much speculation and surprisingly little research. This chapter aims to provide evidence for the various factors that might explain the disparities between white and Mexican-American educational attainment.

In order to understand how and why Mexican-Americans achieve a lower educational level than whites, it is necessary to consider a variety of elements. Some are unique to the situation of Mexican-Americans in the United States; others reflect the general process of educational attainment in the United States. Toward this end, we first summarize the general model of educational attainment that has developed in sociology. Second, we briefly review the educational history of Mexican-Americans. Finally, we construct a model of the process of educational attainment for Mexican-Americans and attempt to identify the differences and similarities in that process for Mexican-Americans and whites.

---

* This work was partially supported by a contract from the National Commission on Employment Policy. We would like to acknowledge the comments of Glen Cain, Carol Jusenius, Alejandro Portes, and Marta Tienda. Any opinions expressed are those of the authors and do not necessarily reflect the position of the Commission.

161

The General Model of Educational Attainment

Formal education is often seen as a process intervening between an individual's family of origin and later occupational and economic attainments (Blau and Duncan, 1967; Duncan et al., 1972; Jencks et al., 1972; Featherman and Hauser, 1978). The amount of education an individual receives is a product of a complex process in which one's background, intelligence, academic performance, and school setting, combined with social–psychological factors such as peer, parental, and teacher encouragement and personal goals in occupation and education, are transformed into educational attainment.

The most important factors affecting an individual's educational attainment are those related to family background (Blau and Duncan, 1967; Duncan et al., 1972; Jencks et al., 1972; Featherman and Hauser, 1978; Mare, 1980). In general, higher-income families, in which parents often have more education and high occupational status, tend to support children in educational endeavors because the parents realize that, in order for their children to prosper economically, they must obtain an education that prepares them for some career. Persons in less affluent families may place less emphasis on education for their children because the costs of college and higher education are too high to meet.

The four variables usually used to index these background factors are father's education, mother's education, father's occupational status, and parental income. Most studies of educational attainment show that these variables exert about equal effects on the child's educational attainment (Hauser, 1971; Duncan et al., 1972; Jencks et al., 1972; Sewell and Hauser, 1975; Shea, 1976). This finding suggests that a variety of mechanisms operate to convert socioeconomic background into educational attainments. Parents' income would seem to most affect the ability of parents to pay for their children's education and related expenses, while parents' education appears to tap the value that parents place on education for their children. Father's occupational status is also an indication of the value placed on education in that professional occupations, which tend to have high status, usually require much training, whereas blue-collar occupations, which have lower status, require less formal training.

Sewell and his associates have tried to clarify more precisely how various social–psychological processes intervene between background and educational attainment (Sewell et al., 1957; Sewell and Shah, 1968; Sewell et al., 1969; Sewell and Hauser, 1975). Their work has attempted to assess how the advantages of background are translated through social–psychological mechanisms into effects on eventual educational attainment. The basic theoretical notion is that an individual's educational attainment will be influenced by his or her relations to other people. Certain people will assume differential significance in a child's life and help shape the educational goals the child holds. Three groups deemed especially relevant to this process are parents, peers, and teachers. Parents and peers are the most important significant others, followed by teachers. Hauser (1971) and Otto and Haller (1979) conclude that the major mechanism by which background is translated into educational achievement is the parents' attitude about what the child's educational goals should be.

Two other variables that help explain educational achievement are intelligence (or, perhaps more accurately, scholastic ability) and academic performance (Hauser, 1971; Jencks et al., 1972; Sewell and Hauser, 1975). Intelligence measurement, however, is related to background, ethnicity, and language in a problematic fashion. High intelligence is more likely to be measured in students who share middle-class backgrounds and values than in those from different ethnic groups that hold nonstandard values, perhaps speak another language,[1] and have different cultural experiences (Cordasco, 1978; Aguirre, 1979).

The school itself aids educational attainment in a number of ways. For instance, class size, facilities, and teacher's motivation are obvious factors that could affect educational attainment. However, after years of trying to show school effects net of student background and neighborhood factors, most researchers have concluded that there has been very little independent impact of schools (Coleman et al., 1966; Hauser, 1971; Jencks et al., 1972; Jencks and Brown, 1975; Hauser et al., 1976). For blacks, research on high school contextual effects (Armor, 1972; Thornton and Eckland, 1980) and school desegregation (Wilson, 1979; Patchen et al., 1980) has been more successful. For Mexican-Americans, there is also evidence suggesting that school-level variables have an independent effect on scholastic performance. Carter and Segura (1979) stress the role of self-fulfilling prophecies due to teacher expectations—that is, since teachers assume that Mexican-Americans are poor students, they behave in ways that hinder these students' achievements.

The remaining factor considered important in the educational attainment process is an individual's educational and occupational aspirations. Indeed, Sewell et al. (1969) report that the best predictor of completed schooling is the student's educational aspirations (but see Alexander and Cook, 1979, for a different view). Occupational aspira-

[1] Jensen (1961, 1980) reports results showing that standard IQ tests are not measuring the scholastic ability of Mexican-American children accurately. He concludes that the inaccuracies stem from the bilingualism of most Chicanos.

tions also determine education, as one's career plans may require a degree. Both educational and occupational aspirations are in turn determined to a large extent by family background, the expectations of significant others, intelligence, academic performance, and the school environment.

In sum, sociological research on educational attainment has clearly demonstrated that social background influences educational outcomes mainly through the transmission of values and attitudes toward education. Parents provide economic, psychic, and emotional support for their children that is translated into educational achievement. Schools appear to selectively reinforce those students who have this kind of motivation and allow them to succeed. Through this complex social–psychological process, student aspirations for education and occupations are shaped, and behavior follows accordingly. The other important pattern to note is that students with higher measured intelligence tend to have higher educational attainment, as do those with higher grades. Academic performance itself is a function of background and values as well as intelligence. Both intelligence and grades are also related to background in that some components of these factors originate in the advantages of growing up in a middle-class environment (Duncan et al. 1972; Sewell and Hauser, 1975).

The Unique Situation of Mexican-Americans

Mexican-Americans have had a history of discrimination in schools (see Carter and Segura, 1979). When the Spanish conquered Mexico, one of the first institutions they destroyed was the indigenous native school (Carter, 1970; Weinberg, 1977a, 1977b; Carter and Segura, 1979). The Spanish set up schools to teach Spanish to the exclusion of the native Indian languages. In 1821 Mexico won its independence from Spain. Although universal education was mandated by the Mexican constitution, it was never implemented in any systematic fashion. The major source of education was the Catholic Church, and most of those who received any formal schooling were of Spanish descent.

Following the war between Mexico and the United States, many Mexicans remained on lands that became part of the southwestern United States. While we today often think of Mexican-Americans as immigrants or non–English-speaking foreigners, the truth is that their presence in the Southwest predates U.S. control of the area. After the U.S.–Mexican war, immigration began. From 1848 to the early part of the twentieth century, Mexican immigration to the United States was rather slow. It increased after the Mexican Revolution (1910–1917) and has fluctuated in a pattern similar to immigration in general since then (Grebler et al., 1970). After World War II, Mexican immigration increased; it reached especially high levels after the *bracero* program (a temporary contract labor program between the Mexican and U.S. governments) was officially terminated in 1964.

Most who have written on the issue have stressed that Mexican-American students have been systematically discriminated against in the schools (see Weinberg, 1977a, 1977b, for an overview). Legally, Mexican-Americans were not subject to discriminatory racial laws, as were blacks. In practice, however, Mexican-American students have attended segregated schools; often their educational facilities are understaffed and lack such basic resources as libraries (Weinberg, 1977a; Carter and Segura, 1979). Several studies (Carter, 1970; Vasquez, 1974; Carter and Segura, 1979) report student underachievement and alienation as a direct consequence of the inferiority of the school setting for Mexican-Americans.

The basic mechanism by which schools have intentionally or unintentionally reduced the likelihood that Mexican-American students will complete high school has been grade delay—repeating a particular grade. By compelling students to repeat grades, schools have made alternatives to schooling more attractive to Mexican-Americans (Carter and Segura, 1979; supported by statistics in U.S. Department of Commerce, 1979). Carter and Segura see this process as one in which the student is pushed out because he or she faces a difficult school situation and is expected to fail. The other part of this process is that, as school becomes less attractive, job opportunities become more attractive. Hence, students may also be pulled out of school by the opportunity for a job (Duncan, 1965; Edwards, 1976; see Nielsen, 1980, for a discussion of push-out and pull-out factors as explanations for Hispanic dropout rates).

A remaining issue is the effect of cultural differences on educational attainment of Mexican-Americans. The argument usually put forward is that Mexican-American cultural values are not conducive to educational attainment. This point of view has both a positive and a negative connotation. Some have argued that the Mexican-American child is culturally deprived, has little intellectual stimulation, is not taught to value education, and has a bad self-image (Bloom et al., 1965; Gordon and Wilkerson, 1966; Heller, 1966). Mexican-American culture has also been characterized as family-centered, patriarchal, and oriented toward the extended family (Grebler et al., 1970). The primary cultural values are thought to be machismo, fatalism, and orientation toward the present.

Educators have tended to view Mexican-American students as victims of this culture, and their low educational achievement is thought to reflect these values and orientations. Most empirical evidence does not, however, support this view of the Mexican family (see, for example, Anderson and Johnson, 1971). Further, there is no evidence that Mexican-American students have a lower self-image than white students (DeBlassie and Healey, 1970).

Ramirez and Castaneda (1974) have expressed a more benign point of view. They argue that each culture possesses a distinct cognitive style by which it relates to and organizes the world. Mexican-Americans are what they call bicultural and have a cognitive style that they refer to as field dependent. The term *bicultural* indicates that Mexican-Americans have had to adjust to two cultures and therefore have learned to express themselves in the cognitive styles of both their own culture and the dominant white culture. *Cognitive style* refers to learning, human relation, and communication. The dominant value-clusters within Mexican-American culture, according to Ramirez and Castaneda, center on family, community, and ethnic group, and focus on interpersonal relations, status and role definition in family and community, and Mexican Catholic ideology. Differing cognitive styles result in different learning styles: Mexican-American children learn better in cooperative rather than competitive settings. They are also more other-oriented in general, and rely more heavily on family, community, and friends for self-perception. The term *field dependence* implies that Mexican-American children do better in verbal tasks and in tasks that relate to other people, whereas white children do better on analytic tasks.

Ramirez and Castaneda's argument suggests that the cultural differences between Mexican-Americans and whites reflect different values concerning what is important in relations with other people. They do not see Mexican-American children as culturally deprived; rather, they have a different culture containing its own set of rules and justifications, whose practices are antithetical to the dominant, white middle-class culture. Thus, as institutions that socialize individuals to the dominant culture, schools become the site of the destruction of Mexican-American culture.

These cultural differences, combined with the schools' perception and treatment of Mexican-American students, go far toward explaining the low educational attainment of Mexican-Americans. Given a hostile school environment and the need to work to help support a household (either one's biological family or one's own children), it is not surprising that Mexican-Americans leave school at an early age (Haro, 1977; Laosa, 1977).

Two other issues arise in discussions of Mexican-American scholastic performance: length of residence in the United States and language. Some studies have found that immigrants tend to be a highly motivated, self-selected group, and therefore show higher achievement, perhaps after an initial disadvantage due to language and customs (Blau and Duncan, 1967; Chiswick, 1978a). Nielsen and Fernandez (1982) and Fernandez and Nielsen (1983) speculate that this high level of motivation may be passed on to the immigrants' children, thus explaining why the children of more recent migrants achieve better in high school. Kimball (1968) and Baral (1979) suggest that long-time residents may become "ghettoized" and therefore achieve poorly compared to more recent migrants. Others (e.g., Featherman and Hauser, 1978, Chapter 8), however, find that immigrants are at a socioeconomic disadvantage, one they attribute to difficulties of language and culture. In addition, 1970 census data show that immigrants have lower levels of education (Jaffe et al., 1980), which can, through the general mechanisms described above, result in lower educational achievements for children.

Past research has found that, owing to language, Spanish speakers in a predominantly English-speaking society experience difficulties in school and work (Garcia, 1980). Other studies have found that bilingualism is an asset, both in school (Peal and Lambert, 1962; Fernandez and Nielsen, 1983; for reviews see also Lambert, 1975; Cummins, 1977, 1981) and in certain job markets (Lopez, 1976; Tienda, 1982). The institutional response for both of these positions has been some form of bilingual education. Many members of the Mexican-American community favor bilingual–bicultural programs that are oriented toward the maintenance of both the English and the Spanish language. Others, with more assimilationist views, emphasize the importance of English proficiency over and above the use of Spanish; they support transitional bilingual programs that are designed to teach English to the Mexican-American child with little regard for maintaining the Spanish tongue. Given these conflicting goals, it is not surprising that there is little agreement about the effectiveness of the different programs that have been implemented (see Fligstein and Fernandez, 1982, for a review of bilingual education programs).

Models of the Educational Attainment Process for Mexican-Americans

It is now appropriate to propose a model of educational attainment in general and to describe how such a model would be modified to take into account the special situations of Mexican-Americans. There are basically two parts to these models: one component consists of variables that have been found to pertain to all subpopulations, and another consists of variables that, in light of the above discussion, can be expected to affect Mexican-Americans disproportionately. The background characteristics common to all groups include father's education, mother's education, father's occupation, family income, and number of siblings. Parental education and father's occupation index both the socioeconomic status of the family and parents' attitudes about the desirability of education, while family income measures the ability of the family to pay for education. Number of siblings indicates how many children must share the family income. Controlling other factors, the larger the family, the more likely that the respondent will be drawn out of school and into the labor force to help support the family (see Rumberger, 1983, for a similar argument). We also include a measure for gender, since past research has shown that men and women vary in educational attainment (Alexander and Eckland, 1974). The social–psychological measures of the educational aspirations and expectations of parents, peers, teachers, and the respondent are also expected to affect educational outcomes.

From the review of the experiences of Mexican-Americans, two additional types of background variables need to be included—migration history and linguistic practices. In both cases, past research (described above) has shown mixed results concerning educational attainment. Much of the discrepancy in these findings may be due to the varying conceptions and measures of migration recency and linguistic practice employed by the different studies. Though we cannot resolve the reasons for the contradictory findings here, we note that it is important to incorporate measures of migration and language into models of educational attainment for Mexican-Americans.

We next suggest a set of school-level variables as predictors of educational transitions. These include whether the school is public or private, the racial and ethnic composition of the school, and such measures of school quality as the dropout rate and the teacher–student ratio. Recently, Coleman et al. (1981) endeavored to show that minorities tend to do better in private schools than in public schools (but see Lewis and Wanner, 1979, for contrary evidence). Our model includes measures of school racial composition (percentage black and percentage Hispanic) because past research on school integration has shown that it has small but positive effects on scholastic achievement for blacks (U.S. Commission on Civil Rights, 1967; Lewis and St. John, 1974; Wilson, 1979). Though we know of no similar research concerning Mexican-Americans, owing to the obvious importance of segregation issues for Hispanics (see Naboa, 1980), we test whether similar effects can be discerned with our data by including percentage Hispanic within the school in our model. As a general measure of the holding power of the respondent's high school, we include the percentage who drop out as a predictor of these educational transitions. Last, in accord with the extensive literature on school effects (e.g., Coleman et al., 1966; Bidwell and Kasarda, 1975; for a review see Spady, 1976), we use the number of students per teacher in the respondent's high school as a measure of school resources.

In addition to these general school variables, which should affect both non-Hispanic whites and Mexican-Americans, we are interested in curriculum measures that should be important for Mexican-Americans (i.e., whether the student was enrolled in a program of English as a second language [ESL] or some form of transitional bilingual education program). As was argued above, it is important to assess whether or not these programs aid in increasing educational attainment.

Finally, we consider some community-related variables. The local unemployment rate in the respondent's area of residence can be considered a measure of the "pull" factors in the local labor market that might draw youth out of school (see Duncan, 1965; Edwards, 1976). Another community variable, urban residence, is included because living in a large city would make one less likely to complete school because of the greater number of nonschool options available in cities.

Analysis

The data set used in these analyses is the U.S. Department of Labor's National Longitudinal Survey (NLS) of 1979 (Borus et al., 1980). The choice of data set presented problems. The ideal data for this project must include information on ethnicity, migration history, family background, language, education, schools and curriculum, educational aspirations and expectations, scholastic ability, and grades, and it must be longitudinal. No data set exists that covers all of these elements. The NLS data, while limited in age range and lacking certain variables, proved to contain the greatest amount of relevant information.[2]

[2] Two other data sets were considered: the Census Bureau's 1976 Survey of Income and Education (U.S. Department of Commerce, 1978), and High School and Beyond (National Center for Education Statistics, 1980). The Survey of Income and Education cannot be used, since it contains limited information on family background and no data on school performance. The High School and Beyond data, collected by the National Opinion Re-

The data analysis strategy requires defining relevant subpopulations and dependent variables. Because the sample members are quite young and many of the respondents are still in school, we divided the data into three groups: those 18 years of age or younger, those aged 19–22, and those who had completed high school. The first group is used to determine which factors are related to the respondent's being in school or having dropped out. The dependent variable is a dummy variable coded zero if the respondent dropped out and one if the respondent was still in school. (Students in this age group who had completed high school were coded as being in school.) The second group is used to determine what factors affect high school completion. The dependent variable here is coded zero if the respondent did not finish high school and one if the respondent did. The third group, composed of those who had completed high school, is used because we are interested in what affects a person's chances of going to college. Since high school graduation is a prerequisite for entrance to colleges and universities, we restricted our attention to the sample of interest (i.e., high school graduates). For these analyses, the dependent variable is coded zero if the respondent did not go to college and one if the respondent did.

We divided the sample in this manner for the following reasons. If we had used completed years of schooling as a dependent variable for these young people, we would have encountered the limitation that many of our respondents had not completed schooling. It makes more sense to consider school transitions, such as staying in school, completing high school, and entering college. Unfortunately, age also plays a role in the schooling process; if we were to consider using only those who had dropped out of high school or who had completed high school, we would truncate our sample by excluding those still in school.[3] By breaking the sample down into age groups, we eliminate this problem. The first group answers the question, "Given that respondents are younger

---

search Center for the National Center for Education Statistics, only samples 10th and 12th graders at one point in time, making it impossible to assess why people completed or did not complete relevant school transitions. When subsequent waves of the High School and Beyond survey become available, it will be the best choice for studying these issues. High School and Beyond oversampled Hispanics and contains detailed language data, achievement test performance, and a broad range of background characteristics.

[3] In essence, this problem can be characterized as a selectivity bias (Heckman, 1979). One could argue that the appropriate econometric solution to this problem is to use a correction for such bias. Unfortunately, in cases where the ultimate dependent variable itself is dichotomous, this correction is not straightforward. It requires use of a technique known as bivariate probit analysis (Ashford and Snowden, 1970), which is not computationally simple. We therefore chose the alternative strategy of splitting the sample.

than 18, what are the causes of their dropping out of school versus their being in school?" The second group assesses the determinants of high school completion among those who are old enough to be eligible to complete high school.

The second dependent variable analyzed for the two high school samples is school delay. We argued earlier that school delay was a major factor in keeping Mexican-American students from completing high school. Since delay and dropping out could be seen as simultaneous events, it might not be reasonable to include delay as an independent variable (although this reasoning may be incorrect, because the sequence usually is that being held back is followed by dropping out; thus the delay could easily be seen as *preceding* dropping out). Nevertheless, it is sensible to examine the determinants of delay. *School delay* is defined as the median age in the population in the highest grade the respondent completed minus the age of the respondent in the highest grade completed.

Two ethnic groups are analyzed separately here: whites and Mexican-Americans. (Hispanic groups other than Mexican-Americans were not included because they did not occur in the sample in sufficient numbers.) We assigned respondents to ethnic groups on the basis of self-identification. T. Smith (1980) shows that, among various methods that have been used to classify respondents into ethnic groups in surveys, self-identification is the most efficient technique.

Two techniques were employed in the data analysis: ordinary least squares (OLS) regression and logistic regression. The OLS regression is used when school delay, a continuous measure, is the dependent variable. Since the transition variables are dichotomous, OLS regressions would result in estimates that are no longer minimum-variance unbiased, because of heteroskedasticity. A logit specification provides an adequate solution to this problem (Theil, 1971, pp. 631–633).

EXPLANATORY VARIABLES

The independent variables are entered into the analyses in two sets: family background, and school and social environment.[4] In our theoretical discussion, we suggested variables relevant to the general population and variables relevant to Mexican-Americans. Here, we incorporate both types of measures into the two sets of variables.

---

[4] The family factors alone produce a reduced-form model. This reduced form provides a baseline from which the effect of potential policy variables (school and environment) can be assessed.

Nine measures of family background are included in the model: (1) father's and (2) mother's education in years of schooling; (3) a dummy variable coded zero if the respondent was female and one if the respondent was male; three dummy variables coded zero if (4) the respondent (5) the mother, and (6) the father were born in the United States, coded one if born elsewhere; (7) a dummy variable coded zero if the interview was conducted in English and coded one if the interview was conducted in Spanish; (8) a dummy variable coded one if the respondent has a non-English mother tongue and zero otherwise; and (9) the number of siblings in the respondent's family. No measures of family income and father's occupation were included because of the high proportion of missing data (over 40%).

The measures of school and social environment reflect characteristics of the surrounding area. The local community is indexed by two measures: the local unemployment rate in 1979, and a dummy variable coded one if the respondent was living in a Standard Metropolitan Statistical Area (SMSA) and coded zero if he or she is not.

The school variables are of two types: school environment and curriculum. The first type measures the quality of the education and the racial–ethnic composition of the school. Only one of the school variables has relatively little missing data. This is a dummy variable coded zero if the respondent attended a public school and coded one for a private school. The other school variables were not assessed for about half of the sample. In order to use the data available, we constructed a dummy variable called "nonresponse school items" that is coded zero if the respondent does not have school data and one if data exist. All variables utilizing the school data are coded zero for those individuals for whom the school data are missing. If those who responded are not systematically more likely to have stayed in school, completed school, or entered college, then this dummy variable should not affect the outcome to a statistically significant degree. From our discussions with the people who collected the data, there is no reason to believe that such bias exists. The four measures of school environment are the percentage of students in high school who are Hispanic, the percentage of students who are black, the percentage of students who dropped out of the high school, and the pupil–teacher ratio.

The curriculum data for individuals were collected independently of the rest of the NLS data. Only about 40% of the respondents have these data, which are taken from high school transcripts. A dummy variable called "nonresponse transcript" was created, coded zero if the respondent did not have transcript data and one if the respondent did. Here too, zero is assigned to the missing transcript data. We should thus be able to assess if the presence of the transcript data is systematically related to the outcomes. The two curriculum variables are coded at the individual level; they are dummy variables coded zero if the respondent did not take a course in English as a second language or bilingual education and coded one if the respondent did.

No measures of social–psychological attributes such as educational aspirations and expectations of peer, respondent, or parent are included in these models, for two reasons. First, some of these variables were not measured. Second, some were measured at the time of the interview, and therefore it is difficult to determine whether the attitude caused the relevant educational transition, or vice versa. To use the measures probably requires longitudinal data.

In sum, the analytic strategy is to examine the causes of schooling outcomes for three relevant age cohorts of non-Hispanic whites and Mexican-Americans. The dependent variables include dropping out of or staying in high school, completing high school, entering college, and school delay. The strategy is first to enter background variables, and next school and community variables. In this way, we should begin to understand the schooling process for the two groups and the ways in which they differ and are similar.

DESCRIPTIVE STATISTICS

Table 5.1 presents means and standard deviations for the subpopulations by ethnic group. Considering the high school populations, we see that Mexican-Americans are less likely to be in school or to have graduated from high school. Most striking is that only 57% of Mexican-Americans over 18 years of age have graduated from high school, compared to 83% of whites. However, when we consider the population of high school graduates, we find that Mexican-Americans attend college at a *higher* rate than whites (66% vs. 58%), despite their generally lower socioeconomic background (see below). The Mexican-Americans who finish high school appear to be a selected group who are motivated to pursue the educational process (see Nielsen, 1980, for an elaboration of this selection argument). This suggests that the primary barriers to Mexican-American school achievement are encountered early in the educational life course—that is, before and during high school.[5] Another indi-

---

[5] This is not to say that there is equality of opportunity for Mexican-Americans to attend college. There is evidence that they are much more likely to attend 2-year colleges than are whites (National Center for Education Statistics, 1980). For a general discussion concerning the plight of minorities in 2-year colleges, see Olivas (1980).

TABLE 5.1
Means for Whites and Mexican-Americans in the Three Sample Populations

Variable	White			Mexican-American		
	≤18 Years	>18 Years	HS Grad	≤18 Years	>18 Years	HS Grad
% in high school	.90	—	—	.83	—	—
	(.30)	—	—	(.38)	—	—
% high school grad.	—	.83	—	—	.58	—
	—	(.37)	—	—	(.49)	—
% enter college	—	—	.58	—	—	.66
	—	—	(.49)	—	—	(.48)
School delay	.50	.68	—	.91	1.11	—
	(.72)	(1.01)	—	(1.00)	(1.32)	—
Father's education	11.73	12.03	12.55	7.29	6.90	8.02
	(3.45)	(3.60)	(3.43)	(4.60)	(4.67)	(4.56)
Mother's education	11.58	11.89	12.28	7.07	6.96	8.17
	(2.56)	(2.62)	(2.45)	(3.99)	(4.31)	(4.21)
Sex	.50	.46	.46	.47	.48	.47
	(.50)	(.50)	(.50)	(.50)	(.50)	(.50)
Number of siblings	3.20	3.22	3.04	4.96	5.16	4.36
	(2.17)	(2.08)	(1.92)	(2.76)	(2.92)	(2.37)
Nativity	.04	.03	.03	.25	.28	.13
	(.19)	(.17)	(.17)	(.43)	(.45)	(.34)
Father's nativity	.05	.05	.05	.41	.45	.36
	(.22)	(.22)	(.22)	(.49)	(.50)	(.48)
Mother's nativity	.06	.05	.05	.45	.47	.39
	(.24)	(.22)	(.22)	(.50)	(.50)	(.49)
Language as child	.11	.13	.13	.93	.94	.93
	(.31)	(.34)	(.34)	(.26)	(.23)	(.25)
Spanish interview	.02	.02	.02	.05	.07	.03
	(.14)	(.13)	(.13)	(.21)	(.25)	(.18)
SMSA	.64	.68	.69	.71	.80	.80
	(.48)	(.47)	(.46)	(.46)	(.40)	(.40)
Unemployment rate	6.34	6.14	6.12	6.64	5.97	6.07
	(2.16)	(2.18)	(2.20)	(3.20)	(2.71)	(2.53)
Nonresponse school items	.54	.51	.53	.47	.40	.49
	(.50)	(.50)	(.50)	(.50)	(.48)	(.50)
% Hispanic in school	3.18	2.89	2.77	31.82	28.13	35.13
	(8.86)	(8.53)	(7.88)	(32.60)	(33.87)	(35.39)
% black in school	6.31	5.63	5.68	4.11	3.23	2.84
	(12.77)	(11.75)	(11.45)	(9.71)	(9.17)	(6.76)

TABLE 5.1 (*Continued*)

	White			Mexican-American		
Variable	≤18 Years	>18 Years	HS Grad	≤18 Years	>18 Years	HS Grad
% dropout in school	11.04 (20.13)	8.28 (14.72)	7.90 (13.72)	13.16 (19.70)	9.98 (15.33)	11.69 (15.65)
Teacher–student ratio	.04 (.02)	.04 (0.03)	.04 (.03)	.03 (.03)	.03 (.03)	.04 (.03)
Public–private	.06 (.24)	.08 (.27)	.09 (.29)	.04 (.19)	.03 (.18)	.04 (.19)
Nonresponse transcript	.70 (.46)	.66 (.47)	.69 (.46)	.58 (.49)	.44 (.50)	.53 (.50)
ESL course	.002 (.05)	.00 (.05)	.00 (.04)	.04 (.19)	.03 (.16)	.02 (.15)
Bilingual education	.02 (.13)	.02 (.15)	.02 (.15)	.07 (.26)	.05 (.22)	.06 (.24)
N	3,465	2,280	1,871	587	296	173

Source: National Longitudinal Survey of Youth, 1979 (Borus et al., 1980).
Note: Standard deviations are in parentheses.

cation of this is that Mexican-Americans are about half a year older in a grade than whites (see the means for school delay in Table 5.1).

The background variables show that Mexican-Americans come from lower-status backgrounds: their parents have much less education than do whites, they come from much larger families, and respondent and both parents are much more likely to be foreign-born. The language measures also show large differences: for all three populations, a small percentage of whites (11–13%) spoke a foreign language as a child; the comparable figure for Mexican-Americans is over 90%. A small percentage (2%) of respondents who identified themselves as white elected to take the interview in Spanish; among Mexican-Americans the range was 3–5%. Since none of those who were interviewed in Spanish spoke English as their mother tongue, we can interpret these two variables as classifying respondents into three language types: Spanish monolinguals (those interviewed in Spanish), bilinguals (interviewed in English and reporting Spanish as the mother tongue), English monolinguals (interviewed in English and reporting English as the mother tongue). Following this interpretation in our sample, the Mexican-American population is largely bilingual, with relatively few at either monolingual extreme (see Skrabanek, 1970, and Garcia, 1980, and Nielsen and Fernandez, 1982, for supporting evidence).

The school and community variables show smaller differences between ethnic groups than do the background variables. Mexican-Americans are somewhat more urbanized than whites and tend to go to segregated schools and to schools with relatively high dropout rates. Not surprisingly, in light of their generally lower-status backgrounds, Mexican-Americans are less likely to attend private school.

Results for Those Aged 14–18

There are two dependent variables in these analyses: whether or not the respondent is enrolled in school, and school delay. We first consider the determinants of the school enrollment variable for each ethnic group, and then compare the models across groups. Finally, we examine the regressions for school delay and compare those results.

SCHOOL ENROLLMENT

For whites in the 14–18 age group, four of the nine family background measures significantly affect the likelihood of being in school (see Table 5.2), including both measures of parental education.[6] Those with more siblings are less likely to be in school, which implies that, other things being equal, respondents from large families are more likely to be drawn out of school in order to help support the family of origin. None of the nativity variables affects the likelihood of being in school, but respondents who were interviewed in Spanish are more likely to be out of school.[7] Two of the measures of school and social environment are significantly related to enrollment in school. One of these, whether or not the individual has a transcript, is of no theoretical interest; as expected, students with transcripts are more likely to be in school. The finding that whites from schools with a high percentage of blacks are less likely to be in school could reflect a number of factors—a poorer neighborhood, a more dangerous school setting, or a poorer-quality educational system.

---

[6] Because mother's and father's educations are highly correlated, multicollinearity could be a problem. In none of our samples is the correlation greater than .46. In analyses not presented here, we investigated the sensitivity of these estimates to the exclusion of one or the other parental education measure. The analyses confirmed that our results are not due to multicollinearity.

[7] Recall that ethnic identity is based on self-report in these data. A small number of respondents who identified themselves as white were interviewed in Spanish (see Table 5.1).

TABLE 5.2
Logit Regression Results for High School Attendance among Whites and Mexican-Americans Age 18 or Younger

Independent variable	Whites		Mexican-Americans	
	Background factors	Background, social, and community factors	Background factors	Background, social, and community factors
Father's education	.16**	.15**	.05	.08*
	(.02)	(.02)	(.03)	(.04)
Mother's education	.10**	.10**	.02	.01
	(.03)	(.03)	(.04)	(.04)
Sex	.07	.06	.05	.11
	(.12)	(.12)	(.24)	(.26)
Number of siblings	$-.11$**	$-.11$**	$-.14$**	$-.16$**
	(.02)	(.02)	(.04)	(.05)
Nativity	$-.27$	$-.17$	-1.65**	-1.81**
	(.43)	(.44)	(.38)	(.42)
Father's nativity	.10	.16	$-.29$	$-.32$
	(.42)	(.43)	(.37)	(.39)
Mother's nativity	.73	.84	1.24**	1.42**
	(.45)	(.46)	(.41)	(.43)
Language as child	$-.05$	$-.04$	.49	.58
	(.23)	(.23)	(.50)	(.54)
Spanish interview	$-.80$*	$-.75$*	-1.46**	-1.27*
	(.31)	(.32)	(.45)	(.52)
SMSA		$-.07$		-1.02**
		(.13)		(.34)
Unemployment rate		.04		$-.04$
		(.03)		(.04)
Nonresponse school items		.14		.75*
		(.16)		(.38)
% Hispanic in school		$-.01$		$-.01$*
		(.01)		(.006)
% black in school		$-.01$*		$-.04$**
		(.004)		(.01)
% dropout in school		$-.004$		.02
		(.003)		(.01)
Teacher–student ratio		3.90		4.14
		(2.92)		(8.57)
Public–private		.04		.30
		(.28)		(.73)

(Continued)

TABLE 5.2 (*Continued*)

Independent variable	Whites		Mexican-Americans	
	Background factors	Background, social, and community factors	Background factors	Background, social, and community factors
Nonresponse transcript		.51**		.69
		(.15)		(.35)
ESL course		−1.34		1.03
		(.99)		(.86)
Bilingual education		1.41		.63
		(.86)		(.72)
Constant	−.27	−.84	1.63	1.95
D^a	.06	.07	.12	.18
N		3,465		587

Source: National Longitudinal Survey of Youth, 1979 (Borus et al., 1980).
Note: Standard errors are in parentheses.
[a] The D statistic is a measure of goodness of fit, analogous to the R^2 statistic in OLS regression. It is bounded by zero and one (Harrell, 1980).
* Statistically significant at the 5% level.
** Statistically significant at the 1% level.

However, neither local economic conditions nor other school or curriculum measures influence high school attendance.

Looking at the results for Mexican-Americans in Table 5.2, the model containing only background variables shows that neither measure of parental education affects the likelihood of being in school. As is the case for whites, respondents with a greater number of siblings are less likely to be in school. This is evidence that young Mexican-Americans may be out of school because their families need additional income. Respondents born in Mexico are also less likely to be in school, although those whose mothers are foreign-born are more likely to be in school.[8] If the interview was conducted in Spanish, the respondent is less likely to be in school. In terms of our discussion above, this might be interpreted as a negative effect of Spanish monolingualism as compared to English monolingualism (the excluded category). The fact that the mother-tongue dummy variable is not significant means that bilinguals are just as likely to be in school as are English monolinguals.

---

[8] In all the analyses that follow, preliminary investigation has shown that the pattern of effects of the nativity variables is not due to multicollinearity.

With the addition of the school and social environment variables, three additional effects appear. Respondents who live in an SMSA are less likely to be in school. This variable may function as a proxy for living in a big city, where employment (albeit at low wages) is usually available. In addition, if students face poor employment prospects after high school graduation, there is little incentive for them to remain in school. (See the argument of Stinchcombe, 1964, regarding the effect of future labor market prospects on behavior in school.) Two school-related measures are significant: a large number of both blacks and Hispanics in the school is related to a lower likelihood of being in school. This is probably a reflection of school quality. Neither of the variables measuring whether or not a respondent was enrolled in a bilingual education or ESL course has a statistically significant effect on staying in school. This result is not surprising, in light of the fact that these programs are quite heterogeneous[9] (see Fligstein and Fernandez, 1982).

In summary, large families, Spanish-language dominance, foreign birth, urban environment, and lower-quality schools all operate to lessen the likelihood that the Mexican-American student will remain in school. The major differences between Mexican-Americans and whites have to do with parental education and nativity. Mexican-American students with highly educated or foreign-born mothers are more likely to be enrolled in school, though the respondent's foreign birth is related to *not* being in school. For whites, both mother's and father's education affect the probability of being in school, while none of the nativity variables affects school attendance. These differences show that being an immigrant lowers Mexican-American school attendance but has no effect for whites. Furthermore, mothers play important roles in the socialization process for Mexican-Americans, as indicated by the effects of mother's nativity and education.

SCHOOL DELAY

The equation predicting school delay for whites 18 and under shows results similar to those predicting school enrollment, although some differences are apparent. In the regression analyses, a negative coeffi-

---

[9] For two reasons, we chose not to combine these measures into one measure that one might call "additional language training." First, ESL and bilingual education programs have quite different goals. Second, being in an ESL course tends to be negatively associated with school outcomes, while bilingual education has positive effects, although both are statistically insignificant. Combining the measures would only introduce greater heterogeneity.

cient indicates less delay and a positive coefficient indicates more delay (see Table 5.3). Education of both parents significantly affects school delay: the more education the parents have, the less delay the student experiences. Male respondents are older in grade on average, as are respondents from large families. For whites, being born in a foreign country increases the probability of being older in grade.

TABLE 5.3
OLS Regression Results for School Delay among Whites and Mexican-Americans Age 18 or Younger

Independent variable	Whites		Mexican-Americans	
	Background factors	Background, social, and community factors	Background factors	Background, social, and community factors
Father's education	−.02**	−.01**	−.02	−.02
	(.004)	(.004)	(.01)	(.01)
Mother's education	−.04**	−.033**	−.02	−.01
	(.006)	(.006)	(.01)	(.01)
Sex	.19**	.18**	.17*	.16*
	(.02)	(.02)	(.08)	(.07)
Number of siblings	.03**	.03**	.06**	.06**
	(.006)	(.006)	(.015)	(.02)
Nativity	.18*	.17*	.66**	.69**
	(.08)	(.08)	(.11)	(.11)
Father's nativity	−.06	−.05	.04	.04
	(.07)	(.07)	(.11)	(.11)
Mother's nativity	.02	.02	−.23*	−.19
	(.07)	(.07)	(.10)	(.11)
Language as child	.04	.04	.13	.13
	(.05)	(.05)	(.15)	(.15)
Spanish interview	.15	.13	.23	.23
	(.08)	(.08)	(.19)	(.19)
SMSA		−.06*		−.26**
		(.03)		(.09)
Unemployment rate		−.006		−.06**
		(.006)		(.01)
Nonresponse school items		.009		.03
		(.03)		(.10)
% Hispanic in school		−.001		.000
		(.001)		(.001)

TABLE 5.3 (*Continued*)

Independent variable	Whites		Mexican-Americans	
	Background factors	Background, social, and community factors	Background factors	Background, social, and community factors
% black in school		.000		.002
		(.001)		(.004)
% dropout in school		.002**		−.002
		(.001)		(.002)
Teacher–student ratio		−1.31*		−.15
		(.54)		(2.20)
Public–private		−.02		−.42*
		(.05)		(.19)
Nonresponse transcript		−.05		−.20
		(.03)		(.10)
ESL course		.28		−.34
		(.22)		(.23)
Bilingual education		−.14		.21
		(.10)		(.17)
Constant	.89	.98	.62	1.25
R^2	.07	.08	.20	.26
N		3,439		580

Source: National Longitudinal Survey of Youth, 1979 (Borus et al., 1980).
Notes: Negative coefficients indicate less delay. Standard errors are in parentheses.
* Statistically significant at the 5% level.
** Statistically significant at the 1% level.

When the school and social environment variables are added, three additional effects appear. Respondents in SMSAs are less delayed, implying that rural schools hold students back more frequently. Two interesting school effects clearly reflect school quality and school strategy. A respondent in a school with a high dropout rate is more likely to be older in grade, which could indicate that those schools use grade retention more frequently and therefore have more discouraged students, who later drop out. There is also a statistically significant effect of the teacher–student ratio; students who attend schools with more teachers per student are less likely to be delayed. Presumably teachers in these schools are able to spend more time with students individually, and students are therefore less likely to fail.

The school-delay regression for Mexican-Americans is similar to the one predicting school enrollment. Those in large families and those of foreign birth are older in grade, and those whose mothers are foreign-born are less likely to be delayed. Variables related to mothers exert effects throughout the Mexican-American equations: mother's education and mother's nativity are strong determinants of children's educational attainment. One difference between the model for school attendance and the model for delay is apparent: young men are more likely than young women to experience school delay.

Among the variables measuring school and social environment, three effects are statistically significant. Respondents who live in an SMSA are less likely to experience school delay. A high unemployment rate is related to less school delay, implying that Mexican-American students may be trading off schooling for work, leaving school when work is available. Mexican-Americans in private schools are less delayed than those in public schools. Whether this is due to self-selection of better students into private schools or to differences in school policies cannot be determined here.

Three conclusions are evident. First, parental education tends to lower school delay for whites, but has little effect for Mexican-Americans. This suggests that school delay for Mexican-Americans is not directly related to socioeconomic background; it may instead reflect other influences—perhaps the school policies emphasized by Carter and Segura (1979). Second, non-U.S. origin is strongly related to delay for Mexican-Americans: being foreign-born increases school delay for Mexican-Americans by almost half a year. Finally, among Mexican-Americans, foreign-born mothers have children who are delayed less in their progress through school. This is consistent with the results for school attendance that show mothers to be important in the educational process of Mexican-Americans.

Results for Those Aged 19–22

Tables 5.4 and 5.5 present models of high school completion and school delay for the older age group.

HIGH SCHOOL COMPLETION

In the equation containing only the background variables (see Table 5.4), for whites we find that the largest effects are those of parental

TABLE 5.4
**Logit Regression Results for High School Completion among Whites
and Mexican-Americans Age 19-22**

Independent variable	Whites		Mexican-Americans	
	Background factors	Background, social, and community factors	Background factors	Background, social, and community factors
Father's education	.15**	.14**	.03	.02
	(.02)	(.02)	(.04)	(.04)
Mother's education	.24**	.23**	.10*	.12*
	(.03)	(.03)	(.04)	(.05)
Sex	−.34**	−.37**	−.02	−.05
	(.12)	(.13)	(.27)	(.29)
Number of siblings	−.14**	−.13**	−.13**	−.15**
	(.03)	(.03)	(.05)	(.06)
Nativity	.38	.47	−1.75**	−1.51**
	(.48)	(.51)	(.42)	(.47)
Father's nativity	1.54**	1.54**	.16	.00
	(.47)	(.49)	(.40)	(.43)
Mother's nativity	−.33	−.16	.57	.41
	(.39)	(.41)	(.41)	(.43)
Language as child	.13	.11	.42	.40
	(.22)	(.22)	(.60)	(.63)
Spanish interview	−.63	−.67	−.23	.36
	(.39)	(.40)	(.60)	(.68)
SMSA		.07		.48
		(.14)		(.39)
Unemployment rate		.02		.04
		(.03)		(.06)
Nonresponse school items		.21		.34
		(.16)		(.41)
% Hispanic in school		−.02*		.014*
		(.006)		(.006)
% black in school		−.001		−.02
		(.005)		(.02)
% dropout in school		.01**		.002
		(.004)		(.01)
Teacher–student ratio		9.67**		−7.17
		(2.91)		(9.21)
Public–private		1.94**		.16
		(.53)		(.88)

(*Continued*)

TABLE 5.4 (*Continued*)

Independent variable	Whites		Mexican-Americans	
	Background factors	Background, social, and community factors	Background factors	Background, social, and community factors
Nonresponse transcript		.30		.69
		(.16)		(.39)
ESL course		−1.37		.06
		(1.27)		(.93)
Bilingual education		.75		1.28
		(.74)		(.84)
Constant	−2.17	−2.69	−.06	−1.25
D^b	.13	.15	.20	.26
N		2,280		296

Source: National Longitudinal Survey of Youth, 1979 (Borus et al., 1980).
Note: Standard errors are in parentheses.
[a] The *D* statistic is a measure of goodness of fit, analogous to the R^2 statistic in OLS regression. It is bounded by zero and one (Harrell, 1980).
* Statistically significant at the 5% level.
** Statistically significant at the 1% level.

education. This result accords with the literature reviewed above indicating that parents' education is a key determinant of children's education. Young men are less likely to complete high school than young women, which could reflect their greater opportunities in the labor market. Respondents from larger families (measured by number of siblings) are also less likely to finish high school, suggesting the importance of family obligations on school continuation decisions. Four of the school variables bear a statistically significant relation to finishing high school. Respondents in schools with a high percentage of Hispanics or schools with high dropout rates tend to finish high school less often. This could reflect school quality, social environment, or a number of other factors. A higher teacher–student ratio positively affects the probability of high school completion. Finally, if other factors are controlled, attending a private school significantly increases one's chances of high school completion. Our data do not permit us to determine whether this is due to selection into private schools of students who are less likely to drop out or to aspects of the school environment that encouraged high achievement.

In the results for Mexican-Americans, we see from the equation with only the background variables that mother's education significantly increases the likelihood of high school completion, whereas father's education does not. As we have noted above, this suggests that Mexican-American mothers play a key role in their children's educational outcomes. The more siblings a respondent has, the less likely he or she is to complete school. Finally, persons of foreign birth finish high school less frequently. Neither of the language measures affects high school completion—that is, English monolinguals are no more likely to finish high school than either bilinguals or Spanish monolinguals. When the school and social environment variables are added, only the percentage of Hispanics in the school affects high school completion to a statistically significant degree. Mexican-Americans in Hispanic schools tend to complete high school more frequently. This could imply that a Mexican-American student culture aids high school completion.

When we compare whites and Mexican-Americans, we find that in general the background variables are more powerful predictors of high school completion for whites. Both parents' education strongly affects high school completion for whites, while only the mother's education does so for Mexican-Americans. White males are much less likely to complete high school than white females, whereas Mexican-American females and males are equally likely to do so. Being in a Hispanic high school aids school completion for Mexican-Americans and deters it for whites. Also, foreign-born Mexican-Americans are much less likely to finish high school than are whites of foreign birth. Taken together, these results show that, for whites, high school completion is highly related to parental education and the respondent's sex, while for Mexican-Americans high school completion is determined mostly by their mother's education and their own nativity.

SCHOOL DELAY

For whites who are older than 18, determinants of school delay are similar to those preventing high school completion (see Table 5.5). In the equation with only background characteristics, parental education is associated with less school delay, and males are more likely to be delayed than females. Respondents from large families experience more school delay. One anomalous result in this table concerns those whites who were interviewed in Spanish: they are more likely to have been delayed in their progress through school. Only 2% of the white sample was in this category, so this coefficient should be interpreted cautiously.

TABLE 5.5
OLS Regression Results for School Delay among Whites and Mexican-Americans Age 19–22

Independent variable	Whites		Mexican-Americans	
	Background factors	Background, social, and community factors	Background factors	Background, social, and community factors
Father's education	−.01*	−.01	−.03	−.02
	(.007)	(.007)	(.02)	(.02)
Mother's education	−.04**	−.04**	.008	.008
	(.01)	(.01)	(.02)	(.024)
Sex	.24**	.24**	.35*	.35*
	(.04)	(.04)	(.15)	(.15)
Number of siblings	.04**	.04**	.10**	.10**
	(.01)	(.01)	(.03)	(.03)
Nativity	.05	.05	.53*	.46
	(.15)	(.15)	(.22)	(.24)
Father's nativity	−.19	−.18	.13	.19
	(.13)	(.13)	(.22)	(.23)
Mother's nativity	.20	.17	−.23	−.11
	(.13)	(.13)	(.21)	(.22)
Language as child	−.04	−.06	.01	−.02
	(.07)	(.07)	(.32)	(.33)
Spanish interview	.39*	.37*	.55	.44
	(.16)	(.16)	(.30)	(.32)
SMSA		−.01		−.33
		(.05)		(.20)
Unemployment rate		−.01		−.02
		(.01)		(.03)
Nonresponse school items		−.09		.19
		(.05)		(.21)
% Hispanic in school		.007**		−.002
		(.002)		(.003)
% black in school		.001		−.001
		(.001)		(.009)
% dropout in school		.001		−.005
		(.001)		(.006)
Teacher–student ratio		−.03		1.55
		(.82)		(4.86)
Public–private		−.01		−.33
		(.08)		(.42)

TABLE 5.5 (*Continued*)

Independent variable	Whites		Mexican-Americans	
	Background factors	Background, social, and community factors	Background factors	Background, social, and community factors
Nonresponse transcript		.05		−.26
		(.05)		(.20)
ESL course		.28		.44
		(.46)		(.50)
Bilingual education		−.11		−.38
		(.15)		(.38)
Constant	1.06	1.16	.41	.85
R^2	.04	.05	.17	.20
N		2,239		287

Source: National Longitudinal Survey of Youth, 1979 (Borus et al., 1980).
Notes: Negative coefficients indicate less delay. Standard errors are in parentheses.
* Statistically significant at the 5% level.
** Statistically significant at the 1% level.

Only one additional effect appears in the equation with the school and social environment variables. Respondents who attended a school with a high percentage of Hispanics were more likely to have experienced grade delay. This could reflect school quality, but it also could be tapping school policy. If the literature on school delay for Hispanics is correct, then schools with Hispanic concentrations may more frequently use grade delay as a policy (see Carter and Segura, 1979).

Only two background variables affect the school delay of Mexican-Americans over age 18: sex of respondent, and number of siblings. Respondents who are male or who come from a large family are more likely to have been delayed in school. Again, the language variables do not affect school delay. None of the school and social environment or curriculum variables has statistically significant effects on high school completion.

Here too, the most interesting difference between groups is that parental education is highly related to school delay for whites, and less so for Mexican-Americans. The lower mean and greater variance of Mexican-American parental educational attainment is perhaps one reason that there is no relationship between delay and parental educational attainment. The school policies that have been alleged to be the major

cause of Chicano school delay (Carter and Segura, 1979) might be another reason. The much smaller R^2's for delay among whites in both age
populations indicate that being delayed is a much more random process
for whites than it is for Mexican-Americans, despite the fact that Chicanos are much more frequently kept back and have much more variance
than do whites (see Table 5.1). Apparently, even without the measures
of school policy that Carter and Segura (1979) emphasize, our model is
much more efficacious for Mexican-Americans than for whites.

Results for High School Graduates

The final set of equations concerns the determinants of college attendance, given that the respondent finished high school (see Table 5.6).
These models are misspecified insofar as parental income is left out of
the equation. Since college costs money, this omission raises problems.[10]

TABLE 5.6
Logit Regression Results for College Attendance by White and Mexican-American
High School Graduates

Independent variable	Whites		Mexican-Americans	
	Background factors	Background, social, and community factors	Background factors	Background, social, and community factors
Father's education	.19**	.18**	−.05	−.06
	(.02)	(.02)	(.05)	(.06)
Mother's education	.18**	.17**	.16**	.17**
	(.03)	(.03)	(.06)	(.06)
Sex	−.02	−.01	−.32	−.49
	(.10)	(.11)	(.36)	(.38)
Number of siblings	−.12**	−.12**	−.06	−.04
	(.03)	(.03)	(.08)	(.09)
Nativity	.23	.29	−.96	−.62
	(.40)	(.41)	(.62)	(.73)
Father's nativity	1.08**	1.05**	.53	.45
	(.35)	(.35)	(.54)	(.58)
Mother's nativity	.78**	.72**	1.39**	1.27*
	(.36)	(.36)	(.53)	(.59)

[10] A measure of parental income was included in the NLS, but, since 60% of the population has missing data, we excluded the variable from our analysis.

TABLE 5.6 (*Continued*)

Independent variable	Whites		Mexican-Americans	
	Background factors	Background, social, and community factors	Background factors	Background, social, and community factors
Language as child	.16	.12	−.48	−.58
	(.18)	(.18)	(.75)	(.79)
Spanish interview	.23	.18	−1.12	−1.23
	(.41)	(.42)	(.91)	(.96)
SMSA		.18		.78
		(.12)		(.49)
Unemployment rate		−.04		.12
		(.03)		(.08)
Nonresponse school items		.09		−1.24*
		(.13)		(.55)
% Hispanic in school		.014		−.001
		(.007)		(.007)
% black in school		.002		−.06
		(.004)		(.03)
% dropout in school		.00		.03
		(.004)		(.02)
Teacher–student ratio		.53		12.65
		(2.12)		(12.64)
Public–private		.97**		.28
		(.21)		(1.23)
Nonresponse transcript		.11		.13
		(.13)		(.46)
ESL course		−.32		−2.66
		(1.47)		(1.45)
Bilingual education		.13		.45
		(.34)		(.97)
Constant	−3.96	−3.85	.21	−1.06
D^a	.16	.17	.12	.19
N		1,871		173

Source: National Longitudinal Survey of Youth, 1979 (Borus et al., 1980).
Note: Standard errors are in parentheses.
* Statistically significant at the 5% level.
** Statistically significant at the 1% level.
[a] The D statistic is a measure of goodness of fit, analogous to the R^2 statistic in OLS regression. It is bounded by zero and one (Harrell, 1980).

The equation with only the background variables for whites shows that both measures of parental education positively affect the likelihood of college attendance. Respondents from larger families are less likely to attend college. (Note that this variable could proxy for the family's ability to pay for college.) Two interesting effects emerge concerning nativity. If either parent was born in a foreign country, the respondent is more likely to attend college. This may be due to immigrants' high levels of motivation (Chiswick, 1978a; Nielsen and Fernandez, 1982; Fernandez and Nielsen, 1983). Only one of the variables concerning school and social environment significantly affects college attendance: if one attends a private school, one is more likely to go to college. This result may reflect the greater affluence of whites who are able to send their children to private schools. Since we do not have a family-income measure, it is difficult to evaluate this effect.

For Mexican-Americans who attend college, only two family background variables affect college attendance: mother's education and mother's nativity. Mexican-Americans with immigrant mothers are more likely to go to college, while the higher the mother's educational attainment, the more likely the respondent is to attend college. When the measures of school and social environment are added, only the dummy variable for the school data significantly influences the likelihood of college attendance.[11]

The major differences across groups for the college equations are the lack of effect of certain variables for Mexican-Americans and the importance of those variables for whites, and the fact that mothers appear to be more important for Mexican-American college attendance, whereas both parents are important to whites.

Summary and Conclusion

How do the educational attainment processes of whites and Mexican-Americans compare? Among whites, the general factor of family background appears to be the major determinant of educational attainment. In particular, parental education and number of siblings significantly affect staying in school, graduating from high school, and attending college. Parents' education to some degree is replicated in their children. Parental nativity also exerts interesting effects. Respondents with foreign-born fathers tend to finish high school more frequently, and those

[11] This measure implies that those with school data were less likely to attend college. Obviously, this is not a substantively interesting result.

with either parent foreign-born enter college more frequently. There also are some school effects on educational attainment of whites. Higher teacher–student ratios reduce school delay and increase high school completion, while respondents in private schools tend to complete school more frequently and attend college more often. Finally, whites stay in school a shorter time and are less likely to finish high school when blacks and Hispanics are present, effects that are probably due to the generally inferior quality of black and Hispanic schools (Coleman et al., 1966; National Center for Education Statistics, 1980).

For Mexican-Americans, general family background factors are also important—family size and parental education, particularly mother's education, are related to school attendance and (negatively) to delay. Among the background variables that we expected could disproportionately affect Mexican-Americans—migration history and language type—only migration history is consistently related to high school and college attendance and to delay in high school.[12] Foreign-born respondents are less likely to be in school and more likely to have been delayed. However, having a foreign-born mother seems to have salutary effects on the respondent's educational attainment. This fact, combined with the importance of mother's education, is evidence that mothers play a critical role in Mexican-American socialization.

When we consider variables measuring the school and social environment, no patterns emerge. The curriculum measures show that those students who at some time were enrolled in ESL or bilingual education courses perform no differently from those never enrolled in such courses. This result is probably due to two problems in our data: (1) the large numbers of missing values on the curriculum variables; and (2) the coarseness of the measures. We do not know what type of bilingual education program the students were enrolled in, the length of the program, or its quality.

It is clear that high school completion is a major barrier to Mexican-American school attainment. Those who do graduate from high school

[12] The fact that language type does not appear as a consistent predictor may be due to the distribution of the language variables. By the criteria listed above, roughly 6–7% of these populations are English monolingual, 3–5% are Spanish monolingual, and the vast majority (87–90%) are bilingual. Though this distribution may make it difficult to identify any effects of language type, it is consistent with other studies (Skrabanek, 1970; Nielsen and Fernandez, 1982) that show somewhat similar distributions, albeit not as small at the monolingual extremes. It is worth noting that the one language effect for Mexican-Americans (i.e., the negative effect of Spanish monolingualism in the population under 18 years of age) is not in conflict with those studies that show positive language effects (Peal and Lambert, 1962; Fernandez and Nielsen, 1983) since the positive results come from studies comparing *bilinguals* with English monolinguals.

go on to college at higher rates than do whites, despite their lower socioeconomic origins. From these analyses, the effects of particular educational policies (as measured by the school and curriculum measures) on the scholastic performance of Mexican-Americans are equivocal. Segregation appears to hurt Mexican-Americans, but little else seems to matter. Most important in explaining the failure of so many Mexican-Americans to complete high school are the general family background factors of low parental education and large family size. Factors more specific to the Mexican-American experience in the United States—language patterns and migration history—also appear to affect Mexican-American educational attainments. There is some evidence that Spanish monolingualism is a hindrance to Mexican-American school achievement, and foreign birth appears to have educational costs. However, while it is important to understand the costs that Mexican-Americans pay, it should be emphasized that they do not suffer from a simple lack of cultural assimilation, for another fact of Mexican-American culture appears as a benefit—that is, mothers who are foreign-born seem to instill higher levels of motivation that lead to better academic achievement.

Although our results are tentative, it is possible to make a number of policy recommendations. First, it is necessary to study the effects of language and language programs (i.e., ESL and bilingual education) on actual school completion. This kind of study should also focus on the quality of various programs and the factors that make programs work. Second, measures to increase educational attainment for Mexican-Americans should focus on high schools because the high rate of noncompletion at that level is at the heart of the problem. The most promising programs seem to be those oriented toward reducing school delay, increasing the numbers of teachers, and generally making it easier for non-English speakers and recent immigrants to adjust. Finally, programs should be set up to aid the transitions of recent immigrants. Even though immigrant mothers appear to influence their children's educational attainments positively, respondents who are recent immigrants (both Mexican-American and white) appear to have difficulties completing high school.

CHAPTER 6

Labor Market Turnover and Joblessness for Hispanic Youth*

Stanley P. Stephenson, Jr.

Introduction

This chapter analyzes the determinants of joblessness of Hispanic American youth using national panel data and focusing on the rates of entering and leaving work and nonwork. A main issue is to estimate how individual and labor market characteristics affect the labor turnover rates of Hispanic youths. For instance, education and skill training for individuals are at the heart of several federal policies to reduce joblessness by improving labor supply, whereas tighter aggregate labor market conditions are associated with efforts to reduce youth joblessness by focusing on labor demand (i.e., maintaining strong aggregate demand for workers primarily by monetary and fiscal policies). Low family income and age have also been used as factors in "targeting" federal employment funds. Because many young Hispanics—Mexicans and Puerto Ricans in particular—drop out of school to enter the labor market, it is relevant to explore their experiences with unemployment, for this may provide insight into the high unemployment rates among adult Hispanics.

Study of jobless experiences among Hispanic youths using a turnover model is in keeping with several other recent studies of youth labor markets. Leighton and Mincer (1979), Flinn and Heckman (1980), Heckman and Borjas (1980), and Stephenson (1982) each used a turnover analysis approach to examine the determinants of high rates of youth joblessness and short periods of job tenure. Each of these studies ex-

* I am grateful for comments from Orley Ashenfelter, Robert Mare, and Finis Welch, and for the computational assistance of Chris Sachsteder and David MacPherson.

tends to youth labor markets the turnover hypothesis of unemployment. All assume that understanding the relatively high rates of youth joblessness begins with examining the determinants of the rates of entering and leaving spells of work and nonwork. This line of thinking can be traced to the work of Hall (1972), and, more recently, Clark and Summers (1979).

The use of maximum likelihood methods to study the determinants of labor market spell durations is especially appropriate because individual labor market duration data are frequently censored (i.e., truncated because some spells are still in process at the time of the interview) and thus cannot be properly studied with standard regression techniques. Advantages of this approach are apparent in several recent empirical papers dealing with unemployment duration—Lancaster (1979), Lancaster and Nickell (1980), Tuma and Robins (1980), and Burdett et al. (1981). This chapter also uses a maximum likelihood approach to estimate parameters in several models of determinants of exit rates from work and nonwork, using continuous time, individual data.

I will first consider several theoretical issues, and then present two different empirical models: a constant hazard rate model, and a model that allows for time dependence. The data are then described. The next section considers empirical results for each model. The final section summarizes some implications of the research for labor policy directed toward Hispanic youth, even though the results are more illustrative than definitive in view of the small sample size and the limitations of the data.

Theoretical Issues

The purpose of this section is to provide a theoretical framework for the empirical analysis. I consider job finding and job leaving in a stationary world, and briefly discuss nonstationary implications. The discussion focuses on the single individual and assumes a two-state environment in which the individual either works or searches for work.

JOB FINDING

Simple job search models have been offered as a foundation for the recent empirical studies of unemployment duration by Lancaster (1979), Flinn and Heckman (1980), Bjorklund and Holmlund (1981). I begin with a similar model. (Readers more interested in the model specification than its derivation may prefer to skip to the empirical Equations 10, 11, and 12.)

Assume that an income-maximizing individual, who is not working, searches for work and receives job offers that are sorted into acceptable and nonacceptable offers. Job offers arrive as a random process, which I assume to be described by a Poisson process with parameter h, or $h(t)$, $t > 0$. Let $h(t)dt$ be the probability of a job offer in a short interval, $(t, t + dt)$, and let $F(w)$ be a known distribution of wage offers. I assume that accepted jobs last forever and that job offers cannot be hoarded (i.e., a once-refused job offer cannot be later accepted, and workers live essentially forever). The key behavioral decision by the searcher is the determination of a reservation wage w^* at time t, because a choice sequence of $w^*(t)$ leads to a sequence of transition probabilities which may be interpreted as job-finding probabilities.[1] The transition probability μ in a short interval $(t, t + dt)$ equals the product of two components $h(t)$, the job-offer probability in that interval, and $[1 - F(w^*(t))]$, the acceptance probability, or

$$\mu = [1 - F(w^*(t))]h(t)dt. \tag{1}$$

A function Θ, called the hazard, or failure rate, is the limiting value of μ as $dt \to 0$. This limiting value provides a linkage between individual search policy and observed durations of spells of unemployment.

Let $G(t)$ be the probability of job finding by an unemployed person at any time before t. Thus, $1 - G(t)$, often called the survivor function, is the probability that a person who began an unemployment spell at a time t remains unemployed until time $t + dt$. I express the relationship between μ and Θ as follows:

$$\Theta(t) = \lim_{dt \to 0} \mu(t, t + dt)/dt$$

$$\Theta t = \lim_{dt \to 0} \Pr(\text{at job at } t + dt \mid \text{unemployed at } t)/dt \tag{2}$$

Equation (2) can be expressed in terms of the survivor function, $1 - G(t)$, and $g(t)$, an associated density function,

$$\Theta(t) = g(t)dt/1 - G(t), \tag{3}$$

and, on integration,

$$1 - G(t) = \exp\left[-\int_s^t \Theta(u)du\right]. \tag{4}$$

Equation (4) is the fundamental relation connecting a search policy

[1] If $w^* < w$, the market wage offer, the job is accepted and search stops.

with unemployment duration; more specifically, Equation (4) relates the sequence of job-finding probabilities associated with choice of $w^*(t)$ to the distribution of unemployment duration (Lancaster, 1979, pp. 940–941). If transition rates are constant over time, a product of the stationary search model (Flinn and Heckman, 1980, p. 7), then

$$1 - G(t) = \exp[-\Theta u] \tag{5}$$

where u, $u = t - s$, is the duration time in the state.

Furthermore, as is well known, the assumed exponential distribution of search times, u, means that the expected duration of nonwork, D, can be written as the reciprocal of the hazard rate, or

$$D = 1/\Theta$$

or

$$D = 1/\lim_{dt \to 0} [1 - F(w^*(t))] \cdot h(t)dt. \tag{6}$$

An optimal search policy, if one assumes an infinite time horizon and a discount rate, r, involves solving for a reservation wage in the familiar expression (see Lippman and McCall, 1976b),

$$c + w^* = (\lambda/r) \int_{w^*}^{\infty} (w - w^*)f(w)dw, \tag{7}$$

where c is the instantaneous (and constant) search cost and $f(w)$ is the known distribution of wage offers. If $w^* < w$, search stops and the offer is accepted. Equation (7) suggests that the searcher should select that w^* that will equate expected marginal costs and marginal revenue from continued search. This is a stationary search process even though w^* may change as other values in (7) change.

A decline in w^* can arise via a leftward shift in the wage offer distribution, an increase in the cost of search, c, a decline in the rate of arrival of job offers, h, or an increase in the discount rate r. Associated with these effects, as Flinn and Heckman have noted (1980, p. 7), are hazard rate changes. The hazard rate $\Theta(t)$ will increase with a rise in search costs, an increase in the discount rate, or a leftward shift in the distribution of wage offers, which means that each of these three effects, other things equal, would reduce expected nonwork duration D.

An increase in h, the rate of job offers, ceteris paribus, would produce two effects of different sign: (1) an increase in D via an increase in w^*, and (2) a decrease in D via an increase in Θ, the instantaneous transition rate. Which effect of an increase in h dominates D cannot be determined a priori. Feinberg (1977), however, notes that the second effect dominates in normal and rectangular wage-offer distributions.

These theoretical issues can be linked to the main analytical point, training versus aggregate demand policy as strategies to enhance job finding for Hispanic youth. I expect a reduction in the local unemployment rate to increase the job-offer arrival rate. This effect on expected nonwork durations is, however, ambiguous, for reasons just stated. More training would also increase the rate of job offers, but I also expect more training to operate as a rightward shift in the job-offer distribution. If w^* did not increase enough to offset this distribution shift, then I would expect that the net effect of greater training would be to reduce nonwork duration. Which effect, training or greater labor demand, would have the greater impact on reducing D is an empirical issue.

JOB LEAVING

In the job-finding discussion, I built on recent developments in job search models used to examine unemployment arising from turnover. To model the rate of leaving a job is more complicated. On the one hand, one might consider a search model of an employed worker similar to the job-finding model in that a currently employed individual would be assumed to compare the best rewards from alternative time uses, w^*, versus keeping a current wage w. Yet such a model has an extra complication; one has to consider the potential actions of both the worker and the current employer in terms of changing the effective rules regarding the quantity or quality of work as well as wage adjustments (Okun, 1981, Chapter 2). To develop such a general model is beyond the scope of the present chapter. On the other hand, more formal presentations, such as that of Flinn and Heckman (1980, pp. 27–30) or Burdett and associates (1981)—papers that utilize dynamic programming methods to derive instantaneous utility-maximization rules for leaving a job—are somewhat disappointing in terms of predictive content. That is, according to Flinn and Heckman (1980, p. 30), if one continues to assume time-stationary value functions, then the hazard function associated with job leaving is independent of time spent at the job! This seems a stiff price to pay in order to achieve a tractable model, but to drop the stationarity assumption sharply undermines one's ability to derive testable propositions.

A reasonable alternative is to estimate the rate of job leaving in an empirical model that is based loosely on economic theory and to test for the presence or not of time dependence, among other determinants. Past research indicates that greater wage rates are associated with a reduced rate of job leaving. Hispanic youths with relatively more work experience, education, and skill training, variables that may be closely associated with a relatively greater market wage, should have a lower rate of job leaving than other Hispanics in the same age group. Past research identified several demographic characteristics and past work efforts that affect the rate of job leaving. For instance, if the individual worker's earnings are relatively important to a family, as might be the case in a low-income family, then one would expect job-leaving rates to be relatively low. Being married, greater fluency in English, older youth, and a more stable past work history, all may reduce the rate of job leaving.

Furthermore, job separations should be affected by several aspects of the labor market. I hypothesize that the rate of job leaving will be affected by the overall tightness of the labor market, although the nature of the effect is unclear, a priori. During an economic downturn, layoffs increase, but voluntary quits presumably will decrease. In geographic areas where market and nonmarket alternatives are relatively numerous, such as a large urban area, one would expect job separations to exceed that for persons from rural areas.

As for the effect of job tenure on the rate of job leaving, the frequent observation (e.g., Leighton and Mincer, 1979) is that persons with relatively more time on the job will have a reduced rate of job leaving. Jovanovich (1979), however, presents a theoretical model of worker and firm sorting in which the separation probability at first rises during the early tenure period and then begins to decline with more and more time on the job. This time-dependence effect is tested below.

Empirical Models of Labor Turnover

In this section I present the basic stochastic model used to study the determinants of early postschool labor mobility. (The Basic Model description closely follows that in Stephenson, 1982.) I assume, following Heckman and Borjas (1980), Robins et al. (1980), and Tuma and Robins (1980), who have presented similar labor turnover models, that the individual is in one of two states at any time, employed or not employed.

THE BASIC MODEL

I begin by describing an individual's work history in some total observation period $(0, T)$. Within this overall time period, one may consider an infinite number of smaller time periods and record the individual's employment state, employed or not employed, in each interval. A spell is a continuous period of time in a state. I consider persons in state i at time t and ask what is the probability that they are in state j at some later time $t + \Delta t$. I assume stochastic movement over time from one state to another. Specifically, I assume a standard first-order, finite state, continuous-time Markov process generates the distribution of state outcomes over time. The probability that a worker who is in state i at time t then switches to state j at a later time $t + \Delta t$, is the transition probability $p_{ij}(t, t + \Delta t)$. The transition rate, $\Theta_{ij}(t)$, is thus defined as

$$\Theta_{ij}(t) = \lim_{\Delta t \to 0} \Pr \text{ (in state } j \text{ at } t + \Delta t \mid \text{in state } i \text{ at } t)/\Delta t$$

$$= \lim_{\Delta t \to 0} p_{ij}(t, t + \Delta t)/\Delta t, \tag{8}$$

where $i \neq j$. The rate of leaving one state $\Theta_i(t)$ is the rate of entering the second state j. The denominator in Equation (8), the probability of remaining in state i until time t, is really $1 - G_i(t)$, where $G_i(t)$ is the probability of leaving state i at any time t. The term $1 - G_i(t)$ is called a survivor function when it gives the probability that a person in state i remains in that state between a start time s and time t. As noted in Equation (5), if the transition rates are time dependent, then the survivor function is expressed as

$$1 - G_i(t) = e^{-\Theta u}, \tag{9}$$

where $u = t - s$. A key assumption is that wait time is exponentially distributed, a standard assumption in survival analysis.

I also assume that the same Θ_{ij} exists only for persons of the same values of an observable, fixed, exogenous vector of X variables. I assume a log-linear relationship between Θ_{ij} and X, or

$$\ln \Theta_{ij} = X\beta_{ij}, \tag{10}$$

I then use the estimated β_{ij} to derive individual Θ_{ij}. The log-linear transformation restricts the Θ_{ij} to be positive.

ALTERNATIVE MODELS

Two alternative model parameters are estimated in this chapter for Hispanic-American youth. (This section is similar to that in Tuma, 1979.) It is instructive to present and briefly describe each model.

Model	Description	
1: $\Theta_{jk}(t) = e^{(\beta_{jk}X)}$	This is the time-independence (time-invariant) model just presented as the Basic Model. Transition rates, Θ_{jk}, are postulated to be log-linear functions of the observed variable vector, X.	(11)
2: $\Theta_{jk}(t) = e^{(\beta_{jk}X+\gamma t)}$	This is a time-dependent model which postulates that transition rates decline exponentially over time until some asymptote is reached. I assume a zero asymptote and that the e_{jk} are the same in each period, but time in a spell does alter exit rates.	(12)

ESTIMATION

I estimate the β_{ij} by a maximum likelihood method and data on observed spell length. Let Y_i be the observed duration of the ith spell. A spell ends when a state change takes place within the reference period or at the end of the sample reference period, in either case $Y_i = 1$; otherwise let $Y_i = 0$. In this two-state case, if I assume time-independent transition rates and independence of observed spells, then the likelihood function for leaving the nonwork state j is

$$L_j = \prod_{i=1}^{n} f_j(u_i \mid \beta_{ij}, X_i)^{Y_i} \cdot (1 - F_j[u_i \mid \beta_{ij}, X_i])^{1-Y_i}, \qquad (13)$$

where n is the observed number of spells in state j. Maximizing with respect to β_{ij} gives maximum likelihood estimates of β_{ij}. With these β_{ij} one can predict individual specific transition rates. In turn, these transition rates can be used to derive various estimates of Hispanic-American youth labor mobility, such as the expected work duration, the expected nonwork duration, and the steady-state employment probability. (See Tuma and Robins, 1980, concerning the mathematical derivations of these outcome measures.)

Data

The primary data sources of this study are the first two waves of the National Longitudinal Survey of Youth (NLS-Youth), which were collected in 1979 and 1980 by the National Opinion Research Center (NORC) in cooperation with the Center for Human Resources Research at Ohio State University (Borus et al., 1980). These data are particularly well-suited to the research goals stated above. First, the overall sample size, 12,693 youths aged 14–21 years, includes 1924 Hispanics. This relatively large sample size permits disaggregation by sex and the application of criteria that are consistent with employment policy analysis. A second advantage is that the sample is national in scope. A third advantage is that the survey design accounts for all time between January 1, 1978, and the spring 1980 interview—that is, all work and nonwork spells are accounted for in this period. These detailed data have been processed for this study into specific periods of three work-history categories: (1) working, (2) not working owing to layoff, and (3) not working for other reasons.[2] A final advantage is the availability of person-specific environmental variables, such as SMSA and county employment rates, industrial characteristics, and labor demand measures, from the *County and City Databook*. These data were matched with the NLS-Youth data.

Sample means of the study group of Hispanic youth used here are shown in Table 6.1. These are individual sample means, although the unit of analysis is a spell of work or nonwork and one individual may have more than one spell.

The main data screens used were age and enrollment in school. Persons selected became 16 years old on or before the spring 1979 interview and did not attend college or high school after January 1, 1978. The sample may be thus described as Hispanic youth aged 15–21 years on January 1, 1978, more than one-half of whom had left school prior to high school graduation.[3] In fact, roughly 30% had at most 9 years of formal schooling and a large proportion of young men and women had been suspended from school and/or had a possible criminal record.

---

[2] In the empircal work, I tried to examine three, not two, states. This choice is technically feasible and exploits the avaialble data more fully.

[3] Because of potential selection bias due to having screened out youth still in school, an adjustment factor was created using a routine developed by Heckman (1979). The auxiliary equations used for that calculation are presented in the appendix to this chapter.

TABLE 6.1
Definitions of Variables and Means

Variables and definitions	Men	Women
1979 interview was conducted in Spanish	.15	.09
	(.36)	(.29)
Believe problem with getting a good job is due to poor	.26	.26
English (interview conducted in Spanish)	(.64)	(.57)
Percentage Spanish in county, 1979	1.98	1.97
	(1.90)	(1.84)
Married, spouse present, 1979 (including common-law	.39	.31
marriage)	(.17)	(.19)
Local unemployment rate, 1979	5.33	5.17
	(1.50)	(1.48)
Percentage population change (1970–75) in county, 1979	60.31	68.91
	(92.62)	(93.81)
Education completed		
0–9 years	.49	.35
	(.50)	(.48)
10 or 11 years	.27	.19
	(.45)	(.40)
12 or more years	.24	.45
	(.42)	(.50)
Age in years	21.16	21.41
	(1.30)	(1.19)
Not U.S. resident at age 14	.27	.24
	(.45)	(.43)
Vocational education received between Jan. 1, 1978, and	.05	.09
Spring 1980	(.22)	(.29)
Ethnic origin		
Mexican or Mexican-American	.69	.70
	(.47)	(.46)
Puerto Rican	.13	.10
	(.34)	(.31)
Other Hispanic	.18	.20
	(.36)	(.21)
Income, net family, 1978	$9,817	$10,188
	(9,663)	(9,663)
Work-limiting health problems, 1979	.07	.05
	(.25)	(.22)
Ever stopped, booked or convicted of crime, 1979	.42	.18
	(.49)	(.38)

TABLE 6.1 (*Continued*)

Variables and definitions	Men	Women
Ever suspended from school	.23	.14
	(.43)	(.34)
λ	.8193	.5176
	(1.073)	(.749)
N	115	96

Source: 1976 Survey of Income and Education (U.S. Department of Commerce, 1978).
Note: Standard deviations are in parentheses.

Empirical Results

This section is organized into four parts. I first provide a brief rationale for the empirical specifications and then present the transition rate results. Next, because the transition rate coefficients may not be readily interpretable, I present several derivations with employment policy implications; these results were calculated with the Model 1 transition rate results. I then present results from Model 2, the time-dependent form of the transition model.

SPECIFICATION

Two empirical models, job finding and job leaving, were estimated with two forms of the transition rate model, the time-invariant and time-dependent specifications, shown as Equations (11) and (12), respectively. The same set of observed variables in the vector X were used in each model. The choice of X variables was guided by concern for economic and demographic issues. The X vector was fixed. That is, in general, I did not include X vector terms whose values changed over particular employment spells. Admittedly, however, some terms, such as marital status, were first measured in the NLS New Youth Cohort only in the spring 1979 interview; consequently they may involve a change since January 1, 1978, the start of the employment history reference period.

In the theoretical discussion of job finding, the search costs, rate of job-offer arrival, and discount rate were linked to the rate of job finding. Direct measures of job search costs and discount rates are not available in the data. I expect, however, that several aspects of psychic costs of job search may be captured in a set of survey questions regarding perceived problems in obtaining (and holding) a good job. These problems may include language problems and not having lived in the United States very long. Thus, I include whether or not the 1979 interview was in Spanish and if the youth lived outside the United States at age 14. As for the discount rate, I expect youth who have been suspended from school or have had an adverse encounter with police (e.g., those who have been stopped, booked, or convicted) to attach relatively greater weight to immediate gratification of needs. One might thus expect such persons to have shorter nonwork durations. Yet job search also involves employers' choices and early school leaving, and a police encounter may lead to fewer job offers by employers (and/or an early dismissal if hired). The net effect on *job finding* of these proxy measures of discount-rate level is thus unclear.

A greater rate of positive job-offer arrivals, h, is also measured by proxy terms, including a lower local unemployment rate, higher individual educational level, relatively greater age, and the absence of a work-limiting health problem. I expect each term to be associated with a faster rate of job finding.

The final specification also included a number of demographic and environmental terms that may alter the individual's relative taste for work, the individual's ability to allocate time for market work, or the market wage rates available to the individual. These factors, which include marital status, family income level (net of the respondent), ethnic origin, educational level, and postschool vocational educational training, may also affect the rate of job finding and job leaving.

RESULTS

Separate transition-rate estimates for Model 1 for the Hispanic male and female youths are shown in Tables 6.2 and 6.3. Each of the models was highly significant statistically as measured by a chi-square ratio. The coefficients indicate changes in the logarithm of the transition rate. As such, it may be more convenient to interpret some coefficients in percentage terms. For example, in Table 6.2, Column 3, note that Puerto Rican men had a statistically significant and lower rate of job finding than other Hispanic young men. The antilog of the -0.79 coefficient implies that young Hispanic men who listed ethnic origin as Puerto Rican had job-finding rates 55% lower than those of otherwise similar Hispanic men in other locations. This particular result illustrates the sort of findings that might be validated with larger samples that permit disaggregated analyses by national origin.

TABLE 6.2
Determinants of Rates of Job Findings, by Sex

	Young women		Young men	
	Model 1	Model 2	Model 1	Model 2
Constant	−21.64**	−19.51**	−2.32	−4.13
	(10.51)	(10.54)	(8.34)	(8.58)
Age	.76	.63	−.05	.02
	(.52)	(.52)	(.40)	(.41)
Income	.04**	.05**	−.01	−.01
	(.02)	(.02)	(.01)	(.01)
Education 0–9 yrs.	.98	.68	−.58	−.48
	(.91)	(.91)	(.91)	(.94)
Education 10 or 11 yrs.	.13	.10	−.09	−.06
	(.31)	(.31)	(.57)	(.58)
Education 13–18 yrs.	−2.17*	−2.17*	−1.17	−1.11
	(1.26)	(1.26)	(.83)	(.83)
Not in U.S. at age 14	.23	.37	−.15	.00
	(.29)	(.29)	(.65)	(.66)
Spanish interview, 1979	.25	.25	−.32	−.34
	(.41)	(.41)	(.30)	(.30)
Mexican-American, Chicano, or Mexican	.25	.38	−.13	−.04
	(.29)	(.29)	(.26)	(.26)
Puerto Rican	−.06	−.02	−.79***	−.68**
	(.43)	(.43)	(.30)	(.31)
Other Hispanic	—	—	—	—
Work-limiting health	−.48	−.55	.74**	.77**
	(.67)	(.67)	(.28)	(.28)
Married, 1979	.16**	.17***	−.04	−.05
	(.06)	(.05)	(.06)	(.06)
Ever suspended	.30	.35	−.013	.18
	(.33)	(.34)	(.219)	(.20)
Ever stopped, booked, or convicted	.33	.46	−.24	−.02
	(.34)	(.36)	(.20)	(.20)
Vocational education received, 1979	−.83**	−.99**	−1.27**	−1.13**
	(.45)	(.46)	(.60)	(.60)
Local unemployment rate, 1979	−.007	−.03	−.16**	−.16**
	(.082)	(.08)	(.06)	(.06)
λ	−.98	−.85	.10	.01
	(.76)	(.76)	(.54)	(.55)

(Continued)

TABLE 6.2 (*Continued*)

	Young women		Young men	
	Model 1	Model 2	Model 1	Model 2
Time dependence γ	—	.0013***	—	.0009***
	—	(.0004)	—	(.0003)
Log likelihood X (-2)	30.31**	38.03***	39.90***	46.57***
Number of spells	105	105	163	163

Source: National Longitudinal Survey of Youth, 1979 (Borus et al., 1980).
Notes: Standard errors are in parentheses. See Table 6.1 for means of variables. Model 1 and Model 2 are described in the text. A dash means the term was omitted from the specification.
  * Statistically significant at the 10% level.
  ** Statistically significant at the 5% level.
  *** Statistically significant at the 1% level.

TABLE 6.3
Determinants of Rates of Job Leaving, by Sex

	Young women		Young men	
	Model 1	Model 2	Model 1	Model 2
Constant	18.45*	15.59	−11.47*	−13.6
	(11.34)	(11.80)	(7.25)	(7.35)
Age	−1.19**	−1.08*	.22	.28
	(.56)	(.58)	(.35)	(.36)
Income	−.03**	−.03**	−.0004	.005
	(.02)	(.02)	(.0104)	(.010)
Education				
0–9 yrs.	−.94	−.80	1.02	1.07
	(.97)	(1.00)	(.86)	(.87)
10 or 11 yrs.	.50	.41	.74	.77
	(.33)	(.34)	(.55)	(.54)
13–18 yrs.	2.11	1.99	−1.34	−1.29
	(1.34)	(1.37)	(1.10)	(1.10)
Not in U.S. at age 14	.02	.03	−.49	−.40
	(.28)	(.29)	(.60)	(.60)
Spanish interview, 1979	−.26	−.25	−.03	.08
	(.39)	(.40)	(.29)	(.30)
Mexican-American,	−.17	−.17	−.08	.015
Chicano, or Mexican	(.33)	(.32)	(.25)	(.25)
Puerto Rican	.21	.20	.11	.19
	(.45)	(.44)	(.32)	(.32)

TABLE 6.3 (Continued)

	Young women		Young men	
	Model 1	Model 2	Model 1	Model 2
Other Hispanic	—	—	—	—
Work-limiting health	−.66	−.72	.42	.34
	(.78)	(.77)	(.29)	(.29)
Married, 1979	−.04	−.02	.12**	.14
	(.06)	(.06)	(.05)	(.06)
Ever suspended	.09	.07	.16	.26
	(.31)	(.31)	(.21)	(.21)
Ever stopped, booked,	.84**	.84**	−.20	−.26
or convicted	(.35)	(.35)	(.18)	(.21)
Vocational education	−.15	−.21	−.98**	−1.13**
received, 1979	(.39)	(.39)	(.73)	(.60)
Local unemployment rate,	−.06	−.06	.12*	−.16**
1979	(.09)	(.09)	(.07)	(.06)
λ	1.54*	1.34	−.35	.009
	(.81)	(.85)	(.50)	(.55)
Time dependence γ	—	.0014***	—	.0020***
	—	(.0005)	—	(.0004)
Log likelihood X (−2)	32.51**	41.67***	39.43***	69.35***
Number of spells	99	99	153	153

Source: National Longitudinal Survey of Youth, 1979 (Borus et al., 1980).

Notes: Standard errors are in parentheses. See Table 6.1 for means of variables. Model 1 and Model 2 are described in the text. A dash means the term was omitted from the specification.

* Statistically significant at the 10% level.
** Statistically significant at the 5% level.
*** Statistically significant at the 1% level.

Age of the youths in January 1978 varied from 15 to 21 years. As frequently observed in other youth labor studies, age has an important and statistically significant effect on female Hispanic youth labor turn-over rates. Older female youth found jobs more quickly and left jobs more slowly than younger persons.[4]

Family income also has a positive and statistical effect on the rate of job finding of Hispanic young women and a negative and statistical effect on their rate of job leaving. To the extent such women consider

---

[4] Inclusion of this age term is also important as a way of mitigating estimation problems resulting from not controlling for initial conditions.

nonmarket activities like child care or home production as normal goods, such a result is somewhat unexpected. That is, a young woman whose family has a relatively greater income may have less need to work in the market and can "afford" to do other things. Yet these young women were selected for inclusion in the sample only if they were not attending school. As noted in Table 6.5 in the Appendix, the selected women had lower average income than those attending school. Also, the sample mean family income for women was only about $10,000 in 1977, a figure well below the U.S. average for white or black families (and 11% below that for other Hispanic families). Thus the positive association of family income and job-finding rate should be interpreted cautiously because of sample selection criteria and possible nonlinear income effects.

Education and training, two important employment policy alternatives of the federal government, are measured here for effects on labor turnover. Education is measured with a set of dummy variables: the reference group has 12 years of education. The only significant relative educational difference is for women. Those with over 12 years of school find jobs more slowly and leave jobs faster than women with 12 years of schooling. Just why this result emerges is not altogether clear, but it is consistent with the notion that women with some higher education are relatively more willing to shop for jobs.

As for training effects on job turnover, work experience prior to January 1, 1978, was tried in earlier versions of the model but was omitted here owing to some measurement problems. Work experience and age have been used by economists as proxy measures for on-the-job training: here I use age. Training is also measured by a dummy variable equal to one if the youth was in a postschool vocational or technical training program. Such training negatively and significantly reduces the rate of job finding for both young men and young women relative to other persons who did not receive this training. This result may be due to such persons being more selective, such persons being less desirable from the employer's viewpoint, or some combination of supply and demand considerations. More research is needed to disentangle these effects.[5]

Unemployment rate at the local level was measured as the 1978 county unemployment rate, a term that is a proxy for the overall tightness of the job market. The intention is that this term will reflect differences in labor demand level or differences in job-offer flow between

---

[5] These education and training effects are described here as person-specific. In fact, the unit of analysis was spells of work and nonwork. To the extent that education and the number of spells are related, these results may be over- or understated.

locations, but, obviously, to the extent that supply-related factors also add to unemployment rates, the measure is not exact. Results here are statistically significant only for Hispanic men: the job-finding rate is slowed if the unemployment rate is greater. Having found a job, however, means that the rate of leaving the job is positively associated with unemployment in Model 1 and negatively in Model 2. The latter effect is probably due to an interaction between unemployment rate level and the time-varying parameter, which changes over duration in a state. The possible interaction, which is not modeled in this chapter, means that the negative sign on unemployment should not be interpreted alone and that greater unemployment rates may still lead to faster rates of job leaving (e.g., more layoffs than quits).

English proficiency and sociocultural adjustments of a recent immigrant are also likely to affect individual job search behavior and potential employment tenure. I assume that persons who answered the 1977 NORC interview in Spanish and were living outside the United States at age 14 had such problems. Results obtained here were not statistically significant for either factor, but this may reflect the crudeness of the English proficiency measure.

Several minor results, especially those that were relatively large and statistically significant, should be listed. Marriage, defined here to include living with a nonrelated adult of the opposite sex, is associated with a faster rate of job finding for women. Another result is that a work-limiting health problem is associated with an increased job-finding rate for men. As for probems with police, it appears that having been stopped, booked, or convicted has a large and significant effect on female rates of job leaving. Specifically, young women who had an adverse police encounter left jobs 130% faster than other women. Whether such women are the first to be asked to leave by employers or whether they quit more readily cannot be determined here. I can only note that a police encounter will increase female chances of being jobless.

PROCESSED RESULTS

One of the advantages to estimating transition rates is that one may use the rate estimates to predict various outcome measures. In this section, I present the expected duration of work, the expected duration of nonwork, and the long-run (or steady-state) probability of joblessness. (Details regarding the mathematical derivations of these expressions are in Tuma and Robins, 1980.) The predictions are calculated as follows: The expected duration in state $k = 1/\Theta_{kj}$; the steady-state probability of being in state $k = \Theta_{jk}/(\Theta_{jk} + \Theta_{kj})$. These outcome measures are computed here by predicting case-specific Θ_{jk} from the β weights in Tables 6.2 and 6.3 and case-specific X values. The average duration of work was 56 weeks for women and 53 weeks for men. Nonwork durations were 33 weeks for women and 22 weeks for men. These nonwork duration differences by sex were the main reason for the steady-state joblessness rate differences, 40% for women versus 32% for men. The high rates of joblessness do vary by economic and demographic factors.

Six different criteria were used to sort the data: ethnic group, local unemployment rate, age, education, English proficiency, and family income. Results shown in Table 6.4 by different groups thus represent not only the differential β weights associated with the criterion variable in question, but also reflect case-specific values of the X terms.[6]

Subgroup differences among the specific Hispanic subgroups listed in Table 6.4 were in general not statistically significant at conventional levels in the transition-rate estimates. The Table 6.4 entry differences for Hispanic subgroups are therefore more suggestive than conclusive. Still, one can note certain differences. Other Hispanic groups, including Cubans, Spanish, and others from Latin America, have lower male joblessness rates than Mexican groups or Puerto Ricans. In turn, Mexican groups stay longer at jobs and find jobs faster than Puerto Ricans.

Local unemployment rate was measured here as a continuous variable in the analysis but was split into a dummy variable to develop the Table 6.4 entries. A greater unemployment rate is associated with a much greater long-run joblessness rate for men (36 vs. 29%), a result that is primarily due to an increased length of an expected nonwork spell. No direct effect of change in a local unemployment rate was found on the joblessness rate of women. Still, the component parts, work and nonwork durations, did change.

Age of the youth is a proxy for a number of employment-related factors. Some employers may prefer older youths or be prevented by state laws or insurance clauses from hiring youths aged 16 or 17 years. Also, older youths may simply be more willing to stay longer at a job, especially if they have car payments, family obligations, and other financial needs. Age was a highly significant determinant of rates of entering

---

[6] Results obtained in another study of work and nonwork spells with one spell per person using the same data base may be relevant. Using data on spells (i.e., not predicting spells), one finds the full work durations of 111 weeks and 115 weeks for young Hispanic males and females, respectively, and nonwork durations of 29 and 82 weeks, respectively. These estimates were obtained as $\Sigma Xi/d$, where Xi is the total number of spells and d is the number of censored spells. This is a much less biased estimator than the frequently reported $\Sigma Xi/n$, where n is the number of spells.

and leaving jobs. Results in Table 6.4 show these effects dramatically. A 3-year age difference (3 years is the difference in the average age in the above-18-year-old group and the below-18-year-old group) is associated with a threefold increase in the expected duration of a work spell for women and a similar but less-sharp change for men. For women, the expected duration of work increases from 17 weeks to 58 weeks between ages 17 and 20. The length of time not working also appears to fall in this period. As a result of both factors, shortened nonwork spells and lengthened work spells, the steady-state joblessness rates fall sharply.[7]

Three other results presented in Table 6.4 concern educational attainment, English proficiency, and family income. I focus here on education and family income, two potential target criteria for employment policies. I do not discuss the English proficiency results because I believe that they were poorly measured.

For both sexes, the long-run joblessness rate for high school graduates and youth with college is about one-half that for youths with at most 9 years of formal education. Greater family income is also associated with a lower joblessness rate, especially for women. The policy implications are that Hispanic youth from low-income families should be aided in some manner, be it training, job-finding assistance, or some other scheme. Also, Hispanic youths who have left school prior to secondary school completion should be encouraged to return to school so as to enhance their subsequent employment chances.

TIME DEPENDENCE

The results presented so far have been for Model 1, which assumes that transition rates do not vary over time. Yet there are several reasons why such an assumption may not be appropriate. For instance, a change in economic conditions during a spell of work (or nonwork) may cause a change during the spell in the rate of job finding (or job leaving). Also, a decline in the reservation wage over the duration of time not working may increase the rate of job finding. If such effects are the only source of time variation, then the time-invariant model has biased constant terms,

---

[7] Of course, some of these processed age results may be due to the effect of other factors such as education or marriage. For example, if older youths are more likely to have graduated from high school and youths with this amount of education leave jobs more slowly, then an age-sepcific subsample work-exit prediction really reflects not only differences in subsample ages weighted by the age coefficient, but subsample differences in education attainment weighted by the work-exit rate coefficient for education. To decompose these components is beyond the scope of this chapter.

TABLE 6.4
Processed Results from Transition Rate Estimates, by Sex and Hispanic Group

	Young women					Young men			
	N	Expected work duration (weeks)	Expected nonwork duration (weeks)	Steady-state nonwork probability		N	Expected work duration (weeks)	Expected nonwork duration (weeks)	Steady-state nonwork probability
Ethnic group									
All	281	56.03 (38.42)	33.41 (23.84)	.40 (.20)		426	52.81 (34.73)	21.99 (11.97)	.32 (.14)
Mexican-American, Chicano, or Mexican	195	54.60 (37.89)	32.11 (24.30)	.39 (.21)		286	52.94 (35.70)	22.21 (12.36)	.32 (.14)
Puerto Rican	29	47.57 (36.81)	35.53 (21.76)	.39 (.18)		55	38.03 (16.05)	27.98 (8.57)	.43 (.11)
Other Hispanic	57	65.22 (39.99)	36.80 (23.19)	.39 (.20)		85	61.96 (37.30)	17.36 (10.71)	.23 (.09)
Local unemployment rate									
0–5.9%	184	58.87 (42.23)	32.72 (18.81)	.40 (.20)		261	49.12 (33.97)	17.79 (9.66)	.29 (.12)
6% or more	97	50.64 (29.32)	34.72 (31.30)	.40 (.20)		165	58.66 (35.27)	28.63 (12.30)	.36 (.15)

Age								
≤18 years	12	16.83	35.94	.67	22	36.47	29.71	.45
		(4.74)	(13.89)	(.05)		(11.49)	(8.20)	(.12)
19+ years	269	57.78	33.30	.39	404	53.71	21.57	.31
		(38.33)	(24.20)	(.20)		(35.37)	(12.01)	(.14)
Education								
0–9 years	111	32.18	36.12	.52	214	47.05	25.93	.38
		(10.07)	(16.31)	(.17)		(23.92)	(8.99)	(.13)
10 or 11 years	65	47.24	31.58	.42	136	49.33	16.21	.29
		(27.37)	(19.56)	(.19)		(41.41)	(8.92)	(.13)
12+ years	105	86.69	31.69	.27	76	75.28	21.22	.21
		(42.44)	(31.62)	(.16)		(38.78)	(18.28)	(.09)
English problem								
Spanish interview	24	57.29	33.17	.40	58	68.94	28.89	.31
		(39.44)	(24.34)	(.20)		(38.15)	(15.97)	(.09)
No Spanish interview	257	42.57	35.91	.46	368	50.27	20.90	.32
		(21.16)	(17.73)	(.18)		(33.54)	(10.85)	(.15)
Family income								
Income ≤$10,000	157	42.58	41.48	.49	304	48.57	21.38	.32
		(20.89)	(26.58)	(.17)		(31.13)	(10.67)	(.13)
Income >$10,000	124	73.06	23.19	.29	122	63.39	23.50	.30
		(47.79)	(14.46)	(.18)		(40.70)	(14.66)	(.16)

Source: National Longitudinal Survey of Youth, 1979 (Borus et al., 1980).
Note: Standard errors are in parentheses.

but the bias in other coefficients is usually slight.[8] I therefore show here the effect of a time-varying parmater only on the constant rate.

The time-varying parameter estimates shown in Tables 6.2 and 6.3 are highly significant statistically for young men and young women. For both sexes and both work and nonwork categories, exit rates increase over time in the state. For youths in a nonwork state, such a result is consistent with several aspects of job-search theory, including a declining reservation wage rate and an expanding area in which job search takes place. As for employed workers, sorting by firms or employees during early tenure could account for this time dependence. Firms need to decide if they wish to keep the worker, while the young worker needs to decide if the job matches his or her career goals. Similar ideas were mentioned earlier by Jovanovich (1979) as to why the rate of job leaving for employed persons need not be monotonically declining, but may increase early in the tenure period. For a sample of mainly teenaged youth, it is not really surprising that positive time dependence is obtained.

Conclusion

In this study I have considered the determinants of the rates of entering and leaving work for a national sample of young Hispanic men and women. Data analyzed were continuous work histories for individuals in the period from January 1978 to spring 1980. Youth studied here, aged 15–21 years at the start of the period, did not attend school in this 2-year period and were unlikely to return to school. Roughly 70% did not have a high school diploma, and 43% had at most 9 years of education. Also, 26% of the youth lived abroad at age 14, and 35% were married. To adjust for special sample selection criteria, I estimated and included Heckman's lambda, which is presented in the Appendix.

I have examined one aspect of Hispanic youth employment problems: the association of high rates of joblessness with high labor turnover rates. Three aspects of the study are important. First, relatively little research has been directed at Hispanic youth employment. This study adds to that literature by describing Hispanic youth labor turnover behavior and by relating a number of economic and demographic issues to

---

[8] See Robins et al. (1980, p. 564). This relatively slight change in rate coefficients between Model 1 and Model 2 is found here, with the exception of the unemployment rate effect in the male results for job leaving.

this behavior. Family income, marital status, and postschool vocational education were found to have substantial and statistically significant effects on turnover rates, especially for women. Age and local unemployment rates also were associated with differential rates of labor turnover. Prior studies have also found these factors to be important determinants of labor market behavior.

Second, two general policy alternatives—labor demand variation (as measured by local unemployment rate) and education and training provisions—were implicitly considered, to evaluate their implications for Hispanic youth rates of entering and leaving employment. While above-average local unemployment rates were associated with lower rates of job finding for men, but not for women, no clear picture emerges as to the relative import of aggregate demand or individual-oriented supply policy. Instead, one is left with a set of policy-relevant observations that are important in their own right, even if they do not seem to form a comprehensive policy plan.

1. Hispanic youth joblessness rates are quite high, between 30 and 40%, and these rates are due primarily to relatively long spells of nonwork after a job loss.
2. Age, education, and family income level all sharply affect Hispanic youth employment behavior and thus call for "targeting" employment policies according to these criteria.
3. Sex differences in labor turnover results also were found, primarily because female nonwork duration was nearly 50% longer than that of young Hispanic men. Employment policy targeting by sex for Hispanic youth may therefore also be appropriate.
4. English-language training may be needed for Hispanic youth, but results obtained here do not support such a policy. Data better suited to measure this effect may suggest that such training is appropriate.

A third and final comment concerns the method of analysis. Most of the results presented were for a time-invariant model, which assumed an exponential distribution of "wait" times at work or nonwork. A time-varying transition rate model was also presented, in which exit rates were found to increase during time at work or not at work. Yet the earlier results obtained with the constant-rate model were affected only slightly in that the main change was in the constant term and not, for example, in the relative effects of education on job finding. More research is needed to understand more fully the nature of this time dependence.

Appendix: An Adjustment for Potential Selection Bias

The main focus of this chapter is the early postschool labor market behavior of Hispanic youth. To create an analysis file from the original longitudinal data file, only youths who had left regular school on or before January 1, 1978, were included. The risk is that systematic subgroup differences in the characteristics associated with school-attenders versus school-leavers may blur one's ability to obtain an unbiased estimate of the relationship between a youth's particular characteristics and rate of job finding (or job leaving). The problem cannot be overcome merely by adding more and more right-hand-side variables, since unobserved subgroup differences may also lead to this bias.

James Heckman (1979) refined a statistical method that enables consistent parameter estimates to be obtained in the case in which one first has a binary choice (include/not include), and, second, has an ordinary least-squares regression for the outcome variable. In the present chapter, the situation is somewhat different. Heckman assumed a bivariate normal distribution of the error terms in the binary choice and the outcome variable models. In this chapter, I estimate λ, Heckman's selection bias adjustment factor, by maximum likelihood probit methods. This much is exactly as Heckman developed it. The difference arises in the second step, in that the outcome variable(s) estimated here is the instantaneous rate of finding or leaving a job, an assumed continuous-time Markov process that I also estimate by maximum likelihood methods. The statistical properties of Heckman's approach in the context of such a turnover analysis have yet to be developed; yet, the second-stage results should also be consistent because of the use of maximum likelihood estimation procedures. See Stephenson (1982) for a related application. Intuition suggests that less bias will be present with λ included than if it is omitted.

Table 6.5 presents sample means for the selected and nonselected subgroups. As noted, the youths here were older, from lower-income families, and had less formal education than those continuing in school or college. In addition, from the other differences listed it appears that those who leave school early may have sharp social, economic, and cultural differences from the nonselected youths. Leaving school early appears to be associated with having lived outside the United States at age 14 and other potential English-language problems, which may in turn be related to early postschool labor market failures.

Table 6.6 shows maximum likelihood estimates computed by Heck-

TABLE 6.5
Sample Means of Selected and Nonselected Hispanic Youth Age 16–21 Years in 1979

	Selected	Not selected
Age	21.33	19.23
	(1.25)	(1.59)
Family income, 1978 dollars ($thousands)	9.986	11.092
	(9.642)	(10.462)
Education		
0–9 years	.43	.25
	(.49)	(.43)
10 or 11 years	.24	.45
	(.43)	(.49)
13–18 years	.04	.13
	(.19)	(.33)
Not in U.S. at age 14	.26	.04
	(.44)	(.21)
Married	.40	.06
	(.49)	(.25)
Interviewed in Spanish	.12	.04
	(.33)	(.18)
Problems in getting a job	.30	.14
due to English	(.46)	(.35)
N	211	433

Source: National Longitudinal Survey of Youth, 1979 (Borus et al., 1980).
Notes: The main sample selection criterion was not to have attended school or college after January 1, 1978. The selected sample includes 115 men and 96 women. The standard deviations are in parentheses.

man's lambda-probit routine. The specification is intended to reflect tastes for schooling and budget constraints. Several points should be noted. First, each model is highly significant as indicated by a chi-square statistic (which is -2 times the difference between the log likelihood ratio of the estimated model from the likelihood based only on the intercept). Second, for both young men and young women, age and, to some extent, education are the dominant variables determining continued enrollment in regular school or not. In addition, for young Hispanic men, not having been in the United States at age 14 is associated with a lower rate of school retention.

These probit coefficients in Table 6.6 were used to predict the probability of being in school for all youth, $F(Z)$ and a λ for each youth was

TABLE 6.6
Probit Coefficient Results for Sample Selection

	Men		Women	
	Probit estimates	Mean	Probit estimates	Mean
Constant	14.47***	1.00	22.69***	1.00
	(3.45)		(3.99)	
Age/10	6.64***	2.00	−10.68***	1.99
	(1.61)		(1.88)	
Family income/($thousands)	−.008	10.75	−.005	10.71
	(.005)		(.009)	
Education				
0–9 years	1.96	.33	−4.38	.29
	(4.42)		(4.86)	
10–11 years	10.08**	.40	−5.00	.35
	(5.11)		(5.11)	
13–18 years	1.50***	.09	2.22***	.11
	(.41)		(.43)	
Not in U.S. at age 14	−1.27***	.12	.10	.11
	(.40)		(.31)	
Education 0–9 years × age	−.18	6.45	.13	5.45
	(.22)		(.24)	
Education 10–11 years × age	−.52**	7.82	.23	6.77
	(.25)		(.25)	
χ^2 with 8 $d.f.$	238.77***		200.03***	
N	321		323	

Source: National Longitudinal Survey of Youth, 1979 (Borus et al., 1980).
Note: Standard errors are in parentheses.
** Statistically significant at the 5% level.
*** Statistically significant at the 1% level.

computed as $f(Z)/(1 - F(Z))$, where $f(Z)$ is the density function evaluated at the estimated probability. This λ was then used as an instrument in the exit rate empirical estimations.

PART III

Labor Supply and Occupational Allocation of Women

Role Incompatibility and the Relationship between Fertility and Labor Supply among Hispanic Women

Frank D. Bean, C. Gray Swicegood, and Allan G. King

Introduction

Recent studies of the relationship between fertility and female labor force behavior in developed societies have focused on the problems of (1) investigating the timing of fertility events in relation to the timing of labor force events (Cramer, 1980; Smith-Lovin and Tickamyer, 1981; Waite, 1981), and (2) disentangling the direction of influence between fertility and labor supply variables, frequently through the use of simultaneous equation procedures (Cain and Dooley, 1976; Waite and Stolzenberg, 1976; Schultz, 1978; Smith-Lovin and Tickamyer, 1978; Fleischer and Rhodes, 1979; Rosenzweig and Wolpin, 1980). It is not certain whether these approaches must be modified in the case of ethnic minorities in developed countries, particularly given that such groups often contain high proportions of immigrants from developing countries (see, e.g., Sullivan and Pedraza-Bailey, 1979) and that often employment opportunities available to recent immigrants and minority workers may differ in several respects from those available to native-born workers and majority group members (Bonacich, 1972; Chiswick, 1978a; Boyd, 1980; Portes and Bach, 1980; Wilson and Portes, 1980).

This chapter focuses on the relationship of fertility to labor supply among women of Mexican, Cuban, and Puerto Rican origin. The concern is with testing a number of specific hypotheses that derive from the general notion that the trade-offs women make between child care and work vary with particular circumstances. We treat fertility explicitly as a

221

determinant of labor supply rather than consider the effects of labor participation and supply on fertility. As noted later, we do this primarily because of the nature of our data, recognizing that these variables may be jointly and simultaneously determined and that under different circumstances the relationship may be the other way around. Further, we argue that because some of the women in the samples under investigation have immigrated to the United States from countries with lower levels of development and, for associated reasons, because they may encounter a structure of employment opportunities different from those available to nonimmigrant and nonminority women, fertility among immigrant women may be less constraining on labor force activity.

Ideas and Hypotheses

The central notion guiding the research is that the demands of child care and of working are often in conflict, an idea that in the sociological literature has often been termed the *role-incompatibility hypothesis* (Stycos and Weller, 1967; Mason and Palan, 1981). A parallel idea derives from the analysis of the allocation of time in the economics literature (Mincer, 1962; Becker, 1965). Stated briefly, the hypothesis predicts an inverse association between fertility and work when women are placed in situations that require "trade-offs between their participation in productive employment and the number of children they bear" (Mason and Palan, 1981, p. 551). The amount of conflict between working and mothering has typically been thought to vary depending upon (1) the organization of production and (2) the organization of child care. To the extent that the industrial organization of employment removes work from the home, thus contributing to the separation of the functions of the family from other institutions, female employment requires nonmaternal arrangements for child care if childbearing and work are to occur at the same time. The availability of parental surrogates in the household serves to diminish this incompatibility and thus to reduce the likelihood of the emergence of a negative association between fertility and female employment. Such alternatives, it is often argued, are more characteristic of the situations of Third World women, and their availability would serve to mitigate conflicts between working and mothering.

Even though it constitutes the point of departure for the present research, the role-incompatibility hypothesis contains a number of deficiencies that require mention. First, the hypothesis is essentially static in nature and thus begs the question of the direction of causality between fertility and labor supply variables—does having more children reduce the paid work of mothers, or vice versa?—and between these two variables and other variables that may jointly affect them. Nonetheless, it is reasonable to hold questions of this nature in abeyance pending further investigation of the conditions that may modify the strength of association between the two variables, particularly in light of the difficulties that beset the estimation of statistical models containing both interactions and jointly endogenous variables.

Another difficulty is that the role-incompatibility hypothesis provides no basis for predicting a positive relationship between fertility and labor force participation (Mason and Palan, 1981)—that is, the more children a woman has, the more she may be gainfully employed. Since positive associations have been reported in the literature (Goldstein, 1972; Weller et al., 1979), the most satisfactory theory would be one that accounts for the full range of observed variation in strength of association. The kinds of considerations invoked in the role-incompatibility hypothesis, however, speak more to the circumstances under which a negative relationship might *not* be found. Because a positive relationship appears to have been observed most typically among rural women in developing societies (Mason and Palan, 1981), a circumstance that is not particularly characteristic of the women under investigation here, the present research focuses on factors that might be expected to mitigate the strength of a negative relationship between fertility and labor supply.

We examine three categories of variables that could modify the relationship of fertility and work in developed countries. These include household composition variables, which we take to indicate variation in the domestic organization of child care, and socioeconomic and ethnicity variables, which we take as indicators of access to the organization of production. In the case of the socioeconomic and ethnicity variables, we assume that certain characteristics of Hispanic women are associated with a relative lack of access to parts of the employment opportunity structure, and that this affects the nature of the trade-offs such women make between fertility and work.

HOUSEHOLD COMPOSITION

The organization of the household to provide child-care substitutes is clearly a factor that might be expected to diminish the incompatibility between maternity and work, and thus weaken the relationship between fertility and work. This factor has usually been measured indirectly (using rural versus urban residence, for example), and one recent study that more directly examined household organization variables generated conflicting findings (Mason and Palan, 1981). Nonetheless, variables that directly or indirectly measure the household organization of child care bear further scrutiny at the individual level, particularly in light of recent findings that the availability of child care outside the household weakens the constraint of fertility on employment (Stolzenberg and Waite, 1981). In general, we would expect that the availability in the household of other persons who might take care of the children will weaken the inhibiting influence of fertility on labor supply.

SOCIOECONOMIC VARIABLES

Women in certain types of occupations, or women with characteristics that qualify (or disqualify) them for certain types of work, may be hypothesized to experience greater conflict in maternal versus work roles. For example, women in higher-status jobs and/or women in the more "central" as opposed to "peripheral" sectors of the economy, where work discontinuities might be more likely to have adverse consequences on earnings and promotion, ought to experience greater role incompatibility and thus be more likely to exhibit a negative relationship between fertility and work. For example, King (1978) has shown that, in a market that offers a range of choices between work and leisure, women with young children are more likely to work. Because an examination of the characteristics of jobs is beyond the scope of the present chapter, we focus on wives' education, the relative lack of which often disqualifies women from jobs where work continuity is important (Polachek, 1975a). Women with lower levels of education are more likely to hold jobs in the peripheral sectors of the economy. Because entry and exit from such jobs produce lower earnings, such women should exhibit a less negative relationship of fertility to work.

A similar pattern is predicted in the case of husbands' incomes, although for somewhat different reasons. Women whose husbands have low earnings often have a greater need to contribute to family income, regardless of level of childbearing (Randall, 1977). In fact, other things being equal, greater childbearing might even be associated among these women with a greater need to work. In short, we hypothesize that as husband's income decreases, role incompatibility becomes less relevant to decisions about whether and how much to work. Hence, holding constant the market opportunities of the wife, fertility should constrain labor force participation less among women whose husbands have low incomes than among those whose husbands have higher incomes.

ETHNICITY VARIABLES

Two variables—nativity and degree of English proficiency—are also hypothesized to modify the relationship between fertility and work. As in the case of female education, lack of knowledge of English and not being born in the United States are more highly associated with limited access to jobs for which work continuity is important (Rodríguez, forthcoming; van Haitsma, forthcoming) and thus that entail greater role incompatibility of maternity and employment. Some immigrant women may even hold jobs that can be performed in the home or in the neighborhood or from which absences are more often tolerated. In addition, some of the immigrant women may be temporarily residing in the United States, either legally or illegally, and the market opportunities they face could be perceived as far more temporary than (and, perhaps, markedly superior to) those prevailing in their countries of origin. The presence of children may be less inhibiting to labor force participation under these temporary conditions than is typical for permanent residents of these ethnic groups. Hence, we expect a less negative association of fertility and work among women not born in the United States and among women with less knowledge of English.

GROUP DIFFERENCES

As is noted below, the number of Puerto Rican and Cuban women in the age range to which the analyses are restricted is relatively small. Nonetheless, the above hypotheses are examined separately for women of Mexican, Puerto Rican, and Cuban origin. No a priori hypotheses are offered about expected patterns of differences among the groups, although it seems reasonable to think that various community structure variables, such as the concentration of Cubans in ethnic enclaves (Sullivan and Pedraza-Bailey, 1979; Wilson and Portes, 1980) may modify the manner in which certain variables mitigate the childbearing constraint on work. For example, some have argued that knowledge of English is not as critical a factor for finding a good job in the ethnic enclave as it is elsewhere (Sullivan and Pedraza-Bailey, 1979). Hence, the predicted effects of this variable may not emerge in the case of Cuban women. In addition, the migration of Cubans to the United States is far more permanent than for the other groups of Hispanics, and the effects of temporary residence may therefore not emerge among Cubans. We should also reiterate that we are focusing here on the manner in which indicators of role incompatibility condition the influence of fertility on labor supply at the microlevel. We therefore do not address here the question of the extent to which differences in role incompatibility among the groups may contribute to explaining differences among them in average levels of labor supply.

Data and Methodology

The analyses are based on data from the 1976 Survey of Income and Education (SIE; U.S. Department of Commerce, 1978) (see the Appendix to Chapter 1 in this volume). The sample for these analyses is restricted to currently married women aged 20–34. This delimitation makes it possible to examine the potential mediating role of husband's income in the relationship of fertility to labor supply. It also takes into account the fact that never married, separated, divorced, and widowed women face a different set of options than do their married counterparts when deciding how their fertility will influence their labor force behavior, including the amount of time they work. The age restrictions placed on the sample are intended to maximize the accuracy of the fertility measures.

MEASURES OF FERTILITY

The SIE does not contain information directly pertaining to fertility. Data on the ages of household members and on family relationships among household members make it possible, however, to allocate children to mother(s) within the household. These data permit the derivation of measures of current and cumulative fertility that are analogous to "own-children" estimates of fertility rates (Grabill and Cho, 1965; Rindfuss and Sweet, 1977; Retherford and Cho, 1978). In this research, analyses are conducted including measures of both *cumulative* and *current* fertility: the number of children under age 15 serves as a measure of cumulative fertility, and the number of children under age 3 as a measure of current fertility.

Similar assumptions to those involved in calculating own-children annual rates apply to these measures. As enumerated by Rindfuss and Sweet (1977, p. 11), four implicit assumptions underlie the calculation of fertility rates based on survey data: (1) that ages of children and women are correctly reported; (2) that all children reside with their mothers; (3) that mortality is negligible for women and children; and (4) that all women and children are covered by the census. The extent to which these assumptions differentially apply to Hispanic groups as compared to other whites has been addressed in depth elsewhere (Bean et al., 1981; Bean and Swicegood, 1982). After a careful examination of the extent to which the assumptions are met for these groups, particularly for those of Mexican origin, it was concluded that own-children procedures generate fertility measures that can be satisfactorily used for studying the determinants and consequences of between- and within-group fertility differentials when they are restricted to women aged 20–34. The restriction does not severely limit the scope of the present analyses, since this age range includes that portion of the life cycle where fertility is highest and where potential role incompatibility might be expected to be greatest.[1]

MEASUREMENT OF LABOR SUPPLY AND OTHER VARIABLES

The analyses are based on (1) the respondent's labor force status during the reference week of the survey and (2) the number of weeks worked by the respondent in 1975 as measures of labor supply, although results are presented only for the latter variable. The pattern of associations involving the participation measure tended to be similar to that involving the number of weeks worked, but the results were less often statistically significant. Measures of the amount of time worked in a given year may vary more strongly with fertility than does a dichotomous participation measure (that is, in the labor force versus not in the labor force), since the amount of time worked allows for the possibility of gradations of incompatibility, whereas a dichotomous status measure does not.

Other variables included in the analyses are measures of ethnicity, household composition, and socioeconomic status. Also, controls are

---

[1] It should also be emphasized that own-children fertility measures, which are the best that can be obtained given the nature of the SIE data, would not provide satisfactory fertility information for women outside the age range 20–34. In the case of the younger women, own-children measures understate actual fertility because many teenage women give their children up for adoption. An own-children-based measure would fail to distinguish these women from those who had never had a child, yet the former women might be much less likely to have worked because of having been pregnant. In the case of older women, own-children measures understate cumulative fertility because teenage children are likely to have left home. Again, an own-children-based measure would fail to distinguish these women from those without teenage children, even though the labor supply consequences for these two types of women may be different. Restricting the analysis to women aged 20–34 eliminates these problems.

included for wife's age and size of place of residence and, in the analyses focusing on the effects of current fertility, for the number of children in the household aged 4–14. The two ethnicity variables are nativity—whether foreign or U.S. born—and English proficiency. English proficiency is measured on a six-point scale ranging from "speaks English fluently" to "speaks no English." Two measures of household composition are included—household complexity and number of children aged 12 and over. Complexity is determined by the number of families in the household, including subfamilies, plus the number of nonrelated adults residing in the household. "Children aged 12 and over" refers to all children in the household. The socioeconomic variables include husband's income and wife's education. The former is the total reported income of the husband in thousands of dollars in 1975; the latter is the number of years of schooling of the wife. Of the control variables, size of place of residence is measured by the rank size of the SMSA (Standard Metropolitan Statistical Area) of residence across the 99 largest SMSAs; women not living in one of these SMSAs receive the maximum rank score of 100. The inclusion of this variable provides a crude control for fertility and labor supply differences across places of varying size (see, e.g., Cooney, 1979). Of the other control variables, wife's age is measured in years, and children aged 4–14 is simply the number of children within this age range in the household.

PLAN OF ANALYSIS

Ordinary least squares (OLS) regression analysis is used to estimate the relationship between the fertility measures and number of weeks worked. Because the latter variable includes zero values for women who are not participants in the labor force, we checked for bias in our estimates by also computing the analyses only for participating women. Very similar patterns of results emerged for the samples of participating women and the total samples of women.[2]

We treat fertility as an independent variable and labor supply as a dependent variable. We do this in part because of a primary interest in labor supply rather than fertility. More important, however, in the case of the cross-sectional SIE data, number of weeks worked is measured for

[2] We pursued this approach rather than the more complex procedure of Heckman. As reported elsewhere in this volume (Chapter 2), the use of Heckman's correction procedure with the SIE data in analyses similar to ours tends not to result in significant λ's. These results corroborate those obtained with our approach.

the previous year, whereas the current and cumulative fertility variables represent the experience of the previous 3 and 15 years, respectively.

The basic statistical model is of the following type:

$$LS = \beta_0 + \beta_1 F + \beta_2 I + \beta_3 (F \cdot I) + \sum_{i=1}^{k} \gamma_i X_i + \varepsilon,$$

where LS is a measure of labor supply, F is a measure of fertility, I is a measure (or proxy for) role incompatibility or some other condition thought to modify the relationship between fertility and work, $F \cdot I$ is the interaction between fertility and role incompatibility (or other condition), the X_i are control variables, and ε is a stochastic disturbance term. Our basic expectation is that β_3 will be significantly different from zero, its sign being determined by the particular variable interacting with fertility. In general, the less the role incompatibility indicated by the variable, the less we expect fertility to be a constraint on the number of weeks worked.

We estimate the OLS regression models for the three Hispanic groups separately. Not only do women of Mexican, Puerto Rican, and Cuban origin exhibit considerably different levels of fertility and patterns of labor force behavior, they also tend to reside in totally different parts of the country. While separate estimates of patterns of relationship could be derived from a single regression estimate based upon pooled samples, this approach seems unwarranted given the heterogeneity of the groups. Hence, separate estimates based upon separate equations are presented.[3]

Empirical Results

Table 7.1 presents descriptive statistics for the variables included in the regression models. The descriptive data contain few surprises and duplicate for the most part the picture of differences among these three groups shown by previous research. Mexican- and Puerto Rican–origin women exhibit lower totals for number of weeks worked than do Cuban women, and Puerto Rican women show a slightly higher value than Mexican-origin women, a pattern that is just the opposite of that when participation rates are examined (see, e.g., Tienda, 1981). Mexican-ori-

---

[3] Because disagreement exists concerning whether to base estimates of statistical relationships among variables on weighted or unweighted samples, we have run our analyses both ways. The results do not differ markedly. In the tables in this chapter, results based on weighted statistics are presented.

TABLE 7.1
Means of Variables Included in Regression Analyses of Currently Married Hispanic Women Age 20–34

Variables	Mexican	Puerto Rican	Cuban
Labor supply			
Weeks worked	18.03	19.28	27.03
	(21.48)	(22.92)	(23.81)
Fertility variables			
Children < 15 years	1.98	1.77	1.55
	(1.46)	(1.28)	(1.27)
Children < age 3 years	.51	.40	.27
	(.65)	(.56)	(.52)
Ethnicity variables			
Nativity (foreign-born)	.30	.78	.95
	(.46)	(.42)	(.22)
English proficiency	4.60	4.29	4.33
	(1.44)	(1.39)	(1.05)
Household structure variables			
Household complexity	1.05	1.02	1.03
	(.24)	(.14)	(.17)
Children ≥ 12 years	.28	.26	.46
	(.75)	(.66)	(1.05)
Socioeconomic variables			
Husband's income	8.86	8.96	12.66
	(5.62)	(5.94)	(9.66)
Wife's education	10.23	10.69	11.72
	(3.30)	(3.12)	(2.85)
Additional control variables			
Rank size of SMSA	57.61	20.30	28.90
	(0.70)	(32.54)	(5.33)
Wife's age	26.89	27.29	28.29
	(4.15)	(4.31)	(4.32)
Children 4–14 years	1.47	1.37	1.28
	(1.42)	(1.33)	(1.25)
N	845	152	53

Source: 1976 Survey of Income and Education (U.S. Department of Commerce, 1978).
Notes: See text for description of the variables. Standard deviations are in parentheses.

gin women have the highest levels of both current and cumulative fertility, followed by Puerto Rican and Cuban women.

A substantially higher proportion of the Mexican-origin women were born in the United States than is the case for the other two groups (almost all of the Cuban women are foreign-born), and perhaps for this reason the Mexican women have a slightly higher average level of English proficiency. Very few of the households in any of the groups contain additional families or nonrelative adults, and the Cuban households are more likely than the Mexican and Puerto Rican households to contain a greater number of children aged 12 and over. Not unexpectedly, the Mexican-origin women tend to have the lowest levels of education and income and the Cuban women the highest; the Puerto Ricans are in between, although much closer to the Mexican levels. The data also reveal that the Puerto Rican and Cuban women are concentrated in larger SMSAs and that the Cubans are somewhat older on average than women in the other two groups.

Before examining the results of the regression models including interaction terms, we first look at the additive models containing the socioeconomic status and control variables (which are included in all models) and each of the ethnicity and household composition variables in turn (Tables 7.2–7.4). Separate sets of regressions are presented for cumulative and recent fertility to ascertain whether the presence of young children has a stronger inhibiting effect on female labor supply than does cumulative fertility. In the case of the regressions involving recent fertility, the number of children aged 4–14 helps to ascertain that any negative relationships between fertility and work do not simply reflect the tendency for women who have already completed their childbearing to work more.

All three groups reveal the expected negative relationship between fertility and female labor supply; the relationship involving cumulative fertility is slightly weaker for Mexican-origin women than for Puerto Rican and Cuban women. Also, when recent fertility as opposed to cumulative fertility is examined, the relationship is considerably stronger, especially among Cuban-origin women. Hence, these results are consistent with the ideas that (1) fertility constrains labor supply among Hispanic married women, and (2) recent fertility has a greater inhibiting influence on labor supply than cumulative fertility, a result that we interpret as owing to the greater child-care demands required for younger children.

Turning to other variables, we find that husband's income exhibits quite different relationships: whether it positively or negatively affects the number of weeks worked varies by national origin. This reinforces the idea that heterogeneity among these groups requires their separate analysis. Among Mexican women, we observe the frequently noted inverse relationship between husbands' income and female labor supply. No statistically significant relationship occurs among Puerto Rican women, while, among Cuban women, higher husbands' income is associated with a greater tendency for wives to work, other things being

TABLE 7.2
Additive Regression Models for Weeks Worked on Fertility and Alternative Independent Variables: Mexicans

Independent variables	Unstandardized coefficients				
	Variables 1–5	Variables 1–5, 6	Variables 1–5, 7	Variables 1–5, 8	Variables 1–5, 9
	Cumulative fertility				
1. Children < 15 years	-3.925*	-3.919*	-3.931*	-4.189*	-4.023*
2. Husband's income	-.494*	-.493*	-.565*	-.474*	-.540*
3. Wife's education	1.042*	1.056*	.416**	1.065*	1.019*
4. Wife's age	.827*	.825*	.882*	.664*	.761*
5. Rank SMSA size	.055*	.055*	.043*	.051*	.051*
6. Nativity	—	.207	—	—	—
7. English proficiency	—	—	2.560*	—	—
8. Children ≥ 12 years	—	—	—	2.553	—
9. Household complexity	—	—	—	—	-11.384*
Constant	-5.893	-6.070	-11.340	-1.894	8.652
R^2	.122	.122	.140	.128	.137
	Recent fertility				
1. Children < 3 years	-9.326*	-9.355*	-8.829*	-8.650*	-9.318*
2. Children 4–14 years	-2.664*	-2.618*	-2.787*	—	-2.783*
3. Husband's income	-.480*	-.477*	-.540*	-.487*	-.524*
4. Wife's education	1.016*	1.092*	.508	1.255*	.994*
5. Wife's age	.452*	.434*	.532*	-.005	.395*
6. Rank SMSA size	.048*	-.051*	.039*	.047*	.049*
7. Nativity	—	1.165	—	—	—
8. English proficiency	—	—	2.086*	—	—
9. Children ≥ 12 years	—	—	—	.123	—
10. Household complexity	—	—	—	—	-10.896*
Constant	-5.620	4.751	.061	-.730	19.323
R^2	.155	.155	.167	.134	.168

Source: 1976 Survey of Income and Education (U.S. Department of Commerce, 1978).
Note: Each regression includes the first five variables—socioeconomic status and control variables. To these are added, one at a time, the two ethnicity measures and the two measures of household composition.
* Statistically significant at the 5% level. ** Statistically significant at the 1% level.

TABLE 7.3
Additive Regression Models for Fertility and Alternative Independent Variables: Puerto Ricans

Independent variables	Unstandardized coefficients				
	Variables 1–5	Variables 1–5, 6	Variables 1–5, 7	Variables 1–5, 8	Variables 1–5, 9
	Cumulative fertility				
1. Children < 15 years	−5.030**	−5.213**	−5.066**	−6.287**	−4.814**
2. Husband's income	.005	.034	.001	.022	.051
3. Wife's education	1.246**	1.327**	1.183**	1.038**	1.225**
4. Wife's age	1.659**	1.595**	1.658**	1.328**	1.591**
5. Rank SMSA size	−.051	−.044	−.050	−.030	−.054
6. Nativity	—	5.413	—	—	—
7. English proficiency	—	—	.260	—	—
8. Children ≥ 12 years	—	—	—	7.434**	—
9. Household complexity	—	—	—	—	11.670
Constant	−29.415	−32.794	−29.742	−18.409	−39.970
R^2	.128	.137	.128	.162	.133
	Recent fertility				
1. Children < 3 years	−11.823**	−11.866**	−12.152**	−10.669**	−11.582**
2. Children 4–14 years	−3.580**	−3.779**	−3.378**	—	−3.377**
3. Husband's income	.092	.118	.109	.047	.137
4. Wife's education	1.092**	1.170**	1.272**	1.244**	1.072**
5. Wife's age	1.055**	1.007**	1.018**	.190	.991**
6. Rank SMSA size	−.069	−.063	−.072*	−.080*	.072*
7. Nativity	—	5.054	—	—	—
8. English proficiency	—	—	.783	—	—
9. Children ≥ 12 years	—	—	—	3.734	—
10. Household complexity	—	—	—	—	11.346
Constant	−10.952	−14.455	−8.776	5.280	−21.298
R^2	.158	.166	.160	.144	.138

Source: 1976 Survey of Income and Education (U.S. Department of Commerce, 1978).
Note: Each regression includes the first five variables—socioeconomic status and control variables. To these are added, one at a time, the two ethnicity measures and the two measures of household composition.
* Statistically significant at the 10% level. ** Statistically significant at the 5% level.

TABLE 7.4
Additive Regression Models for Weeks Worked on Fertility and Alternative Independent Variables: Cubans

Independent variables	Unstandardized coefficients					
	Variables 1–5	Variables 1–5, 6	Variables 1–5, 7	Variables 1–5, 8	Variables 1–5, 9	
			Cumulative fertility			
1. Children < 15 years	-5.203**	-5.002**	-6.032**	-5.171**	-4.850**	
2. Husband's income	.476*	.482*	.312	.474*	.541*	
3. Wife's education	.111	.017	-.710	.099	.079	
4. Wife's age	.274	.253	.894	.278	.310	
5. Rank SMSA size	.220*	.218*	.217*	.220**	.227**	
6. Nativity	—	-4.284	—	—	—	
7. English proficiency	—	—	5.428*	—	—	
8. Children ≥ 12 years	—	—	—	-.119	—	
9. Household complexity	—	—	—	—	15.023	
Constant	13.666	19.054	-14.292	13.715	-4.046	
R^2	.156	.157	.187	.156	.166	
			Recent fertility			
1. Children < 3 years	-17.535**	-17.477**	-18.382**	-17.511**	-17.133**	
2. Children 4–14 years	-2.657	-2.632	-3.486	-3.486	2.332	
3. Husband's income	.627**	.628**	.463*	.620**	.689**	
4. Wife's education	.574	.559	-.249	.378	.542	
5. Wife's age	-.126	-.128	.496	-.317	-.089	
6. Rank SMSA size	.163*	.162*	.160*	.155*	.170*	
7. Nativity	—	-.653	—	—	—	
8. English proficiency	—	—	5.445*	—	—	
9. Children ≥ 12 years	—	—	—	-3.327	—	
10. Household complexity	—	—	—	—	14.373	
Constant	19.353	20.163	-8.688	25.501	2.378	
R^2	.239	.239	.270	.243	.248	

Source: 1976 Survey of Income and Education (U.S. Department of Commerce, 1978).

Note: Each regression includes the first five variables—socioeconomic status and control variables. To these are added, one at a time, the two ethnicity measures and the two measures of household composition.

* Statistically significant at the 10% level. ** Statistically significant at the 5% level.

equal. We return below to an interpretation of this pattern of intergroup differences.

Wife's education tends to be positive and significantly related to number of weeks worked among Mexican and Puerto Rican women, but it shows no significant relationship among Cuban women. For the first two groups, this finding is consistent with the notion that female labor supply varies positively with the female wage rate, if we assume that, among these women, higher education is associated with higher wage rates and greater opportunity costs connected with staying home.[4] Wife's age exhibits a similar pattern of relationship. The coefficients are positive and significant among Mexicans and Puerto Ricans but inconsistent and insignificant among Cubans. The positive relationships may be interpreted as indicating that labor supply increases with the termination of childbearing and as children grow older, thus easing the demands of child care (Waite, 1981).

Finally, it is of some interest to note that among Mexican- and Cuban-origin (but not Puerto Rican) women, living in a larger SMSA is associated with fewer weeks worked. In addition to the possibility that increasing SMSA size may be associated with greater costs of working, thus tending to dampen female labor supply, this finding may reflect two types of seasonal employment. The Cuban women are largely concentrated in Miami, where the economy has a substantial seasonal component. Both Cuban- and Mexican-origin women may find that larger cities offer them the opportunity to take jobs during the school year but to stay at home during the summer. Smaller cities, with less job differentiation, do not offer the same opportunities. In addition, many of the larger SMSAs with Mexican concentrations may have some seasonal component of jobs often performed by women (e.g., food processing in California and Texas). This does not explain the finding among Puerto Rican women. Perhaps Puerto Rican women, like black women, may be trying to acquire "insurance" against the eventual loss of financial support from a husband. The percentage of households headed by women is nearly as large among Puerto Ricans as among blacks.

Focusing next on nativity and English proficiency, we find that having been born outside the United States bears no significant relationship to the number of weeks worked, once other variables are controlled. English language proficiency, however, significantly and positively influ-

[4] It should be noted that we do not include a wage variable in the analyses. This is because a majority of the Mexican-origin women do not work, thus requiring that an attributed wage be calculated for these women. Since we include in the analyses the variables that would be used as predictors in such an equation (e.g., education and English proficiency), we believe that little would be gained by computing attributed wages.

ences labor supply among Mexican and Cuban, but not Puerto Rican, women. The relationship is about twice as strong among Cuban women, perhaps because of the greater range of occupational opportunities available to them (Sullivan and Pedraza-Bailey, 1979).

Of the household composition variables, no significant relationships emerge between number of weeks worked and the number of children in the household aged 12 and over, although the relationships are positive in the cases of women of Mexican and Puerto Rican origin. The measure of household complexity generates quite large coefficients (although not all in the same direction) in all cases. However, the number of observations on which these are based is very small, particularly in the cases of Puerto Rican and Cuban women, thus contributing to their high standard errors. Among Mexican-origin women, the group in which the largest number of complex families occurs, the coefficient is negative, indicating that a greater number of families and secondary adults sharing the same household is, in and of itself, associated with fewer weeks worked. We have no immediately plausible explanation for this finding, except to note that the secondary adults included in our measure are not relatives. Perhaps there is a tendency for such persons to be boarders and/or persons renting a room, thus lessening the need for the wife to work.

Turning to the question of whether fertility is less constraining on number of weeks worked under varying conditions, we present in Tables 7.5–7.7 tests for the hypothesized interaction effects; the tests are presented separately for measures of cumulative and current fertility and separately for the different groups. Table 7.5 shows first the relationships involving interactions between fertility and husband's income and fertility and wife's education. Among Mexicans, the coefficients for the interaction terms exhibit the expected negative sign and are significant in the equations involving cumulative fertility. Taking partial derivatives and following the procedures for interpreting the results of these kinds of models suggested by Stolzenberg (1980), we find that the relationship between fertility and number of weeks worked becomes more negative with both rising husband's income and increasing wife's education.[5] Among Puerto Ricans, cumulative fertility also increasingly inhibits the amount of time worked as wife's education increases. Hence, in the case of cumulative fertility among Mexican- and Puerto Rican–

---

[5] Although we do not present the results here, in the interest of saving space, these effects are not only statistically significant, they are substantively important. To take just one example, having an additional child under age 15 would be estimated to reduce the average number of weeks worked by nearly 2 months more among Mexican-origin women with a college education than among those with a grade school education.

TABLE 7.5
Partial Metric Regression Slopes Relating the Interaction of Fertility and Socioeconomic Variables to Weeks Worked

Independent variables	Mexicans		Puerto Ricans		Cubans	
	Variables 1–4	Variables 1–3, 5	Variables 1–4	Variables 1–3, 5	Variables 1–4	Variables 1–3, 5
	Cumulative fertility					
1. Children < 15 years	-1.734**	2.412**	-6.579**	5.854*	-15.400**	-5.385**
2. Husband's income	.047	-.453**	-.314	.093	-.757*	.476*
3. Wife's education	1.041**	2.319**	1.180**	3.352**	.130	.081
4. Interaction (1 × 2)	-.290**	—	.186	—	.935**	—
5. Interaction (1 × 3)	—	-.703**	—	-1.052**	—	.016
Constant	-10.574	-21.560	-26.244	-55.138	11.563	14.069
R^2	.129	.150	.131	.167	.257	.156
	Recent fertility					
1. Children < 3 years	-8.491*	-7.646*	-20.622*	-1.534	-20.728*	-58.766**
2. Husband's income	-.437*	-.480	-.062	.066	.437	.678*
3. Wife's education	1.017	1.107*	1.004	1.648*	.794	.124
4. Interaction (1 × 2)	-.101	—	.908	—	.278	—
5. Interaction (1 × 3)	—	-.173	—	-.974	—	3.268
Constant	5.356	4.770	-9.383	-15.732	19.350	30.100
R^2	.155	.155	.167	.165	.241	.252

Source: 1976 Survey of Income and Education (U.S. Department of Commerce, 1978).

Note: For each national-origin group, the first column measures interactions between fertility and husband's income, and the second measures interactions between fertility and wife's education. Effects are estimated net of wife's age, rank size of SMSA, and (in the case of models including recent fertility) number of children aged 4–14.

* Statistically significant at the 10% level.

** Statistically significant at the 5% level.

origin women, three of the four tests give results consistent with the idea that fertility is less constraining on labor supply at low levels of socioeconomic status.

By contrast, Cuban women reveal interaction effects that are in the opposite direction, although only one of the four tests attains statistical significance. The interaction of income and cumulative fertility shows that the relationship of fertility to work is most negative for Cuban-origin women whose husbands have lower incomes, and that the relationship becomes increasingly less negative as income rises. Although this result is based on a small number of cases, having larger families is apparently less likely to deter Cuban women from working if their husbands have higher incomes.

Turning to the models that include the ethnicity variables (Table 7.6), we note that among Mexican and Puerto Rican women, seven of the eight tests for interaction effects are statistically significant in the predicted direction. Having been born in Mexico and being less proficient in English both reduce the constraining influence of cumulative and recent fertility on number of weeks worked. Among Cuban women, the opposite pattern occurs once again. Although the number of U.S.-born Cuban women is too small to allow a reliable assessment of the interaction of nativity and fertility, the test based on degree of English proficiency reveals that, while family size sharply constrains working among women with poor English proficiency, it is less and less likely to affect the amount of time worked as English proficiency improves.

The measures of household composition also yield significant results in the predicted direction, but only among Mexican women (Table 7.7). Among Puerto Ricans and Cubans, the number of women living in "complex" family situations is too small to allow reliable assessment of interaction effects involving this variable. The results for Mexican-origin women, however, show that the presence of other persons in the household, either other adults or older children, mitigates the inhibiting influence of fertility on working. For Cuban women, the opposite pattern emerges yet again in the case of the tests for interactions involving number of older children. The presence of older children in the household, who presumably might provide substitute child care, *increases* the likelihood among these women that fertility will have a negative effect on working.

Summary and Conclusions

This chapter has considered the effects of fertility on the labor supply of three groups of Hispanic women in the United States. Drawing on the

TABLE 7.6
Partial Metric Regression Slopes Relating the Interaction of Fertility and Ethnicity Variables to Weeks Worked

	Mexicans		Puerto Ricans		Cubans	
Independent variables	Variables 1, 2, 4	Variables 1, 3, 5	Variables 1, 2, 4	Variables 1, 3, 5	Variables 1, 2, 4	Variables 1, 3, 5
			Cumulative fertility			
1. Children < 15 years	−5.070**	−.452	−9.274**	1.191	—	−23.269**
2. Nativity	−6.267**	—	−1.723	—	—	—
3. English proficiency	—	4.476**	—	2.299	—	−.532
4. Interaction (1 × 2)	3.115**	—	4.965*	—	—	—
5. Interaction (1 × 3)	—	−.861**	—	−1.458*	—	4.024**
Constant	−5.017	5.115	−29.510	−42.250	—	18.013
R^2	.312	.149	.148	.139	—	.224
			Recent fertility			
1. Children < 3 years	−10.504**	−.848	−17.055*	−8.466	—	−41.263
2. Nativity	−5.304**	—	−3.294	—	—	—
3. English proficiency	—	3.427**	—	−.322	—	4.569
4. Interaction (1 × 2)	3.113**	—	5.791**	—	—	—
5. Interaction (1 × 3)	—	−1.901**	—	−.887	—	4.874
Constant	5.801	−4.998	−9.372	−12.254	—	−10.363
R^2	.165	.175	.181	.161	—	.275

Source: 1976 Survey of Income and Education (U.S. Department of Commerce, 1978).

Notes: For each national-origin group, the first column measures interactions between fertility and nativity, and the second column measures interactions between fertility and proficiency in English. Effects are estimated net of wife's age, rank size of SMSA, and (in the case of models including recent fertility) number of children aged 4–14. Fertility and nativity interactions for Cubans were not computed because virtually all respondents (97%) were foreign-born.

* Statistically significant at the 10% level.

** Statistically significant at the 5% level.

TABLE 7.7
Partial Metric Regression Slopes Relating the Interaction of Fertility and Household Composition Variables to Weeks Worked

Independent variable:	Mexicans		Puerto Ricans		Cubans	
	Variables 1, 2, 4	Variables 1, 3, 5	Variables 1, 2, 4	Variables 1, 3, 5	Variables 1, 2, 4	Variables 1, 3, 5
	Cumulative fertility					
1. Children < 15 years	−8.122**	−5.066**	—	−6.351**	—	−3.621
2. Household complexity	−16.283**	—	—	—	—	—
3. Children ≥ 12 years	—	−3.218**	—	6.496	—	16.796*
4. Interaction (1 × 2)	3.869**	—	—	—	—	—
5. Interaction (1 × 3)	—	1.887**	—	.294	—	−4.579*
Constant	13.271	−1.310	—	−18.568	—	17.896
R^2	.140	.139	—	.162	—	.187
	Recent fertility					
1. Children < 3 years	−16.309**	−8.592**	—	−11.725**	—	−16.559**
2. Household complexity	−14.815**	—	—	—	—	—
3. Children ≥ 12 years	—	.207	—	2.823	—	−3.279
4. Interaction (1 × 2)	6.591*	—	—	—	—	—
5. Interaction (1 × 3)	—	−.372	—	8.285	—	−13.876
Constant	23.411	11.212	—	9.164	—	25.623
R^2	.171	.134	—	.151	—	.249

Source: 1976 Survey of Income and Education (U.S. Department of Commerce, 1978).

Notes: For each national-origin group, the first column measures interactions between fertility and household complexity, and the second measures interactions between fertility and children over 12 years old. Effects are estimated net of wife's age, rank size of SMSA, and (in the case of models including recent fertility) number of children aged 4–14. Because so few Puerto Rican and Cuban women were living in complex family situations, interaction terms involving this variable were not computed.

* Statistically significant at the 10% level.
** Statistically significant at the 5% level.

notion of role incompatibility—the degree to which the joint provision of child care and work are in conflict—we addressed the question of whether having characteristics that increase the likelihood of participation in secondary-type labor markets mitigates the effects of fertility on labor supply. The nature of the labor markets to which these women might have access was indexed by the women's English proficiency, generational status, educational level, and husband's income. The role-incompatibility hypothesis directs our attention to the interaction of these variables with the various measures of fertility. In addition, we considered the effects of household composition variables, which record the presence of older children and nonparental adults in the household as factors that lessen the constraint of fertility on female labor supply.

Our results indicate that these variables are significant in their interactions with fertility, particularly among Mexicans, although the signs of the effects are not always in the expected direction among Cuban women. Results for Mexican-origin women seem to conform closely to what we have hypothesized. Cuban women seem to be less deterred from working by the presence of children and by higher socioeconomic status and greater English proficiency.

In general, then, the pattern of the results is consistent with the predictions derived from the role-incompatibility hypothesis. However, an alternative explanation might also be invoked to explain the findings. The more constraining influence of fertility on labor supply among Mexican and Puerto Rican women who have higher socioeconomic status, are U.S.-born, and speak English more proficiently might be interpreted as reflecting a greater desire for children of "higher" quality (de Tray, 1974; Standing, 1978, p. 169) rather than as reflecting greater access to the kinds of labor markets for which the opportunity costs of inactivity are highest. While it might be argued that women with higher education may be more likely to devote time to the informal socialization and education of young children in order to inculcate greater child "quality," it is not so readily apparent why this should hold for English-speaking but not Spanish-speaking women. Perhaps more to the point, among Mexican-origin women (and to a lesser extent among Puerto Rican women) the predicted interaction effects emerge for the ethnicity but not the socioeconomic status variables in the regressions involving recent fertility (which might be argued to be especially likely to pick up quality effects). This pattern suggests that desires for greater child quality probably do not underlie the observed results.

The anomalous results for the Cuban women are based on such a small number of cases that not too much significance should be given to them. Nonetheless, there are some features of the Cuban experience that would seem likely to render distinctive the ways in which fertility affects labor supply in this group. These derive primarily from the fact that the Cuban population is concentrated in an ethnic enclave in Miami. Associated with this are a greater likelihood of self-employment and greater oportunities to employ domestic servants, frequently from among recent immigrants (Portes, 1981, 1982). The less constraining influence of fertility on labor supply that occurs with rising socioeconomic status among Cuban women may simply reflect greater access to the resources required to take advantage of opportunities for alternative child-care arrangements. Further research among Cubans based on larger samples than the ones available here may help to shed further light on these questions.

Finally, we concede that problems exist in our development of entirely satisfactory measures of fertility and labor supply. We find substantial agreement in the results obtained across the various measures employed, as well as support for the notion that Hispanic women are heterogeneous in their patterns of labor supply. Yet the need for refinements is obvious. Also, it would be desirable to consider simultaneously the participation and weeks-of-work decisions, perhaps in the fashion proposed by Heckman (1976). Moreover, it would be worthwhile if our conjectures regarding the nature of work and its complementarity with child care could be evaluated more directly. This seems possible, to a degree, by utilizing the sample of working women and noting the nature of the jobs they hold and their hours of work. If those with English-language deficiencies are concentrated in poorer jobs that may permit more flexible child-care arrangements, then relationships among language proficiency, job characteristics, and hours of work should be apparent in the data.

CHAPTER 8

The Occupational Position of Employed Hispanic Women*

Marta Tienda and Patricia Guhleman

Introduction

Systematic investigation of the labor market experiences of Hispanic-origin women is a relatively new endeavor in the field of social inequality. The few available studies have identified important differences among women of Mexican, Puerto Rican, Central and South American, and Other Hispanic origin along several labor market dimensions, including participation rates (Newman, 1978; Cooney and Ortiz, 1981); returns from work (Reimers, Chapter 2 in this volume); extent of labor force involvement (Guhleman and Tienda, 1981); and employment adequacy (Cooney and Colon, 1979; Guhleman and Tienda, 1981). However, most existing studies are highly descriptive or lack a coherent theoretical framework about the meaning of *Hispanicity* as a dimension of ethnic stratification. No researchers have undertaken multivariate analyses of the determinants of the occupational position of Hispanic women, even though recent studies of sex stratification have considered the role of race (Treiman and Terrell, 1975; U.S. Commission on Civil Rights, 1978; Kemp and Beck, 1981).

Until recently women were routinely excluded from empirical analyses of socioeconomic achievement on the grounds that their labor mar-

* This research was supported by Grant No. 21-55-79-27 from the U.S. Department of Labor and funds granted by the Department of Health and Human Services to the Institute for Research on Poverty, University of Wisconsin—Madison. Institutional support was provided by the College of Agricultural and Life Sciences of the University of Wisconsin—Madison. Computational work was supported by a grant from the Graduate School Research Committee, University of Wisconsin—Madison, and by a grant to the university's Center for Demography and Ecology from the Center for Population Research of the National Institute of Child Health and Human Development.

ket experiences were too complicated for straightforward application of existing research models. Beginning with the benchmark study of sex and the process of status attainment (Treiman and Terrell, 1975), several studies focused on the prestige or socioeconomic status of the jobs women occupy and the array of background, achievement, and life-cycle factors that influence women's initial occupational roles (Featherman and Hauser, 1976; McClendon, 1976; Fligstein and Wolf, 1978; Rosenfeld and Sørensen, 1979; Wolf and Fligstein, 1979; Sewell et al., 1980). However, these studies offer little insight into how the process of stratification may differ among women in different ethnic groups, a serious omission because both ethnicity and sex are major axes of the stratification system (Sullivan, 1978; Hirschman, 1980; Tienda, 1982).

The sex typing of occupations has led some labor market analysts to posit the existence of a distinct female labor market characterized by low-paying jobs, fluid entry and exit, and limited prospects for upward mobility. Studies point to the pronounced concentration of women in a relatively small number of occupations. (For example, see Oppenheimer, 1970; Stolzenberg, 1975; Brito and Jusenius, 1978; Seidman, 1978; Wolf and Rosenfeld, 1978; Beller, 1980; England, 1981, 1982.) Although there is evidence of some decline in the extent of occupational segregation by sex (England, 1981), women continue to be highly concentrated in a few occupations. It is estimated that 70% of all working women would need to change occupations for the occupational distributions of male and female workers to be similar (Williams, 1979).

This study contributes to the research on women's occupational stratification by examining ethnic differentiation among employed Hispanic women. We define occupational position both in terms of status scores and allocation into broad occupational strata. First, we examine the importance of the decision to work, because this conditions the probability that women will have an occupation. We subsequently assess the determinants of occupational status among Hispanic-origin women, correcting for selection bias and emphasizing similarities and differences among nationalities, as well as between Hispanic and non-Hispanic white women. Finally, we illustrate the uneven allocation of female labor according to national origin, and assess the determinants of the occupational configuration for Hispanic and non-Hispanic white women.

Hispanicity and Socioeconomic Differentiation

Table 8.1 provides some information about the economic and demographic characteristics of the female working-age population classified

TABLE 8.1
Selected Characteristics of Women Age 18–64, by National Origin

Selected characteristics	Mexican	Puerto Rican	Central and South American[a]	Other Hispanic	Non-Hispanic white
Age (%)					
18–24	27.2	22.7	22.7	21.5	20.7
	(44.5)	(41.9)	(41.9)	(41.1)	(40.5)
25–34	32.2	34.7	26.5	23.8	24.3
	(46.7)	(47.6)	(44.1)	(42.6)	(42.9)
35–44	19.2	21.2	25.5	20.2	17.9
	(39.4)	(40.9)	(43.6)	(40.2)	(38.4)
45–54	13.9	13.9	17.1	21.0	19.6
	(34.6)	(34.6)	(37.7)	(40.7)	(39.7)
55–64	7.5	7.5	8.2	13.5	17.6
	(26.4)	(26.3)	(27.4)	(34.1)	(38.1)
Mean years of education	9.0	9.1	11.0	11.2	12.3
	(4.0)	(3.6)	(13.6)	(3.1)	(2.5)
Native-born (%)	72.4	17.7	6.3	72.9	94.8
	(44.7)	(38.2)	(24.2)	(44.4)	(22.3)
Mean years since migration					
1 or less	1.9	2.8	5.6	1.0	.2
	(13.7)	(16.4)	(23.0)	(9.8)	(4.9)
2–5	4.6	7.8	17.2	4.4	.4
	(20.9)	(26.8)	(37.8)	(20.5)	(6.4)
6–11	7.0	12.6	37.6	8.7	.8
	(25.5)	(33.2)	(48.4)	(28.2)	(8.7)
12 or more	14.1	59.1	33.3	13.0	4.8
	(34.8)	(49.2)	(47.1)	(33.6)	(19.2)
Mean English-language proficiency score[b]	8.8	8.1	7.7	10.1	11.7
	(2.9)	(2.6)	(2.7)	(2.2)	(1.8)
Mean number of children					
Under 6 years	.6	.5	.4	.3	.3
	(.8)	(.8)	(.7)	(.6)	(.6)
Under 18 years	1.9	1.6	1.1	1.2	1.0
	(1.8)	(1.6)	(1.2)	(1.4)	(1.3)
Female family head (%)	12.9	28.7	10.7	13.6	7.5
	(33.6)	(45.2)	(30.9)	(34.2)	(26.4)
Mean earnings from other family members ($)	7,590	5,490	8,650	9,580	12,000
	(7,290)	(7,800)	(9,130)	(10,080)	(11,090)

(Continued)

TABLE 8.1 (*Continued*)

Selected characteristics	Mexican	Puerto Rican	Central and South American[a]	Other Hispanic	Non-Hispanic white
Disability (%)	12.4	19.4	10.3	14.1	12.8
	(32.9)	(39.6)	(30.4)	(34.8)	(33.4)
Mean area hourly wage rate ($)	4.78	5.59	5.31	5.01	5.14
	(.73)	(.37)	(.56)	(.65)	(.62)
N^c	2,432	554	584	892	20,147

Soure: 1976 Survey of Income and Education (U.S. Department of Commerce, 1978).
Note: Standard deviations are in parentheses.
[a] Includes Cuban-origin women.
[b] See Table 8.2 for definition.
[c] Weighting renders these data comparable to population statistics, but reported N's are unweighted.

by national origin. Hispanic women are clearly disadvantaged with respect to education, a critical resource for labor market success. Mexicans and Puerto Ricans tend to be younger, on average, than non-Hispanic whites, and these two groups also have the lowest levels of educational attainment: about 9 years of graded schooling. Central and South American and Other Hispanic women complete approximately 11 years of school, while non-Hispanic white women complete an average of 12.3 years of school.

Hispanics also differ significantly with respect to their nativity. Central and South Americans are largely an immigrant group: over 90% of these adult women are foreign-born, compared to approximately one-fourth of the Mexican and Other Hispanic women. Also, the proportion of recent arrivals is greatest among Central and South Americans. In contrast, only 5% of the non-Hispanic white female population of labor force age is foreign-born. Although nearly 80% of Puerto Rican women were born on the island, they cannot be considered foreign-born in a strict sense; nevertheless, birth on the island is analogous to being born abroad because these women are likely to have been socialized in a Hispanic environment, including having received their education in the Spanish language. As such, island birth may produce an effect similar to that predicted for foreign birth.

Indices of English proficiency correspond to the birthplace statistics. Central and South American women have the lowest level of English fluency, with an average score of 7.7 (see definitions in Table 8.2), while non-Hispanic whites are most proficient in English, averaging just under the maximum possible score of 12 points. The other Hispanic groups fall between these two extremes.

Fertility, an important determinant of female labor force participation, also differentiates Hispanic women. Mexican women have the highest fertility. On average, Mexican and Puerto Rican women of labor force age have between 0.5 and 0.6 children under 6, and between 1.6 and 1.9 children under 18 years of age. The women of Other Hispanic and Central and South American origin tend to have fewer children at home, and non-Hispanic whites have the fewest children of all groups. Puerto Rican women are considerably more likely than any of the other groups to be family heads, with a headship rate over double that of any other Hispanic group and nearly four times greater than non-Hispanic white women. A high incidence of female headship is frequently associated with high levels of poverty (Tienda and Angel, 1982). Not surprisingly, Puerto Rican women receive the lowest level of earnings from other family members.

These data corroborate the general contention that Hispanics are sufficiently differentiated to require separate analyses of the national-origin groups (Jaffe et al., 1980; Tienda, 1981). What is less well articulated is how national origin should be used in formulating hypotheses about the ways ethnicity stratifies the Hispanic population. There is a dominant tendency in the literature on minority workers to test for the existence of discrimination using residual techniques (Oaxaca, 1973; Polachek, 1975b). Studies conducted within the human capital and status attainment traditions tend to attribute varied labor market outcomes to differences in individual human capital, or achieved characteristics. According to these theoretical perspectives the story is straightforward: Hispanic women with a lower stock of human capital will occupy lower positions in the occupational structure. National origin is relevant within this context to the extent that group differences in achieved characteristics will predict the average level of labor market returns. That is, groups with low average education levels, such as Puerto Ricans or Mexicans, are expected to have low earnings or low occupational status precisely because of the low level of human capital that most members take to their jobs. However the question remains as to why such differences in human capital arise in the first place, an issue we discuss further.

The assimilation literature discusses length of residence in the United States as a form of accumulated human capital. Recently arrived immigrants are often disadvantaged compared with the native-born or long-term residents because they usually lack the knowledge and skills necessary to function efficiently in the U.S. labor market (Gordon, 1964;

Chiswick, 1979; Borjas, 1981). Presumably, with the passing of time and greater opportunity to interact with members of the dominant majority, the initial handicaps associated with migration and residency in a new place should diminish, and immigrants eventually become indistinguishable from their native-born counterparts. Evidence that length of U.S. residence positively influences the labor market success of Hispanic immigrants supports this argument (Chiswick, 1979; Borjas, 1981). However, other authors have suggested that the persisting differences among national-origin groups result from other factors, including differential levels of labor market discrimination and the types of industries in which they are hired. These circumstances explain why some groups are eventually successful in overcoming labor market disadvantages, whereas others are not (Portes, 1979; Wilson and Portes, 1980).

Several excellent critiques of the human capital and assimilation perspectives exist (see, for example, Arce, 1981, pp. 178–182; Treiman and Hartmann, 1981, pp. 18–19), which we do not recount here. For our purposes, it is sufficient to point out that these perspectives emphasize the relevancy of national origin for average labor market outcomes primarily in terms of the level of achieved characteristics.

An alternative interpretation of the disadvantaged labor market position of minorities explicitly recognizes ethnicity as an ascribed characteristic which may serve as a signaling device to employers and to social institutions that confer the resources necessary for success. This "ethnic stratification" perspective differs somewhat from the human capital and assimilation approaches. *Ethnic stratification* refers to a system "wherein group membership (e.g., race, religion, or nationality) is utilized as a major criterion for assigning positions with their attendant differential rewards" (Noel, 1968, p. 157). Within this framework, Boyd (1980) elaborated a rationale for why certain nativity–nationality groups should have greater or fewer advantages in the occupational structure, independent of their varying stocks of human capital. First, such advantages, should they emerge, could reflect the existence of employer discrimination based on prejudice. Second, occupational positions may differ among groups because of varying preferences and opportunities to work. Finally, the occupational allocation of labor by nationality may reflect historically institutionalized practices of recruiting workers for particular jobs on the basis of their ethnicity or nativity. Among Hispanics, this finds a positive expression in the tendency for Cubans to hire other Cubans (Wilson and Portes, 1980), and a negative one in the tendency for non-Hispanic whites in the Southwest to recruit foreign-born, Mexican-origin women for domestic service or agricultural work.

What is missing in this and many other studies conducted from an ethnic stratification perspective is a clear sense of the extent to which various groups exercise differential control over societal resources that in turn facilitate the acquisition of human capital, and how this facet of inequality is produced (see Sullivan, 1978). Obviously, differences in human capital reflect the result of the process, but the main difficulty with cross-section data used to document such outcomes is that causes and consequences cannot be clearly separated. However, it is precisely because *groups* differ in their access to social resources, such as education and wealth, that they can be ranked and predictions can be made about specific social outcomes, such as the chances of securing high-status positions (Sullivan, 1978). Accordingly, in this study we question whether Mexican-origin women as a *group* do better in the U.S. occupational structure than do women of Central and South American or Other Hispanic origin. Patterned differences would indicate the need to ascertain the sources of such differences.

Although our data do not permit an evaluation of the differential control over resources exercised by the Hispanic-origin groups, previous research has demonstrated that Mexicans and Puerto Ricans are much more likely to be in poverty than non-Hispanic white or any other Hispanic–origin groups (Tienda, 1981). Elsewhere, Arce (1981) and Bonilla and Campos (1981), respectively, discussed the limited access to economic, political, and cultural resources among Mexicans and Puerto Ricans. There is also evidence that Cubans who immigrated before 1970 may rank higher in the stratification system than other Hispanic-origin groups because they have formed and maintained their own economic and institutional structure (Sullivan, 1978; Wilson and Portes, 1980). If these differences result from uneven control over and access to social and economic resources, we should discern patterned differences in women's occupational positions according to national origin.

In evaluating the determinants of occupational inequality among employed Hispanic women, the basic issue is whether and how ascribed and achieved characteristics influence their occupational position. This line of questioning suggests two separate but complementary hypotheses. One is that the lower occupational placement of Hispanic-origin women reflects their smaller stock of human resources, most notably those that ensure labor market success, such as education. An alternative but related hypothesis is that Hispanic-origin women occupy a lower position in the status hierarchy because of their ethnicity and nativity. These two hypotheses are not rival explanations; instead they provide a frame of reference from which to interpret socioeconomic differentiation among the Hispanic-origin groups, as well as between Hispanic and non-Hispanic white women. For expository purposes, the first will be called the *achievement hypothesis* and the latter the *ascription hypothesis,* to distinguish the sources of ethnic variation in labor market position. Accordingly, our present task is to evaluate empirically the appropriateness of these explanations of the occupational position of Hispanic-origin women.

Data and Methods

We analyze the occupational position of Hispanic-origin women with data from the 1976 Survey of Income and Education (SIE; U.S. Department of Commerce, 1978). Our analyses are restricted to women aged 18–64 who reported an occupation in 1975. If women were enrolled in school in 1975, they were included only if employed more than 1240 hours. This resulted in a total sample of 13,524, of which 11,341 were non-Hispanic white women used as a comparison group.[1] Of the remaining observations, 1208 were of Mexican origin, 198 of Puerto Rican origin, 332 of Central and South American origin, and 445 of Other Hispanic origin. These samples contain 36–56% of all women aged 18–64 in the SIE.

We base our analysis of occupational position on two measures. One is a measure of social standing based on the socioeconomic content of occupations, and another represents broad occupational strata derived from a grouping of the detailed census occupation codes (see Appendix Table 8A.2 for details). For the former measure, data on respondents' 1975 occupations were converted into socioeconomic status scores as revised by Featherman and Stevens (1982). We denote these TSEI in the analysis. Unlike Duncan's (1961) original socioeconomic index, that computed by Featherman and Stevens is based on the total labor force (men and women). This is important because it addresses a critical issue in the study of female status attainment processes—namely, that the scores based on the male labor force inadequately represent women's location in the status hierarchy.[2]

---

[1] Because the SIE is exceptionally large, a 33% random sample of non-Hispanic white women was drawn for the empirical analyses, mainly for computational efficiency. Sampling weights are not used in the multivariate analyses because weighted samples generate incorrect tests of statistical significance, but descriptive statistics in Tables 8.1 and 8.5 and Appendix Tables 8A.1 and 8A.2 are weighted.

[2] Our decision not to use the Duncan index, which is based only on men's multivariate analyses, results from our appraisal that this metric artificially inflates the mean status levels of Hispanic and non-Hispanic white women. Such upward biases are especially serious when comparisons between men and women are desired, but less so for within-sex comparisons. This criticism does not mean that the male-based Duncan SEI scores are

Socioeconomic status scores reflect the average education and earnings levels of incumbents in specified occupations. Thus, scores based only on the male labor force do not take into account differences in these characteristics between men and women with the same occupation. This difficulty is exacerbated with status scores that represent broad occupational groups, because of the disproportionate concentration of women in two lower white-collar occupations—clerical and retail sales (Powers and Holmberg, 1978; Wolf and Rosenfeld, 1978; Featherman and Stevens, 1982). Powers and Holmberg demonstrated that the status rankings of clerical workers (predominantly women) and crafts workers (predominantly men) are reversed when rankings are based on the total labor force. Failure to acknowledge differences in the underlying occupational distributions between men and women may lead to erroneous conclusions about how the process of stratification depends on sex.

Following recent research in stratification (Beck et al., 1978; Featherman and Hauser, 1978), we depict women's occupational position as a function of individual and labor market characteristics. The extensive literature on the processes of socioeconomic attainment amply documents the value of education and age in providing access to social rewards in a meritocractic system. Education increases skill and access to the social resources necessary for labor market success. In addition, we hypothesize that nativity status, English-language proficiency, and labor supply, represented by a dummy for part-time work, will influence the occupational position of Hispanic women. Table 8.2 provides a summary description of our variables.

Language potentially influences women's occupational placement because other studies show that proficiency in English determines the assignment of men to particular jobs (Garcia, 1979; Grenier, 1981; Tienda, 1982; Tienda and Neidert, 1984) and culturally differentiates ethnic populations (Bowman, 1981). Chiswick (1979) claims that language is also a proxy for the transferability of labor market skills among the foreign-born. We derived our English-proficiency measure from two items with categorical response choices about speaking and comprehension. Each item consists of six categories and the two were summed, generating a proficiency measure with a potential range of 1 to 12, with the high score representing complete fluency. Finally, because important differentials in labor supply patterns exist among the Hispanic na-

---

invalid. It simply means that our analysis shows, as have prior studies, that an occupational status index based on the total labor force is preferable for analyzing the occupational achievements of women (Powers and Holmberg, 1978; Featherman and Stevens, 1982).

TABLE 8.2
Definitions of Variables Used in the Multivariate Analyses

Variable	Definition
Age	A series of dummy variables for the age categories 18–24, 25–34, 35–44, and 45–54. The age category 55–64 is omitted. (0–1)
Education	Number of completed years of schooling. (0–18)
Native-born	Born in the U.S., or on the U.S. mainland for Puerto Ricans = 1. (0–1)
Years since migration	A series of dummy variables for the number of years since immigration to the U.S. or to the U.S. mainland for Puerto Ricans. The native-born constitute the omitted category.
1 or less	Immigrated to the U.S. since 1975 = 1. (0–1)
2–5	Immigrated to the U.S. 1971–1974 = 1. (0–1)
6–11	Immigrated to the U.S. 1965–1970 = 1. (0–1)
12 or more	Immigrated to the U.S. before 1965 = 1. (0–1)
English-language proficiency	A measure of English language proficiency that combines information about understanding and speaking English. A low value indicates low proficiency and a high value indicates high proficiency. (1–12)
Children under 6	The number of own children under 6 years old, related by blood, marriage, or adoption to the family head. (0–6)
Children under 18	The number of own, never-married children under 18 years old. (0–9)
Female family head	If study respondent is the household head and lives with other relatives = 1. (0–1)
Other family earnings	Total family wage and salary earnings minus those of the study respondent, in dollars. (0–80,000)
Disability	Study respondent reported any of the following (= 1): a personal handicap; physical disability, any condition that limits the kind or amount of work, or specified other activities she can do; an illness or disability as the reason for not working in 1975. (0–1)
Area wage rate	The average wage rate in the SMSA, or state nonmetropolitan area, in dollars. (3.62–7.39)
Part-time work	Respondent in the 1975 occupation sample usually worked part time rather than full time in 1975 = 1. (0–1)
Percentage Hispanic	The percentage of the population that is Hispanic in SMSA or state nonmetropolitan area. (00–65)
Periphery sector	Industry where the respondent is employed is in the periphery sector, classified according to Beck, Horan, and Tolbert (1978) = 1. The periphery sector includes labor-intensive industries such as agriculture and highly competitive, nondurable manufacturing and service industries.
TSEI	The socioeconomic status score, as revised by Stevens and Featherman (1979), based on men and women according to 1970 occupational categories. (0–100)

TABLE 8.2 (*Continued*)

Variable	Definition
λ	The inverse of the Mill's ratio predicting membership in the 1975 occupational sample. Table 8.3 shows the variables entered into the probit analysis used to generate the value for each individual. Women are excluded from the occupation sample if they did not report an occupation in response to the question, "What was your longest job in 1975?" They were also excluded if they worked fewer than 1240 hours in 1975 and (1) reported school as their major activity when not working or (2) were in school at the time of the survey. (.14–2.20)

tional-origin groups (Guhleman and Tienda, 1981), we include a measure of part-time work status.

Our functional specification also includes variables representing labor market characteristics to acknowledge that group differences in control over resources also depend on social arrangements over which individual workers exercise little control. Because some Hispanics are highly concentrated in regions according to nationality, recognition of how labor market characteristics might influence female employment outcomes is especially important. We use two indicators, described more fully below, of labor market characteristics: one is an index of labor market crowding, represented by the percentage Hispanic in a Standard Metropolitan Statistical Area (SMSA) or in the state nonmetropolitan area, and another is industry sector location, an index of market segmentation.

The influence of the crowding variable is potentially ambiguous. One possibility is that women residing in areas where Hispanics are concentrated will have greater opportunities to secure higher-status positions because the existence of a large ethnic labor pool increases the chances that at least a few women will secure professional occupations; thus, a positive effect would emerge. Yet it is also plausible that a negative relationship between occupational status and Hispanic concentration would emerge if employers use ethnicity as a queueing device to fill the low-status jobs in particular labor markets. This result would illustrate the merit of the ethnic stratification perspective on labor market outcomes by showing how ascribed characteristics operate to assign workers to occupational positions.

Another way we acknowledge the influence of structural determinants of individual and group positions in the occupational hierarchy is by using a control for labor market sector. This is pertinent because of the growing evidence that workers' insertion in the employment structure determines individual outcomes (Stolzenberg, 1975; Beck et al., 1978; Hodson, 1978; Portes and Bach, 1980; Wilson and Portes, 1980; England, 1982). The segmented market approach suggests that jobs with opportunities for better rewards are concentrated in the oligopolistic, or core, industrial sector. There, firms tend to be large, unionized, and capital intensive. In contrast, competitive industries located in the periphery sector operate on low profit margins, are sensitive to shifts in the wider market, and are labor intensive. Low pay, few opportunities for advancement, lack of job stability, and minimal returns to human capital characterize the inferior working conditions in the periphery. Previous research shows that workers with the weakest labor market positions, namely minorities and women, tend to be overrepresented in the periphery (Kemp and Beck, 1981). This situation reflects a structural constraint on the potential for occupational equality among workers with similar characteristics.[3] In keeping with the basic argument of the market segmentation perspective, we anticipate that women employed in the core labor market sector will have a higher occupational position than those who are employed in the periphery, and that this effect will differ according to nationality groups.

Because we observed occupations only for women who work and who meet the conditions imposed on the sample with respect to school enrollment, analyses based on the subset of women with occupations may be biased. This follows because the expected value of the observed occupation variable is not random but rather is correlated with the errors of the determinants of occupation. One method to correct for selectivity bias, proposed by Heckman (1979), is to estimate a probit model predicting inclusion in the occupation sample, generating the inverse of Mill's ratio, and entering this ratio, denoted λ, in the occupation equations. Accordingly, we estimated reduced-form sample inclusion probits[4] as a

---

[3] While it is true that the dual-sector conceptualization of labor market segmentation tends to blur the extent of within-sector heterogeneity (Hodson and Kaufman, 1981), our decision to consider this aspect of labor market structure in the analyses of occupational stratification reflects our conviction that structural constraints determine individual and group occupational positions, above and beyond the effects that may be attributed to characteristics defining group membership, such as national origin and nativity. As Abowd and Killingsworth (Chapter 3 in this volume) and Reimers (Chapter 2) demonstrate, another pertinent aspect of market structure to consider is the federal–nonfederal sector. Our focus on occupations rather than wages makes the market sector variable more appropriate because it refers to characteristics of jobs that vary systematically by industry rather than to the employer behavior that can translate to higher wages for specific groups.

[4] The general concern of sample selection bias in this case is whether women are in or out of the labor force. However, the status of being in the labor force includes women who

function of women's human capital, family, and economic characteristics. "Other family earnings" represent an exogenous indicator of economic need, which conditions women's decisions to enter the labor market, and "area wage rate" captures the opportunity costs of nonparticipation by indexing potential wages for those who decide to enter the labor force. Table 8.3 reports these results.

Health and the presence of children are uniformly significant determinants of women's inclusion in the occupation sample for all groups. As expected, the presence of children decreases the likelihood that women will work, as does the presence of a limiting health condition. The availability of alternative sources of earnings from other family members lowers the probability that all women, except Puerto Ricans, will work and thus be in our occupation sample, but the point estimates for this effect are very small. Heading a family influences the probability of being in the occupation sample only for non-Hispanic white women; and for them, the effect is positive. The pattern of age effects is not uniform across groups but, in general, participation levels tend to be highest during the prime ages 25–44. Central and South American women continue to exhibit high rates of labor force and sample participation beyond age 44. The insignificance of the age coefficients for this group at earlier ages is partly related to the age distribution of this population.

Surprisingly, education exerts only a modest influence on the likelihood that women will be in the occupation sample, and the point estimates are significant only for Mexican, Other Hispanic, and non-Hispanic white women. Recently arrived Mexican and Central and South American immigrants are less likely than earlier immigrants to work and to have an occupation in 1975, but no similar effect emerges for any of the other ethnicities. For these same two Hispanic groups, the negative effect of recent arrival is offset slightly by high proficiency in English, suggesting that recently arrived Mexican and Central and South American women will be more likely to enter the labor force (and to be in our occupation sample) if they are fluent in English.

Besides providing a general indication of the determinants of labor

---

are unemployed and looking for work, and thus may not have an occupation. The greater the discrepancy between employment and labor force participation, the greater are the differences between those probit estimates for sample-selection bias estimated using the criterion of "in sample" and those using the criterion "in labor force" as the dependent variable. We computed probits using both dependent variables and found some, but not many, differences. Greatest differences appear for Puerto Ricans, the group that experiences the highest rates of unemployment.

TABLE 8.3
Estimated Coefficients of Reduced-Form Probit Equations Predicting Being in
Occupation Sample: Women Age 18–64, by National Origin

Variable	Mexican	Puerto Rican	Central and South American[a]	Other Hispanic	Non-Hispanic white
Age					
18–24	.378**	.409	−.236	.199	.190**
	(.124)	(.308)	(.260)	(.169)	(.031)
25–34	.691**	.655*	.412	.698**	.606**
	(.124)	(.299)	(.256)	(.181)	(.033)
35–44	.768**	.397	.518*	.692**	.603**
	(.127)	(.296)	(.247)	(.174)	(.036)
45–54	.379**	.463	.739**	.555**	.431**
	(.124)	(.296)	(.261)	(.163)	(.031)
Education	.021*	.012	−.033	.090**	.053**
	(.009)	(.022)	(.020)	(.018)	(.004)
Number of children					
Under 6	−.216**	−.255**	−.197	−.312**	−.254**
	(.039)	(.093)	(.106)	(.086)	(.019)
Under 18	−.089**	−.174**	−.236**	−.091*	−.129**
	(.018)	(.047)	(.059)	(.036)	(.009)
Years since migration					
1 or less	−.498	−.373	−.980**	−1.201	−.226
	(.262)	(.422)	(.365)	(.681)	(.208)
2–5	−.118	.048	−.347	−.296	−.044
	(.164)	(.262)	(.283)	(.308)	(.144)
6–11	.106	−.083	−.253	.094	.209
	(.141)	(.240)	(.255)	(.273)	(.108)
12 or more	−.080	.183	.164	−.095	−.051
	(.091)	(.173)	(.248)	(.178)	(.050)
English-language proficiency	.044**	.025	.063*	.015	.002
	(.016)	(.031)	(.029)	(.031)	(.005)
Disability	−.483**	−.690**	−1.094**	−.713**	−.602**
	(.084)	(.175)	(.214)	(.133)	(.028)
Female family head	−.010	−.253	.220	.096	.252**
	(.086)	(.154)	(.214)	(.148)	(.038)
Other family earnings	−.000**	.000	−.000**	−.000**	−.000**
	(.000)	(.000)	(.000)	(.000)	(.000)
Area wage rate	−.008	.060	.006	−.000	.031
	(.041)	(.132)	(.106)	(.085)	(.017)

TABLE 8.3 (*Continued*)

Variable	Mexican	Puerto Rican	Central and South American[a]	Other Hispanic	Non-Hispanic white
Constant	−.667	−1.063	.479	−1.142	−.199
	(.229)	(.835)	(.699)	(.478)	(.116)
N	2,432	554	584	892	20,147

Source: 1976 Survey of Income and Education (U.S. Department of Commerce, 1978).
Note: Standard errors are in parentheses.
[a] Includes Cuban-origin women.
* Statistically significant at the 5% level in a two-tailed test.
** Statistically significant at the 1% level in a two-tailed test.

force participation among Hispanic women, the probit generates the inverse of the Mill's ratio, the correction factor needed to adjust the following analyses of women's occupational positions for sample-selection bias.

Determinants of Occupational Position

Our theoretical discussion of the determinants of the occupational position of Hispanic women indicated that an individual's ascribed and achieved attributes and labor market characteristics are involved. First we evaluate women's occupational position as a function of age, education, nativity, language ability, part-time employment status, the inverse of the Mill's ratio, and two labor market characteristics using the socioeconomic status index. Part-time employment status controls systematic differences in occupational status corresponding to the kinds of jobs available for part-time versus full-time work, and the inverse of the Mill's ratio controls for possible selection bias.

The ascription hypothesis predicts that both nativity and national origin will contribute independently to the occupational placement of Hispanic-origin women. Our analysis is structured to compare occupational status among Hispanic national-origin groups and non-Hispanic whites. This decision was empirically substantiated through a prior analysis based on a pooled regression for the total sample. In the first step, we used the sociodemographic and labor market characteristics to predict occupational status, and subsequently introduced a series of dummy variable interactions between the Hispanic national-origin groups and the other variables in the model. These results confirmed that national origin does make a significant contribution to the explained variance in the occupational status of women, above and beyond that due to differences in levels of human capital among the groups. Thus, we conduct separate analyses for each national-origin group.

Nativity, the second characteristic hypothesized to support the ascription concept, is introduced as an additive term in the equations estimated separately for each group. Additional tests of nativity interactions indicated that nativity does not condition the effects of individual and labor market characteristics in determining socioeconomic status, except among Puerto Ricans. In the interest of parsimony, we do not estimate separate models for native- and foreign-born Puerto Ricans, for whom the nativity distinction is fuzzy, but assume that nativity effects are largely additive for all groups. Appendix Table 8A.1 reports the means and standard deviations of the variables used in the regression analysis.

STATUS ATTAINMENT PROCESS

The functional relationship among the achieved and ascribed characteristics of employed women outlined in Table 8.4 shows how the determinants of occupational status differ among women of Hispanic and non-Hispanic origin. As expected, education positively influences socioeconomic achievement for all groups, but the magnitude of the effect varies according to nationality. Nonminority women receive a status payoff of about 2.8 points on the socioeconomic index for each year of school completed, while Hispanic women receive somewhat lower payoffs for each year of graded schooling. Part-time employment lowers the status rewards of comparably educated nonminority women, although no such effect emerges for Hispanics. Among Hispanics, women of Other Hispanic origin receive the highest status returns to education, averaging 2.5 points for each year completed, while those of Central and South American origin receive the lowest returns, approximately 1.6 points per year of completed schooling. Mexicans and Puerto Ricans receive similar status payoffs to education.

Thus, the lower aggregate status positions of Hispanic-origin women vis-à-vis non-Hispanic whites appear to be due not only to differences in prior achievements, but also to the differential evaluation of educational resources in the U.S. labor market. Being a member of a Hispanic ethnic group confers status disadvantages that are partly transmitted through the differential evaluation of graded schooling. Taking into account linguistic characteristics of the groups does not alter this result because proficiency in English does not affect the occupational status of Hispanic or non-Hispanic white women once differences in education are taken into account.

Nativity has no significant impact on the occupational achievement of Hispanic or non-Hispanic white women, but the ethnic composition of the labor market does. Presence of large proportions of Hispanics confers status advantages to non-Hispanic white women while depressing the status rewards for Puerto Rican women. We hypothesized that the effect of this variable was potentially ambiguous, and this seems to be the case for the other Hispanic-origin groups, for whom the coefficients differ in sign from those of Puerto Ricans. However, because of the large standard errors, we cannot reject the hypothesis that these results are different from zero. For Puerto Ricans, the effects are on the margin of statistical significance, while for non-Hispanic whites, a large and positive coefficient indicates that nonminority women benefit in status from the presence of a large Hispanic labor pool. This result is plausible if minority women are used disproportionately to fill slots in the lower echelons of the occupational hierarchy. In the absence of evidence about significant gains to Hispanics, this finding reinforces the importance of ascription in determining the labor market outcomes of minority and nonminority women workers. Further study of the possibility of employer discrimination in areas containing large minority populations is definitely called for.

The coefficient for sectoral location illustrates the importance of ethnic workers' mode of incorporation into the U.S. labor market. Notice that for every group (nonminority women included), periphery-sector employment results in a sizable disadvantage to workers. The largest penalty accrues to non-Hispanic white and Other Hispanic women, but these women, particularly non-Hispanic whites, are less likely to hold periphery jobs. For both groups, periphery-sector employment produces a 10-point average decrease in the revised socioeconomic status index. For the remainder of the Hispanic nationalities, periphery-sector employment provides a status cost of approximately 6.5 to 8.5 points on the occupational index. Puerto Ricans suffer somewhat more than Mexicans and Central and South Americans from periphery-sector location; but they are also disproportionately located in the core sector relative to women in the other two groups (see Appendix Table 8A.1).

Overall, our results provide strong support for the achievement explanation of socioeconomic status, but there exists sufficient evidence that ascriptive characteristics shape the process of ethnic stratification. Na-

TABLE 8.4

Regressions of Socioeconomic Status Scores on Individual and Labor Market Characteristics, by National Origin: Women Age 18–64 in the 1975 Occupation Sample

Variable	Mexican		Puerto Rican		Central and South American[a]		Other Hispanic		Non-Hispanic white	
	(1)	(2)	(1)	(2)	(1)	(2)	(1)	(2)	(1)	(2)
Age										
18–24	−5.930**	−5.834**	−1.017	−1.501	1.812	2.682	−9.379**	−8.939**	−5.814**	−5.811**
	(1.582)	(1.610)	(4.302)	(4.327)	(3.051)	(3.227)	(2.542)	(2.581)	(.665)	(.666)
25–34	−2.817	−2.648	1.843	1.168	−.087	−.041	−7.743**	−6.777*	−1.302	−1.285
	(1.551)	(1.637)	(4.098)	(4.150)	(2.795)	(2.797)	(2.446)	(2.635)	(.631)	(.654)
35–44	−2.188	−1.990	−3.269	−3.717	−1.241	−1.282	−7.256**	−6.149*	−.408	−.393
	(1.579)	(1.694)	(4.234)	(4.256)	(2.795)	(2.797)	(2.474)	(2.717)	(.669)	(.687)
45–54	−1.888	−1.764	−.494	−1.585	1.440	.855	−7.935**	−6.850*	−.473	−.458
	(1.657)	(1.701)	(4.274)	(4.404)	(2.830)	(2.917)	(2.468)	(2.702)	(.653)	(.672)
Education	1.753**	1.764**	1.833**	1.772**	1.597**	1.631**	2.340**	2.514**	2.842**	2.845**
	(.112)	(.117)	(.294)	(.300)	(.211)	(.215)	(.256)	(.311)	(.084)	(.089)
Native-born	−.937	−.931	2.684	2.766	2.609	2.502	.758	.912	−.711	−.710
	(.971)	(.971)	(2.286)	(2.287)	(2.599)	(2.604)	(2.298)	(2.303)	(.921)	(.922)

	(1)	(2)	(1)	(2)	(1)	(2)	(1)	(2)	(1)	(2)
English-language proficiency	-.310 (.186)	-.293 (.194)	.104 (.402)	.031 (.408)	.321 (.313)	.221 (.335)	.226 (.487)	.232 (.487)	-.179 (.113)	-.179 (.113)
Part-time work	-.729 (.746)	-.750 (.749)	2.253 (2.167)	2.706 (2.211)	1.224 (2.045)	1.786 (2.155)	-.989 (1.460)	-1.261 (1.486)	-1.252** (.440)	-1.262** (.452)
Percentage Hispanic	2.505 (1.963)	2.562 (1.972)	-21.608 (11.418)	-22.975 (11.494)	6.283 (5.982)	6.363 (5.986)	6.025 (4.338)	5.827 (4.343)	6.452* (2.552)	6.459* (2.553)
Periphery sector	-6.502** (.658)	-6.504** (.658)	-8.454** (1.616)	-8.252** (1.628)	-7.685** (1.390)	-7.624** (1.392)	-10.119** (1.351)	-10.218** (1.355)	-10.031** (.415)	-10.032** (.415)
λ	—b	.562 (1.734)	—b	-3.033 (2.957)	—b	-2.251 (2.712)	—b	3.117 (3.159)	—b	.087 (.894)
Constant	24.437	23.597	20.190	24.531	16.153	17.706	21.602	16.607	22.780	22.679
R^2	.321	.321	.394	.398	.354	.355	.352	.354	.186	.186
N	1,208	1,208	198	198	332	332	445	445	11,341	11,341

Source: 1976 Survey of Income and Education (U.S. Department of Commerce, 1978).

Notes: Standard errors are in parentheses. Column (1) in each national-origin group is the effects of each variable unadjusted for nativity, whereas Column (2) coefficients are net of the effects of lambda.

a Includes Cuban-origin women.

b Variable not entered in the equation.

* Statistically significant at the 5% level in a one-tailed test.

** Statistically significant at the 1% level in a one-tailed test.

tionality is clearly instrumental in determining the relative socioeconomic ranking of Hispanic-origin women above and beyond the effects
due to differences in education and other demographic characteristics.[5]
Evidence for the significance of ethnicity is also evident in the different
value of schooling for Hispanic and non-Hispanic white women, but
there is no evidence that nativity directly determines occupational status
after adjusting for differences in socioeconomic characteristics that are
systematically associated with birthplace. Furthermore, our results support the notion that extraindividual characteristics, notably sectoral location but also ethnic composition of the labor market, influence the socioeconomic status of Hispanic-origin women. A remaining question for
further research is to ascertain whether achieved and ascribed characteristics determine sectoral location in the first place. Preliminary evidence
based on men suggests that this is the case (Tienda and Neidert, 1980;
Tienda, 1983).

OCCUPATIONAL ALLOCATION PROCESS

Because socioeconomic status represents but one dimension of occupational position, our conclusions about the role of ethnicity in stratifying Hispanic-origin workers cannot be generalized to all aspects of the
stratification system. Recently there has been considerable debate as to
whether prestige scores and socioeconomic status scores should be used
to evaluate the occupational position of women. For the most part, this
discussion focuses on analyses comparing men and women, but part of
the debate has questioned the significance of the status index per se
(Horan, 1978; Acker, 1980; Horan et al., 1981). Economists, for example,
say that it borders on the tautological to derive socioeconomic index
scores for occupations based on the educational and income characteristics of respondents and then to use education to predict socioeconomic
status. In the light of such sharp criticism, some validation of our empirical results and substantive conclusions is warranted.

In response to criticisms about the value of socioeconomic status
scores as measures of occupational position, we have recomputed our
analyses of occupational position using a categorical measure of occupation. For this purpose, we collapsed the thirteen occupational categories
shown in Appendix Table 8A.2 to form four major occupational strata.

---

[5] The significance of national origin in determining socioeconomic success was based on
pooled regression models that included national origin coded as a dummy variable, which
was subsequently interacted with the independent variables. National origin was a significant predictor of women's occupational status for three of the five Hispanic groups.

These strata, which represent the basic upper white-collar, lower white-collar, and blue-collar groupings conventionally used in studies of occupational mobility (Featherman and Hauser, 1978; Snipp, 1981; Snipp and Tienda, 1982), reflect the distinction between nonmanual and manual workers. The two categories of blue-collar workers include one that combines service and craft workers (due to the small proportion of women in the craft category), and one that combines operatives, laborers, and farm workers. A separate category for farm workers is not justified because only one group, Mexicans, had a nontrivial share of workers assigned to this occupation in 1975. We assigned them to the lower blue-collar stratum.

The allocation of Hispanic and non-Hispanic white female labor among these four occupational strata is presented in Table 8.5, along with the mean socioeconomic status scores corresponding to the aggregated occupational strata. These mean scores impart a sense of the status rankings of the four occupational strata, and serve as a link between the regression and discriminant analyses (which follow). As expected, the highest average status rankings correspond to the professional, managerial, and nonretail sales category, while the lowest levels correspond to the operative and laborer category. This pattern also holds for comparisons *within* ethnic groups, with a minor deviation for non-Hispanic whites. However, owing to differences in the allocation of minority workers among these strata, the average status levels within strata differ among the groups. These differences are most pronounced in the operative and laborer category, where the average status threshold of minority women is on the order of 17 points on the revised socioeconomic index, whereas that of nonminority women is nearly twice as large, or 31 points. A similar pattern emerges in the second and third occupational strata (clerical and retail sales; services and crafts), where the average status level of non-Hispanic white women is about 7 to 10 points higher than the corresponding status level for minority women.

Our discussion of the differential control over social resources exercised by minority and nonminority women suggests that the latter would be more highly represented in the professional, managerial, and nonretail sales category. Lacking access to the resources that confer high-status positions, minority women should be more highly concentrated in the operative and laborer category. This pattern is clearly portrayed in Table 8.5. Whereas about one-fourth of all non-Hispanic white women hold professional, managerial, and sales positions, the proportion of Hispanic incumbents in similar occupations ranges from a high of 19% for those of Other Hispanic origin to less than 8% for Mexican-origin women. At the other extreme, only 12% of all non-Hispanic white

TABLE 8.5

Occupational Allocation of Women Age 18–64 in the 1975 Occupation Sample, by National Origin: Percentage Distribution and Mean Socioeconomic Status Scores

Occupational Category	Mexican		Puerto Rican		Central and South American[a]		Other Hispanic		Non-Hispanic white	
	%	Mean	%	Mean	%	Mean	%	Mean	%	Mean
Professional, managerial and nonretail sales	7.6	59.2 (12.1)	10.5	58.4 (11.1)	11.5	57.4 (11.7)	18.7	60.1 (12.1)	25.9	59.9 (13.2)
Clerical and retail sales	31.3	27.8 (5.7)	28.6	28.1 (3.8)	32.4	28.4 (4.4)	44.4	30.3 (7.2)	44.0	37.6 (19.7)
Service and crafts	26.9	20.0 (4.9)	16.0	21.4 (6.2)	20.2	19.4 (5.3)	22.4	19.2 (4.1)	18.5	27.1 (17.8)
Operative and laborer[b]	34.1	17.1 (2.0)	44.9	17.2 (3.0)	35.8	16.7 (2.2)	14.4	16.8 (2.8)	11.6	31.4 (27.1)
	99.9		100.0		99.9		99.9		100.0	
N	1,208		198		332		445		11,341	

Source: 1976 Survey of Income and Education (U.S. Department of Commerce, 1978).

Note: Standard errors are in parentheses.

[a] Includes Cuban-origin women.

[b] Includes farmers, farm supervisors, and farm laborers.

women are in operative and laborer occupations, as compared to 45% among Puerto Ricans, and roughly one-third of Central and South Americans and Mexicans. Women of Other Hispanic origin are more like nonminority women in that less than 15% held operative and laborer jobs in 1975. Differences among Hispanic and non-Hispanic white women are less pronounced in the clerical and service occupations.

To evaluate the process by which minority and nonminority workers are allocated among the occupational strata and to compare the determinants of occupational position and occupational status among the national-origin groups, we computed a discriminant analysis using the four occupational strata as categorical dependent variables and the same set of independent variables to predict the status dimension of occupational position. This analysis, although problematic in its own way, allows us to ascertain whether our conclusions about the determinants of occupational status are an artifact of the derivation of the socioeconomic index as a measure of occupational status.

Using a four-category dependent variable, the maximum number of discriminant functions possible is three (4 minus 1). The proportion of cases correctly classified ranges from 44 to 60%. Eigen relative-percentage values, which fall between 74 and 92, indicate the overwhelming dominance of the first function in accounting for the pattern of occupational allocation. These statistics show that the fit of the first function is quite good. Even though the second and third discriminant functions produce statistically significant canonical correlations for all groups except Puerto Ricans, their ability to discriminate among the occupational strata is trivial, as indicated by the magnitude of the canonical correlations and the Eigen relative-percentage values. For this reason, we confine our discussion to the first discriminant function.

Results reported in Table 8.6 include the standardized discriminant coefficients for the first function and the statistics required for evaluating the goodness-of-fit of the model. The canonical correlation coefficients, which measure the overall association between the discriminant function and the occupational strata, are fairly consistent across groups, ranging between .6 and .7 for all groups. Group centroids indicate that the first discriminant function best distinguishes employment in the professional, managerial, and sales occupations from employment in operative and laborer occupations. Workers in other occupational strata are distinguishable from one another, but the contrast with the high-status category of professional, managerial, and wholesale workers is not as sharply defined. Another clear message is that the determinants of occupational position differ among the groups, even though there are a great many similarities.

TABLE 8.6
Discriminant Analysis of Women's Allocation into Four Occupational Strata: First
Function Discriminant Coefficients for Hispanic and Non-Hispanic White Women

	Mexican	Puerto Rican	Central and South American[a]	Other Hispanic	Non-Hispanic white
Variables					
Age					
18–24	−.20	−.01	.24	.01	−.19
25–34	−.11	.09	.05	.03	−.07
35–44	−.06	−.30	.17	−.04	−.07
45–54	−.07	.09	.07	−.14	−.03
Education	.85	.56	.54	.62	.90
Native-born	.06	.39	.10	.04	−.03
English-language proficiency	.02	.34	.40	.28	.01
Part-time work	.09	.22	.14	−.06	−.03
Percentage Hispanic	.15	−.06	.08	.33	.07
Periphery sector	−.38	−.39	−.49	−.57	−.34
Statistics					
Eigen value	.44	.91	.77	.65	.51
Eigen relative percentage	84.19	87.32	85.20	74.34	92.03
Canonical correlation	.55	.69	.66	.63	.58
Chi square	534.51	146.88	227.83	312.04	5182.20
p	≤.001	≤.001	≤.001	≤.001	≤.001
Strata centroids					
Professional, managerial, and nonretail sales	1.29	1.47	1.28	1.06	1.11
Clerical and retail sales	.58	.94	.82	.42	−.06
Service and crafts	−.30	.13	−.60	−.86	−.72
Operative and laborer	−.72	−.94	−.90	−1.15	−.92
Percentage of class correctly classified	43.54	60.10	49.10	56.63	50.15
N	1,208	198	332	445	11,341

Source: 1976 Survey of Income and Education (U.S. Department of Commerce, 1978).
[a] Includes Cuban-origin women.

Overall, these results reaffirm those based on the regressions of socioeconomic status scores. Education exerts the dominant influence on the
occupational position of women of all national origins, including non-
Hispanic whites. Without exception, the largest standardized discriminant coefficient corresponds to the schooling variable. This finding cor-
roborates the widely held premise of students of stratification that the
key dimension underlying occupations is socioeconomic (Featherman et
al., 1975). The fact that this result appears for female workers as well as

for men (Snipp, 1981) is significant in its own right. Apparently women, like men, have better chances of entering high-level occupations if they acquire sufficient schooling, but this presupposes equal resources and opportunities for all groups to achieve similar education levels. Clearly, this situation does not exist. Before the occupational position of Hispanic women is improved, it is obvious that measures must be taken to upgrade their educational attainment.

Because the discriminant coefficients have been normalized, strict comparisons cannot be made among the national-origin groups; but the values of the discriminant coefficients relative to the values of the respective group centroids indicate which factors extend greater or lesser influence in allocating women workers among the four occupational strata. The fact that the highest group centroid values correspond to the professional, managerial, and sales category among all groups indicates that women with higher levels of education are more likely to be allocated to this occupational category. However, factors other than education exercise a significant influence on the occupational placement of women. Sectoral location emerges as the second most dominant determinant of occupational placement for all groups. This finding suggests that it is not only worker characteristics but also characteristics of jobs that determine the placement of women in the occupational hierarchy. To the extent that ethnicity interacts with market forces to draw female workers into some slots while excluding them from others, the possibility of securing high-status positions may be reduced.

The magnitude and direction of the group centroids in comparison to values of the discriminant coefficients indicate that Hispanic workers in the periphery sector tend to be excluded from upper white-collar jobs. This result is consistent with existing arguments and evidence about how forms of labor market insertion (Portes, 1979) determine subsequent labor market outcomes, whether these are gauged in terms of earnings (Beck et al., 1978; Portes and Bach, 1980; Tienda and Neidert, 1980; Wilson and Portes, 1980), or occupational position (Stolzenberg, 1975; Wolf and Rosenfeld, 1978). Our analysis does not directly address the question of *why* workers are differentially allocated to the core and periphery, but it does suggest that explanations of inequality that focus on individually achieved and ascribed characteristics must be qualified until the influence of market characteristics is taken into consideration. Presumably, educational differences among the groups play a part in the labor market insertion patterns, but there is more to the story. Moreover, differences in educational attainment among the groups partly reflect differential access to this important social resource.

Results of the discriminant analysis also provide some support for the ascription explanation of labor market location. Only for Puerto Ricans does nativity emerge as an important determinant of women's occupational positions—the second largest discriminant coefficient corresponds to this variable. Perhaps there exists an association between the content and quality of schooling obtained by Puerto Rican women born on the mainland and on the island that continues to differentiate this group within the context of the U.S. labor market. English proficiency is the third most important determinant of occupational placement among Puerto Rican, Central and South American, and Other Hispanic women, reinforcing further the need for adequate linguistic skills for entry into high-level occupations.

Despite their consistency with the results of the regression analysis and their coherence with respect to the determinants of upper white-collar occupational allocation, these findings leave open the question of what determines the allocation of Hispanic women into lower white-collar and blue-collar jobs. Given that so few Hispanic women hold upper white-collar positions, this question is even more critical. Therefore, we recomputed the discriminant analysis, excluding the professional and managerial category. For this analysis, reported in Table 8.7, two discriminant functions are possible, but only the first function is shown because of its dominance in terms of overall discriminating power (Eigen relative-percentage values range from 97 for Puerto Ricans to 78 for Other Hispanic).

The discriminant coefficients reveal three general patterns of influence. As in the previous analysis, the group centroids distinguish between clerical or retail sales workers and the remaining two occupational strata, the clearest demarcation being with the lower-status operative and laborer category. Notice that the magnitudes of the coefficients differ among the groups. For Mexican and non-Hispanic white women, education is the major discriminating factor, with periphery-sector location being the second most important factor, as in the former analysis. By contrast, both education and language proficiency determine the allocation of Central and South American and Other Hispanic women to the clerical and retail versus other occupational slots, and the coefficient for periphery-sector location is large and negative for both groups. In addition, a positive crowding effect appears for the Other Hispanic workers—the presence of a large proportion of Hispanic workers ensures that some women of Other Hispanic origin will find positions in the clerical and retail sales occupations. Yet a third pattern of occupational allocation emerges for Puerto Ricans for whom nativity, education, and language proficiency achieve somewhat uniform weights in differentiating clerical and retail workers from those in blue-collar occupations.

Thus, while education is still an important factor in allocating women to lower white-collar and blue-collar jobs, it is not as dominant a factor

TABLE 8.7
Discriminant Analyses (First Function) of Women's Allocation
into Three Occupational Strata: First Function Discriminant Coefficients for Hispanic
and Non-Hispanic White Women

	Mexican	Puerto Rican	Central and South American[a]	Other Hispanic	Non-Hispanic white
Variables					
Age					
18–24	−.05	.04	.34	.21	−.05
25–34	−.06	−.01	.10	.20	−.08
35–44	−.04	−.32	.26	.04	−.04
45–54	−.04	.13	.09	−.00	.01
Education	.78	.44	.41	.46	.87
Native-born	.12	.45	.10	.09	.07
English-language					
proficiency	.10	.38	.46	.41	.04
Part-time work	.13	.29	.19	−.09	.05
Percentage Hispanic	.18	.07	.05	.48	.19
Periphery sector	−.35	−.32	−.49	−.53	−.39
Statistics					
Eigen value	.31	.72	.60	.51	.16
Eigen relative percentage	84.60	96.97	86.52	77.55	78.92
Canonical correlation	.48	.65	.61	.58	.37
Chi square	351.67	94.28	159.01	196.15	1588.20
p	≤.001	≤.001	≤.001	≤.001	≤.001
Strata centroids					
Clerical and retail sales	.71	1.13	.98	.67	.33
Service and crafts	−.17	.37	−.39	−.60	−.34
Operative and laborer	−.60	−.77	−.72	−1.00	−.64
Percentage of class					
correctly classified	54.41	69.71	59.45	67.49	55.24
N	1,099	175	291	363	8507

Source: 1976 Survey of Income and Education (U.S. Department of Commerce, 1978).
[a] Includes Cuban-origin women.

as it appears to be for professional and managerial positions. The emergence of nativity for Puerto Ricans, and of language proficiency for Central and South Americans and Other Hispanic women, testifies to the importance of additional achieved characteristics that facilitate the incorporation of Hispanic women in the occupational structure. Language is obviously important for professional and managerial jobs, but women who have achieved levels of education sufficiently high to enter these occupations seldom have linguistic difficulties. This is not necessarily the case for incumbents of lower white-collar jobs. Moreover, in ethnic enclaves, retail and clerical jobs may be accessible to individuals who have difficulty with the English language, but who may be quite fluent in Spanish.

Discussion and Conclusions

The results based on the regression and discriminant analyses indicate important differences in occupational positions of Hispanic women according to national origin. Education emerged as the most salient determinant of occupational position for both the interval (TSEI scores) and categorical (occupation groups) metrics, according to the standardized regression coefficients and the discriminant coefficients. However, because the achievement of education itself depends on national origin, it is inappropriate to conclude that the meritocratic bases used to assign female workers their occupational roles are more important than the ascriptive bases of these assignments. This point is made more forcefully through a decomposition of the occupational status gap between Hispanic and non-Hispanic white women.

Our computations reveal that if Hispanic women had the same characteristics as their non-Hispanic white counterparts, only between 27 and 57% of the gap in occupational status would be closed.[6] The remaining portion we assume is due to discrimination (based on ethnicity) or factors we have failed to account for in our models (such as tastes, or intermittent work patterns). Our observed outcomes are undoubtedly related also to preexisting differences in group access to the social and economic resources that provide entry into the highest occupational positions. Failure to recognize this fact will lead to misguided conclusions about the nature and extent of ethnic stratification among women and men alike, as well as about the nature of changes required in public policy to bring about greater parity in labor market outcomes.

Our results provide some support for the ascription explanation of ethnic stratification. There is nothing inherently hierarchical about national origin or nativity to predict the location of specific groups in the

[6] The specific results for the various groups are as follows:

	Total status gap (TSEI points)	Share due to characteristics (TSEI points)	% of Gap closed
Mexican	18.62	5.02	27
Puerto Rican	16.42	9.39	57
Central and South American	16.50	6.27	38
Other Hispanic	9.25	2.74	30

occupational structure. Rather, groups are ranked socioeconomically in terms of their status achievements, which largely reflect their differential access to resources. To the extent that foreign-born women arrive with low levels of the resources necessary for obtaining high-level occupations in the U.S. labor market, birthplace should influence labor market outcomes, at least until the foreign-born acclimate their labor market skills to the U.S. occupational structure. Nativity does not significantly influence the socioeconomic status or occupational location of most Hispanic-origin women, once differences in educational and linguistic characteristics are accounted for, but there is weak evidence that nativity still matters for Puerto Rican women. The fact that native- and foreign-born women have differential access and control over social resources, including education and market skills, contributes to ethnic stratification, and we should not endeavor to explain it away or pretend that it is relatively unimportant. With appropriate policy interventions, foreign-born women can overcome their labor market handicaps more rapidly, especially if programs emphasizing skills that can be transferred are given priority. But, equalizing groups in terms of their achieved characteristics will reduce the occupational status gap between Hispanic and non-Hispanic white women only by 27 to 57%.

The question that needs to be addressed is why some groups continue to acquire low levels of resources, especially education. It is this line of questioning that lies at the core of the ethnic stratification perspective, because differences in achieved characteristics are themselves determined by ascribed characteristics. Our analyses do suggest promising avenues for further investigation into the question of why some ethnic groups are more successful in gaining access to the resources that permit subsequent labor market success. One approach likely to render new insights is a study of the role and function of ethnic enclaves in shaping labor market outcomes. More generally, further analysis of the role of structural factors in stratifying ethnic workers of both sexes might further clarify which groups are able to experience mobility as a *group,* and why. Obviously, census data are not appropriate for empirically testing these ideas, so future researchers should be prepared to utilize methodologies that can blend individual and structural factors in a single analysis of group and individual outcomes. Such information may provide new insights about why the socioeconomic differentiation among Hispanic-origin women takes the form it does, and how this might be changed in the future. In addition, future analysts should strive to determine to what extent employer discrimination contributes to the uneven labor market outcomes demonstrated here. An ensuing step entails outlining policy measures to eliminate discriminatory practices, but this area of investigation is still in its infancy.

APPENDIX: ADDITIONAL TABLES

TABLE 8A.1
Selected Characteristics of Women Age 18–64 in the 1975 Occupation Sample, by National Origin

Variable	Mexican	Puerto Rican	Central and South American[a]	Other Hispanic	Non-Hispanic white
Age (%)					
18–24	26.8	24.8	15.4	19.6	19.4
	(44.3)	(43.3)	(36.1)	(39.7)	(39.6)
25–34	33.6	36.4	27.7	25.4	26.7
	(47.3)	(48.2)	(44.8)	(43.6)	(44.2)
35–44	21.8	19.2	27.4	23.6	18.7
	(41.3)	(39.5)	(44.7)	(42.5)	(39.0)
45–54	13.1	15.2	22.9	22.5	20.5
	(33.7)	(36.0)	(42.1)	(41.8)	(40.4)
55–64	4.7	4.6	6.6	9.0	14.7
	(21.2)	(20.9)	(24.9)	(28.6)	(35.4)
Age continuous (mean years)	33.3	33.5	37.4	37.3	38.1
	(11.1)	(10.9)	(11.0)	(12.3)	(13.1)
Education (mean years)	10.0	9.8	11.2	11.7	12.6
	(3.5)	(3.4)	(3.5)	(2.7)	(2.4)
Native-born (%)	82.3	21.2	7.2	86.1	95.3
	(38.2)	(41.0)	(25.9)	(34.7)	(21.3)
English language proficiency score (mean)	9.7	8.6	8.2	10.5	11.7
	(2.3)	(2.6)	(2.5)	(1.7)	(1.7)
Part-time work (%)	22.3	17.2	11.1	27.4	26.7
	(41.6)	(37.8)	(31.5)	(44.7)	(44.3)
Percentage Hispanic in area	18.6	8.2	12.8	18.2	5.1
	(15.9)	(7.2)	(11.0)	(15.7)	(7.5)
Periphery sector (%)	53.6	45.0	53.3	44.5	37.8
	(49.9)	(49.9)	(50.0)	(49.8)	(48.5)
λ	.74	.91	.57	.70	.64
	(.23)	(.31)	(.32)	(.285)	(.250)
TSEI	25.2	25.7	26.2	40.0	40.4
	(12.9)	(14.0)	(14.1)	(16.2)	(22.5)
N	1,208	198	332	445	11,341

Source: 1976 Survey of income and Education (U.S. Department of Commerce, 1978).
Note: Standard deviations are in parentheses.
[a] Includes Cuban-origin women.

TABLE A8.2

Detailed Occupational Distribution of Women Age 18–64 in the 1975 Occupation Sample, by National Origin (percentages)

Occupational group	Mexican	Puerto Rican	Central and South American[a]	Other Hispanic	Non-Hispanic white
Stratum I					
Professional, technical, and kindred	5.1	6.6	8.9	13.9	18.7
Managers and administrators[b]	2.1	3.8	2.0	4.1	5.4
Nonretail sales workers	0.3	0.1	0.7	0.7	1.8
Stratum II					
Self-employed managers and administrators	0.7	0.1	0.0	1.8	1.2
Retail sales workers	3.4	4.2	1.9	3.8	5.1
Clerical and kindred	27.3	24.3	30.5	38.8	37.7
Stratum III					
Crafts and kindred	1.8	0.7	2.7	0.9	2.0
Service					
Private household	3.4	1.3	4.2	3.5	1.5
Other service	21.8	14.1	13.3	18.0	15.0
Stratum IV					
Operative[c]	27.1	43.0	35.2	13.6	9.9
Nonfarm laborers	2.1	0.4	0.6	0.4	0.9
Farmers and farm managers	0.2	0.0	0.0	0.0	0.2
Farm laborers and supervisors	4.8	1.4	0.0	0.4	0.6
	100.0	100.0	100.0	99.9	100.0
N^d	1,208	198	332	445	11,341

Source: 1976 Survey of Income and Education (U.S. Department of Commerce, 1978).

[a] Includes Cuban-origin women.

[b] Excludes farm and self-employed workers.

[c] Includes transportation workers.

[d] Weighting renders these data comparable to population statistics.

PART IV

Labor Market Studies

The Migration of Mexican Indocumentados as a Settlement Process: Implications for Work*

Harley L. Browning and Nestor Rodríguez

Indocumentados as Settlers

"Illegal aliens," "*mojados*," "undocumented workers"—there is not even agreement as to what they should be called.[1] Few features of American life in the last decade or so have generated as much interest and concern as the large-scale movement of Mexican nationals without papers who cross the U.S. border in search of employment. The mass media, especially in the Southwest, regularly run stories on this group, sometimes of an alarmist tone, and on the political level both President Carter and President Reagan formulated plans to attempt to deal with this problem.

Even the scholarly community, somewhat tardily, has begun to look

---

* Although this chapter bears the names of two contributors, it is really a product of a larger group, the members of the Texas Indocumentado Study, who have contributed much to the development of the approach taken here. In particular, we wish to acknowledge the contributions of Rogelio Núñez, co-director, as well as those of David Benke, Waltraut Feindt, and Harriet Romo. We are also indebted to the discussants at the conference, Solomon Polachek and Robert Bach. Bach, in particular, raised some important points that have stimulated us to reconsider our argument. Our thanks to Humberto Muñoz and Orlandina de Oliveira, who provided timely encouragement and suggestions.

[1] Let us immediately set forth our own preferences for labels to be attached to the populations we will review. Our choices are *indocumentados* (shorter and more descriptively correct than the English term "undocumented workers," not all of whom are workers); *Chicanos* (admittedly not the choice of all Mexican-descent citizens of the United States, but it too is less clumsy than the English "Mexican-Americans"); and *Mexicanos* (to denote all those born in Mexico but resident in the United States).

closely at this phenomenon.[2] As a result, it is no longer possible, as would have been the case in the 1970s to state that the ignorance about indocumentados is almost total. Yet our knowledge is still fragmentary and therefore likely to provide a somewhat distorted view of the subject. Most studies of indocumentados have taken one of two quite different approaches: the individual (micro) level or the global, international (macro) level. Characteristically, the individual level is tapped by questionnaires administered to those apprehended in attempting to cross the border or to those contacted in some other manner. The survey approach permits the compilation of population profiles by aggregating the individual responses to a range of questions (sex, age, birthplace, method of crossing, jobs in the United States, use of social services, etc.).[3] At the other extreme are analysts who pose broad questions such as, What is the impact upon the capitalist systems of Mexico and the United States of this type of geographical mobility? This political economy approach takes the individual as given and makes problematic the structures—economic, political—through which that person moves.[4]

Each approach is legitimate, offering perspectives and insights that the other cannot consider. But even when considered together (which is rarely the case),[5] they provide an incomplete understanding of the situation of indocumentados. A full perspective requires consideration of a number of intermediate levels that lie between the individual and the international level. A list of the levels, from macro to micro, might cover the following elements: (1) international, (2) national, (3) regional (especially the Southwest), (4) community, (5) workplace, (6) welfare and leisure institutions, (7) interethnic relationships (especially Chicano–indocumentado), (8) neighborhood (barrio), (9) family or household, (10) individual. No single research project can be expected to devote equal attention to all 10 levels, but researchers should be aware of how changes introduced in one level (e.g., the national level through implementation of the Reagan program) would have significant impacts on many of the other levels.

The Texas Indocumentado Study has chosen to concentrate on Levels 4–9, from the community to the family or household. During several

---

[2] This chapter is not intended as a survey of the growing literature: see, for example, Cornelius (1978), Corwin (1978), and Select Commission on Immigration and Refugee Policy (1981). As a point of reference for the Chicano population, see Tienda (1981).

[3] Still the most frequently cited study based on this approach is North and Houston (1976).

[4] A recent effort to provide the "big picture" of international migration on a global basis is Portes (1981).

[5] The work of Castles and Kosack (1973) is a formidable attempt to analyze international migratory labor in Western Europe by utilizing the two approaches.

years of field experience, our attention has shifted from the traditional emphasis on the individual—the "classic" depiction of young, unattached men coming across the border for a limited period of time and then returning to Mexico—to those indocumentados who may be characterized as settlers because their actions are likely to lead to permanent settlement (although they themselves would not necessarily say that this was their intent).

The shift of emphasis from the temporary migrant to those involved in settlement involved changes to broaden the study design. A central alteration is the unit of analysis, which shifted from the individual to the family or household. Family formation is a major consideration and introduces factors that are not present in dealing with individuals.

Illegality, a basic identifying characteristic of these people, takes on a different meaning for families. An unattached man or woman, in the country for only a few months, can be rather nonchalant about the prospect of being apprehended by the *Migra* (as the U.S. Immigration and Naturalization Service is called), but the situation for families is much more complex and uncertain. The costs of getting back across the border are higher, and there is always the possibility of family separation. The longer the family remains in the United States the greater is the pressure to acquire legal status, for the lack of it raises problems and obstacles at every turn.

The length of U.S. residence of the family unit also generates new conditions that must be met. The short-term migrant has no ambivalence about his or her status as a Mexican, but for those who have resided for years in the United States the matter of self-identity becomes more ambiguous, and for the children born or brought up in this country, the question of identity—Mexican or Chicano—inevitably produces uncertainties and tensions within the family.

The shift to a focus on the settlement process thus introduces many new aspects and requires a broader research design. In particular, time as an analytic variable becomes more significant. Short-term migrants often do not change the pattern of their activities, even if they engage in repeat migrations. The temporal parameters of the individual life cycle serve to characterize this kind of migration, but when dealing with the family unit the family life cycle must be introduced with its inherently more complex relationships that change over time.

Historical time also is important. The periods when migrants come across must be related to changes in the national economy, especially labor market conditions in the area of destination, as well as developments during the stay of the migrants. These factors must be evaluated in a different way from the experience of short-term migrants.

In confronting the analytically challenging task of assembling data from a variety of sources, ordering them, and then developing a coherent interpretation of the settlement process of indocumentados, we have elaborated an analytic framework that has proved, in our judgment, useful in dealing with the complexity of the situation. Our framework incorporates time as an explicit dimension and can be used for multiple levels of analysis. More important, it examines two fundamental social processes: social reproduction and resource accumulation. The former addresses the question of how the indocumentados reproduce themselves both demographically and socially, while the latter involves the manner by which indocumentados, in the process of their incorporation into U.S. society, acquire and utilize financial, work, social, and cultural resources.

In this chapter we briefly describe some features of the Texas Indocumentado project. We then attempt to find what analytic leads emerge from a consideration of the settlement process that will help us understand the work conditions of indocumentados. We discuss the relationship of the household to work participation, the ways in which employers make use of indocumentado labor, and factors affecting job mobility.

The Texas Indocumentado Study

THE LOCALES

Over a period of more than 3 years (1980–1982), the Texas Indocumentado Study has carried out fieldwork in the metropolitan communities of Austin and San Antonio.[6] Both are far enough from the border (150 miles and more) that they do not share the characteristics peculiar to the border zone, but are close enough to be convenient destinations for indocumentados. San Antonio has a 1980 city population of 785,000, 54% of Mexican origin; Austin has a 1980 city population of 345,496, with a Mexican-origin population of 19%.[7] The two communities differ not only in population size, but also in the relative, and of course the absolute, size of the "host" community, the Chicano population. They also differ in their historical development. San Antonio can be characterized as an "old" community of destination for Mexican migrants, legal

[6] The study is financed by two sources, the Mexico–United States Border Research Program at the University of Texas at Austin, directed by Stanley Ross, and a grant from the Population Division of the National Institute of Child Health and Human Development.

[7] We report the city rather than the metropolitan area populations because indocumentados tend to congregate in the inner cities, where we concentrated our investigations.

and illegal, for it is possible to trace the migratory flows back for many decades. Labor recruiters were sent to Mexico in the early decades of the century to contract for workers (see Reisler, 1976). In contrast, Austin may be termed a "new" community of destination, with fewer and more recently arrived indocumentados.

Because of these and other factors, Austin and San Antonio differ in what may be termed the *opportunity structures* that confront indocumentado migrants upon their arrival. Each community presents a different industry-occupation mix of employment opportunities. Both have a higher than average number of government service industries, but of different kinds: the military in San Antonio, state government and the university in Austin. Consequently, San Antonio is more a blue-collar metropolis and Austin is more a white-collar community. None of the government-based industries directly hires many indocumentados, but the industries do provide substantial employment for Chicanos.

In terms of the respective labor markets, Austin and San Antonio differ in the mix of industry jobs for indocumentados. San Antonio has more opportunities in the garment industry, certain food processors, and wholesaling (it is a major processor and distributor of Mexican-American food products), and Austin has the mining industry of lime production and the manufacturing industry of cement precasting. Both are strong in construction and in restaurant and hotel employment. What is striking in both communities is the virtual absence of indocumentado employment in white-collar positions and its concentration in the secondary labor market sector (i.e., in unstable, low-paying jobs with little opportunity for advancement), even when Chicanos are employed in the primary sector.

FIELDWORK PROCEDURES

Study of the indocumentado population presents an array of difficulties not generally encountered in social research. Sampling, establishing contacts, and the "protection of human subjects" pose many problems. This is not the place for a full discussion of these difficulties and how we attempted to cope with them. Suffice it to say that these unusual conditions make the study of indocumentados in the field a slower and less efficient process than is generally the case. Since conditions and procedures did not allow us to draw a representative sample, we cannot say with certainty anything about the total indocumentado population of Austin and San Antonio, much less of other parts of the United States. Nor do we attempt to demonstrate the extent of individual variation within these populations. Our goal has been to understand basic patterns for indocumentado populations: how they get to communities of destination, what kinds of jobs they find, their patterns of consumption, the ways they relate to Chicanos, and what happens to their children. There is no one response for any of these questions, but there is enough commonality of experience to permit the basic patterns to be determined.

The first fieldwork in San Antonio was on a small scale and was exploratory in nature. Contacts were made through key informants, who introduced us to indocumentados. This resulted basically in a snowball sampling design, working through the social networks of our sponsors. We made a special effort to contact women, and we interviewed several *coyotes* (those who guide the indocumentados across the border) for their experiences in getting indocumentados across, but we did not at that time concentrate on those who were part of the settlement process.

We originally planned to carry out as many as 1200 interviews, but we shifted from a survey emphasis to one more ethnographic in nature when we began work in Austin. We made the shift for theoretical and methodological reasons. We became intrigued with the problems posed by the settlement process, which had received little attention in other research. We shifted from questionnaires not because they are impossible to carry out with this group, although they are difficult to execute on a large scale and in a short time, but because we believe it is difficult to fully identify and characterize the patterns of indocumentado adjustment with survey instruments. Our Chicano interviewers found that it took repeated contacts before indocumentados developed enough trust to say what they really believed.

In Austin we worked intensively with about 50 families.[8] We obtained information on all the approximately 250 members of the households, and on the structure of the households themselves. In-depth and semi-structured interviews were carried out, generally with recorders; the interviews were then transcribed.

Social Reproduction

Reproduction always has been a central preoccupation of demographers. A population will perpetuate itself by ensuring that the "exits"

[8] In part, this was due to fortuitous circumstances. Codirectors Rogelio Núñez and Nestor Rodríguez had, before the grant award, begun an informal school for the children of indocumentados, and through them entrée was gained to their parents.

from it (deaths and outmigration) will at least be balanced by the "entries" (births and inmigration). But it is not enough to ensure a supply of warm bodies; there must also be a reproduction of the many statuses and positions that make up a social structure.

DEMOGRAPHIC FACTORS

Reproduction is not a simple matter, even under the simplest of conditions—a closed, stationary population undergoing minimal social change—and the special circumstances of the indocumentados make them particularly difficult to capture under the rubrics of demographic and social reproduction. Figure 9.1 should make this clear. Indocumentado population change is not just a function of three demographic variables: fertility, mortality, and migration. It is also essential to take into account legal status and time in the United States.

The top panel of Figure 9.1, "Temporary Migrants," depicts the older, "classic" form of indocumentado migration. Young unattached men, originating mainly in about a dozen Mexican states, cross the border to work for limited periods and then return to Mexico. (Sometimes the same individual will repeat the process several times.) As the arrows indicate, entries and exits are virtually equal, with the result that there is a continual turnover of the indocumentado population. Few go on to become legal aliens and even fewer become U.S. citizens.

The second panel, "Adult Settlers," is more complex; it represents the various ways by which migrants from Mexico construct settlement patterns. The key feature is the formation of stable unions, legal or consensual, which usually produce offspring. Some ostensibly temporary migrant men join this category. Their chances for unions are enhanced by the growing numbers of unattached women crossing the border. Either sex, however, may form unions with legal aliens or American citizens. In addition, unattached migrants may reconstitute family units by arranging for the missing members to be brought across. Finally, there are entire nuclear families coming into the country as a unit. However formed, these family units are more likely than are unattached migrants to remain in the United States (save for visits to Mexico). They want to regularize their situation by becoming legal aliens, but few believe it necessary or desirable to become U.S. citizens.

The children of these families are of special interest, with a complexity all their own. Four groups can be distinguished. Those children born in Mexico and brought to the United States in late adolescence (ages 13–17) behaviorally belong in the "Adult Settlers" category, for they are consid-

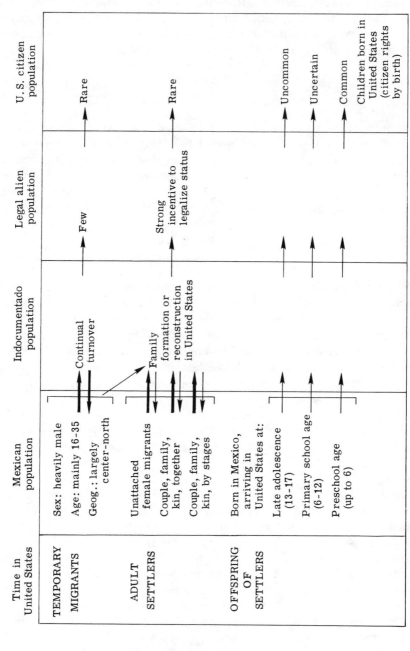

Figure 9.1 Population change among migrants in terms of legal status and time in the United States.

ered both by their parents and by themselves to be adults rather than adolescents. Too old to be easily incorporated into the school system, they generally get full-time jobs, continue to speak Spanish, and maintain their Mexican identity, just as do their parents. In the second group are those of school age (ages 6–12), who often enroll in schools, although the older ones experience considerable difficulty "fitting into the system." The third group, preschool children (ages birth through 5), adjust best to the school system and spend their formative years (ages 6–14) in the United States. They resemble most the fourth group, those children born in the United States, except that the latter are U.S. citizens by virtue of their birth.[9] Culturally, the great majority of the last two groups will grow up to be Chicanos, since they lack direct contact with Mexico and will acquire competency in English at an early age. In contrast, the late adolescents, and some of the school-age children, like their parents, will continue to consider themselves Mexicans no matter how long they live in the United States.

SOCIAL FACTORS

Social reproduction must take into account two social structures—that in Mexican-origin communities and that in U.S.-destination communities. Fully developed, this could lead us to consider such distinctive features of Mexican peasant communities as the fiesta system or, in the United States, the role of voluntary associations in integrating individuals within the community, all of which lie beyond the scope of this chapter. We concentrate on two crucial features of indocumentado social reproduction: family and kinship networks, and work patterns.

Family and Kinship Networks

Even in the period of massive structural change that Mexico has experienced over the past 40 years or so, the Mexican family and kinship structure remains at the center of an individual's existence. The question is to what extent indocumentados are able to reproduce their family–kin situations in the United States. The critical distinction between indocumentados who come for brief periods (sojourners) and those who choose to settle is that the former have less need to reproduce family or kin structures in the United States because they are only transient, while

[9] This is not to say that they are fully able to take advantage of their rights. Undoubtedly, their parents' lack of legal status, along with other conditions associated with minority status, affects their ability to do so.

the latter must try to constitute such structures. A nuclear family can be formed in the United States or introduced from Mexico, but it is impossible for the full range of the kinship network to be reproduced north of the border.

What is critical is that enough of the extended kin system exists to facilitate the incorporation of the migrants into American society. The pattern of indocumentado migration to the United States displays similarities with internal migration within Mexico, particularly movements from villages to metropolises such as Monterrey (see Balan et al., 1973). We have come to recognize that migration is very much a social process in which people migrate to places where there is someone, most often a relative, whom they already know. In the case of Austin, a number of families originated from one village. A migratory chain was formed between it and Austin, and as a result new arrivals to Austin counted on assistance.

Social networks are a kind of lubricant that facilitates adjustment and adaptation and reduces personal stress. In the context of indocumentado migration, the successful operation of the social network does not directly depend upon its size or complexity. To illustrate, one indocumentado family upon arrival obtained all the help it needed in settling in and finding work from just one family of relatives already living in the community, whereas another incoming family called upon three or four families and *compadres* for assistance.

Work Patterns

The social network is especially important in finding jobs. Some have argued that indocumentados experience difficulties in reproducing their skills in the United States, because the organization of work differs greatly from that in Mexico. Yet none of our indocumentado respondents mentioned any problems of this nature. The explanation is that in both countries the kind of work these people are called upon to do is manual labor, ranging from such basic skills as wielding a shovel to the more advanced skills of bricklaying, carpentry, painting, and so forth. Such work is common in Mexico and is easily transferred to a work site in the United States. Moreover, language need not be an obstacle for such work. One of the most remarkable features of the entire indocumentado story is the rapidity and relative ease by which indocumentados obtained jobs, generally within a few days of arrival. This was made possible because the social networks provided reliable up-to-date information on the existence of jobs that could be filled by indocumentados.

What about the social relations on the job? One could suspect that the change from the small-scale work situation in Mexico to the large bureaucratic structures of the United States contributes a major difference. Typically, indocumentados do not work in large-scale enterprises; when they do, it is often in enclave situations that shield them from the full impact of large bureaucracies. Often our respondents were found in patron relationships and if their patron was sometimes harsh and exploitive of the workers, this was also all too familiar a pattern in Mexico. In that country also, there is little job security; fringe benefits are few; the work is physically demanding; and the hours long. Thus, in terms of skills and social relations, indocumentados find situations in the United States not greatly different from those in Mexico.

Four Forms of Resource Accumulation

Four forms of capital are acquired in the resource accumulation process:[10] (1) financial resources—either in liquid form (money) or in the form of salable assets (property, goods, etc.); (2) work resources—the various skills needed to execute work tasks, acquired in formal educational institutions or on-the-job training; (3) social resources—the development of interpersonal bonds that not only facilitate overall social adjustment in a new locale, but also enhance the opportunities for other forms of resource accumulation; and (4) cultural resources—acquisition of information about the community of settlement that permits a better adaptation to it (growing "savvy" about where to go and how to get things done). In particular it includes language acquisition (in this case, English).

It is axiomatic that the long journey to destinations within the United States requires financial capital (resources). Even the young unattached man who hitches rides to the border, swims across the river on his own, and then walks several hundred miles to his destination, needs a stake. But the do-it-yourself approach has become increasingly rare, even among our young man respondents. Now virtually everyone makes use of the services of a *coyote* to get across the border and to be delivered by

[10] In the conference version of this chapter we used the term *capital accumulation*, our intent being to take a concept familiar in the economics literature and then to extend it to other areas of behavior. In France, Bourdieu (1977) has taken a similar direction, and, although we have tried to work out our formulation independent of his efforts, it seemed a good idea to suggest a certain continuity in approach. Unfortunately, capital accumulation as a concept has connotations that are not necessary for us to assume and that serve to cloud rather than clarify the issues. Marxists see capital as something that is appropriated, but we do not make this assumption. On the other hand, neoclassical economists consider capital accumulation in a more restricted sense than our intent. It therefore is more prudent to switch from capital accumulation to resource accumulation, the latter being a more general concept, less freighted with specific meanings.

motorized vehicle to the community of destination. This service is not cheap, the cost varying by distance from destination to border. In 1981, for destinations in Texas 200 to 300 miles beyond the border, the going rate for an adult was $350, for children somewhat less. A family of four would require a sum in excess of $1000, a sizable amount of money for rural or blue-collar urban Mexicans.

Indocumentados obtain this money from savings, by selling valuable assets such as crops, animals, or land, or by loans from relatives, friends, and, more rarely, from moneylenders. Seldom do coyotes delay collection of their fee until the client obtains a job in the United States and is able to pay off the debt by installments. Indocumentados also must have some financial resources to defray costs while they settle in and find a job. Fortunately, this is often not a major consideration, since they can frequently count on the hospitality and help of kin and friends.

The last point introduces another resource form, social resources. As mentioned earlier, the existence of social networks, basically made up of kin, explains why so many of the families in our Austin study came from Bejucos, a village on the border of the states of Mexico and Guerrero. Individuals in social networks provided food and shelter to the newly arrived, and were also critical for finding first jobs. As the newcomers gained experience in the community and expanded their cultural resources, they customarily expanded their social networks beyond those of kin, thus providing themselves with options that were not available upon first arrival.

Work resources have their own characteristics and logic. As noted, most jobs available to indocumentados rarely demand skills not already acquired on the job in Mexico, even in "traditional" agrarian communities. Such jobs do not require schooling or formal training, and the work resources are quite portable. Moreover, some indocumentados utilized migration within Mexico to acquire work resources that subsequently enabled them to secure well-paying positions in the United States. One man, for example, moved from Bejucos to Mexico City, where he received training as a cook in a restaurant. Upon migrating to the United States, he was able to translate this experience into a high-paying position ($1300 a month at the time of our study) in a restaurant specializing in Mexican food. He had complete authority in the kitchen, hiring a six-man staff (all indocumentados), buying the foodstuffs, and organizing the kitchen routine.

Cultural resources are largely acquired on the U.S. side of the border. Over time indocumentados learn a variety of things—where to get a certain product or service, techniques useful in approaching various local bureaucracies such as hospitals and schools—that make life easier. Most adult indocumentados do not learn English in any systematic fashion, but acquire a minimal basic vocabulary of 100 or fewer key words and phrases enabling them to perform adequately on the job and in routine shopping situations. This does not make them literate, for it does not enable indocumentados to deal with the written word, and their minimal vocabulary often actually inhibits them from making the sustained effort necessary to become literate. Nonetheless, it provides the rudimentary communicative skills necessary to move about in American society.

All four forms of resources can be used up as well as accumulated. Since the main motivation in coming to the United States is financial, indocumentados sometimes are able, by working long hours, to acquire a fairly sizable nest egg. But as illegal aliens they must be prepared for an unforeseeable sharp drop in their financial assets. They or other members of their family may be apprehended and sent back to Mexico; they often return quickly, but getting back entails costs. Also, as part of their social network, they may be called upon to help others meet the costs associated with apprehension. Both kinds of calls may come at any time. For example, one indocumentado for months had been planning a trip back to his village of origin but unexpectedly had to help out a member of his social network and thus depleted his financial reserves to the point that he was forced to cancel the trip. Those desiring to regularize their status by becoming legal aliens must pay attorney fees and other costs running to thousands of dollars.

Work resources may atrophy if skills acquired in Mexico are not utilized. If one had been a carpenter or bricklayer in Mexico but became a dishwasher in the United States, the pay level could be higher, but skills could deteriorate. Social resources also may be lost if the social networks are not actively maintained through continued interaction and the recruitment of new members to replace those who leave.

We believe that it is helpful from an analytic standpoint to use one noun, resources, to depict various forms of accumulation, but homogenization is far from our intent. We believe that financial, work, social, and cultural resources differ sufficiently so that it makes little sense to seek a common metric or to strive to develop an overall resource accumulation scale. Rather, we wish to emphasize that there is a strong interactive relationship among the four resources and that a strictly additive model would be inappropriate.[11]

[11] A number of criticisms have been raised regarding the resource accumulation model suggested here. Robert Bach, discussant of the first version of the essay, was unhappy with our practice of "calling everything capital—it homogenizes by definition rather than analysis the social relationships in which each activity develops." Our switch of terms from capital to resources doubtless would not stay his criticism. We acknowledge that the concept can be abused by overextension, but our intent is to formuate concepts to help

Implications of the Process of Social Reproduction and Resource Accumulation

ADJUSTMENTS OF FAMILIES

Nothing serves to define the settlement process more sharply than that of the family as contrasted with the unattached migrant. An individual here for only a short time can engage in all kinds of "unnatural" behavior (e.g., working 70 or more hours a week, sharing a room with two or three migrants, saving and sending home one-half or more of income). This is possible because the time horizon is short, obligations in the United States are few, and goals are limited—to earn as much money as possible in a short time.

A family changes all this. The settlement process requires a different set of strategies. Paradoxically, the family may serve to increase the ability of its members to sustain themselves while at the same time increasing their vulnerability. Several members may contribute to family income and the performance of household tasks, but vulnerability is increased because the needs of families become more diversified and difficult to satisfy.

Indocumentado families must develop their strategies under a number of unfavorable conditions. First, by not having legal status they are not eligible in large measure for the range of social services available to poor families in the United States. None of our indocumentado families lives in public housing; none has unemployment compensation, and few have regular access to food stamps.[12] Second, most of the families have been rather recently formed, and the children are therefore mostly still too young to contribute to family income. This means these families are at the most vulnerable stage of the family life cycle, when child costs (hospital delivery, infant illnesses, etc.) are often high. Third, indocu-

---

account for the conditions that do or do not lead to the incorporation of the individual, family, or household into American society. All that we wish to sugget by the term *incorporation* is simply this: to the degree that individuals and families or households can accumulate the four kinds of resources, the more successful they will be in providing themselves a reasonably secure existence in the United States.

[12] Food stamps are available only for legal residents of the United States. Heer and Falasco (1982) present some startling results from their study of Los Angeles County, California. For the period August 1980 through March 1981, they estimate that 13.2% of *all* county births were to indocumentado mothers. They also report that 19% of the indocumentado mothers received food stamp income and 20% were enrolled in the Medi-Cal Program (California's version of Medicaid).

mentados have low-paying jobs characterized by instability of employment and by wide swings in hours of work.

How do indocumentado families strive to overcome their disadvantaged situations? Basically, they try to maximize the number of contributors, both to household income and to the fulfillment of household
maintenance chores. This effort takes several forms. First, they share
housing. Only a small fraction of our families lived in households limited to the nuclear family. Most lived with related or nonrelated individuals, and there were several multiple-family households. Some of the
latter resulted when newly arrived migrants moved in with relatives. In
these cases it was made clear that after a short settling-in period (a
couple of weeks) the recently arrived indocumentados were expected to
contribute to the financial maintenance of the household. Even close
relatives who were invited to come were expected to do their share.
Taking boarders is a common way of guaranteeing a steady income
when wages of the head of the household fluctuate.

A second way to maximize household income is to ignore the Mexican
norm that a mother with children should not work outside the home.
Among our families, the woman who did not work was the rarity. Many
indocumentado women had very full "double days": working full time
and assuming the major responsibility at home for child care, food preparation, and household chores, including shopping. (The fathers helped
around the house and with the shopping, after work, but did little
cooking or child care.)

A third way is through the utilization of the labor of children. Families
fortunate enough to have teenage children often encouraged them to
enter the labor force full time, simply skipping school. (Other families,
however, believe their children, even the olders ones, must have schooling if they are to have any success in American society, so they forgo the
income these children could contribute). Even young children, especially girls, were given major responsibility for the care of infants and
younger children while the mother worked outside the home. When
such labor was not available or the older children were in school, the
parents paid neighbors (sometimes Chicana women) to look after the
children. Household chores and preparation of meals were often assigned to the older children.

One consequence of these strategies is a high degree of household
compositional instability and turnover. The core nuclear family may lose
its boarders or relatives, and sometimes the joint-family households
split up. Members may return to Mexico for some months or even per-
manently, while others move to another part of the country. Newly
arrived indocumentados leave to set up their own households. Obvi-

ously, this turnover introduces considerable uncertainty.[13] In one instance the head of the household controlled the incomes of six adult contributors and was able to make payments on two pickup trucks and several major household appliances. Within a year, however, household turnover had reduced the contributors to two, and the man was in severe financial straits.

Turnover with the accompanying moves from one residence to another entails substantial costs in making deposits on apartments or housing and for utilities. Among our respondents, the common practice was for the current residents to pay under the name of the first indocumentado who occupied the residence. Phones were an exception. Indocumentados maintain regular contact with relatives in Mexico by phone, and in doing so run up substantial bills. No one wants to get stuck with large, unpaid bills, so each family establishes service under its own name.

In linking work and the family or household, it is the resource accumulation process that has the greatest salience. It shows how the various members of the family or household can be mobilized not only for multiple contributions to financial resources, but also how social and cultural resources can be useful in accumulating financial and work resources.

RESPONSES TO EMPLOYERS

Employers are virtually unanimous in categorizing indocumentados as good workers, and they often compare them very favorably with native workers, especially Chicanos. This should come as no surprise because indocumentados, if for no other reason than their illegal status, are quite tractable workers, and are very responsive to their employers' desires. Employers take advantage of the indocumentados by using work practices unacceptable to native-born workers. They speed up the work pace and in some instances fail to provide indocumentados with the rest periods that other workers receive. They hire indocumentados at one level and then require them to do higher-level work at no increase in pay.

Employers expect indocumentados to be on call whenever needed and to work overtime. In a landscaping company indocumentados

---

[13] It is the indocumentados who face uncertainty. Employers, who consider this labor homogeneous, are not uncertain. Consistent with the position taken by Piore (1979), it is our belief that employers act on the assumption that there is an unlimited supply of undocumented workers.

worked up to 77 hours per week, but were not paid for overtime hours. A produce-packing company required workers to be on call at any time of the day or night when the produce arrived. Those who did not show were suspended for several days. In a *tortilleria* where the antiquated machinery frequently broke down, workers were not paid while they waited for the machines to be repaired.

Employers also skimp on investments that would provide for more pleasant and safer working conditions. For example, in several food-preparation businesses, workers had to labor in hot and poorly ventilated areas where not even fans were provided. A cement precasting fabricator had indocumentados loading large cement columns onto trailers. Not provided with gloves or steel-toe shoes, they experienced broken toes and fingers.

Employers also manage to save on wage costs when employing indocumentados. This is more complex than simply paying less than the minimum wage. The majority, though not all, do pay minimum wages, but they hold down their labor costs in a number of ways. The practice of making deductions for services not rendered is common. In restaurants, for example, workers were charged for meals they had no time to eat. Indocumentados do not receive overtime or various fringe benefits (e.g., insurance, retirement). In addition, they are often kept at minimum wage levels for long periods. One national manufacturing corporation maintained indocumentados at the minimum wage for the first year and a half of employment. The few who earned $4.00 or more an hour usually had supervisory or semisupervisory responsibilities or had proven themselves over several years.

Temporary migrants, who are the most tractable, tend to put up with these conditions without complaint, but those who have more experience and are in the United States as part of a settlement process sooner or later question and sometimes resist such work practices. The change is partly a matter of cultural resource accumulation—as they learn how native workers are treated—and partly a matter of unwillingness to accept poor conditions over an indefinite period of time. Thus we find that over time indocumentados did come to resist what they saw to be unfair and exploitive practices.

Their efforts to assert themselves, however, were not often successful. Many employers continued to operate on the assumption that there is an unlimited supply of indocumentado labor. If workers complained or resisted, then it was simply a matter of getting rid of them and hiring others. And employers could always threaten to turn indocumentados in to the Immigration and Naturalization Service to keep them in line.

Still, we believe that to the extent the settlers represent an increasing proportion of the total indocumentado population, there is a greater likelihood that indocumentado workers will be less tractable to employer control.

SOCIAL MOBILITY

When indocumentados are hired they can be considered either as individuals or as members of a social group. When hired as individuals, indocumentados are a numerical minority in the firm and are individually incorporated into various work crews. Employers do not systematically make demands on them on the basis of their illegal status. When hired as members of a social group, indocumentados make up the majority of the work force, or at least their work crews are made up entirely of indocumentados. Employers consider them as a distinct social group and often try to make extra demands on them because of such an identification.

One might assume that wherever possible indocumentados will seek to be hired on an individual rather than a group basis, for it would be to their advantage to be treated just like other workers. But this is not generally the case. Indocumentados tend to form homogeneous work groups. Why? We believe part of the answer is to be found in the manner in which indocumentados interact with Chicanos; they form an enclave within an enclave. Most indocumentado immigrants to a community make use of the social network linking this community to the one of origin in Mexico. This pattern has a decisive impact on how they find jobs. In effect, indocumentados recruit other indocumentados, thus increasing the homogeneity of the work group. This may occur even if employers do not make deliberate efforts to hire indocumentados, but often the two practices are complementary. Our evidence clearly indicates that indocumentados will strive for homogeneity within the work group, to the extent of refusing to cooperate with Chicanos. This in-group character of much of indocumentado employment serves to inhibit job mobility, and we found little occupational or job mobility among indocumentados, either in Austin or San Antonio. Women were almost always in low-status, dead-end jobs, and, though a few men obtained responsible and well-paying positions, they were truly exceptional. Most men started at the minimum wage (then $3.10) and waited months for nickel and dime wage increases up to about $3.75 an hour. The few indocumentados earning $4.00 an hour or more had either the seniority of 3 or more years experience or had taken on supervisory responsibilities, generally of an informal nature.

It was not occupational or job mobility that served to differentiate indocumentados socially. Status changes come mainly by financial accumulation in the form of property. The ability to buy a car, for example, gives indocumentados a higher status because it shows that they have control over an important part of their existence—transportation. A late model can heighten one's status by advertising the owner as financially resourceful. Those without cars spoke of those with them as having to "struggle less."

Possessing a car confers distinction upon the family as well as the individual, but even more of a status symbol is the conversion of rented houses or apartments into "homes." (Two or three indocumentado families were buying their own homes, but this was not a realistic consideration for the typical family.) This transformation consists of getting enough financial security so that boarders are no longer needed. Household improvements are introduced—buying furniture, putting down floor coverings, getting new curtains, adding household appliances. Indocumentado wives are especially concerned with improving their homes, and they will explicitly compare their house furnishings with those of other indocumentado families.

Other than following the changes in the material possessions of indocumentado familes, our respondents did not engage in much discussion of social mobility. Probably their reluctance to do so was related to the recognition that the chances for any really significant social mobility depended upon something not directly linked to their work skills or household management skills, but rather to their legal status. Several respondents reported that they believed they could not effectively improve their employment situations until they had acquired the proper legal status. They said that they knew this, as did their employer.

It is for this reason that indocumentado families follow closely the efforts of the national government to formulate a national policy concerning indocumentados. Obviously, those now in the settlement process would welcome the opportunity to acquire legal status quickly and cheaply. Paying a lawyer to guide their case through the long and convoluted legal process costs thousands of dollars, with no guarantee that the petition will be successful. Even though it is a major drain on their financial resources, some families were willing to take the risk, because so much hinges on legal status.

There is one way to promote social mobility that also enhances one's prospects for obtaining legal status. Unfortunately, its rewards entail a considerable delay. Throughout the world one of the incentives for undertaking rural-to-urban migration and international migration is not the prospect of intragenerational mobility but rather intergenerational mobility. In other words, many indocumentados are realistic enough to recognize and admit that their own prospects for job mobility are very poor, but they are much more optimistic that their children will do well. If the children are born in the United States, they are automatically U.S. citizens, and their status provides preferential consideration in getting the parents' legal status changed.

In conversations, indocumentados made it clear that they expected their children to have better economic opportunities than their own. This viewpoint is reflected through two independent but related factors. The first is that their children will be better *preparados*. That is, their children's work resources (skills) will be superior (generally stated as "knowing how to do other jobs"). There is a somewhat vaguely expressed notion that the United States is a more open and resourceful society than Mexico, and therefore the opportunity structures available to their children are more diversified and richer.

The first reason is linked to the second and is in an important sense dependent upon it. The principal mechanism by which their children may obtain better jobs is through education. But education has a special meaning to indocumentados; it is the ability to handle English in its spoken and written forms. Independent of any vocational skills acquired, competence in English will permit the children of indocumentados to open doors that will always remain closed to their parents. So indocumentado parents tend to be quite positive and supportive in seeing that their children enter and stay in school whenever possible. Younger children are more likely to enter and complete school than are older children, partly because the latter have to contribute to household income, and partly because their experience in school—delay resulting from their poor grasp of English—serves as a disincentive to continuing their education. (An indication of the commitment on the part of these parents is that enrolling their children in schools potentially makes them more exposed to the risk of apprehension.) For the parents, the full payoff will be some time in the future, but even quite young children who know English are valuable intermediaries between their parents and Anglo society.

Conclusion

The major premise of this chapter is that the shift from the individual sojourner to the family that is involved in a settlement process requires different and more complex perspectives for the analysis of Mexican undocumented migration. We have explored some of the many implications for work and its articulation with family–household structures. We have noted the paradox that the family offers enhanced possibilities for survival and economic betterment of its members because of its potential for utilizing the labor of various family individuals, while the vulnerability of the family is at the same time increased because it has more varied needs (i.e., education, housing) to satisfy.

Because of the special circumstances of Mexican indocumentados, families and households are forced to exploit, sometimes to the limit, the labor capacities of their members. Not only are the indocumentados restricted to inferior, low-paying jobs that often are of uncertain duration and subject to wide fluctuations in weekly hours and pay, but their illegal status very largely excludes them from access to the welfare services provided by the state for the native-born poor. Hence, we find among them a high incidence of working wives and mothers, full-time employment of adolescent children, and utilization of younger children to babysit and do house chores. Doubtless, these actions serve to strengthen family solidarity as well as increase income in many cases, but the short-term advantages should be viewed in the context of long-term effects that are often deleterious.

CHAPTER 10

Changing Composition and Labor Market Location of Hispanic Immigrants in New York City, 1960–1980*

Saskia Sassen-Koob

Immigrant Work Force and Economic Decline

The 1980 census counted 14.6 million persons of Hispanic origin, representing 6.5% of the total population of 226.5 million (U.S. Department of Commerce, 1981b, Table 3). The Hispanic population of the Northeast, numbering approximately 2.6 million in 1980, is quite distinct from that of the Southwest in that most of the Hispanics are immigrants from South America and the Caribbean Basin or citizens from Puerto Rico. Because of the volume of recent immigration to New York City and its surrounding area, Central and South American immigrants may come to outnumber Puerto Ricans, and already have, if we include a medium-high estimate for the undocumented. Although Hispanic-origin persons constitute only 5.3% of the total population in the Northeast, they are quite significant in New York State and New York City, where they represent 9.4 and 19.9%, respectively, of the residents.

Between 1960 and 1980, New York City not only received a large pool of Hispanic immigrants, but also lost a significant number of jobs. Ac-

* I thank the Center for Latin American and Caribbean Studies of New York University for supporting this research through grants from the Tinker Foundation and the Ford Foundation. I am particularly grateful to Christopher Mitchell and Catherine Benamou of the Center, Evelyn Mann and Frank Vardy of the Population Division of New York City's Department of City Planning, and Eric Kruger of the Port Authority of New York and New Jersey.

cording to census figures, New York City's Hispanic population increased by 10% from 1970 to 1980, when it reached 1.4 million (U.S. Department of Commerce, 1981b). Civilian employment in New York City, on the other hand, declined from 3.7 million in 1970 to under 3.3 million in 1980 (U.S. Department of Labor, 1981c). Of particular relevance to the immigrant work force is the 35% decline in manufacturing jobs during the 1970s (Ehrenhalt, 1981, p. 44), which accounted for almost three-fifths of the city's half-million job loss between 1970 and 1980 (City of New York, 1982, pp. 18, 21).

The increase in the immigrant population during this period, coupled with the decrease in the number of jobs, would seem to exceed the absorption capacity of the declining sector of the economy, the one that typically employed immigrants. Furthermore, the coexistence of significant job losses and a large immigrant influx is both historically and analytically unusual: analytically, because the migration literature posits economic growth as one of the main pull factors drawing immigrants to the United States; historically, because the major migratory labor flows have, indeed, typically been directed toward growth areas. Examples include the United States at the turn of the century, Western Europe during the post–World War II reconstruction, and the OPEC countries during the 1970s. The market model, which has explicitly but also unwittingly shaped the analysis of international labor migrations, posits a direct relation between labor flows and capital flows, or the inflow of labor into areas of high economic growth. However, this model less adequately explains the coexistence in a given location of job outflows and the inflow of workers traditionally employed in the kinds of jobs prevailing in the job outflow. It would seem that the new immigrants should settle in the Sunbelt rather than New York City. Although many do, a substantial proportion do not.

This raises the question about the capacity of New York City's economy to absorb a large immigrant pool under conditions of pronounced job losses in precisely those sectors of the economy likely to draw immigrant workers. Though available studies do not directly address this issue, the migration literature does contain insights into this question. Most salient are explanations that emphasize (1) the weight of push factors (e.g., lack of employment opportunities in countries of origin); (2) the existence of immigrant networks that draw the migratory flows even under less-than-optimal economic conditions; and (3) the internal differentiation of the labor market in advanced industrial societies, which allows high unemployment among native workers to coexist with a demand for cheap immigrant workers. While essentially correct, the explanations contained in the immigration literature are incomplete, particularly as regards the last point.

The possibility of absorbing the new immigrant work force in the face of a continuing loss of jobs suggests a need to refine the notion of economic decline and to specify the process of labor market differentiation so that it captures both decline and growth trends. I attempt such a specification and argue that the new immigration is primarily associated with a process of socioeconomic recomposition in major urban centers that is characterized by two major growth sectors: producer services and downgraded manufacturing. Although very different, both generate a large array of low-wage jobs, with few if any requirements for skills and language proficiency and with few advancement opportunities, and thus generate conditions conducive to the absorption of a large influx of immigrants. To this should be added the increase of low-wage jobs brought about by the general shift to a service economy. The argument can be extended to include major urban centers on the West Coast and, with qualifications, in the Southwest. In the case of major cities in the Southwest, Mexican immigrants are a key component in the new labor demand, as reflected by their growing presence in urban low-wage service jobs. In the case of major West Coast cities, this role is filled by new Asian and continuing Mexican immigration.

The following section discusses New York City's changing economic structure, with a particular focus on decline and growth trends. The next section then discusses the expansion of the Hispanic immigration to New York City, comparing 1970 and 1980 census tract data as well as the results of a survey of six immigrant groups in Queens (the borough in New York City with the largest concentration of the new Hispanic and Asian immigration). Juxtaposing the results of these two sections, the conclusion attempts to outline how the labor market location of immigrants has become internally differentiated.

Economic Recomposition: Conditions for the Absorption of the Immigrant Work Force

The massive expansion of Hispanic and Asian immigration to New York City occurred in a context of large losses of factory and office jobs in the northern and northeastern regions. New York City was disproportionately affected by the movement of jobs abroad and to the Sunbelt. Furthermore, there were particularly large job losses in sectors of the economy likely to employ immigrants. Netzer (1974) estimated that, between 1968 and 1972, New York City lost 334,000 goods-handling jobs and 99,000 retail and consumer services jobs. Between 1969 and 1977, Manhattan's central business district experienced a 30% decline in factory employment, down from 570,000 to 400,000, besides a 15% decline in office employment, down from 910,000 to 770,000 (Tobier, 1979, pp. 15–16). Table 10.1 provides further information on New York City's employment distribution over the past two decades.

The disaggregated data on economic decline reveal three general trends that are consistent with an economic base capable of absorbing an expanded immigrant work force. First, the highly specialized service sector has expanded significantly, particularly after 1976 (U.S. Department of Labor, 1981c). This sector provides many low-wage jobs that often involve night and weekend shifts. Second, foreign investment in New York City increased significantly after 1976 and played a central role in the growth and recovery of certain sectors of the economy, including manufacturing and construction (Port Authority of New York and New Jersey, 1981). Third, the departure of capital from the area affected labor-intensive industries unevenly. In fact, what I call a *downgraded manufacturing sector*—that is, one where sweatshops and industrial homework are common forms of production—has expanded. This downgrading has affected not only the garment industry, but also the toy, footwear, and electronics industries (New York State Department of Labor, 1982a, 1982b).

One consequence of these trends is increased socioeconomic polarization in the city's occupational structure, especially in the borough of Manhattan. This polarization consists in an expansion of high-income professional jobs, a decline of middle-income blue-collar and white-col-

TABLE 10.1
New York City Wage and Salary Employment by Major Industry, 1960–1981 (in thousands)

Industry	1960	1970	1977	1980	1981[a]
Manufacturing	946.8	766.2	538.6	498.7	485.5
Construction	126.9	110.1	64.2	74.7	75.8
Transportation, communications, and public utilities	318.1	323.3	258.2	257.2	257.2
Wholesale and retail trade	744.8	735.4	620.1	614.9	611.2
Finance, insurance, and real estate	384.4	458.2	414.4	445.8	478.0
Services and miscellaneous	609.2	787.3	784.6	890.4	917.5
Government	408.2	562.8	507.8	516.6	516.9
Total	3,538.4	3,743.3	3,187.9	3,298.3	3,342.1

Source: The Port Authority of New York and New Jersey (1982, p. 18), and the City of New York (1982, pp. 18 and 21).

[a] Preliminary estimates.

lar jobs, and an increase of low-wage service and manufacturing jobs. It is in this restructuring of labor demand that we find the conditions for the absorption of the large immigrant influx (Sassen-Koob, 1981, pp. 76–77). However, declining industries in need of cheap labor for survival, typically viewed as a key source of employment for immigrants, account for only a part of the supply of low-wage jobs. This will become evident as I discuss each of the three trends that has altered the structure of labor demand in New York City over the past two decades.

GROWTH AMID DECLINE:
THE PRODUCER SERVICES

A disaggregation of employment data points to sharp increases in certain sectors in spite of the overall employment decline. Between 1977 and 1980, employment in nine white-collar service industries increased. Two-fifths of the jobs in these industries are in the higher-pay, higher-status professional, technical, managerial, and administrative occupations (U.S. Department of Labor, 1980, 1981a). Between 1977 and 1980, employment increased by 7.7% in finance, insurance, and real estate, by 9.4% in communications and media, and by 24.7% in business services. Also, employment expanded by 8.9% in educational services and research institutions, by 7.4% in entertainment, culture, and tourism, and by 3.9% in social services (U.S. Department of Labor, 1982a).[1]

These growth rates together with the decline in office and manufacturing jobs point to a recomposition of the city's economy. In 1950, manufacturing supplied almost one job in three while services supplied one in seven. By 1980 these figures were reversed. There was a parallel loss of office jobs, particularly headquarters office jobs, which declined by 41% between 1969 (highest employment) and 1980 (Ehrenhalt, 1981, p. 46).

The sharp rise in domestic and worldwide demand for highly specialized services is a key stimulus to the large relative growth of the producer services. Two major conditions for this growth are the internationalization of the U.S. economy and the technological transformation of the work process (Sassen-Koob, 1984). Both have made producer ser-

---

[1] A more detailed analysis of the service sector shows that between 1977 and 1980 the highest growth rates were in computer services (51.8%), personnel agencies and temporary employment agencies (65.5%), management consulting and public relations (31.1%), engineering and architecture (24.2%), accounting (18.8%), protective services (19.9%), securities dealers (19.5%), theaters (excluding movie theaters) (21.0%), and in outpatient care facilities (48.4%) (U.S. Department of Labor, 1982a).

vices the most dynamic sector in the national economy. Furthermore, the characteristics of production of advanced services induce agglomeration, thus they tend to be concentrated in major trade centers (Conservation of Human Resources Project, 1977).

International trading is an important source of earnings for numerous service industries in the United States, including accounting, advertising, banking, communications, computer services, construction and engineering services, consulting and management services, educational services, franchising, health services, insurance, leasing, legal services, motion pictures, shipping and air transport, tourism, and the overseas development of hotels and motels (U.S. Department of Commerce, 1980b, pp. 2–4).[2] The production of these services tends to be concentrated in New York and other major urban centers (Knight, 1973; Stanback, 1979; Sassen-Koob, 1984). The growing importance of the international trade in services led to the establishment in 1978 of the International Services Division within the Department of Commerce and to intensified pressure to lift trading barriers (U.S. Senate, Committee on Banking, Housing, and Urban Affairs, 1982).

Of particular significance for New York City is the weight of producer services in the expansion of service employment, particularly as employment in other major services, such as public, distributive, and consumer services, has leveled off since the middle or late 1960s. Producer services continued to grow throughout the 1970s, with business services the fastest growing segment of the U.S. economy. In New York City, producer services accounted for almost 31% of all employment in 1981; in contrast, in a city like Detroit, they account for under 13% of all employment (Sassen-Koob, 1984).[3]

The weight of producer services in the expansion of employment and the characteristics of this type of economic activity explain both the high concentration in New York City, and why, amid an overall decline in employment levels, the city can support a thriving, export-oriented producer service sector. The extension of international banking to New

---

[2] The earnings of service industries from foreign trade are often very high. For example, for the top 83 advertising firms in the United States, gross income from sales abroad represented 37.6% of their total income in 1980; for the 10 largest, this share was 51.7% (Economic Consulting Services, Inc., 1981, p. 85). The top 8 accounting firms made 40% of their income from sales abroad in 1977, and in 1978 the 2 largest firms made over half of their revenues from such sales (U.S. Department of Commerce, 1980b, pp. 13–15).

[3] Mostly producer services include the following industries (Standard Industry Codes): 60–67, 73, 81, 86, and 89.

York City in December 1981 further added to the growth of producer services,[4] as have the rapidly increasing foreign investments in banking in New York City. This growth of producer services in New York City is further underlined by the fact that although a large number of *Fortune* 500 firms moved their headquarters out of the city over the past 15 years, those that remained showed higher growth, especially in international activity, than those that left.

The significance for immigrant employment of dynamic growth in the producer services is the concomitant growth of service jobs that require low skill levels, minimum language proficiency, often involve undesirable night or weekend shifts, and typically offer limited or no advancement prospects. The growth of specialized service industries brings about an increase not only of experts but also of cleaners, stock clerks, messengers, and other low-skill jobs that are integral to almost any industry. The expansion of the producer service sector also generates an indirect demand for low-wage workers to service the lifestyles of the very high-income workers it employs. Among these are residential building attendants, workers producing services or goods for specialty shops and gourmet food shops, dog walkers, domestic service workers, and so on. Many of these jobs fall outside any of the major industry counts, not so much because they may involve illegal immigrants, but because they are part of the underground economy.

Immigration can be seen as a significant source of labor for the vast infrastructure of low-wage jobs underlying the expansion of the specialized service sector and the high-income lifestyles of its upper-level employees. It is not only their willingness to accept low wages that make immigrants a suitable source of labor for these jobs, but also their willingness to staff these generally undesirable positions (Sassen-Koob, 1980). Thus, continued immigration appears to contribute both to the maintenance and expansion of a polarized economic system, while also lowering the costs of operating such a system. This is done directly by providing cheap labor and indirectly by lowering the cost of living of top-level personnel.

---

[4] The establishment of International Banking Facilities (IBFs) encourages international transactions by domestic banks and branches of foreign banks by removing Federal Reserve regulations or reserve requirements and interest rate ceilings. IBFs that locate in New York City are also exempt from state and city taxes. Of the 140 IBFs announcing they were going into business in December 1981, 100 were in New York City (City of New York, 1982, p. 18).

THE RISE IN FOREIGN INVESTMENT AFTER 1976

One of the central factors in the rapid growth trends beginning in 1977 was a pronounced increase in foreign investment in several important New York City industries: banking, real estate, hotels and restaurants, and manufacturing. The importance of this investment at a time of massive departures by domestic capital and an all-time low in employment levels has increasingly been recognized by government officials and the private sector (Goldmark, 1979; the Conference Board, Inc., 1981; Port Authority of New York and New Jersey, 1981, 1982; City of New York, 1982). There are sound reasons for foreign investors to locate in the United States, especially when the dollar is cheaper and there is a threat of import restrictions into what is still the largest single market in the world. Thus, the large increase in foreign investment in the Sunbelt states would seem to need little explaining, particularly given the massive move of domestic capital to those same areas. The choice to locate in New York City, however, requires more explanation.

One can argue that the massive departure of capital from the North, including New York City, has created once again conditions for profitable investment in depressed areas. The massive loss of jobs has put pressure on northern workers to accept wage cuts, forfeit benefits, and tolerate speed-ups, entrenchment, and automation as a way to save some jobs (Tabb, 1982). Capital's bargaining position improved both in the factory and with respect to city government. In New York City, the loss of capital was accompanied by a decline in the tax base, which in turn had a decisive role in getting the city to cut services and welfare rolls and to lay off municipal workers. These interventions were not only accepted, but had an air of legitimacy about them that they would not have had in the 1960s.[5]

Foreign investors in the United States have shown a preference for buying plants or building new ones in the old manufacturing centers

---

[5] These developments acquire particular significance in the light of recent trends in the Sunbelt cities. The Sunbelt is beginning to experience some of the problems that were instrumental in the departure of capital from the North (Mollenkopf, 1977). The area of urban sprawl is increasingly costly to service efficiently. Though desirable as a tax base, continuous incorporation of newly developed areas in the metropolitan unit creates the need for a very large service operation. This is likely to increase unionization rates of municipal workers. Both servicing and increased unionization will increase the operating budgets of these cities. In addition, northern unionized labor is intensifying its efforts to organize the South. In sum, the explosive growth in the Sunbelt is generating a number of trends that may have the effect of diminishing the pull for capital to relocate, while the increased power of capital in the North, resulting from its own departure, may become a new pull factor.

that have experienced severe decline, especially in areas with high unemployment rates.[6] Rather than leveling off in response to the worsening situation in the northern manufacturing centers, foreign investments actually increased through the decade of the 1970s. The current value of foreign investments in U.S. plants and equipment has more than doubled since 1973. In 1979 alone, over 400 foreign firms built or bought manufacturing facilities in the United States, a large share of these located in the Northeast (Port Authority of New York and New Jersey, 1981, 1982). Nationwide, New York and New Jersey had 18.6% of all foreign-owned manufacturing plants in 1980. This is a significant share given the severe manufacturing crisis in this region, and considering that booming states such as Texas and Georgia have 5.8 and 3.9%, respectively (see Table 10.2). Furthermore, New York had the largest net increase in foreign-owned manufacturing firms of all states between 1976 and 1980—196 plants added, compared to 161 in California, 87 in Texas, and 94 in North Carolina. The data in Table 10.2 on foreign-owned plants are an undercount because they cover only plants employing 50 or more workers. Factories with fewer than 50 employees are common in New York City (Goldmark, 1979, p. 6).

Foreign investment in construction and tertiary sector activities was a central factor in the construction boom of offices, hotels, and residences during the second half of the 1970s (Goldmark, 1979; Port Authority of New York and New Jersey, 1981, 1982). Furthermore, there has been a rapid increase in the number of foreign banks and in foreign purchases of major retail establishments, such as Saks Fifth Avenue in Manhattan. From 1978 to 1980, 21 new foreign bank branches and agencies were added in New York City, representing an increase of 17%. Assets of all foreign banks and branches increased by 42.6% over that same period, going from $79.1 billion in 1978 to $112.8 billion by June 1980. "What distinguishes the recent influx of foreign investment is its strong influ-

---

[6] A 1976 study for the Conference Board (Bauer, 1980) found that over one-quarter of all investments by foreign firms made between 1968 and 1975 were in New England states and mid-Atlantic states (New York, New Jersey, and Pennsylvania), a region with a high incidence of domestic capital emigration and more than 5000 factory closures over that period. A study for the Federal Reserve Bank of Boston (Little, 1978) found that, adjusting for differences in population and land area of individual states, the northern industrial areas had received the largest share of foreign investments. Similarly, Cohen (1979) found that 64% of foreign-owned manufacturing facilities operating in urban areas in 1974 were located in economically distressed areas. Cohen also found that nearly 60% of announced investments for 1977 and 1978 occurred in distressed urban areas; German, English, and Swiss firms were most likely to locate facilities in such areas, while Japanese firms were less likely to do so.

TABLE 10.2
Foreign-Owned Manufacturing Plants, Selected States and Regions, and U.S. Total, 1980

	Cumu-lative total through 1975	1976	1977	1978	1979	1980	Cumu-lative total through 1980	% of U.S. total	Net increase 1976–80
New York State	222	42	45	36	50	23	418	11.4	196
New Jersey	178	13	21	16	17	18	263	7.2	85
NY–NJ metro-politan region	234	9	17	18	28	16	322	—	88
California	103	16	22	43	50	30	264	7.2	161
Texas	82	6	14	16	31	20	169	5.8	87
North Carolina	90	6	11	16	25	36	184	5.0	94
Pennsylvania	125	10	16	14	19	30	214	4.6	89
Georgia	68	5	5	20	22	23	143	3.9	75
Illinois	92	10	5	6	10	13	136	3.7	44
All other	1006	137	135	191	210	194	1873	51.2	867
U.S. Total	1966	245	274	358	434	387	3664	100.0	1698

Source: The Conference Board, Inc. (1981); The Port Authority of New York and New Jersey (1981, p. 3).

ence on the recovery of the economy of New York City and the region following the significant loss of jobs and population between 1969 and 1976" (Goldmark, 1979, p. 4).

There are strong inducements for foreign investment in the United States generally. Firms with sizable exports to the United States may benefit from direct production here to consolidate and expand their markets and to avoid import restrictions, especially in view of continuing U.S. merchandise trade deficits. The declining value of the dollar during the 1970s made investments, acquisitions, and construction of plants in the United States relatively more profitable to outsiders. An additional factor is the intense competition and active lobbying on the part of local governments to draw domestic and foreign investors. Equally important is the nature of the labor supply in the Northeast generally, and New York City in particular. The availability of a skilled industrial work force politically weakened by the closing of factories is one factor promoting foreign investment in manufacturing. So too is the large presence of a politically powerless immigrant labor pool that can either replace native supplies of low-wage workers, who became highly politicized in the 1960s, or occupy the new jobs created by the transformation of the industrial structure.

RECOMPOSITION PATTERNS IN OLD INDUSTRIES

Two pronounced trends are evident in the city's manufacturing base over the past decade. One is the large loss of manufacturing jobs associated with the closure or migration of plants; the other is the expansion of a downgraded manufacturing sector, often involving the same branches but using different forms of production and organization of the work process. This process of recomposition was accompanied by a considerable decline in New York City's average wage levels for factory production workers as a share of the national average (U.S. Department of Labor, 1980, 1981a).[7]

An important distinction for my argument is that backward sectors of capital may be declining or experiencing dynamic growth. The garment industry in New York City illustrates both aspects well. It is still the single largest manufacturing employer in the city. This industry, one of the first to undergo internationalization, shows a variety of patterns: (1) development of large, rather automated operations, mostly in the Southwest, that have come to incorporate jobs once existing in New York City; (2) the loss of medium-sized operations, typically unionized, that constituted the core of the city's industry; and (3) the growth of sweatshops and industrial homework.

Worth mentioning is the case of the footwear industry because of its importance to the Northeast as a whole and because it illustrates the development of a polarized mode of recomposition. This recomposition has assumed the form of large, mostly mechanized factories that monopolize domestic production, coupled with an expansion of sweatshops and industrial homework. Medium-size plants, mostly unionized, are the ones that have disproportionately experienced closings. Of added significance to New York City is the fact that the replacement of a large share of domestic production with imports has generated service jobs in import and distribution activities, many of which are located in New York City, while the lost production jobs were mostly located outside the city.

Not all components of labor-intensive industries were affected equally by capital emigration. In the case of the garment industry, the larger shops with standardized production were the ones most likely to move. The less-mechanized branches, as well as the industry's marketing and design operations, have remained in New York City. While the produc-

---

[7] From 1961, wage rates for factory production workers held at about 94% of the national average, reaching an all-time high of 95.5% in 1970. By 1981 the wage rate for factory production workers was down to 85.9%, probably a significant overestimate, since it excludes sweatshops and industrial homeworkers.

tion of shirts, undergarments, and work clothing has moved to the Sunbelt, branches that are more tied to fashion, have higher seasonal requirements, and demand more tailoring skill have remained in the north. These shops are usually small, employing between 5 and 30 workers, are subject to intense competition, and specialize in highly fashionable or very cheap, fast-moving garments. Highly specialized finishing work also remains in New York City. (For more detailed data see North American Congress on Latin America, 1978; U.S. Executive Office of the President, 1978; and Waldinger, Chapter 11 in this volume.) The experience of the garment industry over the past 20 years shows that components of labor-intensive industries have remained in the old manufacturing centers, notwithstanding high overall capital mobility, as indicated in Table 10.3.

A key variable explaining both the emigration of garment industry jobs and their continued presence in an old center is the nature of the production process. The possibility of "de-skilling" a share of the jobs, lowering ratios of fixed assets per worker, and limited economies of scale can dramatically alter the nature of the production process. In other words, it is easy to move an apparel factory because the necessary investment is relatively small; it does not require a highly skilled labor force, and those components of the production process that demand high skills can be separated from the rest.

The apparel industry was one of the first to undergo internationalization of production. One requisite for internationalization is the possibility of breaking down production tasks to isolate low-skilled operations for export to areas where labor costs are lower. The very simple, basically unchanging technology of the industry has two important consequences. The basic fixed asset is the sewing machine, which makes possible a pronounced fragmentation of the production process (unitized production) without sacrificing economies of scale. It makes economic sense to open up a plant with 5 to 30 sewing machines, an impossibility in many types of industries where scale determines economic feasibility. Furthermore, the practice of subcontracting and section work, which started in the late 1800s, created a type of organization of work that later facilitated the export of certain jobs. Subcontracting and section work entailed the replacement of highly skilled workers who prepared a whole garment by semi- or unskilled workers who mass-produced one piece. This practice permits taking advantage of dispersed production sites.

From this derives the second consequence: the possibility of starting an apparel factory with a small amount of initial capital. According to a report in the *Wall Street Journal* (October 18, 1976), starting an "efficient"

TABLE 10.3
Employment in the Apparel Industry, United States and Selected States, 1958–1980 (in thousands)

Year	United States	New York	New Jersey	Penn-sylvania	North Carolina	Georgia	Alabama	Florida	Texas	Cali-fornia	All other states
1958	1171.8	329.0	76.7	157.8	27.1	41.8	21.5	7.3	32.5	54.5	423.6
1960	2233.2	318.9	77.7	168.1	35.3	47.6	25.8	8.7	35.7	59.5	455.9
1965	1354.2	291.4	77.3	180.1	57.1	63.4	37.4	13.2	47.1	65.6	521.6
1970	1364.6	249.2	72.3	171.2	75.1	70.0	44.9	23.7	61.3	72.7	524.2
1975	1243.3	180.8	57.9	132.7	75.4	66.7	48.4	27.5	69.8	91.6	492.5
1980	1265.8	170.0	55.3	124.2	87.9	72.4	53.9	34.1	75.0	107.0	486.0

Source: U.S. Department of Labor (1981a, 1982b).

dress operation requires $300,000—a relatively small amount compared with initial capital requirements in most other industries. A large apparel factory, which is uncommon, may have as much as $15,000 worth of assets per worker. This contrasts markedly with the situation in advanced industries, where assets per production worker range between $40,000 and $70,000. The typical garment shop has 50 production workers and about $6000 in fixed assets per worker—the figures proposed by the government study to establish an efficient operation, but a North American Congress on Latin America study (1979) found that apparel factories can start on much less and do so in cities like New York.

In addition to unitized production and skill standardization—two conditions that facilitate plant relocation—the weight of labor costs is a third factor in explaining internationalization. Though in recent years a few big U.S. apparel companies have become more automated, for most of the 15,000 apparel companies labor accounts for about 27% of production costs, compared with 10% for manufacturing as a whole. Thus, this factor is of major significance for profit levels, and partly explains the continued decline in wages over the past 30 years as a means of maintaining profit levels. In 1947, the average wage of apparel workers was 95% of average manufacturing wages; by 1977 it had declined to 64% (U.S. Executive Office of the President, 1978, p. 27). It is the nature of the production process (one in which labor costs play such a significant role) that explains this decline in wages, not simply the availability of cheap immigrant labor per se.

The same characteristics of the production process that explain the facility and desirability of plant relocation in the garment industry also explain why during the past few years the industry began to expand again in a place like New York City, with its outmoded physical plants, its fiscal precariousness, and its scarcity of and highly priced commercial space. Highly skilled or fashion-linked components of the production process can be isolated and carried out on a small scale and with minimal initial investments. Finally, the availability of an abundant low-wage labor supply that can be drawn into industrial homework and sweatshops makes possible production of cheap garments for a mass market. A parallel argument can be developed for the footwear industry (see Evans, 1979).[8]

[8] The overall picture that emerges in the case of the footwear industry is one of growing concentration, in which a few large companies control the market through domestic production, production abroad, and control over imports. Some components of the domestic footwear industry are thriving, while others are declining severely. Insofar as domestic producers are heavily involved in the import trade, certain components of the industry are expanding.

The overall relevance of this discussion to my central argument is that disaggregated data on capital emigration from the Northeast, especially from New York, show that (1) certain branches within labor-intensive industries such as apparel and footwear continue to operate in the Northeast, and are actually expanding; (2) the types of production that make relocation easy and desirable are also conducive to continued operation in places like New York City, which have highly skilled and cheap unskilled labor pools; and (3) the severe shrinking of the production base of an industry such as footwear through expanding imports may generate a whole range of new jobs associated with import trade. This development may be particularly significant to New York City as a commercial center because the transfer of production jobs from an area outside of the New York SMSA (Standard Metropolitan Statistical Area) to foreign countries has generated a new set of jobs within the city. These three trends do not by any means overcome the devastating impact of capital emigration from New York City during the past two decades, but they are elements of an explanation that seeks to resolve the apparent contradiction of the coexistence in one place of a massive job loss and a massive influx of immigrants.

The New Hispanic Immigration to New York City

The data of the U.S. Justice Department's Immigration and Naturalization Service (INS) for the past two decades indicate a changing composition of immigrant streams from a preponderance of immigrants from high-wage countries of origin during the 1950s to one of inflows from low-wage countries of origin. Moreover, there has been a substantial increase in annual entries, even excluding undocumented immigrants. Finally, the INS data show a tendency for immigrants to concentrate residentially in a few large cities: South Americans and West Indians (excluding Cubans) in New York City; Mexicans in Chicago, Los Angeles, and major Southwest cities; and Asians in San Francisco, Los Angeles, and New York City. New York City and Los Angeles, the two major recipients of the new immigration, both experienced severe job losses in their older, established industries and had fiscal crises. (For a comparison of Los Angeles and New York City see Sassen-Koob, 1984.)

The available evidence for New York City suggests that a large share of the Hispanic population furnishes labor for low-wage jobs. Census data for 1980 show that median family income of Hispanics in New York City was $10,300, that one out of three Hispanics was below the poverty threshold, and that almost half had an elementary school education or less. These aggregate socioeconomic indicators include Puerto Ricans, known to have low incomes and high unemployment rates. However, special studies on South and Central American immigrants in Queens, where the highest share of new immigrants reside, indicate a polarized occupational distribution consisting of some representation in professional and middle-level jobs while over half hold low-wage service and manufacturing jobs. The large share of economically active women among recent Hispanic immigrants contributed to the high representation of this group among low-wage jobs (Castro, 1982; Cohen and Sassen-Koob, 1982).

This section documents the expansion of the Hispanic population in New York City and analyzes the available evidence on the employment distribution of Hispanics in the city, including the results of two studies of immigrant groups in the borough of Queens (Cohen and Sassen-Koob, 1982; Beshers and Sassen-Koob, 1982). The purpose is to juxtapose this information with that provided in the previous section on the types and availability of low-wage jobs known or likely to employ immigrants.

HISPANIC POPULATION GROWTH AND RESIDENTIAL DISTRIBUTION

There is a pronounced tendency, both in the past and today, for immigrants to be concentrated geographically in certain areas, a fact that accentuates their effects on the labor market. About 40% of all (legal) immigrants live in the 10 largest cities, which together account for less than 10% of the total U.S. population (U.S. Department of Justice, 1978, pp. 76–85). In the early 1900s, New York, Pennsylvania, and Illinois attracted most of the immigrants (Immigration Commission, 1911, p. 105). Up to 1975, New York was still the largest recipient of immigrants, followed by California, currently the main destination of recent Mexican and Asian immigrants (U.S. Department of Justice, 1978, p. 75). Together, these two states receive almost half of all new immigrants. Between 1966 and 1976, New York City received about one-fourth of all new arrivals, a level remarkably higher than that of the cities with the next largest concentrations—Los Angeles with 4.7% and Chicago with 4.4%. If we add the immigrant population of New Jersey during the past few years (the third or fourth largest recipient of immigrants), and consider the fact that many New Jersey residents actually work in New York City, then the impact of immigration on the New York labor market may be even greater.

The preliminary and court-contested 1980 census figures show a total population for New York City of 7.1 million. Of these, 1.4 million were Hispanics. The 1970 census counted 1.2 million Hispanics in New York City, representing 16% of the population. The increase in the number and share of Hispanics in New York City is particularly impressive in view of a 10.4% decline in the city's total population between 1970 and 1980.

Census tract data for New York City show an increase from 1970 to 1980 in the number of tracts containing Hispanic residents, and in the number of tracts with over 50% of Hispanic residents. Comparing 1970 and 1980 census tracts with a large number of Hispanics, the most marked increase took place in Queens and Staten Island (see Table 10.4). The decline in the Hispanic populations of Brooklyn and the Bronx masks the fact of an increase in non–Puerto Rican Hispanics that compensated for a large decline in Puerto Ricans. The figures for Manhattan reflect a similar replacement, only on a more massive scale. The increases in Queens and Staten Island, on the other hand, reflect almost exclusively the new Hispanic immigration as well as Puerto Rican additions. An examination of residential patterns suggests that the expansion of the Hispanic-occupied areas in Queens spilled over into Brook-

TABLE 10.4
Population of Spanish–Hispanic Origin or Descent in New York City by Boroughs, 1970–1980

Borough	1970	1980	Change	
			Number	Percentage
Bronx	407,322	396,730	−10,592	−2.6
Brooklyn	392,575	392,118	−457	−0.1
Manhattan	312,722	335,803	23,081	7.4
Queens	153,691	262,422	108,731	70.7
Staten Island	12,320	18,884	6,564	53.3
Total New York City	1,278,630	1,405,957	127,327	10.0

Source: City of New York (1980).

lyn, which accounts for part of the increase in new Hispanics in that borough (Beshers and Sassen-Koob, 1982).

Annual legal entries of Hispanics (excluding Mexicans) have increased over the past few years and reached their highest levels ever. Entries between 1955 and 1979 describe a bimodal curve: a substantial increase after 1960, a decrease in the first half of the 1970s and a new increase in the second half of the 1970s. This pattern also holds for West Indians, another major immigration stream mostly directed to New York City. Total entries of South and Central Americans and West Indians were 522,369 from 1965 to 1969; they declined to 467,515 from 1970 to 1974 and rose to 643,254 from 1975 to 1979 (U.S. Department of Justice, 1981). This pattern holds for each of the three major groups and for specific nationalities, notably Colombians and, to a lesser extent, Dominicans. Such a pattern most likely holds for illegal immigrants as well. The sharp rise after 1965, which had already begun after 1959, is largely a function of the changed immigration law, whereas the increase after 1975 may also be associated with the expansion of jobs for which immigrants are especially suited.

HISPANIC LABOR MARKET POSITION, 1980

Information from studies based on localized samples (Beshers and Sassen-Koob, 1982; Castro, 1982; Cohen and Sassen-Koob, 1982; Urrea Giraldo, 1982) shows New York City Hispanics concentrated in service and manufacturing jobs, particularly when we exclude Puerto Ricans. Cohen and Sassen-Koob (1982) found that the new Hispanics (i.e., excluding Puerto Ricans) were more highly concentrated in factory and service jobs than the other ethnic groups in a survey from Queens (see Table 10.5). While similar shares (about 11%) of Puerto Ricans, Colombians and other Hispanics hold managerial jobs, a significant difference emerges for professional jobs. Only 3.8% of Colombians compared with over 13% each of Puerto Ricans and Other Hispanics hold professional jobs. Among Asians the other major new immigrant group, almost 42% are employed in this occupational stratum. Colombians, on the other hand, were well represented in crafts jobs, about 15.4%, compared with 3.3% of Puerto Ricans, 7.7% of blacks and between 6 and 9% of the major European groups. The highest concentration of new Hispanics is in both operative and service jobs: half of all Colombians and 42% of Other Hispanics. A considerable share of South American immigrants hold professional positions, confirming INS reports. They also provide a

TABLE 10.5
Percentage Distribution of Ethnic Groups, by Occupation: Queens, 1980

	Blacks	Jews	Italians	Irish	Other European ethnics	Puerto Ricans	Colombians	Other Hispanics	Asians	Others
Management	8.9	13.4	8.6	11.4	14.7	11.7	11.5	11.3	2.8	7.9
Professional and technical	24.6	31.0	18.0	31.4	21.5	13.3	3.8	13.6	41.7	22.8
Sales	6.0	8.8	7.0	1.0	5.1	11.7	3.8	3.4	8.3	7.9
Clerical	14.1	27.2	18.0	24.8	24.9	21.7	15.4	15.9	22.2	18.5
Crafts	7.7	4.2	6.2	5.7	9.0	3.3	15.4	12.5	0.0	13.6
Operatives and laborers	14.5	3.1	18.0	5.7	7.9	16.6	19.2	20.5	8.3	9.3
Transport	4.8	2.3	6.3	2.9	1.7	1.7	0.0	1.1	0.0	2.9
Services	19.4	10.0	17.9	17.1	15.2	20.0	30.9	21.7	16.7	17.1
	100.0	100.0	100.0	100.0	100.0	100.0	100.0	100.0	100.0	100.0
N	248	261	128	105	177	60	26	88	36	140

Source: Cohen and Sassen-Koob (1982, p. 9).

labor supply for clerical and low-level managerial jobs, especially in small firms (Urrea Giraldo, 1982).

Furthermore, Cohen and Sassen-Koob (1982) found that two-worker households were more prevalent among the new Hispanics, about 30% compared with 15 to 20% among the other ethnic groups in their Queens sample. Both Urrea Giraldo (1982) and Castro (1982) also found a very high incidence of multiple-earner households among Colombians. This characteristic helps explain why the average family income of the new Hispanics is not much different from that of other ethnic groups in our sample even though their occupational distribution is much more disadvantaged.

Comparing the occupational distribution of Hispanics generally and other major ethnic groups in the New York City SMSA for 1979 (U.S. Department of Commerce, 1980b) with that of the new Hispanics in our Queens sample reveals that the new Hispanics exhibit one of the highest concentrations in service jobs (see Table 10.6). Blacks are most concentrated in services, partly due to their higher share of transport jobs, which is 4.8% compared with about 1% among the new Hispanics in our sample. Second, all Hispanics and the new Hispanics in our sample hold an above-average share of manufacturing jobs. A similar pattern emerged from a comparison of the occupational distribution of the Queen's sample with that of the national Hispanic population. These various employment patterns strongly suggest that the new Hispanic immigration is a labor supply directed toward service jobs and a downgraded manufacturing sector. The considerable decline in the average industrial wage for factory workers in New York City over the past 10 years suggests that manufacturing jobs are increasingly unattractive.

TABLE 10.6
Percentage Distribution of Major Ethnic Groups, by Occupation:
New York City (1979) and Queens (1980)

Occupation	New York City (SMSA) 1979				Queens (NYC) 1980	
	All	Whites	Blacks	Hispanics	Puerto Ricans	New Hispanics
White-collar	60.8	64.0	50.2	35.7	58.4	42.1
Blue-collar	20.8	20.9	20.7	38.6	19.9	33.3
Services[a]	18.4	15.1	29.1	25.7	21.7	24.6
	100.0	100.0	100.0	100.0	100.0	100.0

Sources: U.S. Department of Labor (1982c); Cohen and Sassen-Koob (1982).
[a] Transport included in Services.

Preliminary 1980 census data (see Table 10.7) reveal Hispanics in New
York City to be economically disadvantaged compared with Hispanics
residing in other major cities (see also Bonilla and Campos, 1982). A
comparison of selected characteristics of Hispanics in major SMSAs with
a population of 1 million or more and 25,000 or more Hispanics shows
New York City to rank second in size of the Hispanic population,
twelfth in family income, second in numbers of families below the poverty level, and thirteenth in the share of Hispanics 25 years of age and
over with a high school degree. This information is problematic if we
consider that Hispanics in two cities as diverse as Miami, with its large
Cuban population, and Houston, with its large Mexican population,
have relatively similar rankings.

TABLE 10.7
**Selected Characteristics of Populations of Spanish–Hispanic Origin or Descent in SMSAs
of 1,000,000 or More with 25,000 or More Hispanics, 1980**

SMSA	Hispanic median family income Rank	$	Hispanics below the poverty level Rank	%	Hispanics, age 25 and over with a high school degree Rank	%	Size (Rank)	Total Hispanics
Los Angeles–Long Beach, Calif.	7	15,447	6	21.2	10	39.1	1	2,066,103
New York, N.Y.–N.J.	12	10,347	2	39.3	13	35.4	2	1,492,559
Chicago, Ill.	4	16,551	8	19.5	11	36.1	3	580,467
Miami, Fla.	5	16,133	10	15.9	5	53.3	4	580,427
San Antonio, Tex.	11	13,284	5	26.9	9	40.5	5	481,378
Houston, Tex.	3	17,185	9	18.1	8	44.9	6	424,957
Dallas, Tex.	6	15,754	7	20.1	12	35.8	7	247,937
Newark, N.J.	8	14,596	4	30.1	7	45.2	8	131,655
Philadelphia, Pa.–N.J.	10	13,287	3	33.4	4	56.8	9	116,869
Washington, D.C., Md.–Va.	1	22,834	13	10.6	1	74.5	10	93,686
Boston, Mass.	13	9,586	1	42.0	3	57.3	11	65,696
Fort Lauderdale–Hollywood, Fla.	2	19,174	12	12.2	2	62.5	12	40,345
Cleveland, Oh.	9	14,502	11	15.3	6	49.3	13	25,475

Source: Prepared from data distributed by the City of New York, Department of City Planning,
Population Division, 1980.

Conclusion

The internal differentiation of the economic structure of New York City seems to correspond to shifts in the economic location of Hispanic immigrants. The notion of economic decline adequately describes what is happening with many industries that were central components of the Northeast economy. However, it fails to capture the emergence of new kinds of manufacturing, the expansion of sweatshops, and more fundamentally, the expansion of highly specialized services. The notion of capital flight adequately describes what is happening with many of the manufacturing firms and corporate headquarters that had traditionally operated from New York City, yet it disregards the new trends in capital investment for which New York City is a suitable and desirable location: professional services; banking; hotels and restaurants; the construction of offices and luxury and high-income residential buildings, with all of their associated services; specialized manufacturing firms directed toward a small, identifiable clientele; the art market; and so forth.

A parallel argument can be made for the changing composition of immigration. Arguing that immigration provides inexpensive, reliable labor is correct, but this oversimplifies the supply and demand relationship. Declining sectors of the city's economy contain low-wage jobs and, as the migration literature has shown, firms in these sectors often depend on immigrants who accept low wages for sheer survival. Workers demanding higher wages have contributed to the closing of such firms. But low-wage jobs are also contained in the highly dynamic growth sector of the economy. It is this fact that partly resolves the conflict between a growing labor pool due to immigration coupled with an absolute and relative loss of jobs. If we juxtapose the large immigrant influx during the past 15 years in New York City and the large job loss over that same period of time, one would conclude that low-wage jobs in the declining sector of the economy could not absorb additional immigrant labor. However, the available evidence for New York City shows that a large share of immigrants find employment in low-wage jobs. This is accomplished in several ways, three of which I summarize in closing.

First, immigration provides labor for the low-wage service and manufacturing jobs that support (1) the expanding, highly specialized, export-oriented service sector, and (2) the high-income lifestyles of the growing top-level professional work force employed in that sector.

Second, the 35% decline in manufacturing jobs recorded in official counts between 1970 and 1980 masks the recomposition taking place in the manufacturing sector. The evidence shows both (1) the consolidation of certain decline trends, notably the shrinking in the supply of the more secure manufacturing jobs, those typically unionized and paying well above minimum wages, and (2) the expansion of what I have called a downgraded manufacturing sector, one where sweatshops and industrial homework are important components. This recomposition makes wages in New York City competitive with those in Third World countries.

A third major labor market mechanism making possible the increased absorption of immigrants in the city's economy, one not dealt with in this chapter, is the formation of an enclave employment sector, one consisting of jobs generated and controlled by the immigrant community (Sassen-Koob, 1979; Wilson and Portes, 1980; Waldinger, Chapter 11 in this volume). These jobs include not only those that are temporary until mainstream jobs can be secured, but also a large array of professional and technical jobs that service the expanding and increasingly income-stratified immigrant communities in the city, as well as those producing services and goods for the consumption of members of the ethnic community. The goods and services directed toward the ethnic community contribute to lowering the costs of survival—both for the immigrants and for their employers. Finally, the immigrant communities generate jobs to meet the demand for low-cost goods and services, a demand that originates in the so-called modern sector of the economy.

This brings to the fore an important distinction blurred by the concept of an "underground economy." Part of the production in the so-called underground economy is aimed at the subsistence of its members, but part (and one wonders how large a part) is actually aimed at mainstream consumption. In the case of New York City, the latter type of production involves not only garments but all kinds of goods and services, such as food for specialty shops, cleaning and repair services carried out at workers' homes, decorative items sold at high prices in chic boutiques, and so on. There are, then, two spheres of circulation for this production: one internal and the other external to the communities where this production takes place.

In sum, the socioeconomic recomposition taking place in New York City entails a restructuring of labor demand: an expanded need both for high-income professional workers and for low-wage workers willing to work at low-paying, dead-end jobs. This restructured labor demand is not a distortion created by the decline of traditional components of the city's economy. Rather, it is an integral part of the major growth trends visible in the city: the expansion of the producer services and of the downgraded manufacturing sector. This recomposition brings into sharp focus two important distinctions. One is the distinction between growth sector and job characteristics. There has been a tendency to view growth sectors as generators of "modern" jobs. The second is the distinction between growth trends and backward sectors of capital. Again, there has been a tendency to view backward sectors as typically undergoing decline. The rapid expansion of a downgraded manufacturing sector shows that backward sectors may be highly dynamic growth sectors.

Whether this restructuring of labor demand is the essence of the immediate future is difficult to establish, but it seems to be a strong possibility. In this context, the large increase in immigration since the middle of the 1960s and the pronounced recomposition of the influx from a preponderance of high-wage countries of origin in the 1950s to one of low-wage countries of origin during the 1970s assumes added meaning. Push factors can only partly explain the reason for this flow. The expanded demand for low-wage workers willing to have dead-end, often odd-shift jobs contains the conditions for the absorption of the large immigrant influx in a major city such as New York. Native workers, socialized to expect better working conditions, move out of the city or become "unreliable" (i.e., dissatisfied). Immigrants, in making the decision to emigrate, have made a second decision, that of taking any job. But, insofar as they are part of a growth sector of the economy, especially in the case of the low-wage jobs in the producer services, immigrants could raise their cost to employers without endangering the survival of these firms. Under these circumstances, immigrants would behave approximately as native workers do. Herein lies a significant policy implication that is lost when we emphasize the employment of immigrants in declining industries, where raising labor costs endangers a firm's survival.

CHAPTER 11

Immigration and Industrial Change in the New York City Apparel Industry

Roger Waldinger

Introduction

This chapter explores the relationship between immigration and in-dustrial change through a case study of the New York City apparel industry. This industry presents a paradox for both conventional and structuralist perspectives of the causes and significance of international migration. One part of the puzzle involves the temporal and contextual pattern: Hispanic immigrants from the Caribbean and Latin America, and Asian immigrants from China and Korea, apparently came to domi-nate the apparel labor force at a time of shrinking labor demand and declining job opportunities for the city's minority residents who had previously been employed in these trades. Problematic from the struc-turalist perspective of migration (see Petras, 1981; Portes and Walton, 1981) are more recent developments: the stabilization of New York's market position, coupled with increasing ownership by immigrants of small competitive enterprises.

The paradox is here addressed in terms of an argument about ethnic enterprise and those complex interactions between immigration and the structure of the economy that produce immigrant-owned firms. The central hypothesis is that the structure of competitive industries gener-ates opportunities for ethnically organized small-business activities. Eth-nicity comes into play as a resource that immigrants mobilize to exploit these opportunities and secure a protected market niche. Although the immigrant enterprise is clustered in peripheral industries, it is not a subspecies of the secondary firm but rather a specific category of pro-duction effecting a distinctive organization of the labor process.

I briefly elaborate a model of ethnic entrepreneurial development and discuss the procedures used in the study. Then I examine the transformation of the New York apparel industry and review the implications of industrial change for labor market integration processes. In the final section I discuss the research issues raised by the case study.

A Model of Ethnic Entrepreneurial Development

The crux of the model of ethnic entrepreneurial development is an argument about the relationship between production technologies and product market structures.[1] In a market characterized by the demand for standardized products, mass production tends to be the prevailing technique. But instability and variability in the structure of demand tend to limit the extent of that mass market. Whatever the case, flux and small market size render the techniques of mass production and mass distribution inappropriate. Product variations and discontinuous runs deter producers from using specialized machines, reduce economies of scale, and militate against assembly-line methods.

Segmentation affects the opportunities for entrepreneurship in several ways. First, because demand is unstandardized and susceptible to unpredictable variations, the optimal scale of enterprise is small and capital barriers are generally low. Small size minimizes problems of delegation and administration, while the production techniques concomitant with small business draw on traditional methods requiring little technical expertise. Second, the volatile economic environment to which the small firm is linked makes flexible industrial relations practices optimal. But in the small firm, where management and labor interact on a face-to-face basis and work routines are unstable and subject to idiosyncratic rearrangements, the employment relationship tends towards conflict (Piore, 1969; 1973; Edwards, 1979). Antagonism is likely to be transcended if there "is a congruence between the worker's orientation to work and the mode of control operated by the employer" (Newby, 1977, p. 62). That congruence can be heightened if owner and employee share connections and meanings that originate outside the work situation; these can then be deployed within the workplace to redefine the employment relationship beyond simple exchange terms. Thus, for reasons fully developed below, immigrant firms that combine

---

[1] This section is extracted from a much broader statement presented in Waldinger (1983a), which also contains an extensive discussion of the literature.

social and economic roles through family ownership, network recruitment, and the employment of fellow nationals may surmount organizational barriers that impede performance among ethnically diverse competitors.

First, the small business provides a vehicle for converting informal labor market relationships into business capital. In competitive industries, investment in training is imperiled because attachment to a single firm is tenuous and skills are general (Doeringer and Piore, 1971). However, the risk calculus takes a different form in the immigrant concern, since social ties are reproduced within the workplace. When shop size is small, labor market mechanisms are superseded by family relations (Kim, 1981; Bailey, 1983). And when labor requirements make it necessary to reach beyond the family circle, jobs can be filled by fellow townsmen (Herman, 1979) or, at the limit, by common nationals. These preexisting connections to the ethnic labor force provide privileged information about worker attributes, useful in predicting behavior on the job. And the same ties also furnish a source of norms and sanctions needed to promote cohesiveness and guard against turnover—especially important during expansionary periods when the competition for labor stiffens.

Second, ethnic, friendship, or kinship connections lend themselves to alternative job arrangements that compensate for the managerial or technical deficiencies of primitively capitalized firms. Wilson and Portes (1980) show that Cuban-owned concerns generate significantly more favorable attitudes among their workers than do nonimmigrant, secondary-type firms that also employ immigrant workers. Since the employment relationship is further characterized by customary obligations of a sponsor–client kind (Herman, 1979, Wong, 1979, Lovell-Troy, 1981), reciprocity makes it possible to substitute informal and contingent practices for rules designed to constrain both managerial and worker behavior.

Finally, network hiring insulates ethnic firms from wider economic influences, with important competitive advantages. Following Hechter (1978), occupational distinctiveness promotes ethnic identity and solidarity by creating a niche in which interaction among culturally similar individuals is maximized. Homogeneity at the workplace also produces social distance. Even if new, ethnic firms enter into complementary rather than competitive relationships with "majority" concerns, the fact of general ethnic subordination fosters a broader group identity that tends to eclipse relationships of authority and exploitation at the workplace (Wong, 1979). And the salience of ethnic identity further reduces the appeal of groups that make class-based claims, such as unions, while also generating norms of solidarity that shield ethnic firms from the purview of state regulation.

Procedures Followed in the Study

This chapter brings together various parts of a 3-year study of immigrants in the apparel industry in New York City.[2] That study involved close observation of industry trends and patterns over the entire study period; continued interaction with key informants in labor and management; and an exhaustive search through trade journals, government reports, and primary and secondary studies of industry structure, labor force trends, industry history, and technology.

More detailed information on market structure, locational patterns, and the role of immigrants was gathered through interviews with businessmen and employer and labor representatives from each of the major apparel subindustries—men's tailored clothing, women's and misses' outerwear, women's and children's undergarments, children's outerwear, and pocketbooks (handbags). In each case, extensive discussions were held with the heads of the relevant employee associations and labor organizations and with at least four businessmen whose firms represented the differences in organization, form, and product specialization.

The women's and misses' outerwear industry, the most important component of New York's apparel complex, received primary attention. The research procedure reflects the industry's particular characteristics. The most important distinction is between *manufacturers*, which are firms that design clothing, purchase the textiles out of which clothes are made, and then merchandise the finished goods, and *contractors*, which are specialized firms that generally sew and finish garments to the specifications set by the manufacturers. Three different sources among these various groups provided information for this industry case study:

[2] The study covers all of the apparel industries clustered in New York City. Most of the apparel products fall into four main categories in the Standard Industry Code: men's tailored clothing (SIC 231), women's and misses' outerwear (SIC 233), women's and children's undergarments (SIC 234), and children's outerwear (SIC 236). Pocketbooks (SIC 317), strictly a leather-goods rather than an apparel industry, is also included. This deviates somewhat from the conventional classification. However, market structure and location patterns in the pocketbook industry are much more similar to apparel than they are to the other leather-goods industries. Technology is substantially the same in pocketbooks and apparel, and both industries have been affected by the same labor force trends.

The mode of aggregation chosen follows the classification developed by Lichtenberg (1960) for his volume in the New York Metropolitan Region Study. See his discussion on pages 252–273 and elsewhere throughout that volume.

1. In-depth interviews were obtained with 20 major outerwear manufacturers that primarily used New York City production facilities. Interviews focused on relationships with suppliers and buyers, organizational practices, factors influencing technology, and extent and type of markets. In addition, interviews conducted with three industry "majors" producing outside the New York area were supplemented by interviews with textile suppliers, retailers, machinery manufacturers, and officials of labor and employer organizations.

2. A survey was carried out of 45 firms engaged in the actual production of women's outerwear. On-site interviews were conducted with the owner of each firm; only one interview was conducted by telephone. These interviews collected data on company histories, patterns of recruitment and training, production practices and technology, linkages with manufacturers and suppliers, and labor relations.

3. A second survey provided data on 96 firms owned by Hispanic immigrants. On-site interviews covered the topics that were discussed with nonimmigrant businessmen; coverage was expanded, however, to include issues relating to ethnic, friendship, and kinship connections, linkages with other immigrant-owned firms, and the occupational and migration experiences of the owners.

This chapter uses materials generated by the two surveys for typological purposes. The concern is not with distributions or frequencies, but rather with a series of salient characteristics that define an "ideal type."

Industrial and Labor Force Changes in the New York City Apparel Industry

Immigrant-owned firms in the New York City apparel industry emerged out of an interaction between changes in the opportunity structure and new patterns of labor recruitment. This involved shifts on both the demand and supply sides: the transformation of New York's market position and the large-scale influx of immigrants into New York's labor market.

DEMAND FACTORS

The persistence of apparel manufacturing in New York is a by-product of the city's historical role as an incubator for small-scale, labor-intensive industries. Making small quantities of highly variable goods under intense time pressures, the apparel industries clustered in a central location where inputs could be shared, transport costs minimized, and accessibility to the labor force maximized. Agglomeration generated significant advantages in each stage of the apparel-manufacturing process: designing, where it permitted quick and inexpensive flows of information; selling, where it reduced the costs of attracting customers; and production, where it facilitated trade with a multiplicity of suppliers, reduced overhead expenses, and accelerated the actual production of finished goods (Hoover and Vernon, 1959).

As Sassen-Koob shows (Chapter 10 in this volume), changes in the international division of labor undermined the viability of New York's manufacturing base. In apparel, the process of industrial dispersion involved a constant dynamic between restructuring—the emergence of large, capital-intensive firms—and relocation. Initially, the outflow of apparel jobs from New York was limited to the lowest-price, labor-sensitive lines in which product variation played an insignificant role. Even then, the importance of proximity to New York's merchandising and designing activities kept firms within the Northeast (Lichtenberg, 1960). But the growth of large firms, abetted by changes in the structure of demand, transformed the locational tie in even those product categories keenly influenced by fashion. Constant changes in production technology—chiefly mechanization and de-skilling—made firms more sensitive to labor costs. Large size also generated internal economies of scale, allowing firms to standardize inputs and outputs and make bulk transactions, thus freeing them from dependence on local suppliers and customers. Intraregional competition between New York and areas of labor surplus in the Northeast assumed interregional dimensions, as first the South and then the Southwest became poles of industry growth. Despite this internal shift, foreign producers penetrated deeply into the American market. The growth of the overseas industry competed with even the largest American producers. These responded in turn by either setting up their own foreign subsidiaries, or by intensifying their search for low-wage domestic sources of labor that were free of union control.[3]

---

[3] For example, *Business Week* (1979) reported that Kellwood, a large manufacturer of women's apparel dominated by Sears, Roebuck, and Co., had increased its imports from virtually nothing to 8% of sales after having built plants in Mexico and Nicaragua, and was expecting to open similar ventures in the Orient (p. 62). Schmenner (1980) shows how the response to import competition also takes the form of a stepped-up search for low-labor-cost facilities in the United States. For a more detailed analysis of the processes of relocation and restructuring in apparel, and their effects on metropolitan production activity, see Waldinger (1983b). Sassen-Koob (Chapter 10 in this volume) presents a more general treatment of locational trends and their implications for industrial activity in New York City.

In the 1970s these broader trends in the spatial division of labor transformed a gradual process of dispersion away from New York into a massive loss of jobs. With the intensification of international competition and a slowdown of economic growth, the older, higher-wage facilities, which New York had in abundance, were squeezed economically. Between 1969 and 1975, New York City lost 289,000 manufacturing jobs; the apparel complex, where employment declined by one-third, lost more than 81,000 jobs.

By the end of the period, New York producers had rendered substantial parts of their markets to Sunbelt and overseas competitors. Between 1969 and 1975, New York's share of national apparel employment declined from one-sixth to one-eighth, as Figure 11.1 shows. Yet, imports had also climbed precipitously: in women's apparel, imports equaled 36% of domestic production as compared to 22% in 1969. Even in men's tailored clothing, a more skilled and expensive line, import penetration had risen from 11 to 26% over the same time span (Allison, 1977; International Ladies' Garment Workers Union, 1980).

After 1975, however, the performance of New York's manufacturing sector notably improved. Though industrial employment continued to drop, sinking from 536,000 in 1975 to 499,000 in 1981, the decline was considerably slower. More important, those components of the apparel complex that survived the crisis appeared to represent a bedrock of employment involving activities firmly linked to New York. As indicated by the data on Figure 11.1, the apparel industries sustained a competitive position vis-à-vis the rest of the nation. In contrast to 1969, when the national recession sent New York's market share tumbling, the city retained its share of employment even after the nation's economy faltered in 1979.

What accounts for the resilience of the remaining apparel complex? One answer, congruent with the arguments developed earlier in this volume by Sassen-Koob, is that New York firms can still compete successfully in the production of unstandardized goods. This explanation links constraints on capital mobility to the structure of demand, suggesting that only a portion of the demand for apparel has proved susceptible to standardization. Handling the remaining unstable portion is both too costly and too risky for large firms with unwieldy and dispersed multiplant operations. The logistics of size and organization increase the costs of disrupting planned operations to meet short-term shifts in demand. But, given the uncertainty in demand, stocking goods to supply the less-predictable portion represents too speculative an alternative. The risk in the system is thus absorbed by the remaining small-firm segment, which either produces unstandardized goods or else fills in shortages of mass-produced items.

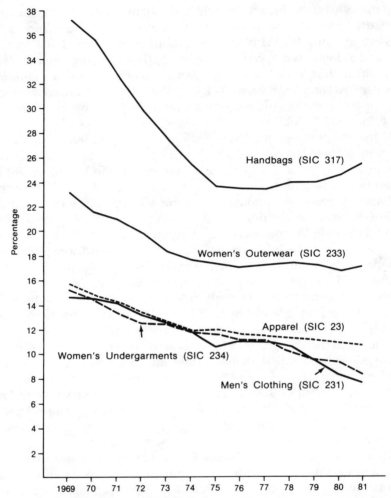

Figure 11.1 New York City's share of national employment in apparel industries, 1969–1981. National employment levels are from the U.S. Department of Labor (1979b, pp. 547–592, 682–707; 1982b, pp. 235–262, 320–329). Local employment levels are from the U.S. Department of Labor (1979c, pp. 423–435; 1981a, pp. 165–167) and the New York State Department of Labor (1982c, pp. 14–15). Figure by the University of Wisconsin Cartographic Laboratory.

Instability of demand derives from two sources. Owing to styles in fashion, consumer wants at the individual level are short-lived and prone to radical and sudden changes. But a quantitatively more significant factor—and one that explains the stabilization of New York's market position—grows out of the distinctive characteristics of the wider economic environment during the present period. These aspects—an endemic and seemingly uncontrollable rate of inflation accompanied by a slow-growing, often faltering economy—have decisively upset the stability needed to pursue standardization. High interest rates have heightened the costs of accumulating inventory, while the uneven performance of the economy has steered consumer behavior on an erratic path, forcing both large chains and their major suppliers into costly liquidations.

To hedge against inventory buildups, the retail chains have attempted to shunt the burden of risk back to domestic producers, buying close to the actual selling season, ordering in small quantities, and calibrating reorders to inventory flows. In turn, large manufacturers, compelled either to dispose of promotional goods or else sell to off-price discounters at disadvantageous prices, have cut back sharply on their more speculative production runs. Collectively, these risk-averse strategies have created the space for a spot market that fills in late-developing and unpredictable portions of demand. While this primarily affects the volatile segments of New York's apparel complex, uncertainty also shields the remaining standardized lines. Manufacturers have been reluctant to make permanent commitments in new plants and equipment, thus leaving in place older facilities using labor-intensive methods.

As New York has been transformed into a spot market, the structure of activity within the area has also changed. Manufacturers, in particular, have sought new ways to cope with uncertainty. Typically, they have done so by disposing of directly owned operations, thus increasing the importance of external economies of scale provided in the supply of fractional services. As the environment has become increasingly unstable, New York firms have moved textile-cutting departments and inexpensive pleating operations to specialized firms, and have closed in-house sewing operations in favor of separate sewing contractors.

Ultimately, New York's ability to capture a protected niche stems from the infusion of new blood into its labor force. Immigration has lessened the labor costs associated with a New York location. And it has also furnished a supply of entrepreneurial labor endowed with an orientation toward risk-bearing activities and the organizational capacity needed to exploit market opportunities.

SUPPLY FACTORS

The quintessential immigrant city, New York has remained a principal port of entry for the new immigrants who have come to the United States in growing numbers since 1965. Approximately 800,000–850,000 legal immigrants arrived in New York City between 1970 and 1980. To these can be added an indeterminate, though certainly considerable, number of illegal immigrants. Despite economic crisis and aggregate population decline, immigration mounted toward the second half of the last decade, when both the level of legal immigration and the numbers of foreign visitors—an indirect indicator of illegal immigration—rose (U.S. Department of Justice, 1970–1979; Tobier, 1982).

The New York–bound migration stream constitutes a group quite distinct from that received by the rest of the nation. Despite the city's large European ethnic population, migration from Europe has dropped off more sharply than in the country at large. Though they are important sources of immigration nationally, Cuba and especially Mexico contribute relatively little to the New York migration flow. Newcomers from Western Hemisphere countries dominate New York's recent immigrants. Among these, Hispanics from the Caribbean and Central and South America predominate, but this population is extremely varied both in terms of countries of origins and social background. The Dominican Republic, followed by Ecuador and Colombia, have been the most important source countries; yet there are considerable numbers of Hispanic immigrants from other Caribbean and Latin American countries as well (U.S. Department of Justice, 1970–1979).

Occupationally, New York's immigrant population appears to be of preponderantly low-level origin. In part this is an artifact of its national composition, since Asians, the most educated group among the new immigrants, generally settle elsewhere. However, even in comparison to migrants of similar national backgrounds, New York's newcomers were less likely to have been previously employed in professional and technical jobs. And the percentage of such immigrants with higher-level training has declined among all immigrant groups, including Hispanics (Tobier, 1982).

Immigrants were initially drawn to New York by the opportunities paradoxically created by the decline of the city's apparel complex. (This summarizes a more extended treatment developed in Waldinger, 1983b.) As external competition intensified, wages and related job configurations (work standards, hours, employment stability) fell increasingly out of line with the rest of New York's blue-collar base in service and manufacturing. Moreover, apparel had traditionally been identified as an "immigrant" job, and there is an extensive body of evidence, albeit anecdotal, suggesting that status considerations persistently impeded the recruitment of native workers, whether minority or white. Thus, as compensation sank below the reservation rate, native workers (blacks,

Puerto Ricans, and ethnic whites) dropped out of the effective labor supply pool.

Though scanty, the evidence suggests that employers also responded to the shortage of labor by the familiar search for new sources of supply.[4] That new immigrants provided the alternative is indicated by the variety of corroborating demographic and ethnographic materials. Accounts by Gonzalez (1970), Hendricks (1974) and Chaney (1976), based on research conducted in the late 1960s or early 1970s, all underline the centrality of apparel for the employment of Hispanic immigrants. Tabulations from the 1% Public Use Sample of the 1970 census indicate that 21% of the Hispanic female immigrant population were employed in apparel. Thus, by this date immigrants had already become a numerically important part of the industry's labor force: more than a quarter of the area's female operatives—of whom most were employed in apparel—were immigrants from Latin America and the Caribbean.

However, once this initial immigrant population was in place, a somewhat different set of dynamics came into play. In part, this involved the simple phenomenon of chain migration. The costs of migration are less severe at a later stage, since newcomers arrive under the auspices of a settled population possessing its own information networks and well-established job connections. But a more important consideration is that the influx of immigrants mitigated the cost disadvantages confronted by New York producers. What partially accounts for this invigorating effect is the quantitative expansion in the labor supply of low-level workers. Because they need constant income to send to relatives at home, and because they are subject to deportation if they lose their jobs, immigrants are less likely than comparable minority residents to be unemployed; they also have higher rates of female labor force participation and a lower incidence of welfare usage (Jaffe et al., 1980, pp. 236–238, 305–306; Dixon and Storper, 1981, pp. 17–18; Tobier, 1982, p. 175).

A more important explanation of the viability of New York's apparel sector is that immigration has dampened the upward pressure on wages. Though segmentation in the product market partially differentiates the product of New York firms from standardized goods manufactured abroad or in the South, market boundaries are not sharp. On the

---

[4] Koshetz (1969) reported an increase in illegal homework among Hispanics in the South Bronx and a proliferation of Hispanic contractors employing Dominicans and Hondurans. Wrong (1974) indicates that apparel employers expressed a preference for Hispanic over black recruits; Hispanics were seen as more willing to accept inferior conditions and respond to directives without question.

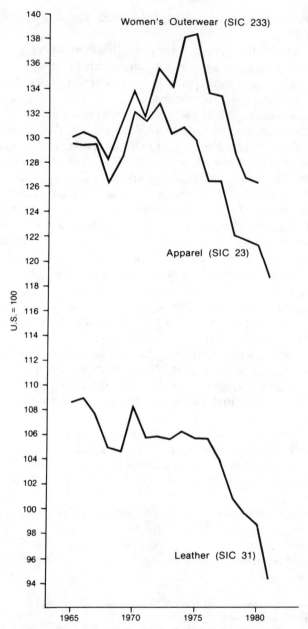

Figure 11.2 Average hourly earnings in New York City apparel industries, 1965–1981. See Figure 11.1 for sources. Figure by the University of Wisconsin Cartographic Laboratory.

contrary, given the clear resistance of consumers to increases in the price of apparel, the price elasticity of apparel is high. Immigrants thus provide a low-cost resource to firms that are thinly buffered from competition with lower-price, standardized producers. As Figure 11.2 indicates, the relative cost of apparel labor is no longer as great as it previously was. New York's wage differential, which edged upward in the early 1970s, moved downward in the second half of the decade. In women's outerwear, the increases in the average hourly wage were outpaced by the gains registered elsewhere; in leather, the difference in hourly wages between New York and the rest of the nation was almost entirely eclipsed. Immigration also relaxed the internal competition for low-level labor, as indicated by the continual slippage of apparel labor costs past the remainder of New York's depressed manufacturing sector (see Figure 11.3).

Another supply-related factor derives from the patterns of labor market incorporation caused by New York's changed relationship to the national industry. By keeping a narrow ceiling on establishment size and reducing the technical requirements of production, market instabil-

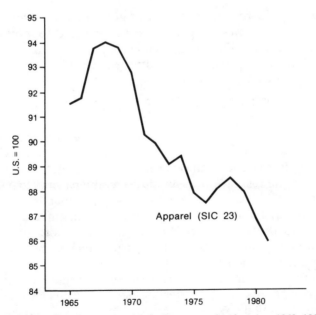

Figure 11.3 Relative earnings in New York City apparel industries, 1969–1981. From the U.S. Department of Labor (1979c, pp. 423–435; 1981a, pp. 165–167) and the New York State Department of Labor (1982c, pp. 14–15). Figure by the University of Wisconsin Cartographic Laboratory.

ity has facilitated the emergence of new immigrant-owned firms. The volatility in the demand for New York's products has enlarged the space for immigrant-owned firms, which absorb seasonal fluctuations and thus fill the large excess between baseline and peak production flows. In the proliferation of these immigrant firms lies a final explanation for the improvement in New York's competitive position. Because production technology is organized around the social relationships of kinship, friendship, and nationality, the immigrant firms gain the flexibility needed to maneuver in markets with quick turnaround times and rapidly fluctuating product flows. Ethnic encapsulation also allows these firms to lower variable costs by evading the full effects of unionization, minimum wage laws, and labor standards. Thus, immigration has not simply slowed the pace of New York's decline, but has also provided the organizational resources needed to secure a more viable, if still highly competitive, market niche.

Labor Market Integration Processes

The apparel industry has several distinguishing features that serve to integrate immigrants into its operations. These include opportunities for entrepreneurship, recruitment mechanisms, job structure, industrial relations, and ownership patterns, features discussed below.

OPPORTUNITIES FOR ENTREPRENEURSHIP

Firms in the garment industry fall into two categories: manufacturers, which design and merchandise clothing, and contractors, which produce clothing to the specifications set by manufacturers. While low in comparison to the rest of American industry, the barriers to entry at the manufacturer level vastly exceed the resources that immigrants can amass. However, the divison of labor between manufacturer and contractor reduces the contractor's functions to the more basic tasks of providing and organizing labor; this in turn facilitates the emergence of small, immigrant-owned firms.

Even at the contracting level, patterns of entrepreneurship are circumscribed by constraints of capital, technology, and skill. Although it does not take much capital to open a contracting factory producing higher-priced dresses, there is no evidence of Hispanic business activity in this line. What impedes the emergence of immigrant-owned firms, it appears, are the complex tasks of preparing textiles for sewing, using difficult and costly inputs, and providing the design advice required in this type of business. Similarly, immigrant firms have not successfully penetrated the mass production lines—coats, pants, undergarments, pocketbooks. Here, there is a determinate production flow in which each item is broken down into sections and then reassembled by operators performing repetitive tasks. Setting up this kind of production line requires technical assistance and training. In any case, the costs of capitalizing a fairly large factory using specialized machines are sufficiently high to deter potential immigrant entrepreneurs.

Immigrant firms are clustered in low-priced product categories, where volatility keeps the barriers to entry low. In these lines, almost any existing factory space—basements, storefronts, or apartments—will suffice. Low-cost space is still amply available, either in the vacant lofts of New York's manufacturing districts, where lofts in marginal buildings are let on a month-to-month basis, or else in the empty storefronts that line the decaying commercial streets of the immigrant neighborhoods.

Specialization at the low end of the market keeps both equipment and labor investments to a minimum. As in the high-price lines, variable product requirements sharply limit capital outlays. Where the high-fashion firms substitute for capital with costly labor inputs, the market position of the immigrant firms virtually obviates the need for skilled labor, thus generating savings on both the capital and labor sides. With few of the time-consuming and costly finishing operations that higher-priced firms undertake, the immigrant concerns can utilize special, high-speed sewing machines for which workers can be quickly trained. Similarly, many immigrant firms work on cheap, synthetic materials that enable them to use industrial hand irons in place of the heavier machine presses that are standard equipment among larger nonimmigrant firms. Some immigrant concerns even ship for delivery without pressing the newly sewn products. In this way the immigrant concerns not only lower investment capital, but minimize related fixed and variable costs as well, such as the installation fee for a steam-driven machine press, costly ancillary equipment, and, most important, the skilled labor required to operate the more complicated piece of machinery.

RECRUITMENT

Recruitment in the nonimmigrant sector is primarily a market process and only secondarily a social one. Most firms hire walk-ins or workers attracted by "help wanted" signs posted on factory buildings. Gate recruitment generates a sizable flow of applicants, and one can often observe casual job seekers walking from one shop to the next in the dense, multistoried loft areas of the central business district. Although employers hire from this casual, shared labor pool for all jobs, only those completely unskilled jobs for which turnover costs are minimal are filled exclusively from this source.

To secure experienced sewing machine operatives and skilled workers, employers seek to mobilize the social networks among the workers already in their employ. Network hiring serves two functions. It works as a predictive device in that employers use the attitudes and behavioral patterns of the existing work force as a guide for screening potential recruits. It also acts as a mechanism of stabilization that implicates workers in the recruitment process, inducing them to screen out unqualified recruits and then exercise their own informal controls over behavior in the workplace. Network recruiting thus integrates new workers into an environment structured by preexisting social relations. Frequently, network hiring assembles a series of friendship groups or family relations—cousins, siblings, and mother–daughter pairs. One 40-person plant in a heavily Dominican neighborhood, for example, employed six members of a single family along with a scattering of smaller family groups.

In the nonimmigrant sector, network recruiting competes with more formal processes that play a particularly important role in filling more skilled positions. In the manufacture of pocketbooks, for example, the union hiring hall responds to most of the labor demands, thus furnishing what is in effect a shared labor pool. Recruitment networks also rarely extend beyond the primary level: plants tend not so much toward ethnic homogeneity as toward a multiplicity of fluid networks feeding in from a variety of ethnic sources. Most important, network recruiting does not offer privileged access to the labor supply. Although employers seek to control their labor supply by mobilizing immigrant networks, they are unsuccessful at manipulating the immigrant labor pool. Instability in both work and settlement patterns makes the immigrant labor supply inherently fluid, and ethnically dominant work force groups tend to replace one another in a process of ethnic succession that employers only perceive after the fact. As the owner of one sportswear firm put it: "I woke up one day and realized that my Puerto Rican workers, who used to make up two-thirds of the plant, had all moved out of the shop." Employers are also stymied in their attempts to recruit highly encapsulated immigrant groups, of whom the Chinese and the Koreans are the best examples.

In contrast, the organization of the immigrant firm systematically combines social and economic roles. Business activity is typically a family enterprise in which spouses, siblings, or relatives share ownership responsibilities. Firm size makes it necessary to recruit beyond familial ranks. Still, work relationships remain firmly embedded within the orbit of friendship and ethnic ties, because immigrant firms hire through informal networks, building on the social structures that connect immigrants to settlers and reproducing and cementing such structures within the workplace. For example, migration chains regularly link Dominican-owned factories to a common hometown in the Dominican Republic.

Some cases from the interviews indicated how social ties can be utilized in the work context. Relatives and friends composed the entire work force in one 18-person factory owned by three brothers from San José de las Matas, Dominican Republic. In a family-owned firm in which parents and their two adult children worked together, half of the workers came from the owners' hometown in the Cibao (Dominican Republic), and the remaining employees came from small towns in the vicinity. A 28-year-old Dominican who had migrated illegally in 1976 from Santiago employed an exclusively Dominican work force of which half consisted of hometown acquaintances or friends. Similarly, all of the workers in a small factory in Brooklyn had previously lived together as neighbors in the same Santiago barrio. While encapsulation within the larger immigrant population seems characteristic of all of the ethnic firms, the survey of Hispanic businesses revealed clear differences in the ability of the various national-origin groups to mobilize these informal networks. Recruitment through national or village networks is most pronounced among the Dominicans. Other groups, being less numerous at large, but also less heavily concentrated in apparel, appear to lack the critical mass needed to combine social and economic roles in this way.

By hiring friends and relatives, immigrant firms obtain a work force whose characteristics are largely known, thus screening out unqualified or inappropriate recruits. "I never put up a 'help wanted' notice," commented an owner who emigrated from Santiago in 1967. "I only hire through friends. That way I have greater control." Since the immigrant factory has a simple division of labor requiring general skills applicable throughout the industry, social ties to new recruits are needed to justify investment in training. One Dominican owner, with a factory located in a heavily immigrant neighborhood, explained his recruitment practices in these terms: "I won't provide training to unknown workers who come in looking for a job. When I need somebody, I ask the workers to bring in a relative. That way, one worker helps another, and I don't have to worry about training someone who will later go find work in another shop."

Network recruiting also lends a social dimension to the employment exchange that alters the expectations of labor and management alike. "It's been a tradition to hire the relatives of our workers," explained one immigrant owner who announced all vacancies to his workers. "We consider them our friends." But the employers who principally hired the friends and relatives of their employees also claimed that this promoted a "better relationship." What they meant by this was that the reciprocity involved in the recruitment process improves performance, strengthens attachment, and facilitates adjustment to tight and varying production schedules. As one South American owner pointed out, "It's one way of getting workers to stay longer and work harder."

JOB STRUCTURE

The mass production industries—pocketbooks, men's clothing, and undergarments—tend toward a bimodal job structure. In pocketbooks, for example, skilled and unskilled workers form two distinct classes of labor: sewing machine operatives, whose skills are high, owing to costs of raw materials and constant product variations; and unskilled table-workers, engaged in pasting or cemeting pieces of leather together. The operators are mainly middle-age women with considerable industry experience and lengthy attachment to the firm. By contrast, young women in their late teens or twenties dominate the unskilled group, and it is among these workers that turnover is concentrated. There is virtually no movement from one category to the other; nor is there an organized pattern of mobility through the hierarchy of skilled jobs. Rather, training takes place on a haphazard basis: workers may get instruction from friends doing skilled work, or they may exploit free time by sewing on scrap materials during lunch, break periods, and after work. Consequently movement into skilled categories involves a series of lateral moves among firms. Frequently, the path leads from large firms, which maintain modest training programs for less-demanding operating jobs, to smaller concerns, where recruitment difficulties dilute entry-level job requirements.

Though also discontinuous, the job hierarchy is not as severely segmented in men's clothing, women's outerwear, pocketbooks, and undergarments. In the production of women's outerwear, there is a cluster of standardized operations involving simple, repetitive tasks that link unskilled sorting and finishing jobs to highly delicate and intricate sewing operations. But although the job structure offers opportunities for advancement, the pattern of progression is not necessarily smooth. Since these firms alternate long production runs with short-lived unsuccessful styles or limited-run special orders, production flows lack continuity. This minimizes the amount of standardized work for which unskilled workers can be easily trained. Though openings in skilled sewing jobs are more frequently filled by less-proficient operators from within, gaps tend to appear in this part of the job ladder as well. There is neither a bidding process nor are there seniority rights. Workers with skills in specialized operations or experience in working particular machines can enter at all rungs of the job ladder.

The critical difficulty for firms owned by nonimmigrants lies in adjusting rigid job structures to a labor force characterized by poor work habits and unstable job attachments. In certain subindustries, a particular department absorbs the bulk of instability: pleating departments in large pleating and stitching plants, or tablework sections in pocketbook factories are prone to high levels of turnover. Here, hiring practices fall into a casual mode. Firms that specialize in highly standardized clothing items experience comparable retention problems: a large plant in a ghetto neighborhood reported annual turnover of 100%; in an 80-person firm making running shorts, two-thirds of the workers had been employed for 3 years or less; and in a blouse plant employing 60 workers, one-third of the work force consisted of a "permanent" group with no more than 3 years of seniority, and the remaining positions were filled by short-term workers prone to high quit rates. In more variable and skilled lines, turnover can be confined to that portion of the work force engaged in manual jobs or simple operative tasks. But it is the rare plant that contains more than a handful of workers with extensive seniority levels dating back 10 years or more.

Absenteeism and lack of punctuality disrupt normal work routines. As one employer put it, "absenteeism is unreal, punctuality is hopeless." The universal assumption is that some workers will not show up to work on any given day. But the failure to enforce rules governing attendance and punctuality largely reflects the problems that nonimmigrant employers face in mobilizing the new immigrant labor force. "You can't get operators," noted the owner of a new and highly successful firm, "so you tolerate absenteeism." Another owner who also complained about poor work habits explained that "you can't fire sewing machine operatives because they're skilled workers."

Absenteeism and irregular attendance impose additional production costs. Since section work is the prevailing technique, jobs are interdependent. Unpredictable work habits threaten the continuous flow of sewn textile parts through the production line. To prevent excessive downtime and avoid bottlenecks, most employers use overstaffing as a technique to keep the line moving.

The extensive division of labor among apparel firms owned by nonimmigrants is not found in the immigrant sector. The job structure in the immigrant sector is characterized by the virtual absence of positions at either extreme of the skill hierarchy. Producing low-price, volatile products, immigrant firms make minimal use of skilled processes while tending toward a primitive division of labor that dispenses with low-skilled preparatory and finishing jobs. Simplicity in the technical division of labor generates significant organizational advantages for both management and labor. Unlike the large sectionalized factory in which tasks are broken down and then organized in an orderly production flow, the immigrant firm requires little planning. Moreover, there are few ancillary or supervisory functions to carry out, and thus overhead costs can be more easily contained. The labor process is also compatible with instability on both the demand and supply sides. Since jobs are relatively independent, changes in staffing can be accommodated without disruption to established work routines or the redesign of jobs. Similarly, flexible or irregular work habits are compatible with normal work routines. Neither absenteeism nor lateness results in downtime for the entire factory, allowing immigrant concerns to absorb part-time workers with minimal readjustments in work flows.

INDUSTRIAL RELATIONS

The nonimmigrant sector in the New York apparel industry is almost entirely organized. The most important unions are the International Ladies' Garment Workers Union, the Amalgamated Clothing and Textile Workers Union, and the Pocketbook Workers Union. Since union organization is extensive, the formal bargaining relationship tends toward cooperation. But in light of differences in size and stability, labor organizations exercise a dominant role in labor–management relations. However, this same asymmetry makes it difficult to institutionalize control. Organized union resources must be spread over a multiplicity of units; within each factory, union interests are represented informally. The ability of the unions to enforce compliance has diminished as the industry's position has weakened. Confronted with a decreasing number of ever more vulnerable firms, union officials now show considerable reluctance to assert control.

In their relationship with the labor force, employers in the nonimmigrant sector pursue two distinguishable strategies. The first more closely approximates the conventional portrayal of managerial approaches in low-wage industries. Here the style tends toward a harsh exercise of authority and an attempt to regulate the work pace through direct discipline, resembling Edwards's (1979) characterization of "simple control": "Bosses exercise power personally, intervening in the labor process often to exhort workers, bully and threaten them, reward good performance, hire and fire on the spot, favor loyal workers, and generally act as despot" (p. 19). "Simple control" techniques prevail among those firms tied to low-price, standardized-product markets, where price competition is keen. Since these firms contain few skilled jobs, work-force instability is a matter of little economic significance. By the same token, the intrinsic qualities of the jobs, particularly the repetitive nature of the work and the absence of meaningful opportunities for advancement, spark considerable worker discontent, to which employers typically respond in an authoritarian way. Thus, the employment relationship takes the form of a vicious circle in which management's harsh and rigid exercise of discipline reinforces tendencies toward conflict, weakening workers' commitment to the job.

But in firms linked to less-stable markets, flux induces an alternative managerial strategy, one designed to secure authority through consent. Employers seek to forge personal bonds that engender loyalty and flexibility among a core of key workers. While network hiring provides a vehicle for stabilizing employment, employers also adopt a paternalistic strategy in an attempt to foster a "family atmosphere." The owner of a large contracting factory explained, for example, that his forelady scheduled free appointments at the union clinic for his Dominican workers and that he often helped his employees to fill out forms or resolve minor consumer problems or disputes. In another instance, an employer chose to establish his factory in a particular location in order to develop a "neighborhood shop" in which closer employer–employee ties could be created. A third employer assisted workers in preparing immigration forms.

Ultimately, even this strategy proves of limited usefulness in counteracting disaffection and instability. Small firm size and direct managerial involvement in production provide personal interaction between owner and worker. Yet production cycles and changing product flows sharply intensify production pressures. Even where owners effect a paternalistic style, the tenor of relationships quickly alters under duress. As one employer noted, in explaining the reasons for the turnover: "The truth is, if people want to work for us, we insist that they work hard. And a substantial portion of turnover occurs because they can't adjust to us or we won't adjust to them."

In the ethnic firm, industrial relations take a different form, due to the interpenetration of economic and social roles. Here, the employment exchange includes a social component that extends beyond the cash nexus. Immigrant employers tend to act as intermediaries, intervening to assist their employees with social, economic, and legal problems. As one Dominican employer explained, "The shop is like a family—people bring me problems every day. I help them with applications, fill out their immigration papers, call the hospital to find out about relatives, and help with anything involving English." Ownership also gives the employer strategic importance in immigration matters, an asset that can be used to assist workers in bringing over relatives from the home country and that also lends itself to more formal types of sponsorship, as when immigrant owners promise to provide employment for prospective immigrants seeking permanent residency. Bonds of common nationality are reinforced when the factory becomes a fulcrum for political organizing—a frequent occurrence among Dominican-owned firms, reflecting the pervasive influence of island politics in the mainland community.

Similarly, employment practices are compatible with the needs of special labor force groups. Social connections between owners and newly arrived workers, we have seen, facilitate job seeking and the acquisition of skills. The pervasive tendency to pay employees by results also obviates the need to establish strict norms governing attendance and punctuality. As one employer observed: "This is a piecework shop. We don't care about hours. As long as they are working, we just count the production. We don't count how many hours they work." Moreover, family involvement at the ownership level provides the resources needed to compensate for unstable work habits. "Most of the women workers are married," noted one Dominican owner who was in partnership with three of his brothers. "Often, there are family problems that force them to miss work. But that's not a difficulty, since my brothers and I know all the machines and can make up the production ourselves." Thus, immigrant firms can adjust work rules without undermining performance, thereby widening access for mothers, students, and other workers with conflicting social roles and part-time employment needs.

Finally, the employment of immigrants in a context in which obligations are understood to be both informal and reciprocal discourages unionization. Kin and friendship ties virtually immunize the immigrant firms from organizing efforts, and the owners, who evince strong antipathy toward the idea of unionization, succeed with few exceptions in remaining nonunion. When organizing occurs, it is almost always more a response to external pressure than to attempts from within. Virtually all of the organized immigrant concerns had signed union agreements in order to retain contracting agreements with unionized manufacturers.

Coming "over the top," unionization primarily involved a change in the relationship between firms. Within the firm, unionization had little impact, and several unionized employers indicated that only a small portion of the work force had actually become union members.

IMMIGRANT AND NONIMMIGRANT OWNERSHIP

There is a strong element of inertia in the continued activity of nonimmigrant firms in New York's outerwear industry. Many of these firms grew up when the locational advantages of a New York operation were considerably greater than they presently are. Most are family-owned, and consequently personal considerations make them resistant to relocation. The age and experience of the owners go far in accounting for continued persistence. Most have succeeded in finding a market niche where direct competition with firms that have lower labor costs can be minimized. Extensive information networks and long-standing connections with buyers and suppliers help contain direct competition with large, out-of-town producers of standardized goods.

But the market position of these firms is becoming increasingly disadvantageous. Most lack the continuity needed to train new workers; the same factors make it difficult to attain optimal operating efficiencies. Stabilizing the employment relationship among a core of skilled operators is a common goal. Yet the stock of incentives that firms can use to induce stability is limited. While the aim may be to create a "family atmosphere," ethnic differences and conflicts generated during the course of production are disruptive.

More important, there is little potential for greater flexibility at a time when market conditions have become increasingly unstable. Unlike immigrant-owned firms, these companies do not enjoy comparable access to workers who are linked by social ties and whose labor can be used intensively to attain quick responses and sustain short production cycles. Although specialized machinery might be used to reduce turnaround times, variable production flows limit this option. Moreover, most of the nonimmigrant firms are unionized and are thus saddled with variable costs that are considerably higher than those of their immigrant-owned competitors.

The transformation of New York into a spot market that supplies the last-minute portions of demand has precipitated the emergence of a new industry sector characterized by immigrant ownership. As we have seen, market instability promotes the proliferation of immigrant-owned firms that need little capital investment or technical proficiency in order to begin operations. A number of significant competitive advantages accrue to these immigrant-owned firms. Production technology is organized around the social relationships of kinship, friendship, and common nationality. These relationships provide privileged access to the immigrant labor market, ensuring a steady supply of workers. This in turn cements job attachment and promotes investment in training.

By hiring through the immigrant network, the immigrant firms also induce work arrangements that compensate for managerial, technological, and capital deficiencies. The reproduction of the immigrant network within the firm provides the flexibility needed to maneuver in markets with quick turnaround times and rapidly fluctuating product flows. Moreover, ethnic encapsulation allows firms to lower variable costs by evading—partially or completely—the effects of unionization, minimum wage laws, and labor standards. The advantages associated with this organizational form promote further growth, and the potential for entrepreneurship strengthens the employment relationship, since expansion creates new opportunities in which immigrants can exploit past investments in skills.

Research Issues

Research within the emerging structuralist framework has emphasized the functions of immigrant labor for the economies of the immigrant-importing countries. The case of the New York City apparel industry is partly consistent with that framework. In apparel, industrial decline undermined the stability of apparel's domestic sources of labor; this shortage on the supply side provided the catalyst for the influx of new immigrants. Subsequently, immigrant workers came to furnish the apparel industry with a low-cost resource, shielding the industry from both internal and external wage competition.

The structuralist framework captures an important dimension of the labor market experience of immigrant workers, but, because it is static, it leaves unanswered such apparent anomalies as the proliferation of immigrant-owned firms. This study has attempted to develop a dynamic framework that captures the interaction between immigrant labor and the structure of the economy. Although the framework only applies to certain segments of the economy, it suggests that, in specified markets, risk and uncertainty can create small-business opportunities that are congruent with informal resources mobilized through migration subprocesses. The case of the apparel industry illuminates the processes at work in various businesses in which immigrant entrepreneurs have been successful. In this instance, the transformation of New York from a production center to a spot market has created new opportunities for immigrant entrepreneurship. This entrepreneurial development has also reinvigorated that segment of the apparel industry remaining in New York. The mobilization of ethnic resources through the immigrant network mitigates New York's cost disadvantage while strengthening its ability to service rapidly changing and unstable portions of demand.

The case study also suggests a number of areas for further research in the field. The delineation of the market structure conducive to small immigrant businesses introduces a refinement to the dual labor market framework. As Bailey (1983) has pointed out, small firm size and competition—the defining features of the secondary sector—are precisely the conditions that create the opportunities for small entrepreneurship. Thus, in those segments of New York's apparel industry where capital–labor ratios are relatively high, there has been little replacement of non-immigrant by immigrant firms. Rather, opportunities for entrepreneurship are concentrated in those volatile product categories where flexibility and informal organizational resources play an important role.

On a broader scale, one can hypothesize a relationship between entrepreneurial opportunities and the structure of competitive industries. Mexican commuter workers employed in the highly mechanized pants factories of El Paso are unlikely to have the same success in moving into small businesses as the Dominican or Latin American immigrant contractors that specialize in fashion-sensitive lines (Rungeling, 1969). Similarly, Asian refugees working in assembly-line jobs in the highly competitive semiconductor industry are apt to encounter a job structure more closely resembling the division of labor in the pocketbook industry than the informal work arrangements of the immigrant sector.

It is also important to know how opportunities for entrepreneurship are decreased or increased by the changing structure of the economy. Indeed, recent evidence suggests a relationship between the emergence of small enterprises and broader structural trends. Small firms now furnish the major share of new jobs generated in the United States (Birch, 1981). Large companies, by contrast, seem generally stagnant and, if growing, tend to expand by opening small, single-purpose plants (Schmenner, 1980). One hypothesis, consistent with the evidence reported here, links the shift toward small business to the breakup of mass markets and the proliferation of smaller markets serviced by a multiplicity of specialized producers (Piore and Sabel, 1981).

Identifying opportunity structures appropriate for immigrant entrepreneurship leads in turn to aspirational issues. For native members of the labor force, the ideal of self-employment appears to be diminishing.

Why, then, the attraction for immigrants? The critical factor, it would seem, is a much smaller range of opportunities. Immigrants suffer from a variety of impediments in the labor market: lack of facility in English, inadequate or inappropriate work skills, and, often, discrimination. Lacking the same opportunities as natives for stable career forms of employment, immigrants are more likely to opt for self-employment and the substantial risks entailed. Moreover, immigrants may attach a higher value than natives to income-generating opportunities and be less sensitive to considerations of leisure and status (Waldinger, 1982).

In the past, certain ethnic groups, in particular Jews, Italians, and Greeks, have been overrepresented in small business. Although these groups continue to tend toward entrepreneurship (Goldscheider and Kobrin, 1980), the process of assimilation has produced an overall trend toward convergence with the rest of the population. As Glazer and Moynihan (1963) noted for Jews, the problem of succession in low-status, but profitable, family businesses seems pervasive.

The apparel industry exemplifies this shift in aspirational patterns among previously dominant entrepreneurial groups. Ownership of contracting facilities, in particular, is concentrated among middle-age Jews and Italians, who often followed a parent into the business but whose children are now engaged in managerial or professional careers. This weakening of the entrepreneurial tradition, one can hypothesize, has exercised an independent influence on the decline of New York's apparel complex. By the same token, the emergence of new groups with a risk-bearing tradition or outlook adds to or strengthens the external economies in a competitive industry like apparel. Moreover, in groups that are new to this cycle of entrepreneurship, success in self-employment is likely to build on itself, strengthening rather than weakening the interest in small-business activities.

Apart from the factors that promote entrepreneurial opportunities, further attention should be devoted to the implications of employment in the immigrant small-business sector. Bonacich has expressed reservations, arguing that immigrant entrepreneurs fulfill "middleman" functions by exploiting their own national group in the interest of larger firms in the monopoly sector (Bonacich, 1980). Alternatively, on the basis of a regression analysis on the earnings of a sample of 590 Cuban émigrés in Miami, Wilson and Portes (1980) concluded that income determination processes are in fact similar in immigrant-owned and monopoly-sector firms.

While these conflicting interpretations serve to underline the still-preliminary state of research in this field, this chapter suggests a framework for assessing the relationship between entrepreneurship and mobility. In apparel, specialization in the production of novelty items or late-developing runs of mass-production goods tends to obviate direct competition with larger, more heavily capitalized firms. However, maintaining that protected position depends on the possibilities that consumers enjoy for substitution. This, in turn, confronts the small apparel producer with constant pressure on wages and other variable costs. In fact, the success of the immigrant firms is due in no small measure to their ability to contain labor costs, a process that does not simply involve lowering the wage, but also evading a variety of different labor standards and fending off unionization. Visits to immigrant-owned factories for this case study uncovered a pattern of systematic violation of the labor codes, as evidenced by the prevalence of cash payments, lax reporting procedures, and the use of home workers. Immigrant-owned factories in two of the neighborhood study areas were cited by state officials for abuses of wage and safety codes.

However, the situation may be different in the service sector. As in manufacturing, instability and differentiation in the demand for service also create favorable conditions for small immigrant firms. In the retail grocery trade, large national chains may cede parts of the markets to local independents who are more attuned to the needs of smaller, often ethnically dominated, market segments (Cournoyer, 1980). In the restaurant industry, enterprises in which immigrants play important ownership and labor roles outperform larger, capital-intensive restaurants by providing a full-service menu to the ethnic and higher-priced components of demand (Bailey, 1983). Yet, for all the similarity, external competitive pressure does not really come into play, since services, unlike manufacturing, are produced and consumed in situ. If these local-economy aspects of the service industry militate against the types of competition existing in manufacturing, the ease with which new service businesses can be established suggest that internal pressures may be almost as severe. The Chinese restaurant trade, for example, is notoriously competitive and characterized by low earnings, long hours, and mandatory overtime (Neustadt, 1980).

At this point, the evidence on immigrant entrepreneurship is only beginning to emerge. But if the image of the immigrant firm as sweatshop is overdrawn and incomplete, it seems fair also to guard against an overly benign portrait of entrepreneurship as a cherished form of self-help. Issues of immigrant small business and entrepreneurship have only begun to attract serious scholarly attention. Further progress is likely to come as a result of continued attempts to develop systematic models of ethnic entrepreneurial development, and of efforts to apply those models in studies that cut across both industry and immigrant-group boundaries.

References

Abowd, A. M. 1983. *Sample selectivity adjustments and fairness considerations for direct wage regressions.* Unpublished manuscript, Graduate School of Business, University of Chicago.

Abowd, J. M., and Killingsworth, M. R. 1981. *An analysis of Hispanic employment, earnings and wages in the federal and nonfederal sectors with special reference to Puerto Ricans.* Technical Report No. 21-36-78-61, U.S. Department of Labor, Employment and Training Administration. Washington, D.C.: Government Printing Office.

Acker, J. 1980. Women and stratification: A review of recent literature. *Contemporary Sociology, 9,* 25–39.

Aguirre, A. 1979. Intelligence testing and Chicanos: A quality of life issue. *Social Problems, 27,* 186–195.

Alexander, K., and Cook, M. 1979. The motivational relevance of education plans: Questioning the conventional wisdom. *Social Psychology quarterly, 42,* 202–213.

Alexander, K., and Eckland, B. K. 1974. Sex differences in the educational attainment process. *American Sociological Review, 39,* 668–682.

Allison, E. 1977. *The impacts of imports on the men's clothing industry.* New York: Amalgamated Clothing and Textile Workers Union.

Anderson, J. G., and Johnson, W. H. 1971. Stability and change among three generations of Mexican-Americans: Factors affecting achievement. American Educational Research Journal, *8,* 285–309.

Arce, C. 1981. A reconsideration of Chicano culture and identity. *Daedalus, 110,* 171–191.

Armor, D. 1972. School and family effects and black and white achievement: A reexamination of the USOE data. In *On equality of educational opportunity,* eds. F. Mosteller and D. P. Moynihan. New York: Vintage Books.

Arrow, K. J. 1973. The theory of discrimination. In *Discrimination in labor markets,* eds. C. Ashenfelter and A. Rees. Princeton, N.J.: Princeton University Press.

Ashford, J., and Snowden, R. 1970. Multivariate probit analysis. *Biometrics, 26,* 535–546.

Bailey, T. 1983. *Labor market competition and economic mobility in low-wage employment: A case study of the restaurant industry.* Ph.D. dissertation, Department of Economics, Massachusetts Institute of Technology, Cambridge.

Balan, J., Browning, H., and Jelin, E. 1973. *Men in a developing society.* Austin: University of Texas Press.

Baldus, D. C., and Cole, J. W. L. 1980. *Statistical proof of discrimination.* New York: McGraw-Hill.

Baral, D. 1979. Academic achievement of recent immigrants from Mexico. *NABE Journal, 3,* 1–13.

Bauer, D. 1980. The question of foreign investment. *New York Affairs, 6,* 52–58.

Bean, F. D., and Swicegood, G. 1982. Generation, female education, and Mexican American fertility. *Social Science Quarterly, 63,* 131–144.

Bean, F. D., Swicegood, G., and Linsley, T. F. 1981. Patterns of fertility variation among Mexican immigrants to the United States. In *U.S. immigration policy and the national interest: Staff report, Appendix D.* Washington, D.C.: Select Commission on Immigration and Refugee Policy.

Beck, E. M., Horan, P., and Tolbert, C. M., II. 1978. Stratification in a dual economy: A sectoral model of earnings determination. *American Sociological Review, 43,* 704–720.

Becker, G. S. 1965. A theory of the allocation of time. *Economic Journal, 75,* 493–517.

Becker, G. S. 1981. *A treatise on the family.* Cambridge, Mass.: Harvard University Press.

Beller, A. H. 1980. *Occupational segregation by sex: Determinants and changes.* Unpublished manuscript, Department of Family Living, University of Ilinois at Champaign-Urbana.

Beshers, J. M., and Sassen-Koob, 1982. *Micro social ecology and social distance: Residential patterns of six immigrant groups in Queens, New York City, 1970–1980.* Unpublished manuscript, Department of Sociology, Queens College, City University of New York.

Bidwell, C., and Kasarda, J. 1975. School district organization and student achievement. *American Sociological Review, 40,* 55–70.

Birch, D. 1981. Who creates jobs? *The Public Interest, 65* (Fall), 3–14.

Bjorklund, A., and Holmlund, B. 1981. The duration of unemployment and unexpected inflation. *American Economic Review, 71,* 121–131.

Blau, F., and Kahn, L. 1981. Race and sex differences in quits by young workers. *Industrial and Labor Relations Review, 34,* 563–577.

Blau, P., and Duncan, O. D. 1967. *The American occupational structure.* New York: John Wiley.

Blinder, A. S. 1973. Wage discrimination: Reduced form and structural estimates. *Journal of Human Resources, 8,* 436–455.

Bloom, B., Davis, A., and Hess, R. 1965. *Compensatory education for cultural deprivation.* New York: Holt, Rinehart, and Winston.

Bloom, D. E., and Killingsworth, M. R. 1982. Pay discrimination research and litigation: The use of regression. *Industrial Relations, 21,* 318–339.

Bonacich, E. 1972. A theory of ethnic antagonism: The split labor market. *American Sociological Review, 37,* 547–559.

Bonacich, E. 1980. Middleman minorities and advanced capitalism. *Ethnic Groups, 2,* 211–220.

Bonilla, A. F., and Campos, R. 1981. A wealth of poor: Puerto Ricans in the new economic order. *Daedalus, 110,* 133–176.

Bonilla, A. F., and Campos, R. 1982. Imperialist initiatives and the Puerto Rican worker: From Foraker to Reagan. *Contemporary Marxism, 5,* 1–18.

Borjas, G. J. 1978. Discrimination in HEW: Is the doctor sick or are the patients healthy? *Journal of Law and Economics, 21,* 97–110.

Borjas, G. J. 1981. Hispanic immigrants in the U.S. labor market: An empirical analysis. In *Hispanic-origin workers in the U.S. labor market: Comparative analyses of employment and earnings,* ed. M. Tienda. Final report to the U.S. Department of Labor, Employment and Training Administration, Washington, D.C. (Available from National Technical Information Service, Springfield, Va. 22151.)

Borjas, G. J. 1982. The earnings of male Hispanic immigrants in the United States. *Industrial and Labor Relations Review, 35,* 343–353.

Borjas, G. J. 1984. The substitutability of black, Hispanic, and white labor. *Economic Inquiry, 21,* 93–106.

Borus, M., Crowley, J., Rumberger, R., Santos, R., and Shapiro, D. 1980. *Pathways to the future: A longitudinal study of young Americans. Preliminary report: Youth and the labor market—1979.* Columbus, Ohio: Ohio State University, Center for Human Resource Research.

Bourdieu, P. 1977. *Reproduction in education, society and culture.* Beverly Hills, Calif.: Sage.

Bowman, C. 1981. *Language, identity and relational ethnicity shifts among Chicanos.* M.S. thesis, Department of Sociology, University of Wisconsin—Madison.

Boyd, M. 1980. *The double negative: Female immigrants in the Canadian labor force.* Paper presented at the annual meetings of the Population Association of America, Denver.

Briggs, V. M. 1973. *Chicanos and rural poverty.* Baltimore: Johns Hopkins University Press.

Brito, P. K., and Jusenius, C. L. 1978. Sex segregation in the labor market: An analysis of young college women's occupational preferences. In *Women, work, and family: Dimensions of change in American society,* ed. F. L. Mott. Lexington, Mass.: Lexington Books.

Burdett, K., Kiefer, N., Mortensen, D., and Neumann, G. 1981. *A Markov model of employment, unemployment and labor force participation: Estimates from DIME data.* Paper presented at the summer meeting of the Econometric Society, San Diego.

Business Week. 1979. Apparel's last stand. May 14.

Cafferty, P. S., Chiswick, B. R., Greeley, A. M., and Sullivan, T. A. 1983. *The dilemma of American immigration: Beyond the golden door.* New Brunswick: Transition.

Cain, G., and Dooley, M. D. 1976. Estimation of a model of labor supply, fertility and wages of married women. *Journal of Political Economy, 84,* S179–199.

Carter, T. 1970. *Mexican Americans in school: A history of educational neglect.* New York: College Entrance Examination Board.

Carter, T., and Segura, R. 1979. *Mexican Americans in school: A decade of change.* New York: College Entrance Examination Board.

Castles, S., and Kosack, G. 1973. *Immigrant workers and class structure in Western Europe.* London: Oxford University Press.

Castro, G. M. 1982. "Mary" and "Eve's" social reproduction in the "Big Apple": Colombian voices. *Occasional Papers,* No. 35. New York: New York University, New York Research Program in Inter-American Affairs.

Chaney, E. 1976. Colombian migration to the United States. *Occasional Papers,* Vol. 2, No. 2. Washington, D.C.: Interdisciplinary Communications Program.

Chiswick, B. R. 1978a. The effect of Americanization on the earnings of foreign-born men. *Journal of Political Economy, 86,* 897–921.

Chiswick, B. R. 1978b. A longitudinal analysis of the occupational mobility of immigrants. *Proceedings of the 30th Annual Winter Meeting, Industrial Relations Research Association.* Madison, Wis.: Industrial Relations Research Association.

Chiswick, B. R. 1979. The economic progress of immigrants: Some apparently universal patterns. In *Contemporary economic problems,* ed. W. Fellner. Washington, D.C.: American Enterprise Institute.

Chiswick, B. R. 1980. The earnings of white and coloured male immigrants in Britain. *Economica, 47,* 81–87.

Chiswick, B. R. 1982. *The employment of immigrants in the United States.* Unpublished manuscript, Department of Economics, University of Illinois at Chicago Circle.

Chiswick, B. R. 1983. An analysis of the earnings and employment of Asian American men. *Journal of Labor Economics, 1,* 197–214.

City of New York. 1980. Computer printout, City of New York, Department of City Planning.

City of New York. 1982. *Report on economic conditions in New York City: July–December 1981.* New York: City of New York, Office of Management and Budget and Office of Economic Development.

Clark, K. B., and Summers, L. H. 1979. Labor market dynamics and unemployment: A reconsideration. *Brookings Papers on Economic Activity,* No. 1, pp. 13–60.

Cohen, M., and Gruber, W. 1970. Variability by skill in cyclical unemployment. *Monthly Labor Review, 93* (August), 8–11.

Cohen, R. 1979. *The impact of foreign investment on U.S. cities and regions.* Washington, D.C.: U.S. Department of Housing and Urban Development.

Cohen, S. M., and Sassen-Koob, S. 1982. *Survey of six immigrant groups in Queens.* Research report, Department of Sociology, Queens College, City University of New York.

Coleman, J. S., Campbell, E. Q., Hobson, C. J., McPartland, J., Mood, A. M., Weinfeld, R. D., and York, R. L. 1966. *Equality of educational opportunity.* Washington, D.C.: U.S. Government Printing Office.

Coleman, J. S., Hoffer, T., and Kilgore, S. 1981. *Public and private schools.* Mimeo, University of Chicago. Report to the National Center for Education Statistics, Washington, D.C.

Conference Board, Inc. 1981. *Announcements of foreign investments in U.S. manufacturing industries (first quarter, second quarter and third quarter).* New York: Author.

Conservation of Human Resources Project. 1977. *The corporate headquarters complex in New York City.* New York: Columbia University, Conservation of Human Resources Project.

Conway, D. A., and Roberts, H. V. 1983. Reverse regression, fairness, and employment discrimination. *Journal of Business and Economic Statistics, 1,* 75–85.

Cooney, R. S. 1979. Intercity variations in Puerto Rican female participation. *Journal of Human Resources, 14,* 222–235.

Cooney, R. S., and Colon, A. E. 1979. Puerto Rican labor utilization: 1970–1977. *Research Bulletin* (Hispanic Research Center), 2 (July), 5–7.

Cooney, R. S., and Ortiz, V. 1981. Hispanic female participation in the labor force: A comparative analysis of Puerto Ricans, Mexicans, and Cubans. In *Hispanic-origin workers in the U.S. labor market: Comparative analyses of employment and earnings,* ed. M. Tienda. Final report to the U.S. Department of Labor, Employment and Training Administration, Washington, D.C. (Available from National Technical Information Service, Springfield, Va. 22151.)

Cooney, R. S., and Ortiz, V. 1983. Nativity, national origin, and Hispanic female labor force participation. *Social Science Quarterly, 64,* 510–523.

Cordasco, F. 1978. *The bilingual-bicultural child and the question of intelligence.* New York: Arno.

Cornelius, W. A. 1978. *Mexican migration to the United States: Causes, consequences and U.S. responses.* Revised and expanded version of a paper presented to the Study Group on Immigration and U.S. Foreign Policy, Council on Foreign Relations, Washington, D.C., June.

Corwin, A., ed. 1978. *Immigrants—and immigrants: Perspectives on Mexican labor migration to the United States.* Westport, Conn.: Greenwood Press.

Cournoyer, P. 1980. *The New England retail grocery industry.* (Available from National Technical Information Service, Springfield, Va. 22151.)

Cramer, J. C. 1980. Fertility and female employment: Problems of causal direction. *American Sociological Review, 45,* 167–190.

Cummins, J. 1977. Viewpoint: Psycholinguistic evidence. In Center for Applied Linguistics, *Bilingual education: Current perspectives;* Vol. 4: *Education.* Arlington, Va.: Center for Applied Linguistics.

Cummins, J. 1981. Empirical and theoretical underpinnings of bilingual education. *Journal of Education, 163,* 16–29.

DeBlassie, R., and Healey, G. 1970. *Self-concept: A comparison of Spanish-American, Negro, and Anglo adolescents across ethnic, sex, and socioeconomic variables.* Las Cruces, N.M.: New Mexico State University.

DeFreitas, G. 1979. *The earnings of immigrants in the American labor market.* Ph.D. dissertation, Department of Economics, Columbia University.

DeFreitas, G. 1982. *The earnings and labor force behavior of immigrants.* Report prepared for the National Institute of Child Health and Human Development, Washington, D.C.

de Tray, D. N. 1974. Child quality and the demand for children. In *Economics of the Family: Marriage, children, and human capital,* ed. T. W. Schultz. Chicago: University of Chicago Press.

Dixon, L., and Storper, M. 1981. *Trends in the characteristics of AFDC families in New York City: 1969–1979.* New York: City of New York, Human Resources Administration.

Doeringer, P. B., and Piore, M. J. 1971. *Internal labor markets and manpower analysis.* Lexington, Mass.: D. C. Heath.

Duncan, B. 1965. Dropouts and the unemployed. *Journal of Political Economy, 73,* 121–134.

Duncan, O. D. 1961. A socioeconomic index for all occupations. In *Occupations and social status,* ed. A. Reiss, Jr. New York: Free Press.

Duncan, O. D., Featherman, D. L., and Duncan, B. 1972. *Socioeconomic background and achievement.* New York: Seminar Press.

Economic Consulting Services, Inc. 1981. *The international operations of U.S. service industries: Current data collection and analysis.* Washington, D.C.: Author.

Edwards, L. 1976. School retention of teenagers over the business cycle. *Journal of Human Resources, 11,* 1–13.

Edwards, R. 1979. *Contested terrain.* New York: Basic Books.

Ehrenberg, R. G. 1979. *The regulatory process and labor earnings.* New York: Academic Press.

Ehrenberg, R. G., and Oaxaca, R. 1976. Unemployment insurance, duration of unemployment, and subsequent wage gain. *American Economic Review, 66,* 754–766.

Ehrenhalt, S. M. 1981. Some perspectives on the outlook for the New York City labor market. In *Challenges of the changing economy of New York City 1981,* The New York City Council on Economic Education. New York: The New York City Council on Economic Education.

England, P. 1981. Assessing trends in occupational tax segregation, 1900–1976. In *Sociological perspectives on labor markets,* ed. I. Berg. New York: Academic Press.

England, P. 1982. The failure of human capital theory to explain occupational sex segregation. *Journal of Human Resources, 17,* 358–370.

Evans, P. 1979. Shoes, OPIC, and the unquestioning persuasion: Multinational corporations and U.S. Brazilian relations. In *Capitalism and the state in U.S.–Latin American relations,* ed. R. R. Fagen. Stanford, Calif.: Stanford University Press.

Featherman, D. L., and Hauser, R. M. 1976. Sexual inequalities and socioeconomic achievement in the U.S., 1962–1973. *American Sociological Review, 41,* 562–583.

Featherman, D. L., and Hauser, R. M. 1978. *Opportunity and change.* New York: Academic Press.

Featherman, D. L., Jones, F. L., and Hauser, R. M. 1975. Assumptions of social mobility research in the United States: The case of occupational status. *Social Science Research, 4,* 329–360.

Featherman, D. L., and Stevens, G. 1982. A revised socioeconomic index of occupational status: Application in analysis of sex differences in attainment. In *Social structure and behavior: Essays in honor of William H. Sewell,* ed. R. M. Hauser, D. Mechanic, A. O. Haller, and T. S. Hauser. New York: Academic Press.

Feinberg, R. 1977. Search in the labor market and the duration of unemployment: Note. *American Economic Review, 67,* 1011–1013.

Fernandez, R. M., and Nielsen, F. 1983. *Bilingualism and Hispanic scholastic achievement: Some baseline results.* Unpublished manuscript, Department of Sociology, University of Arizona, Tucson.

Finkelstein, M. O. 1980. The judicial reception of multiple regression studies in race and sex discrimination cases. *Columbia Law Review, 80,* 737–754.

Flanagan, R. J. 1978. Discrimination theory, labor turnover, and racial unemployment differentials. *Journal of Human Resources, 13,* 187–207.

Fleischer, B. M., and Rhodes, G. F., Jr. 1979. Fertility, women's wage rates, and labor supply. *American Economic Review, 69,* 14–25.

Fligstein, N., and Fernandez, R. M. 1982. *The causes of Hispanic educational attainment: History, patterns, and analyses.* Report to the National Commission on Employment Policy. Mimeo.

Fligstein, N., and Wolf, W. 1978. Sex similarities in occupational status attainment: Are the results due to the restriction of the sample to employed women? *Social Science Research, 7,* 197–212.

Flinn, C., and Heckman, J. J. 1980. *Models for the analysis of labor market dynamics.* Discussion Paper No. 80-3, Chicago Economic Research Center, National Opinion Research Center.

Fogel, W., and Corwin, A. 1978. Shadow labor force: Mexican workers in the American economy. In *Immigrants—and immigrants: Perspectives on Mexican labor migration to the United States,* ed. A. Corwin. Westport, Conn.: Greenwood Press.

Garcia, S. 1979. *Language usage and the status attainment of Chicano males.* M.S. thesis, Department of Sociology, University of Wisconsin—Madison.

Garcia, S. 1980. *Language usage and the status attainment of Chicano males.* Working Paper No. 80-2. University of Wisconsin—Madison, Center for Demography and Ecology.

Garvey, N., and Reimers, C. W. 1980. Predicted vs. actual work experience in an earnings function for young women. In *Research in labor economics,* Vol. 3, ed. R. G. Ehrenberg. Greenwich, Conn.: JAI Press.

Gilroy, C. 1974. Black and white unemployment: The dynamics of the differential. *Monthly Labor Review, 97* (February), 38–47.

Glazer, N., and Moynihan, D. P. 1963. *Beyond the melting pot.* Cambridge, Mass.: MIT Press.

Goldmark, P. C., Jr. 1979. Foreign business in the economy of the New York–New Jersey metropolitan region. *City Almanac, 14,* 1–14.

Goldscheider, C., and Kobrin, F. 1980. Ethnic continuity and the process of self-employment. *Ethnicity, 7,* 256–278.

Goldstein, S. 1972. The influence of labour force participation and education on fertility in Thailand. *Population Studies, 26,* 419–436.

Gonzalez, N. 1970. Peasants' progress: Dominicans in New York. *Caribbean Studies, 10,* 154–171.

Gordon, E., and Wilkerson, D. 1966. *Compensatory education for the disadvantaged.* New York: College Entrance Examination Board.

Gordon, M. 1964. *Assimilation in American life: The role of race, religion and national origins.* New York: Oxford University Press.

Grabill, W. H., and Cho, L.-J. 1965. Methodology for the measurement of current fertility from data on young children. *Demography, 2,* 50–74.

Gray, L. S. 1975a. The jobs Puerto Ricans hold in New York City. *Monthly Labor Review, 98* (October), 12–16.

Gray, L. S. 1975b. *A socio-economic profile of Puerto Rican New Yorkers.* Regional Report 46. Washington, D.C.: U.S. Department of Labor, Bureau of Labor Statistics.

Grebler, L., Moore, J., and Guzman, R. 1970. *The Mexican American people*. New York: Free Press.

Grenier, G. 1981. *An analysis of the effect of language characteristics on the wages of Hispanic American males*. Paper presented at the meetings of the Société Canadienne de Science Économique, Sherbrooke, Quebec, Canada, May 13–14.

Guhleman, P., and Tienda, M. 1981. *A socioeconomic profile of Hispanic-American female workers: Perspectives on labor force participation and earnings*. Working Paper No. 81-7. Madison: University of Wisconsin—Madison, Center for Demography and Ecology.

Hall, R. E. 1972. Turnover in the labor force. *Brookings Papers on Economic Activity*, no. 3, 709–756.

Hamermesh, D. 1977. *Jobless pay and the economy*. Baltimore: Johns Hopkins University Press.

Haro, C. 1977. Introduction [to a special issue], *Aztlan, 8*, 1–10.

Harrell, F. 1980. *The LOGIST procedure*. Statistical Analysis System Supplemental Library Users' Guide, 1980 ed. Cary, N.C.: SAS Institute.

Hashimoto, M., and Kochin, L. 1979. A bias in the statistical estimation of the effects of discrimination. *Economic Inquiry, 18*, 478–486.

Hauser, R. M. 1971. *Socioeconomic background and educational performance*. Washington, D.C.: American Sociological Association.

Hauser, R. M., Sewell, W. H., and Alwin, D. F. 1976. High school effects on achievement. In *Schooling and achievement in American society*, ed. W. H. Sewell, R. M. Hauser, and D. L. Featherman. New York: Academic Press.

Hechter, M. 1978. Group formation and the cultural divisions of labor. *American Journal of Sociology, 84*, 293–318.

Heckman, J. 1976. The common structure of statistical models of truncation, sample selection and limited dependent variables and a simple estimator for such models. *Annals of Economic and Social Measurement, 5*, 475–492.

Heckman, J. J. 1979. Sample selection bias as a specification error. *Econometrica, 47*, 153–161.

Heckman, J. J., and Borjas, G. J. 1980. Does unemployment cause future unemployment? Definitions, questions and answers from a continuous time model of heterogeneity and state dependence. *Economica, 47*, 247–283.

Heckman, J. J., Killingsworth, M. R., and MaCurdy, T. 1981. Empirical evidence on static labour supply models: A survey of recent developments. In *The economics of the labour market*, ed. Z. Hornstein, J. Grice, and A. Webb. London: Her Majesty's Stationery Office.

Heer, D. M., and Falasco, D. 1982. *The socioeconomic status of recent mothers of Mexican origin in Los Angeles county: A comparison of undocumented migrants, legal migrants, and native citizens*. Paper prepared for the annual meetings of the Population Association of America, San Diego, Calif.

Heller, C. 1966. *Mexican-American youth: Forgotten youth at the cross-roads*. New York: Random House.

Hendricks, G. 1974. *Dominican diaspora*. New York: Teachers College Press.

Herman, H. 1979. Dishwashers and proprietors: Macedonians in Toronto's restaurant trade. In *Ethnicity at work*, ed. S. Wallman. London: Macmillan.

Hirschman, C. 1980. Theories and models of ethnic inequality. In *Research in race and ethnic relations*, Vol. 2, ed. C. Marrett. Greenwich, Conn.: JAI Press.

Hodson, R. D. 1978. Earnings in the monopoly, competitive and state sectors. *Politics and Society, 8*, 429–480.

Hodson, R. D., and Kaufman, R. L. 1981. Circularity in the dual economy: Comment on Tolbert, Horan, and Beck. *American Journal of Sociology*, 86, 881–887.

Hoover, E., and Vernon, R. 1959. *Anatomy of a metropolis.* New York: Doubleday.

Horan, P. M. 1978. Is status attainment research atheoretical? *American Sociological Review*, 43, 534–541.

Horan, P. M., Tolbert, C. M., and Beck, E. M. 1981. The circle has no close. *American Journal of Sociology*, 86, 887–894.

Immigration Commission (The Dillingham Commission). 1911. *Abstract of reports of the Immigration Commission. U.S. Senate, 61st Congress.* Washington, D.C.: U.S. Government Printing Office.

International Ladies' Garment Workers Union. 1980. *General Executive Board report.* New York: Author.

Jaffe, A. J., Cullen, R. M., and Boswell, T. D. 1980. *The changing demography of Spanish Americans.* New York: Academic Press.

Jencks, C., and Brown, M. 1975. Effects of high schools on their students. *Harvard Educational Review*, 45, 273–324.

Jencks, C., Smith, M., Acland, H., Bane, M. J., Cohen, D., Gintis, H., Heyns, B., and Michelson, S. 1972. *Inequality: A reassessment of the effect of family and schooling in America.* New York: Basic Books.

Jensen, A. 1961. Learning abilities of Mexican-American and Anglo-American children. *California Journal of Educational Research*, 12, 147–159.

Jensen, A. 1980. *Bias in mental testing.* New York: Free Press.

Jovanovich, B. 1979. Firm-specific capital and turnover. *Journal of Political Economy*, 87, 1246–1260.

Kamalich, R. F., and Polachek, S. W. 1982. *Discrimination: Fact or fiction? An examination using an alternative methodology.* Unpublished manuscript, Department of Economics, University of North Carolina, Chapel Hill.

Kemp, A. A., and Beck, E. M. 1981. Female underemployment in urban labor markets. In *Sociological perspectives on labor markets*, ed. I. Berg. New York: Academic Press.

Kiefer, N. M., and Smith, S. P. 1977. Union impact and wage discrimination by region. *Journal of Human Resources*, 12, 521–534.

Kim, I. 1981. *The new urban immigrants: Korean immigrants in New York City.* Princeton, N.J.: Princeton University Press.

Kimball, W. L. 1968. *Parent and family influences on academic achievement among Mexican-American students.* Ph.D. dissertation, Department of Education, University of California, Los Angeles.

King, A. 1978. Industrial structure, flexibility of working hours, and women's labor force participation. *Review of Economics and Statistics*, 60, 399–407.

Kmenta, J. 1971. *Elements of econometrics.* New York: Macmillan.

Knight, R. 1973. *The metropolitan economy.* New York: Columbia University Press.

Koshetz, H. 1969. A major labor shortage squeezing New York garment center. *New York Times*, August 10.

Lambert, W. 1975. Culture and language as factors in learning and education. In *Education of immigrant students*, ed. A. Wolfgang. Toronto: Ontario Institute for Studies in Education.

Lancaster, T. 1979. Econometric methods for the duration of unemployment. *Econometrica*, 47, 939–956.

Lancaster, T., and Nickell, S. 1980. The analysis of reemployment probabilities for the unemployed. *Journal of the Royal Statistical Society*, series A, 143, 141–165.

Laosa, L. 1977. Inequality in the classroom: Observational research on teacher–student interactions. *Aztlan, 8,* 51–68.

Leighton, L., and Mincer, J. 1979. *Labor turnover and youth unemployment.* Working Paper No. 378. Cambridge, Mass.: National Bureau of Economic Research.

Levy, M. B., and Wadycki, W. 1973. The influence of family and friends on geographic labor mobility: An international comparison. *Review of Economics and Statistics, 55,* 198–203.

Lewis, L. S., and Wanner, R. 1979. Private schooling and the status attainment process. *Sociology of Education, 52,* 99–112.

Lewis, R., and St. John, N. 1974. Contributions of cross-racial friendship to minority group achievement in segregated classrooms. *Sociometry, 37,* 79–91.

Lichtenberg, R. J. 1960. *One-tenth of a nation.* Cambridge, Mass.: Harvard University Press.

Lippman, S. A., and McCall, J. C. 1976a. The economics of job search: A survey. *Economic Inquiry, 14,* 155–189.

Lippman, S. A., and McCall, J. C. 1976b. Job search in a dynamic economy. *Journal of Economic Theory, 12,* 365–390.

Little, J. S. 1978. Locational decision of foreign direct investors in the U.S. *New England Economic Review* (Federal Reserve Bank of Boston), July–August, pp. 43–63.

Lopez, D. 1976. The social consequences of Chicano home/school bilingualism. *Social Problems, 24,* 234–246.

Lovell-Troy, L. 1981. Ethnic occupational structures: Greeks in the pizza business. *Ethnicity, 8,* 82–95.

McClendon, M. 1976. The occupational status attainment processes of males and females. *American Sociological Review, 41,* 52–64.

McFadden, D. 1974. Conditional logit analysis of qualitative choice behavior. In *Frontiers in econometrics,* ed. P. Zarembka. New York: Academic Press.

McFadden, D. 1975. The revealed preferences of a government bureaucracy: Theory. *Bell Journal of Economics, 6,* 401–416.

McKay, R. 1974. Employment and unemployment among Americans of Spanish origin. *Monthly Labor Review, 97* (April), 12–16.

McManus, W., Gould, W., and Welch, F. 1983. Earnings of Hispanic men: The role of English language proficiency. *Journal of Labor Economics, 1,* 101–130.

Maddala, G. S. 1977. *Econometrics.* New York: McGraw-Hill.

Malkiel, B. G., and Malkiel, J. A. 1973. Male–female pay differentials in professional employment. *American Economic Review, 63,* 693–705.

Mare, R. 1980. Social background and school continuation decisions. *Journal of the American Statistical Association, 75,* 295–305.

Mason, K. O., and Palan, V. T. 1981. Female employment and fertility in peninsular Malaysia: The maternal role incompatibility hypothesis reconsidered. *Demography, 18,* 549–575.

Mincer, J. 1962. Labor force participation of married women. In *Aspects of labor economics,* ed. H. G. Lewis. Princeton, N.J.: Princeton University Press (for the National Bureau of Economic Research).

Mincer, J. 1974. *Schooling, experience and earnings.* New York: Columbia University Press (for the National Bureau of Economic Research).

Mollenkopf, J. 1977. *The rise of the Southwest: Problem and promise.* Paper presented at the Roundtable Conference of the Southwest, Phoenix, Arizona. Washington, D.C.: U.S. Department of Commerce, Economic Development Administration, Urban Technical Assistance Office.

Moncarz, R. 1973. A model of professional adaptation of refugees: The Cuban case in the U.S., 1959–70. *International Migration*, 11, 109–114.

Naboa, A. 1980. Hispanics and desegregation: A summary of ASPIRA's study of Hispanic segregation trends in U.S. school districts. *Metas*, 1, 1–24.

National Center for Education Statistics. 1980. *The condition of education for Hispanic Americans*. Washington, D.C.: U.S. Government Printing Office.

National Commission for Employment Policy. 1982. *Hispanics and jobs: Barriers to progress*. Washington, D.C.: U.S. Government Printing Office.

Neidert, L. J., and Tienda, M. 1981. Converting education into earnings: The pattern among Hispanic-origin men. In *Hispanic-origin workers in the U.S. labor market: Comparative analyses of employment and earnings*, ed. M. Tienda. Final report to the U.S. Department of Labor, Employment and Training Administration, Washington, D.C. (Available from National Technical Information Service, Springfield, Va. 22151. Also issued as Center for Demography and Ecology, Working Paper No. 81-31, University of Wisconsin—Madison.)

Netzer, D. 1974. The cloudy prospects for the city's economy. *New York Affairs*, 1, 22–35.

Neustadt, D. 1980. They also serve: Waitering, a changing union, and Chinatown struggles. *Village Voice*, May 12.

Newby, H. 1977. Paternalism and capitalism. In *Industrial society: Class, cleavage, and control*, ed. R. Scase. New York: St. Martin's Press.

Newman, M. 1978. A profile of Hispanics in the U.S. work force. *Monthly Labor Review*, 101 (December), 3–14.

New York State Department of Labor. 1980. *Occupational employment statistics: Services, New York State, April–June 1978*. Albany: State Department of Labor.

New York State Department of Labor. 1982a. *Report to the Governor and the legislature on the garment manufacturing industry and industrial homework*. New York: State Department of Labor.

New York State Department of Labor. 1982b. *Study of state–federal employment standards for industrial home-workers in New York City*. Albany: State Department of Labor, Division of Labor Standards.

New York State Department of Labor. 1982c. *Employment Review*, Vol. 35, No. 6.

Nielsen, F. 1980. *Hispanic youth in U.S. schools: A design for analysis*. Mimeo. Report to the National Center for Education Statistics, Washington, D.C.

Nielsen, F., and Fernandez, R. M. 1982. *Achievement of Hispanic students in American high schools: Background characteristics and achievement*. Washington, D.C.: National Center for Education Statistics.

Noel, D. J. 1968. A theory of the origin of ethnic stratification. *Social Problems*, 16, 157–172.

North, D., and Houston, M. 1976. *The characteristics and role of illegal aliens in the U.S. labor markets*. Washington, D.C.: Linton.

North American Congress on Latin America. 1978. Capital's flight: The apparel industry moves South. *Latin America and Empire Report*, 11, No. 3 (special issue).

North American Congress on Latin America. 1979. Undocumented immigrant workers in New York City. *Latin America and Empire Report*, 12, No. 6 (special issue).

Oaxaca, R. 1973. Male–female wage differentials in urban labor markets. *International Economic Review*, 14, 693–709.

Oaxaca, R. 1976. Male–female wage differentials in the telephone industry. In *Equal employment opportunity and the AT&T case*, ed. P. Wallace. Cambridge, Mass.: MIT Press.

Okun, A. 1981. *Prices and quantities: A macroeconomic analysis*. Washington, D.C.: Brookings Institution.

Olivas, M. 1980. *The dilemma of access: Minorities in two-year colleges.* Washington, D.C.: Howard University Press.

Oppenheimer, V. K. 1970. *The female labor force in the United States: Demographic and economic factors governing its growth and changing composition.* Berkeley: University of California Press.

Osterman, P. 1979. Sex discrimination in professional employment: A case study. *Industrial and Labor Relations Review, 32,* 451–464.

Otto, L., and Haller, A. 1979. Evidence for a social-psychological view of the status attainment process. *Social Forces, 57,* 887–914.

Parsons, D. 1972. Specific human capital: An application of quit rates and layoff rates. *Journal of Political Economy, 80,* 1120–1143.

Patchen, M., Hoffman, G., and Brown, W. 1980. Academic performance of black high school students under different conditions of contact with white peers. *Sociology of Education, 53,* 33–51.

Peal, E., and Lambert, W. 1962. The relation of bilingualism to intelligence. *Psychological Monographs: General and Applied, 76,* 1–23.

Petras, E. 1981. The global labor market in the modern work economy. In *Global trends in migration,* ed. M. M. Kritz, C. B. Keely, and S. M. Tomasi. Staten Island, N.Y.: Center for Migration Studies.

Piore, M. 1969. On-the-job training in a dual labor market. In *Public–private manpower policies,* ed. A. R. Weber, F. H. Cassell, and W. L. Ginsburg. Madison, Wis.: Industrial Relations Research Association.

Piore, M. 1973. *The role of migration in industrial change: A case study of Puerto Rican migration to Boston,* Working Paper No. 112. Cambridge: Massachusetts Institute of Technology, Department of Economics.

Piore, M. 1979. *Birds of passage: Migrant labor and industrial societies.* Cambridge: Cambridge University Press.

Piore, M., and Sabel, C. 1981. *Italian small business development: Lessons for U.S. industrial policy.* Working Paper No. 288. Cambridge: Massachusetts Institute of Technology, Department of Economics.

Polachek, S. 1975a. Discontinuous labor force participation and its effect on women's market earnings. In *Sex, discrimination, and the division of labor,* ed. C. Lloyd. New York: Columbia University Press.

Polachek, S. 1975b. Potential biases in measuring male–female discrimination. *Journal of Human Resources, 10,* 205–229.

Port Authority of New York and New Jersey. 1981. *Inventory of foreign-owned firms in manufacturing, by major industry in the New York–New Jersey metropolitan region.* New York: Port Authority of New York and New Jersey, Planning and Development Department, Regional Research Section.

Port Authority of New York and New Jersey. 1982. *Regional perspectives: The regional economy, 1981 review, 1982 outlook.* New York: Port Authority of New York and New Jersey, Planning and Development Department, Regional Research Section.

Portes, A. 1979. Illegal immigration and the international system: Lessons from recent legal immigration from Mexico. *Social Problems, 26,* 425–438.

Portes, A. 1981. Modes of structural incorporation and present theories of labor immigration. In *Global trends in migration,* ed. M. M. Kritz, C. B. Keely, and S. M. Tomasi. Staten Island, N.Y.: Center for Migration Studies.

Portes, A. 1982. Immigrants' attainment: An analysis of occupation and earnings among Cuban exiles in the United States. In *Social structure and behavior: Essays in honor of*

William H. Sewell, ed. R. M. Hauser, D. Mechanic, A. O. Haller, and T. S. Hauser. New York: Academic Press.

Portes, A., and Bach, R. 1980. Immigrant earnings: Cuban and Mexican immigrants in the United States. *International Migration Review, 14*, 315–341.

Portes, A., and Walton, J. 1981. *Labor, class and the international system*. New York: Academic Press.

Powers, M. G., and Holmberg, J. J. 1978. Occupational status scores: Changes introduced by the inclusion of women. *Demography, 15*, 183–204.

Ramirez, M., and Castaneda, A. 1974. *Cultural democracy, bicognitive development, and education*. New York: Academic Press.

Randall, N. H. 1977. *Women's need for income: Their employment and earnings*. Working Paper No. 77-2. Madison: University of Wisconsin—Madison, Center for Demography and Ecology.

Reimers, C. W. 1980. *Sources of the wage gap between Hispanic and other white Americans*. Working Paper No. 139. Princeton, N.J.: Princeton University, Industrial Relations Section.

Reimers, C. W. 1983. Labor market discrimination against Hispanic and black men. *Review of Economics and Statistics, 65* (Nov. 1983), 571, 574–577, Table 4.

Reimers, C. W. 1984. Sources of the family income differential between Hispanics, blacks, and white non-Hispanics. *American Journal of Sociology, 89*, 889–903.

Reisler, M. 1976. *By the sweat of their brow*. Westport, Conn.: Greenwood Press.

Retherford, R. D., and Cho, L.-J. 1978. Age-parity-specific birth rates and birth probabilities from census or survey data on own children. *Population Studies, 32*, 567–581.

Rindfuss, R. R., and Sweet, J. A. 1977. *Postwar fertility trends and differentials in the United States*. New York: Academic Press.

Roberts, H. V. 1979. *Harris Trust and Savings Bank: An analysis of employee compensation*. Report 7946. Chicago: University of Chicago, Center for Mathematical Studies in Business and Economics.

Roberts, H. V. 1980. Statistical biases in the measurement of employment discrimination. In *Comparable worth: Issues and alternatives*, ed. E. R. Livernash. Washington, D.C.: Equal Employment Advisory Council.

Roberts, H. V. 1981. *Reverse regression and employment discrimination: Rationale and criticisms*. Unpublished manuscript, Graduate School of Business, University of Chicago.

Robins, P. K., Tuma, N. B., and Yaeger, N. B. 1980. Effects of the Seattle and Denver income maintenance experiments on changes in employment status. *Journal of Human Resources, 15*, 545–573.

Rodríguez, N. Forthcoming. The utilization of *indocumentado* labor. In *Navigando in unfamiliar waters*, ed. H. Browning, R. Núñez, and N. Rodríguez. Manuscript in preparation.

Rogg, E., and Cooney, R. 1980. *Adaptation and adjustment of Cubans: West New York, New Jersey*. New York: Hispanic Research Center.

Rosenfeld, R. A., and Sørensen, A. B. 1979. Sex differences in patterns of career mobility. *Demography, 16*, 89–101.

Rosenzweig, M. R., and Wolpin, K. I. 1980. Life-cycle labor supply and fertility: Causal inferences from household models. *Journal of Political Economy, 88*, 320.

Rumberger, R. 1983. Dropping out of high school: The influence of race, sex, and family background. *American Educational Research Journal, 20*, 199–220.

Rungeling, B. 1969. *Impact of the Mexican alien commuter on the apparel industry of El Paso, Texas*. Springfield, Va.: Clearinghouse for Federal Scientific and Technical Information.

St. Marie, S., and Bednarzik, R. 1976. Employment and unemployment during 1975. *Monthly Labor Review, 99* (February), 11–20.

Sassen-Koob, S. 1979. Formal and informal associations: Dominicans and Colombians in New York. *International Migration Review, 13,* 314–332.

Sassen-Koob, S. 1980. Immigrant and minority workers in the organization of the labor process. *Journal of Ethnic Studies, 8,* 1–34.

Sassen-Koob, S. 1981. Towards a conceptualization of immigrant labor. *Social Problems, 29,* 65–85.

Sassen-Koob, S. 1984. The new labor demand in global cities. In *Cities in transformation,* ed. M. P. Smith. Urban Affairs Annual Reviews. Beverly Hills, Calif.: Sage Publications.

Schmenner, R. 1980. *The location decision of large, multi-plant corporations.* Cambridge, Mass.: MIT–Harvard Joint Center for Urban Studies.

Schneider, P. A. D. 1974. *The central personnel data file.* Unpublished manuscript, Bureau of Management Information Systems, U.S. Office of Personnel Management, Washington, D.C.

Schultz, T. P. 1978. The influence of fertility on labor supply of married women: Simultaneous equation estimates. In *Research in labor economics,* Vol. 2, ed. R. G. Ehrenberg. Greenwich, Conn.: JAI Press.

Seidman, A., ed. 1978. *Working women: A study of women in paid jobs.* Boulder, Colo.: Westview Press.

Select Commission on Immigration and Refugee Policy. 1981. *U.S. immigration policy and the national interest.* Supplement to the Final Report. Washington, D.C.: Author.

Sewell, W. H., Haller, A., and Portes, A. 1969. The educational and early occupational attainment process. *American Sociological Review, 34,* 82–92.

Sewell, W. H., Haller, A., and Strauss, M. A. 1957. Social status and educational and occupational aspiration. *American Sociological Review, 22,* 67–73.

Sewell, W. H., and Hauser, R. M. 1975. *Education, occupation, and earnings: Achievement in the early career.* New York: Academic Press.

Sewell, W. H., Hauser, R. M., and Wolf, W. C. 1980. Sex, schooling and occupational status. *American Journal of Sociology, 86,* 551–583.

Sewell, W. H., and Shah, V. P. 1968. Social class, parental encouragement, and educational aspirations. *American Journal of Sociology, 73,* 559–572.

Shea, B. 1976. Schooling and its antecedents: Substantive and methodological issues in the status attainment process. *Review of Educational Research, 46,* 463–526.

Skrabanek, R. L. 1970. Language maintenance among Mexican-Americans. *International Journal of Comparative Sociology, 11,* 272–282.

Smith, S. P. 1977. *Equal pay in the public sector: Fact or fantasy?* Research Report No. 332. Princeton, N.J.: Princeton University, Industrial Relations Section.

Smith, T. 1980. Ethnic measurement and identification. *Ethnicity, 7,* 78–95.

Smith-Lovin, L., and Tickamyer, A. R. 1978. Nonrecursive models of labor force participation, fertility behavior, and sex role attitudes. *American Sociological Review, 43,* 541–556.

Smith-Lovin, L., and Tickamyer, A. R. 1981. Fertility and patterns of labor force participation among married women. *Social Biology, 28,* 81–95.

Snipp, C. M. 1981. *The structure of mobility: An alternative approach to social mobility and achievement.* Ph.D. dissertation, Department of Sociology, University of Wisconsin—Madison.

Snipp, C. M., and Tienda, M. 1982. New perspectives on Chicano intergenerational occupational mobility. *Social Science Journal, 19,* 37–49.

Sowell, T. 1978. *Essays and data on American ethnic groups.* Washington, D.C.: Urban Institute.

Spady, W. G. 1976. The impact of school resources on students. In *Schooling and achievement in American society*, ed. W. H. Sewell, R. M. Hauser, and D. L. Featherman. New York: Academic Press.

Stanback, T. M., Jr. 1979. *Understanding the service economy*. Baltimore: Johns Hopkins University Press.

Standing, G. 1978. *Labour force participation and development*. Geneva: International Labour Office.

Stephenson, S., Jr. 1982. A turnover analysis of joblessness for young women. In *Research in labor economics*, Vol. 5, ed. R. G. Ehrenberg. Greenwich, Conn.: JAI Press.

Stinchcombe, A. L. 1964. *Rebellion in a high school*. Chicago: Aldine.

Stolzenberg, R. M. 1975. Occupations, labor markets and the process of wage attainment. *American Sociological Review, 40,* 645–665.

Stolzenberg, R. M. 1980. The measurement and decomposition of causal effects in nonlinear and non-additive models. In *Sociological methodology, 1980,* ed. K. Schuessler. San Francisco: Jossey-Bass.

Stolzenberg, R. M., and Waite, L. J. 1981. *Labor market characteristics and the labor force participation of individuals*. Rand Paper Series P-6705. Santa Monica, Calif.: Rand Corporation.

Stycos, J. M., and Weller, R. H. 1967. Female working roles and fertility. *Demography, 4,* 210–217.

Sullivan, T. A. 1978. Racial-ethnic differences in labor force participation: An ethnic stratification perspective. In *The demography of racial and ethnic groups,* ed. F. D. Bean and W. Parker Frisbie. New York: Academic Press.

Sullivan, T., and Pedraza-Bailey, S. 1979. *Differential success among Cuban American and Mexican American immigrants*. Final Report to the U.S. Department of Labor, Employment and Training Administration, Washington, D.C.

Tabb, W. K. 1982. *The long default: New York City and the urban fiscal crisis*. New York: Monthly Review Press.

Theil, H. 1971. *Principles of econometrics*. New York: John Wiley.

Thornton, C., and Eckland, B. 1980. High school contextual effects for black and white students: A research note. *Sociology of Education, 53,* 247–252.

Tienda, M. 1980. Familism and structural assimilation of Mexican immigrants in the United States. *International Migration Review, 14,* 383–408.

Tienda, M. (ed.) 1981. *Hispanic-origin workers in the U.S. labor market: Comparative analyses of employment and earnings*. Final report to U.S. Department of Labor, Employment and Training Administration, Washington, D.C. (Available from National Technical Information Service, Springfield, Va. 22151.)

Tienda, M. 1982. Sex, ethnicity, and Chicano status attainment. *International Migration Review, 16,* 435–473.

Tienda, M. 1983. Market characteristics and Hispanic earnings: A comparison of natives and immigrants. *Social Problems, 31,* 59–72.

Tienda, M., and Angel, R. 1982. Female headship and extended household composition: Comparisons of Hispanics, blacks and non-Hispanic whites. *Social Forces, 61,* 508–531.

Tienda, M., with Bowman, C., and Snipp, C. M. 1981. *Socioeconomic attainment and ethnicity: Toward an understanding of the labor market experiences of Chicanos in the U.S.* Report to the U.S. Department of Labor, Employment and Training Administration, Washington, D.C. (Available from National Technical Information Service, Springfield, Va. 22151.)

Tienda, M., and Neidert, L. 1980. Segmented markets and earnings inequalities of native and immigrant Hispanics. In *1980 Proceedings of the American Statistical Association, Social Statistics Section.* Washington, D.C.: American Statistical Association.

Tienda, M., and Neidert, L. 1984. Language, education and socioeconomic achievement of Hispanic origin men. *Social Science Quarterly, 65,* 519–536.

Tobier, E. 1979. Gentrification: The Manhattan story. *New York Affairs, 5,* 13–25.

Tobier, E. 1982. Foreign immigration. In *Setting municipal priorities,* eds. C. Brecher and R. Horton. New York: New York University Press.

Treiman, D. J., and Hartmann, H. I. (eds.). 1981. *Women, work, and wages: Equal pay for jobs of equal value.* Washington, D.C.: National Academy Press.

Treiman, D. J., and Terrell, K. 1975. Sex and the process of status attainment: A comparison of working women and men. *American Sociological Review, 40,* 174–200.

Tuma, N. B. 1979. *Invoking rate.* Unpublished manuscript, Department of Sociology, Stanford University, July.

Tuma, N. B., and Robins, P. K. 1980. A dynamic model of employment behavior: An application to the Seattle and Denver income maintenance experiments. *Econometrica, 48,* 1031–1052.

Urrea Giraldo, F. 1982. *Life strategies and the labor market: Colombians in New York in the 1970s.* Mimeo, New York Research Program in Inter-American Affairs, New York University.

U.S. Commission on Civil Rights. 1967. *Racial isolation in the public schools,* 2 vols. Washington, D.C.: U.S. Government Printing Office.

U.S. Commission on Civil Rights. 1976. *Puerto Ricans in the continental United States: An uncertain future.* Washington, D.C.: U.S. Government Printing Office.

U.S. Commission on Civil Rights. 1978. *Social indicators of equality for minorities and women.* Washington, D.C.: U.S. Government Printing Office.

U.S. Commission on Civil Rights. 1982. *Unemployment and underemployment among blacks, Hispanics, and women.* Washington, D.C.: U.S. Government Printing Office.

U.S. Department of Commerce (Bureau of the Census). 1977. *Technical documentation of the 1976 Survey of Income and Education.* Washington, D.C.: U.S. Government Printing Office.

U.S. Department of Commerce (Bureau of the Census). 1978. Microdata from the Survey of Income and Education. Data Access Description No. 42.

U.S. Department of Commerce (Bureau of the Census). 1979. *Persons of Spanish origin in the U.S.: March 1978.* Current Population Reports, Population Characteristics, Series P-20, No. 339. Washington, D.C.: U.S. Government Printing Office.

U.S. Department of Commerce (International Trade Administration). 1980a. *Current developments in U.S. international services industries.* Washington, D.C.: U.S. Government Printing Office.

U.S. Department of Commerce (Bureau of the Census). 1980b. *Persons of Spanish origin in the United States: March 1979.* Current Population Reports, Population Characteristics, Series P-20, No. 354. Washington, D.C.: U.S. Government Printing Office.

U.S. Department of Commerce (Bureau of the Census). 1981a. *Age, sex, race, and Spanish origin of the population by regions, divisions, and states: 1980.* 1980 Census of Population and Housing, Supplemental Report No. 1, PC80-S1-1. Washington, D.C.: U.S. Government Printing Office.

U.S. Department of Commerce (Bureau of the Census). 1981b. *Census of population and housing, 1980: P.L. 94-171, population counts.* Machine-readable data file. Washington, D.C.: Bureau of the Census.

U.S. Department of Justice (Immigration and Naturalization Service). 1970–1980. Various years. *Annual report.* Washington, D.C.: U.S. Government Printing Office.

U.S. Department of Justice (Immigration and Naturalization Service). 1981. *Tabulation of immigrants admitted by country of birth, 1954–1979.* Unpublished manuscript.

U.S. Department of Labor (Bureau of Labor Statistics). 1977. *Handbook of labor statistics, 1976.* Washington, D.C.: U.S. Government Printing Office.

U.S. Department of Labor (Bureau of Labor Statistics). 1979a. *Employment and training report of the President.* Washington, D.C.: U.S. Government Printing Office.

U.S. Department of Labor (Bureau of Labor Statistics). 1979b. *Employment and earnings, United States, 1909–78.* Bulletin 1312–11. Washington, D.C.: U.S. Government Printing Office.

U.S. Department of Labor (Bureau of Labor Statistics). 1979c. *Employment and earnings, for states and areas, 1939–78.* Bulletin 1370–13. Washington, D.C.: U.S. Government Printing Office.

U.S. Department of Labor (Bureau of Labor Statistics). 1980. *News.* New York: U.S. Department of Labor, Bureau of Labor Statistics, Middle Atlantic Region.

U.S. Department of Labor (Bureau of Labor Statistics). 1981a. *Employment and earnings, for states and areas, 1939–78.* Bulletin 1370–15. Washington, D.C.: U.S. Government Printing Office.

U.S. Department of Labor (Bureau of Labor Statistics). 1981b. *Geographic profiles of employment and unemployment, 1980.* Washington, D.C.: U.S. Government Printing Office.

U.S. Department of Labor (Bureau of Labor Statistics). 1981c. *News.* New York: U.S. Department of Labor, Bureau of Labor Statistics, Middle Atlantic Region.

U.S. Department of Labor (Bureau of Labor Statistics). 1982a. *News.* New York: U.S. Department of Labor, Bureau of Labor Statistics, Middle Atlantic Region.

U.S. Department of Labor (Bureau of Labor Statistics). 1982b. *Supplement to employment and earnings, revised establishment data.* Washington, D.C.: U.S. Government Printing Office.

U.S. Department of Labor (Bureau of Labor Statistics). 1982c. *Geographic profile of employment and unemployment, 1980.* Bulletin 2111. Washington, D.C.: U.S. Government Printing Office.

U.S. Executive Office of the President (Council on Wage and Price Stability). 1978. *A study of textile and apparel industries.* Washington, D.C.: Council on Wage and Price Stability.

U.S. Senate, Committee on Banking, Housing, and Urban Affairs. 1982. *Foreign barriers to U.S. trade: Service exports.* U.S. Senate, 97th Congress, Hearing before the Subcommittee on International Finance and Monetary Policy of the Committee on Banking, Housing, and Urban Affairs. Washington, D.C.: U.S. Government Printing Office.

van Haitsma, M. Forthcoming. *Indocumentado* family patterns. In *Navigando in unfamiliar waters,* ed. H. Browning, R. Núñez, and N. Rodríguez. Manuscript in preparation.

Vasquez, J. A. 1974. Will bilingual curricula solve the problem of the low achieving Mexican-American students? *Bilingual Review, 1,* 236–242.

Wagenheim, K. 1975. *A survey of Puerto Ricans on the U.S. mainland in the 1970s.* New York: Praeger.

Waite, L. J. 1981. Working wives and the family life cycle. *American Journal of Sociology, 86,* 272–294.

Waite, L. J., and Stolzenberg, R. M. 1976. Intended childbearing and labor force participation of young women: Insights from nonrecursive models. *American Sociological Review, 41,* 235–251.

Waldinger, R. 1982. The integration of the new immigrant. *Law and Contemporary Problems, 45,* 197–222.

Waldinger, R. 1983a. *Ethnic enterprise: A critique and reformulation.* Paper presented to the annual meetings of the American Sociological Association, Detroit, September.

Waldinger, R. 1983b. *Ethnic enterprise and industrial change: A case study of the New York garment industry.* Ph.D. dissertation, Department of Sociology, Harvard University, Cambridge.

Wall Street Journal, Oct. 18, 1976.

Weinberg, M. 1977a. *A chance to learn: The history of race and education in the United States.* Cambridge: Cambridge University Press.

Weinberg, M. 1977b. *Minority students: A research appraisal.* Washington, D.C.: U.S. Government Printing Office.

Welch, F. 1973. Black–white differences in returns to schooling. *American Economic Review,* 63, 893–907.

Weller, R., Bertrand, W., and Harter, C. 1979. *Female employment status and fertility in Cali, Colombia.* Paper presented at the annual meetings of the Population Association of America, Denver.

Williams, G. 1979. The changing U.S. labor force and occupational differentiation by sex. *Demography,* 16, 73–87.

Wilson, K. L. 1979. The effects of integration and class on black education attainment. *Sociology of Education,* 52, 84–98.

Wilson, K. L., and Portes, A. 1980. Immigrant enclaves: An analysis of the labor market experiences of Cubans in Miami. *American Journal of Sociology,* 86, 295–319.

Wolf, W., and Fligstein, N. 1979. Sexual stratification: Differences in power in the work setting. *Social Forces,* 58, 94–107.

Wolf, W. and Rosenfeld, R. (1978). Sex structure of occupations and job mobility. *Social Forces,* 56, 823–844.

Wong, B. 1979. *A Chinese-American community.* Singapore: Chopmen.

Wrong, E. G. 1974. *The Negro in the apparel industry.* Philadelphia: University of Pennsylvania, Wharton School, Industrial Research Unit. (Distributed by University of Pennsylvania Press.)

Yancey, W. L., Ericksen, E. P., and Julian R. N. 1976. Emergent ethnicity: A review and reformulation. *American Sociological Review,* 41, 391–403.

Index

Institute for Research on Poverty
Monograph Series

Published

George J. Borjas and Marta Tienda, Editors, *Hispanics in the U.S. Economy.* 1985

Joel F. Handler and Michael Sosin, *Last Resorts: Emergency Assistance and Special Needs Programs in Public Welfare.* 1983

Irwin Garfinkel, Editor, *Income-Tested Transfer Programs: The Case For and Against.* 1982

Richard V. Burkhauser and Karen C. Holden, Editors, *A Challenge to Social Security: The Changing Roles of Women and Men in American Society.* 1982

Jeffrey G. Williamson and Peter H. Lindert, *American Inequality: A Macroeconomic History.* 1980

Robert H. Haveman and Kevin Hollenbeck, Editors, *Microeconomic Simulation Models for Public Policy Analysis, Volume 1: Distributional Impacts, Volume 2: Sectoral, Regional, and General Equilibrium Models.* 1980

Peter K. Eisinger, *The Politics of Displacement: Racial and Ethnic Transition in Three American Cities.* 1980

Erik Olin Wright, *Class Structure and Income Determination.* 1979

Joel F. Handler, *Social Movements and the Legal System: A Theory of Law Reform and Social Change.* 1979

Duane E. Leigh, *An Analysis of the Determinants of Occupational Upgrading.* 1978

Stanley H. Masters and Irwin Garfinkel, *Estimating the Labor Supply Effects of Income Maintenance Alternatives.* 1978

Irwin Garfinkel and Robert H. Haveman, with the assistance of David Betson, *Earnings Capacity, Poverty, and Inequality.* 1977

Harold W. Watts and Albert Rees, Editors, *The New Jersey Income-Maintenance Experiment, Volume III: Expenditures, Health, and Social Behavior, and the Quality of the Evidence.* 1977

Murray Edelman, *Political Language: Words That Succeed and Policies That Fail.* 1977

Marilyn Moon and Eugene Smolensky, Editors, *Improving Measures of Economic Well-Being.* 1977

Harold W. Watts and Albert Rees, Editors, *The New Jersey Income-Maintenance Experiment, Volume II: Labor-Supply Responses.* 1977

Marilyn Moon, *The Measurement of Economic Welfare: Its Application to the Aged Poor.* 1977

Morgan Reynolds and Eugene Smolensky, *Public Expenditures, Taxes, and the Distribution of Income: The United States, 1950, 1961, 1970.* 1977

Fredrick L. Golladay and Robert H. Haveman, with the assistance of Kevin Hollenbeck, *The Economic Impacts of Tax-Transfer Policy: Regional and Distributional Effects.* 1977

David Kershaw and Jerilyn Fair, *The New Jersey Income-Maintenance Experiment, Volume I: Operations, Surveys, and Administration.* 1976

Peter K. Eisinger, *Patterns of Interracial Politics: Conflict and Cooperation in the City.* 1976

Irene Lurie, Editor, *Integrating Income Maintenance Programs.* 1975

Stanley H. Masters, *Black–White Income Differentials: Empirical Studies and Policy Implications.* 1975

Larry L. Orr, *Income, Employment, and Urban Residential Location.* 1975

Joel F. Handler, *The Coercive Social Worker: British Lessons for American Social Services.* 1973

•Glen G. Cain and Harold W. Watts, Editors, *Income Maintenance and Labor Supply: Econometric Studies.* 1973

Charles E. Metcalf, *An Econometric Model of Income Distribution.* 1972

Larry L. Orr, Robinson G. Hollister, and Myron J. Lefcowitz, Editors, with the assistance of Karen Hester, *Income Maintenance: Interdisciplinary Approaches to Research.* 1971

Robert J. Lampman, *Ends and Means of Reducing Income Poverty.* 1971

Joel F. Handler and Ellen Jane Hollingsworth, *"The Deserving Poor": A Study of Welfare Administration.* 1971

Murray Edelman, *Politics as Symbolic Action: Mass Arousal and Quiescence.* 1971

Frederick Williams, Editor, *Language and Poverty: Perspectives on a Theme.* 1970

Vernon L. Allen, Editor, *Psychological Factors in Poverty.* 1970